"Ford details the endless connections driven by the almighty dollar and what it can buy in addition to more money: power, status, and 'safety' through policing. For this equation to hold, Black lives were indispensable in creating a world built on the backs of their labor, a world whose profits and privileges they would never reap. Clyde W. Ford's *Of Blood and Sweat* is a timely and authoritative narrative replete with sorely needed historical truth telling. A wordsmith of the first order. The depth of his research and scope of his knowledge on myriad topics, including economic history and theory, are astounding."

—Elizabeth Dowling Taylor, *New York Times* bestselling author of *A Slave in the White House* and *The Original Black Elite*

"Ford weaves in stories of resistance, noting, for instance, that a Black ship captain 'helped foment the largest slave rebellion in South Carolina history'; explains complex financial instruments in lucid terms; and paints vivid scenes of Black life in the U.S. The result is an essential reckoning with the roots of the racial wealth gap in America."

—*Publishers Weekly* (starred review)

"A compelling argument for long-overdue reparations—though much more than that alone."

—*Kirkus Reviews*

"Ford's forceful arguments and writing will compel readers to face the facts of the long history of exploitation and appropriation that have defined so much of America's struggle with itself to give substance and meaning to its promise of 'freedom' for all."

—*Library Journal*

OF BLOOD AND SWEAT

ALSO BY CLYDE W. FORD

Where Healing Waters Meet

Compassionate Touch

We Can All Get Along

The Hero with an African Face

The Long Mile

Red Herring

Deuce's Wild

Precious Cargo

Boat Green

Whiskey Gulf

Think Black

OF BLOOD AND SWEAT

BLACK LIVES AND THE MAKING OF
WHITE POWER AND WEALTH

CLYDE W. FORD

AMISTAD

An Imprint of HarperCollinsPublishers

In Memory of

Vincent Gordon Harding (1931–2014)

Lerone Bennett, Jr. (1928–2018)

HarperCollins books may be purchased for educational, business, or sales promotional use. For information, please email the Special Markets Department at SPsales@harpercollins.com.

FIRST HARPERCOLLINS PAPERBACK PUBLISHED IN 2023

Designed by Leah Carlson-Stanisic

Library of Congress Cataloging-in-Publication Data is available upon request.

ISBN 978-0-06-303852-3

23 24 25 26 27 LBC 5 4 3 2 1

CONTENTS

INTRODUCTION

Phillip Corven's case against Charles Lucas came before the Virginia Supreme Court on the afternoon of June 16, 1675, for final disposition, Lieutenant Governor Sir Henry Chicheley presiding. Opposing counsels may have argued the case a few days earlier, on June 12, to the full court of Governor Sir William Berkeley. Most cases landed at the Virginia General Council (the colonial-era supreme court) on appeal. Either the petitioner, Corven, or the defendant, Lucas, presumably contested an adverse ruling by the lower Warwick County Court, which is how the case came up for final review by judges Henry Chicheley (knighted by Charles I), Thomas Bacon, James Bridger, Phillip Ludwell, James Bray, and William Cole.

We know for certain that Phillip Corven was a Black man, his case officially annotated as the "Petition of a negro for redress, etc." In his initial filing, Corven presented details of how he had been treated like property: Anne Beasley bequeathed him to her cousin, Humphrey Stafford, who then sold him to Charles Lucas.

Phillip Corven, however, asserted he was not a slave. Beasley's will stipulated an eight-year indenture, after which Corven was to have been given his freedom. But Lucas, his present master, had forced Corven to work three years longer than the terms of that will. Then, after those eleven years of service, Lucas forced Corven to sign an indenture for an additional twenty years, under "threats & a high hand," Corven said.

At that point, Phillip Corven had had enough. He took his case to the judicial system of colonial Virginia, demanding not only his freedom but also the three barrels of corn and a suit of clothes promised him in Anne Beasley's will; that promise was widely known in colonial America as "freedom dues."[1]

Chicheley handed down the supreme court's ruling, from which there would be no subsequent appeal: Petitioner's twenty-year indenture? Vacated. Petitioner's request for freedom? Granted. Petitioner's request for court costs paid by defendant Lucas? Granted. Petitioner's request for freedom dues from defendant? Granted.

Freedom dues is an idea as old as America. Not expressed in the Declaration of Independence, nor enshrined in the Constitution, nor enumerated in the Bill of Rights, freedom dues, nonetheless, arrived on America's shores with the first colonists: a belief that power and wealth created from the labor of others entitled those who helped create that power and wealth to their fair share.

Stolen from Africa, hoodwinked, captured, or voluntarily signed on from Europe, in the early 1600s, indentured servants worked in the fields of colonial planter-masters without pay. But unlike slaves, bound in perpetuity, the labor of indentured servants had limits. They entered into contracts with their masters, offering their service for four, five, seven, eleven, fourteen years, and in some cases longer.

At the end of their bondage, indentured servants expected not only their freedom but also their freedom dues—some combination of land, seed, tools, and clothes to help them begin anew. Freedom dues represented a promise: for a very few, a path up from poverty into the wealth, security, and prominence of the privileged planter class; for most, at least the bare essentials of subsistence living, enough to keep poverty at bay.

This book focuses on the clash and convergence of two fundamental human conditions—freedom and bondage—and how that clash and convergence has played out in America.

The clash between freedom and bondage is obvious.

Not surprisingly, many masters, like Charles Lucas, refused to pay freedom dues, especially when it came to land grants. This failure to pay freedom dues was but one of many means by which landholding masters thwarted the aspirations of indentured servants—brutal working conditions, refusing to abide by contracts, arbitrary extension of the terms of indenture were others.

But landowners fought most bitterly to prevent those formerly bonded to them, Black or White, from owning land, which, after all, was the basis of colonial-era power and wealth. So, in this conflict between those who owned land and those who felt deserving of land lies another, equally potent force coursing through early America— the amassing of wealth and power by a few, and the denial of even a portion of that wealth and power to many.

Here is the earliest glimmer of the 1 percent in America, for the roots of wealth inequality lay in this gathering and holding tight of land. Here, too, lay the earliest roots of the 99 percent calling for a reversal of this inequality in the form of freedom dues. And this contest between masters and servants; between the landed and the landless; between those denying freedom dues and those demanding them; between freedom and bondage, has animated America ever since.

The convergence between freedom and bondage is less obvious.

In his books and lectures, the late Edmund S. Morgan, a professor of American history at Yale University, captured this convergence succinctly. In America, Morgan said, freedom presupposes bondage; in other words, there is no freedom without bondage. Here's what Morgan was getting at. Take any of the slaveholding Founders, for example: Washington, Jefferson, or Madison. In previous generations, they were considered heroes because of the lofty ideals of freedom and equality they espoused. The fact that they owned slaves was never an issue, even though slavery was diametrically opposed to freedom. In modern times, the fact that most Founders owned slaves looms large; for some, this hypocrisy looms larger than the ideals of freedom they espoused. On one hand, freedom is most important. On the other hand, bondage is most important.

Morgan would say that either position misses a deeper truth, a truth that is both more revealing and more damning.

Without slavery, the Founders would not have been able to pontificate on the lofty ideals of freedom that made their way into documents like the Declaration, the Constitution, and the Bill of Rights. They would have been so tied to their land, growing their crops, mostly tobacco, that they simply would not have had time for anything else. Cultivating tobacco, it turns out, even with slave labor, was incredibly time-consuming. Thus, freedom in early America was a privilege that derived from slavery.

This idea of an inextricable link between freedom and slavery proves to be extremely useful. It's a means for understanding why almost 25 percent of the US Constitution is related to the support of slavery, while the word *slavery* is never mentioned in the original text. It's a tool for examining the Emancipation Proclamation, and Lincoln's motives, then realizing the proclamation itself did not free a single slave. And, it's the basis for understanding how Black labor built White power and wealth.

If, historically speaking, there was no freedom without slavery in America, then the institutions of power and wealth that emerged in America owe themselves to the slavery upon which America established its freedom. Pick an institution, any institution—agriculture, politics, jurisprudence, religion, medicine, policing, finance, transportation, military—apply Morgan's rule, and you'll discover that as a means of power and wealth, that institution is rooted in slavery. In fact, that's exactly what this book intends to do—examine how American institutions of power and wealth came about as the result of Black labor, which before 1865 meant, for the most part, slavery.

Sometimes, the answer to the question of how Black labor built a particular institution of White power and wealth will be direct. Take agriculture. Black labor, slave labor, by working in farm fields, literally built the agricultural industry in America as one of the first institutions of power and wealth. At other times, the answer to this question will be indirect. Like policing. Black men and women had no direct hand in creating the institution of policing, an obvious instance of power used to protect White wealth. But the institution of policing was created to control the labor of Black men and women. Without the need of White slave owners to control their slave populations, policing may not have developed in America the way that it did. And occasionally, the answer will be both direct and indirect. How did Black labor build Wall Street? Turns out slaves actually built the wall, but slavery was also the basis for many of the financial instruments and investment vehicles used by brokers on the Street.

I approach this book by plotting a course along the river of American history, and at each stretch examine the institutions being born and trace their connections to Black labor at the time. But the method has its disadvantages. Principally, the river of American history is vast—wide, deep, ever-flowing, with many side streams and tributaries. How do you chart a course?

Black history is a strong current within this river of American history. So primarily, that's the course I chose. I began with the capture of Africans in West Africa as slaves in the seventeenth century, and their arrival in Virginia in 1619. And I ended about a decade after the Civil War, a decade after the end of slavery. Within this large sweep of time most of the key institutions of power and wealth in America were established, and the role that Black men and women played in their creation can be seen.

A key tenet of human systems theory is that in any interaction between the members of a group one finds essential elements of every interaction between those members, essential elements that do not vary over time.[2] Groups, in this view, refer to collections of people that share deep interdependencies and bonds. When applied to racial groups in America, this tenet serves as a tool to help understand how Black lives matter in creating White power and wealth, and how Black Americans have not shared in the wealth and power they have helped to create.

A pattern of racial interaction began well before there even was an America, in the late fifteenth and early sixteenth centuries in West Africa. There, Europeans first met Africans, and, for the most part, those Europeans viewed the African men and women they encountered not as humans but as resources to be exploited, like the gold and exotic spices they coveted and also found.

The "Age of Exploration" was not a time of beneficent contact between Europeans and new peoples and civilizations. The Portuguese, the Spanish, the English, the Dutch, and many other European countries and monarchies sent expeditions beyond the horizon for two reasons—to secure power and to obtain wealth. The two goals were fundamentally intertwined. Wealth came from trade. Trade came from shipping. Shipping came from the power to control the seas and from the power to control and subjugate the people Europeans encountered in this quest for power and wealth.

From slavery in the seventeenth century to the designation "essential workers" in the time of a pandemic in the twenty-first century, the essential elements of racial interaction in America have not changed: Black lives are a means to an end for all too many White Americans. That end? Greater wealth. To protect the acquisition of greater wealth? Greater power.

We will witness a similar racial interaction time and time again, starting in Africa in the sixteenth century and continuing through the post–Civil War period in America. Whites interacted with Blacks based on how Blacks could help create White wealth, and Whites developed systems of power to protect this wealth creation. Time and again, when Blacks asked for their fair share of this wealth or power—asked for their freedom dues—that request was met with outright betrayal and brutality, met with deception, violence, and death.

This present volume ends a decade after the Civil War with the election of 1876. For reasons I hope will become clear to the reader, the election of 1876 is so sharp a line of demarcation that it's possible to speak of how Black lives created White wealth and power before, and after, that election. From the Great Migration to eugen-ics to the Black Freedom Struggle to the killing of George Floyd, nearly everything that has happened since 1876 has deep roots in the period before. But leading up to the Civil War and the period just after, it seems as though new institutions of wealth and power were coming into being at a surprising rate. Rarely, if ever, does the history of that period trace these institutions back to the principal role that Black lives played in their creation.

In this regard, *Of Blood and Sweat* is also a story about the his-tory and emergence of White privilege in this country. At the mere mention of the term "White privilege," the eyes of many Americans glaze over. "What, me? I have not lived a privileged life. I've worked hard for everything I've obtained. The playing field is level. If you work hard, you can attain the same, too." That's how the reason-ing goes, and while this is the essence of the American Dream, it is also the substance of an American Nightmare. The playing field has never been level for Black Americans and other Americans of color. There has always been a privileged class in America, and that privilege has long been based on skin color.

White wealth. White power. White privilege. These are fascinat-ing ideas to explore at this unique moment in American history. In all likelihood, before the close of the current century, reparations for slavery will be made to Black Americans as a gesture, an overture, at closing the yawning income inequality gap, and recognizing their contribution to the institutions of power and wealth in America. How were White wealth, power, and privilege created? How should wealth be distributed? Who gets to decide? To answer these ques-tions is to maintain a better grasp on why reparations for slavery are justified and why the income inequality gap needs to be closed.

But Americans, for the most part, are not enamored of history even when it might offer insights into current issues and predica-ments. As an alternative to a lifeless and dry history of facts and fig-ures, I want to tell the story of how Black labor created White power and wealth through the actual stories of men and women who did the creating. Like the story of Phillip Corven, suing for his freedom dues; or the story of Antoney and Isabella, whose African names we do not know, but who were captured and thrown together on that first ship which appeared off Point Comfort, Virginia, in 1619 carrying "20. and odd Africans." Antoney and Isabella were later married, went into indentured servitude, and had the first Black child born in America.

I am also writing this book in the midst of the novel coronavirus pandemic. So the question of how disease shapes the course of human history and institutions is not far away; and the rise of slavery, for example, is directly related to the smallpox and measles pandemics of the sixteenth and seventeenth centuries, as I discuss.

I've been in self-isolation while working on this book. Even in isolation it is impossible to be insulated from the protests and calls for change sweeping across the country, and around the world; calls for racial equity, an end to police brutality, and an end to income inequality. These pressing present issues all have deep roots in America's past. And I hope, in some small way, *Of Blood and Sweat* will contribute to the ongoing discussion of how to understand and best address them.

Of Blood and Sweat scours the past for clues about the present and the future. As a student of history, how I wish I could walk the shores of colonial Virginia in late August 1619. I'd like to peer over the shoulder of Sir John Rolfe, husband-turned-betrayer of Pocahontas, as he pens entries into his ledger of the Flemish man-of-war *White Lion*, anchored in the James River off modern-day Fort Monroe, Virginia, with its cargo of "20. and odd Negroes." I'd like to row out to speak with Captain John Colyn Jope, in command of the *White Lion*, to inquire of him the sea battle he engaged in with the *São João Bautista*, a Portuguese slaver that had acquired its human cargo in present-day Luanda, Angola; booty, it appears, from Portuguese wars with the Angolan kingdom of the Ndongo.

What student of history would not want to travel back in time to be physically present during an epoch of interest? But even if we could time travel, we would still bring our present biases into the past.

For example, it is not possible to tell the story of *Of Blood and Sweat* without encountering the words *negro* and *nigger*, which appear everywhere throughout the extensive historical documents related to Black Americans. As a Black American myself, I have an implicit bias against these words, and as a student of history, I've also worked hard at overcoming this bias throughout the years. The word *negro*, for example, was not used in colonial America in the same way it was used in eighteenth-century America, nor twentieth-century America, nor the way it is thought of today. If we are to crack the code of how Black labor created White power and wealth, we must also begin to crack the code of the language used around race. And at the beginning of this book, I want to attempt that by examining my relationship to the word *negro*, as an example of addressing implicit historical bias.

As a child of the turbulent and radical 1960s, the clenched fist raised by John Lewis or Stokely Carmichael at a Student Non-Violent Coordinating Committee (SNCC) rally, or Eldridge Cleaver marching with a group of Black Panthers, or Tommie Smith and John Carlos at the Olympics, spoke to me more deeply than the use of *negro* by Martin Luther King, Jr. on the steps of the Lincoln Memorial. Yet, much like music across generations, the word *negro* fueled a radical departure for my parents and grandparents from the term *colored*, used to describe African Americans a generation before me. If *Black* or *Afro-American* or *African American* was radical for me, *negro* was radical for them. Yet, I heard echoes of *nigger* in the word, and I abhorred it.

Some time ago, I had the chance to write a book about African mythology, and as part of that book I became fascinated with the mythology of black and white. How did "white" come to connote goodness and purity, and "black" to connote evil and filth? What I discovered forever changed my relationship with the word *negro* and all words related to it, even the word *nigger*.

For it turns out that *niger*, a Latin root from which the words *negro* and *nigger* derive, has origins as a vowel-less Egyptian Semitic word, *ngr*, the similarity of the Semitic and Latin words unmistakable. Linguists have no real idea how *ngr* was pronounced in ancient Egypt, hence its representation absent vowels. But *ngr* referred to the grace and power of the Nigretai, a fierce clan of Libyan charioteers admired for the beauty of their black skins. And *ngr* also referred to the Niger River, whose strange, U-shaped course led many early observers to believe the river terminated in desert sands. Linguists tell us that *ngr* originally meant "water to flow into sand" and the Black people along the river were the "people of the water to flow into sand."[3]

This was a wholly new and unexpected discovery of the real meaning of *negro*, which shook me at first. I fully understood how *negro*, for some, referred to Black subservience and *nigger* was used to convey hate. But, in the ancient history of the words, I'd also discovered a meaning which was poetic and beautiful; a meaning I readily embraced.

Therein, I feel, lies one secret to addressing implicit bias: the ability to hold competing truths simultaneously. I will probably always recoil, at first, upon hearing *negro* or *nigger*; and yet I will also recover after a moment, recognizing that unlike many people, I also have knowledge that provides me with a deeper understanding of both words.

And so, when approaching historical records, as was so necessary in writing *Of Blood and Sweat*, I do recoil, at first, upon encountering the words *negro*, *negroe*, *neggar*, and *nigger* as they appear so frequently in the writings of the White and Black men and women in early America. But I also recover after a period of time, with my own understanding of the deeper meaning behind these words, and also an understanding they were not used with the same meaning in the seventeenth century as they are today.

Prior to 1640, when slavery was firmly established in the American colonies, the words *negroe* and *neggar* were usually no more than descriptions of people with dark skin from Africa, and sometimes they were simply called *Africans*. As the American colonies embraced slavery, the words took on new meaning as substitutes, or code words, for the word *slave*. With the abolition of slavery, *negro* and *nigger* became Jim Crow terms for referring to Blacks pejoratively with regard to their prior status as slaves; a reminder they still occupied the lowest rung on the ladder of the American hierarchy of race and class. And, in modern times, a similar usage of the words continued, though after the rise of eugenics in the early twentieth century, there was an added element of hatred that came from wanting to eliminate these undesirable people from the ranks of the American population. So, in some ways, the story told in *Of Blood and Sweat* also could be told by simply tracking the evolutionary use of these N-words.

As a scholar deeply interested in history, I have long been at odds with the idea that history should be told in dispassionate, removed terms. This way of thinking about history goes something like this: (a) events took place in the past; (b) you, the historian, have a hypothesis about what happened and why; (c) you assemble the facts of those historical events that might prove (or disprove) your hypothesis; and (d) you remove yourself as much as possible from the presentation of those events and let others decide whether you have successfully proved, or disproved, your hypothesis. This is history as a courtroom drama.

My starting point is somewhat different. Yes, events happened in the past but those events are more like stones thrown into a body of water creating ripples that move out from the center. Those ripples travel forward into the future, interacting with the ripples from other stones thrown into the water. All of those intersecting ripples affect us today. I cannot but be affected, for example, when I am personally touched by the strictures of a world caught in the throes of a pandemic but also reading about a world four hundred years ago also in the midst of a pandemic. In this book, in that case, I'm going to draw parallels between both times, and comment on them personally as it seems appropriate. Similarly, when I hear outside my door chants of "Black Lives Matter," then read of a 1672 colonial law which allowed for the taking of Black lives with impunity, I'm going to draw parallels and comment, and it's going to be personal.

I know this approach to history breaks with the ranks of those who feel the "scientific method" should be applied to the study of history, and the personal opinions of the historian should be left out. But I also feel so many people, particularly Americans, take perverse pride in saying, along with Sam Cooke, "don't know much about history" precisely because it tends to be overly academic and sanitized. And one way to reverse this disdain for the past is by making it relevant to current times and also making it personal.

As a writer, I find the historical use and evolution of the English language fascinating. Most readers have no idea that just a few hundred years ago written English was so different than it is today. In the early parts of the book I have resisted the temptation to modernize word spellings and usage as they appear in the original sources.

In seventeenth- and eighteenth-century America, writers frequently spelled words as they heard them. Add to this, English in those times still showed influences from Old English, German, Latin, and other languages: f, for instance, is often used in place of s; v is occasionally used in place of u, and vice versa; y is sometimes found where we might expect an i; e is tacked onto words in a seemingly random fashion. And there are many other spellings and usages that seem foreign and wrong by today's standards. This particularly effects the spelling of names. Thomas Key, for example, might be spelled Thomas Keie, Keye, or Kaye, or sometimes all three spellings within the same document, still referring to the same person.

So, instead of saying, "It appears to us that she is the daughter of Thomas Key based on several pieces of evidence," the original statement might have been written, "It appeareth to us that shee is the daughter of Thomas Keie by severall Evidences."

It might take a moment longer to read and comprehend such statements, but this archaic English language and spelling allows me to better connect with that past moment in time and it *seemes to Mee to adde Hystoricale colour to what myhte bee an Otherwyse drye Storye.*

Similarly, when using slave narratives from the Library of Congress collection, I quote the words of individuals as they were written. These narratives are a rich source of personal stories from the Black men and women who lived during some of the times covered in this book. They were recorded near the end of their lives in the late 1930s, by writers working with the New Deal Works Progress Administration (WPA) Writers' Project. These chroniclers were instructed to scour the south for older Black men and women, who grew up during slavery. A few had massive, portable recording devices wired to heavy batteries weighing down the trunks of their cars and made actual audio recordings of these ex-slaves. But most had only pen and paper, or perhaps a typewriter. They tried to capture the words the ex-slaves spoke. So the English is full of *dat*s and *dem*s and *dey*s. I have made no effort to change or standardize the spellings, which are unique to each WPA writer.

Some consider this use of English reflective of the uneducated, ignorant state of these men and women—a belief I completely reject. In fact, I actually find it amusing to contrast the strange English used by White men in historical documents with the equally strange English used by ex-slaves in telling their stories. While they are not the same, they both bring me closer to the individuals behind the words.

Where possible, *Of Blood and Sweat* is based on primary sources. What that means is the book uses, as much as possible, original documents contemporary to the time period under consideration. Sir John Rolfe's ledger entry for August 20, 1619, that the captain of the *White Lion* anchored off Fort Monroe "brought not anything but 20. and odd Negroes," is an example of a primary source document. When such source documents are not available, then secondary or tertiary sources are used. These include recognized experts in various fields of study writing about historical events or about the findings of other recognized experts.

Writing about historical events is akin to working on a jigsaw puzzle where many pieces are either missing or damaged. You piece together what you can, then make reasoned assumptions and conjectures about the absent puzzle parts. Rolfe's statement about the arrival of Africans is a case in point. Does "20. and odd Negroes" mean exactly twenty Africans or approximately twenty Africans? Some researchers examining other documents from colonial Virginia in August 1619 note a count of twenty-two or twenty-three Africans, so the figures vary. But then recent discoveries point to the arrival of a second ship, *Treasurer*, four days after *White Lion*, which may have left two or three Africans, so the count of Africans at the end of August 1619 may have conflated these two groups.

Of course, a more important question is does it matter if we know exactly how many Africans arrived in Virginia in August 1619? As a student of history, I feel that accuracy does matter; that the more accurate we are, even in the smallest of details, the more reliable we will be when forced to move beyond facts and details into the realm of assumptions and conjectures.

There's another reason I prefer to use original source material when it is available. In reading the works of others writing about the past, time and time again, I found that the actual historical documents were misquoted, misspelled, or taken out of context. Even people I deeply respect, like my mentors and past teachers, made such errors. In the past, references to source documents would be buried in footnotes, which required a researcher to have the books the author cited, or travel to a library to get them. That was a time-consuming process that few readers, or other authors, engaged in. We simply trusted the principal writer as long as they included a footnote to a quoted source. Now, however, it's quite easy to type a phrase into a search engine and see what results are returned. When I did that, it surprised me how often what the author wrote varied in some meaningful way from the original; surprised me to the point that I checked and double-checked nearly every secondary or tertiary reference I used.

Throughout the book, when I dispute the claims and assertions of other researchers from my own reading of the historical record, for the most part, I move that commentary into endnotes, so as not to interrupt the main flow of the narrative. Some of this commentary is quite long. While students and lovers of history may find these comments interesting and engaging, those less interested in such historical details may simply skip over them with little sacrifice.

Many years ago, as a young student at Wesleyan University in Connecticut and the Institute of the Black World in Atlanta, I had the great privilege of studying with two towering scholars of Black history, the late Drs. Vincent Harding and Lerone Bennett, Jr. Both would become mentors and friends. They shaped my understanding of the importance and power of Black history, and through them I learned how history needn't be a dry and lifeless recounting of facts, for they were both masterful storytellers who wove compelling tales from the facts of the Black American experience they assembled.

Of Blood and Sweat owes much to these men. The book covers events and people that both Bennett and Harding covered numerous times in their scholarship. I am thrilled to be able to retake a journey for which these two men served as my first guides, as I am also thrilled to be able to contribute something of my own to that journey. History is continually being rewritten as historical finds are made. More is available to me now, as I reconsider the formative years of America, than was available to Bennett and Harding when they wrote. While *Of Blood and Sweat* updates and corrects the historical account of Black Americans, it also adds to this account insights from my own scholarship. And, the book applies the historical record of how Black lives mattered in building White power and wealth to issues central to public discourse today, such as police brutality, income inequality, and reparations, that were not as central to the public discourse when Bennett and Harding wrote.

History, it is said, is written by the victors. And Black folks, more often vanquished than victorious, have only infrequently woven their own place into the fabric of the American story. *Of Blood and Sweat* seeks to do justice to the many ways in which Black Americans have fundamentally contributed to and shaped the American story. *Of Blood and Sweat* is not a top-down story of American triumphalism and exceptionalism. It is a bottom-up people's account of how this American story was fashioned and molded based on the presence of a marginalized group considered unworthy and undeserving of full inclusion.

That said, I am mindful that *Of Blood and Sweat* does not account for all the marginalized groups that form the warp and weft of the American fabric. Notably absent in this present account is the full story of Native Americans, the story of Whites who were not part of the ruling class, and the story of women. Their stories are essential. Fortunately, there are scholars better equipped than I am, researching and telling these stories.

I strongly support reparations to Black Americans, for having suffered many decades of slavery, then endured the brutality of post-slavery America to the present day. But *Of Blood and Sweat* is not written simply to make that case, nor to make the case to eliminate or reduce wealth inequality, nor to completely refashion American policing, all of which I also strongly support. Still, it's my hope that *Of Blood and Sweat* tells a powerful tale about how Black Americans helped to build White power and wealth while never receiving their fair share and, in so doing, contributes to discussion of these important issues.

Clyde W. Ford
May 2021
Bellingham, Washington

1

ANTONEY AND ISABELL

"Antoney, Negro, and Isabell, Negro" is how they were known in the 1625 ledger of Captain William Tucker of Elizabeth City, Virginia.[1] In all likelihood, they also had African names only the ages know now. They may have been baptized shortly after birth, and their anglicized names conferred then by Portuguese priests who'd ventured deep into the interior of Angola, where Catholicism was well established by the sixteenth century. Or, Portuguese priests may have performed obligatory baptisms and christenings of these two young people as they were herded into the hold of the *São João Bautista*, a Portuguese slave ship at anchor in Luanda Bay off the coast of Angola, in the late central-African rainy season of 1619. Let's call them Anthony and Isabella, for our narrative.[2] Two among the "20. and odd Negroes" Sir John Rolfe recorded aboard the Dutch man-of-war *White Lion*, lying at anchor on August 20, 1619, at the mouth of the James River off Point Comfort.[3]

Anthony and Isabella carried within them the germinal cells of the first Black child born in America, though on that fateful day in August 1619 they probably did not know that, nor did they know his name. Nor could they have known that symbolically they also carried within them the germinal cells of Scipio and Crispus and Nat and Sojourner and Maggie and Frederick and Booker T. and W.E.B.

and Marcus and Langston and Duke and Yardbird and 'Trane and Malcolm and Martin and Rosa and Barack and Trayvon and Eric and Breonna and George . . . and me . . . and countless millions who, in some measure or part, were torn, like them, from Africa's soil.

Anthony and Isabella stepped from the decks of the *White Lion* into a pinnace, bobbing in the surf off Point Comfort, Virginia; a small boat that would carry them to the White planters and merchants and colonists waiting ashore, men who had just determined their worth in terms of salted meat and vegetables and grain and the other provisions needed by the captain of the *White Lion*. What they did not know then, could not know then, is that in being handed over to these men, they were about to embark on a journey of unimaginably epic proportions; a heroic journey in which, during their lives, they would endure great hardships and privations; a symbolic journey that would see their work lay the foundation of the economics, politics, religion, medicine, education, industry, law enforcement, and technology of a new nation; and, a hard-earned journey that would generate great power and wealth for some that, sadly, Anthony and Isabella, and those like them, for the most part, would never share.

In their interaction with those White men ashore lay the embryonic maps of many roads, some surveyed and taken, others surveyed and deemed unworthy: American slavery, American freedom, Bacon's Rebellion, the Revolutionary War, the Constitution, the Declaration of Independence, the Bill of Rights, Nat Turner's Rebellion, the cotton gin, the Age of Sail, the Civil War, Reconstruction, Jim Crow, the Great Migration, railroads, mines, oil drilling, cars, racism, lynching, Red Summer, two world wars, two Marches on Washington, the murders of Malcolm and Martin, the gunning down of Trayvon and Ahmaud, the killing of George Floyd, and the many other events shaped by the interaction of Black folks and White folks in America. Anthony and Isabella did not know this then, and neither did the men onshore, like Captain

William Tucker, who would acquire and settle the couple to work on his farm near present-day Hampton, Virginia.

But today, we can know what became of those seeds, real and symbolic, which Anthony and Isabella carried within them; we can know of the roads taken and those that were not. And where they could not know, we must not forget.

Anthony and Isabella were Angolan; they came from the Kimbundu-speaking, Bantu Ndongo people of the highlands surrounding the modern-day city of N'dalatando, a little over one hundred miles inland from the coastal capital Luanda.

We may never know if they knew each other in Angola, but I can imagine they did; that their families also knew each other. And that their love may have even begun in the Angolan highlands, survived a savage capture by the Portuguese, a "death march" to the coast, the ravages of the Middle Passage, to be consummated in a strange new land.

We can say, however, that Anthony and Isabella knew each other as *malungu*.

Malungu, originally a Kimbundu word meaning "watercraft," is how Angolans referred to their fellow captive shipmates. Eventually, *malungu* was extended to mean a close companion, compatriot, or friend. The word found its way into the Portuguese as *melungo* ("shipmate") and into English as *Melungeon*.[4] Initially, in English, it referred to an ethnically diverse group of people originating in early-seventeenth-century Virginia, Carolina, Maryland, and Delaware from Bantu Africa, with some combination of eastern Native American and northern European ancestry. Recent DNA testing has shown that Melungeons possess significant African and European DNA markers with little discernible evidence of Native American DNA.[5] Others have made claims, with varying degrees of scientific and historical evidentiary support, that Abraham Lincoln, Tom Hanks, Ava Gardner, Elvis Presley, Heather Locklear, Rich Mullins, and comedian Steve Martin are also Melungeon.[6]

Ultimately, Melungeons settled Kentucky, Tennessee, Ohio, Louisiana, and Texas. They are often called the "Lost Tribe of Appalachia." Some historians and heritage societies have labored to obliterate or obscure their African roots, preferring instead to describe Melungeons as having descended from the "Lost Colony of Roanoke"[7] or from Mediterranean settlers. They have traced the word to *melun jinn* (from the Arabic meaning "evil spirit") or the French *mélange* (meaning "mixture") without ever mentioning the Kimbundu word *malungu*.[8]

But, in 1880, the Portuguese philologist Macedo Soares, citing a 1779 Portuguese dictionary, gave the definition of *malungo*, poetically, as: "*Malungo, meu malungo . . . chama o preto a outro cativo que veio com ele na mesma embaracao.*" ("Malungo, my malungo . . . one black calls to another captive who came with him on the same ship.")[9]

I, too, am malungu.

I know this from the surprising results of DNA testing, which showed only one genetic hot spot in Africa on both my mother's and my father's side of the family, where I thought there might be two. That hot spot: Angola. On the maternal side of my family, I am descended from Africans who lived across the James River from Jamestown, forty miles upstream from that fateful anchorage at Point Comfort, in Surry, Virginia.

I would also be considered a Melungeon.

Curious about what DNA showed of my European roots, I was equally surprised to find, once again, only one major hot spot for both my mother's and father's side of the family. This hot spot was in northern Europe, in the Scottish Highlands.

No abstract tale from a time long ago, the story of Anthony and Isabella *is* my story; a story borne in my blood, which starts in Angola in the late sixteenth and early seventeenth centuries.

Anthony and Isabella resided in the Kingdom of Ndongo, a principality of the well-organized Kingdom of Kongo, founded in the late sixteenth century by Ngola Kiluanje, chief of a Kimbundu-speaking clan, and a migrant from Kongo. Throughout the sixteenth and early seventeenth centuries, the kingdoms of Ndongo and Kongo were at odds with each other, and also with the Portuguese.[10]

Both factions, however, viewed the Portuguese as arbiters of their conflict, and Christianity as the currency of that arbitration. So, seeking a declaration of independence from Kongo, between 1518 and 1571 the Kingdom of Ndongo sent three missions to Lisbon asking for missionaries, offering to be baptized, and seeking military assistance in fighting their Kongo rulers. In response, Portugal sent three military missions in return; one in 1520 and another in 1560 ended in retreat. The third, in 1571, was led by Paulo Dias de Novais, grandson of Bartolomeu Dias, the famous explorer who'd first rounded the Cape of Good Hope in 1488.

Dias operated under brutal orders from King Sebastian I of Portugal and Pope Nicholas V in Rome. Dias founded the port city of *São Paulo da Assunção de Loanda* (present-day Luanda) in 1576, and pushed his way inland along the Cuanza River, blessed by Lisbon to subjugate the Kingdom of Angola and by a papal bull "to invade, search out, capture, vanquish, and subdue all Saracens and pagans whatsoever, and other enemies of Christ wheresoever placed, and the kingdoms, dukedoms, principalities, dominions, possessions, and all movable and immovable goods whatsoever held and possessed by them and *to reduce their persons to perpetual slavery . . .*"[11]

Religion could not hold its own against the powerful forces of profit and greed unleashed by the slave trade. A Catholic bishop, Manuel Bautista Soares, living in Angola at the time of Anthony and Isabella's capture, lodged a complaint with the Holy See against Portuguese raids on the Ndongo, and the plunder of slaves, but to no avail.[12] A Calvinist minister and ship captain, John Colyn Jope, would finally deliver Anthony, Isabella, and the other captives to a settlement in colonial Virginia.[13] Jewish merchants, escaping the Portuguese Inquisition for the Dutch lowlands, held contracts, known as *asientos*, to deliver slaves to Spanish colonies.[14] And Muslims ran a massive Trans-Saharan, Indian Ocean slave trade, where by some estimates as many as 80 to 90 percent of the estimated six to seven million captured Black Africans died before reaching their final destinations.[15] Muslims also participated directly in the transatlantic slave trade to America. In places like Senegal, Ghana, and Nigeria, slaves were captured by Muslim African communities at war with other Africans they considered nonbelieving infidels.[16] With profits to be made, and scores to be settled, all the children of Abraham were complicit.

Dias failed in his second attempt to vanquish the Kongo and the Ndongo in 1560. Ever a soldier in service of God and country, he went back again, but experience taught him he needed a better plan. So, he made alliances with both the kingdoms of the Kongo and Ndongo, often pitting one against the other in service of Portugal conquering and controlling territory. Back-and-forth conflict ensued among all three parties for more than a quarter century. A Portuguese force was ambushed and massacred by Kongo forces in 1579, leading to the narrow defeat of a subsequent Kongo invasion and a foray by Portuguese forces in 1582 up the Cuanza River whereby many Ndongo riverine principalities switched their allegiance from the Ndongo to the Portuguese.

Eventually, the Portuguese settled on the Kingdom of Kongo as an ally, and the Kingdom of Ndongo as their mortal enemy. A 1590 offensive by the Portuguese against the Ndongo capital of Kabasa was repulsed owing to an alliance between the Ndongo and the nearby Matamba, and many of the formerly pro-Portuguese principalities along the Cuanza returned to the control of the Ndongo.[17]

By the start of the seventeenth century, this teeter-totter warring had ceased, and a border had been formalized between the Portuguese colony of Angola centered in Luanda and the Kingdom of Ndongo. A tenuous truce prevailed, even as the Portuguese continued their expansion into Ndongo lands along the Cuanza River. In 1611, when Bento Banha Cardoso took over as governor, he once again pursued war with the Ndongo, but unlike his predecessors, he enlisted a new, lethal weapon. Cardoso made a fateful, strategic decision to align with a ruthless, feared group of nomadic raiders, neither of Kongo nor Ndongo origin, known as the Imbangala, intent on sacking and pillaging the Ndongo countryside.[18]

Imbangala societies were based on military, not kinship, bonds. In Imbangala *kilombos* (war camps) brutal control was exercised over members through a strict set of *yijila* (codes) that included real and symbolic infanticide, persecution of women, real or symbolic cannibalism, and the grooming of child soldiers through alcohol and terror.[19] Many of the Imbangala's tactics of control are still in use by groups in Nigeria, Uganda, Afghanistan, Colombia, and other countries around the world where child soldiers are groomed for conflict today.

Imbangala warriors smeared an ointment, *maji a samba*, over their bodies, believed to anoint them with invincibility.[20] By the early seventeenth century, Portuguese merchants, with the insights and assistance of an English sailor named Andrew Battell, who lived as a captive among the Imbangala, were buying Imbangala war captives, mostly Ndongo, whom they sold as slaves to Iberian colonies in Central and South America.[21]

In the Imbangala, the Portuguese found the perfect mercenary force for their battle with the Ndongo. In 1617, Governor of Angola Luís Mendes de Vasconcelos, a successor to Cardoso, first rejected an alliance with the Imbangala before committing to it. Under Portuguese guidance, the Imbangala conducted a series of raids against the Ndongo: sacking the capital city of Kabasa, forcing King Ngola Mbandi to flee to the island of Kindonga in the Cuanza River, and capturing thousands of Ndongo subjects, royalty and commoners alike, who were then acquired by the Portuguese for sale on the other side of the Atlantic.[22]

Anthony and Isabella were among those Ndongo captured by the Imbangala, then marched in irons the hundred or so miles to the coast. One can only imagine them cresting a hill for their first view of the Atlantic near Luanda, seeing slave ships riding anchor in the bay, like hungry beasts with empty bellies waiting to be fed.

In the early seventeenth century, from New England to New Spain (Mexico), prior to the British engaging in a direct slave trade of their own, most Africans in the Americas came from the Ndongo region of Angola.

• • •

Christopher Columbus's original plan failed. Had it succeeded, it's doubtful that as many Africans would have been taken from inland Angola on death marches to the coast, and from there into the horrific Middle Passage bound for the Americas. Had it succeeded, Anthony and Isabella may never have been acquired from the Imbangala by the Portuguese for sale in Spanish colonies. Had it succeeded, the couple may have never been captured by the *White Lion*, then sold for victuals to Virginian colonists. Had Columbus's original plan succeeded, the African slave trade may have not taken on the shape and magnitude, the brutality and savagery, it did. But Columbus's original plan did fail, failed spectacularly, and one of the reasons it failed is that Columbus and his men were asymptomatic carriers of pandemics from Europe to the Americas.

When he first arrived on the island of Hispaniola in 1492, Columbus noted a friendly and peaceful indigenous Taino people. But Columbus had ventured to the Americas not for peace but for profit and for the establishment of Spain as an international power. Hispaniola's land was fertile. The island's climate good. Talk swirled of nearby gold. So, the Spaniards dispossessed the Taino of their land and enslaved them to work that same land and dig in the Spanish mines.

Munitions benefited the conquistadores. Taino warriors, outfitted with only clubs and spears, bows and arrows, even though poison tipped, were no match for Spanish gunpowder and rifles. But microbes benefited the conquistadores as well. For they brought with them to the New World two viral diseases ravaging the Old World: measles and smallpox.

The Taino, and the other indigenous Arawak people of Central and South America, had no biological defenses against the novel diseases, no "herd immunity," no antibodies. Columbus touching down in the Americas unleashed what historians and epidemiologists call a "virgin soil epidemic,"[23] also referred to as "the Columbian Exchange," whereby potatoes, corn, medicinal plants, other fauna and flora, and culture passed bidirectionally between Europe and the Americas during the sixteenth century, but disease passed unidirectionally from Europe to the indigenous populations of the New World.[24]

Numbering a million when Columbus first arrived, the population of Taino on Hispaniola succumbed so quickly to the munitions and microbes of the Spanish that by 1520 they'd dwindled to a mere fifteen thousand.[25] But the Spanish still had economies to open and profits to be made. This meant replacing Columbus's failed plan to use indigenous slave labor with a new plan to bring in slave labor from outside of New Spain.

Africa, on the other hand, was not "virgin soil" for smallpox or measles. By the time Columbus arrived on Hispaniola in 1492, the Portuguese had already been in West Africa for nearly a century; had already comingled with West African societies, who consequently had already developed immunities similar to Europeans. West Africans, some also the beneficiaries of smallpox vaccines developed by Arabic medicine, were not nearly as susceptible to European disease as were the indigenous populations of the Americas. Thus, the Spanish turned to the Portuguese to supply them with slave labor, and the Portuguese turned to West Africa.[26]

A pandemic not only spreads disease, but also leaves a fundamentally altered world in its wake. At nearly 360 nanometers in length, the smallpox virus is three times the size of the novel coronavirus, which causes COVID-19. More than a half trillion coronavirus particles could fit on the head of a pin. Roughly, a couple of hundred million smallpox virus particles could occupy a similar space. So, Anthony and Isabella would never have known, nor could they have ever seen, that their fate was, in a strangely significant way, tied to that of a microbe that spread disease from Europe to the indigenous people of the Americas.

Ripples from a pebble dropped into a body of water flow in all directions. Apart from an unseen microbial assailant, unknown ripples ensnared Anthony and Isabella, and the others marching with them in irons toward the coast and the *São João Bautista*. From one direction came ripples from events colliding to give rise to their capture, like the Portuguese conflict with the Ndongo. Waiting, where ripples had not yet reached, events were yet to unfold, like their sale in Virginia and work on Captain William Tucker's plantation. These first ripples were direct, touching not only these two young souls but the Imbangala mercenaries and the Portuguese military as well.

Yet, in these first ripples one catches the initial wavering glimpses of Black labor creating White power and wealth. Military success in Angola strengthened the Portuguese alliance with the Imbangala. It established the Imbangala as a powerful, fierce, and feared fighting force. It consolidated the Portuguese grip on power in Angola, establishing Portugal as the preeminent European power on the west coast of Africa in the sixteenth century. Victory kept wealth flowing into political and military coffers, enriching colonial governors and military commanders. With coastal Angola protected, merchants began moving to Luanda, building fabulous *casas* on the cliffs overlooking the Atlantic, enriching themselves as middlemen in the trade among Spanish and Portuguese New World colonies, Africa, and Europe through the sale of spices, ore, and, principally, human beings. Africa, more specifically Africans, became the currency of Portuguese power and wealth.

For Anthony and Isabella, and the people who lost them, these initial ripples were, no doubt, devastating. Overnight, they were ripped away from people they loved and societies they'd known. In Luanda Bay, slave ships waited for them, pirouetting around their anchors at the mercy of the wind and waves. Here, now, we first glimpse the indirect effects of building power and wealth that came into play with this traffic in human beings; and, surprising as it may be, the role that millions of Africans like Anthony and Isabella, soon-to-be African Americans, would play in creating new industries of White power and wealth in America, that land still far away. But first, we need to examine how Anthony and Isabella, and those like them, shaped and created new industries and institutions, new power and wealth in Europe. For New World colonies, before they were independent countries, were extensions of Old World Europe.

The *São João Bautista* (*Saint John the Baptist*), awaiting Anthony and Isabella, and some 350 other captive Ndongo natives, in Luanda Bay, bore the distinctive markings of a Dutch-designed and built *fluyt* (pronounced like the English word *flute*): three masts, a high stern or aftcastle, a narrow deck, and a compensatory bulbous, pear-shaped hull below her waterline. All business. Dutch naval architects and shipwrights from the city of Hoorn designed and built fluyts for cargo not conflict, for war booty not war-making, maximizing cargo space, minimizing the space or need for crew. The larger the cargo hold the more ore and spice a ship could hold, but also the more human beings; therefore, the more profit to the ship's owners.[27]

But in the lines of a sixteenth-century Dutch fluyt, like the *São João Bautista*, one can also see technological innovations built from the lines of fifteenth-century carracks or caravels, vessels that themselves were innovations on the cogs plying the Mediterranean in prior centuries.

Early European explorers and merchants faced a problem: Human and natural resources awaited exploitation along the west coast of Africa, and beyond, but how to harvest them and safely return? Prevailing trade winds made voyages south around Cape Verde, the westernmost tip of Africa, relatively easy. But on the return leg, a cog became a "pig," what sailors sometimes call a vessel barely capable of sailing into the wind. Cogs needed fair winds directly behind their sails, and this required tacking west almost to the coast of present-day Brazil to catch a ride home to Europe on prevailing trade winds. This was long, difficult, and dangerous. Vessels were lost, and so, too, profits.

Carracks and caravels, designed from cogs, had three or four masts, deeper drafts, and enlarged cargo holds. Carracks and caravels handled rough seas better, sailed closer to the wind, and made for shorter and safer return voyages from West Africa. Magellan, da Gama, Dias, Columbus—all of the early navigators sailed either carracks or caravels. With their enlarged cargo holds, most of the early slave ships bound from Europe to Africa, then across the Atlantic for Portuguese and Spanish colonies in the Americas, were carracks or caravels. But technology proceeded relentlessly, in the sixteenth century as it does today, and carracks and caravels yielded to a newer, sleeker, less expensive, more specialized design: the Dutch fluyt.

Slavery drove technological innovation, and that created an additional stream of European power and wealth. In spurring new shipbuilding, Anthony and Isabella and their malungu drove the profits made by merchants who paid for the construction and use of new ships. But, behind these merchants were the profits made by bankers, or kings and queens and royals, who laid out the funds for the merchants to construct the ships that would be used to transport captured Africans to uncertain fates in the New World.

Ripples expanded ever wider from the drops of African blood in Angola. European power and wealth grew. Non-shipbuilding businesses in cities like Hoorn thrived off the shipwrights building slave ships. Banking houses and financial institutions in Amsterdam and London grew fat from the profits they made, then invested those profits in non-slave-trade-related businesses. In effect, laundering blood money. Take the hypothetical owner of a seventeenth-century Amsterdam bakery who needed capital to expand his shop. Perhaps he secured a loan from a Dutch bank at a fair interest rate, then hired workers to construct an addition to his store. He would most likely never realize how his shop's expansion was fundamentally linked to the capture of Africans by the Imbangala, and their death march from inland to the coast.

And, we have yet to consider even more distant ripples. How, once bartered or sold in the New World, slaves built the agricultural economies of the colonies that created further European wealth. We will examine these details in later chapters.

Such ripple effects, in generating power and wealth, are not trivial. Economic analysis is based on them. Modern-day national and international economies are built from them, and destroyed by them in times of economic crisis. An understanding of how Black labor built White power and wealth begins with them—like the capture of Anthony and Isabella, and the start of their harrowing journey to America.

• • •

Who was this couple, captured and enslaved, who would then travel an ocean to begin building the power and wealth of a country, power and wealth they would not share? We know where they came from. We know many details about their passage. We know the circumstances of their arrival. Yet, we know almost nothing about who they really were. No journals of Anthony and Isabella survive. No books of their travails are known. No contemporaneous newspaper accounts of them have ever surfaced. Must they remain only names on the muster of their master?

Anthony and Isabella did have a son, William, and descendants of William Tucker have been found.[28] So, we do know something about Anthony and Isabella's family tree, but that still leaves us knowing little about them. I don't believe we should throw up our hands and claim there's nothing more to know. We may not be able to understand their unique traits as individual human beings, but there's a powerful way of understanding them, and their malungu, as a whole—through the stories, more specifically the myths, that were told in the region of Africa from where they were taken.

"The myth is the public dream," said Joseph Campbell, "and the dream is the private myth."[29] And both myths and dreams are portals into the psyche, as Carl Jung showed.[30]

So, for a brief moment, I want to venture into the myths that Anthony and Isabella carried with them as they headed out to sea and into the maw of the Middle Passage. For these myths may be the only portals we have into the psyches of the men and women who would then go on to build power and wealth in a New World.

Anthony and Isabella, and their malungu, did not face this long, hard, torturous passage unarmed. Nor did the families and friends and villages they left behind face their disappearance unprepared. Though in 1619 Ndongo villages had succumbed to the war hatchets and battle clubs of the Imbangala, and Ndongo men and women had been rounded up as chattel set on death marches to Portuguese ships lying off the coast, the Ndongo possessed a superior weapon that neither the Imbangala nor the Portuguese could ever capture: a deep, abiding, and widespread spirituality grounded in mythic wisdom. While this mythic wisdom connected the Ndongo in Africa, it kept them connected through the horrors of the Middle Passage, and even on the other side of the Atlantic in the Americas as well. Malungu was not based solely on a shared geography of kinship and blood, but more important, on a shared mythology of convictions and beliefs.[31]

Ndongo spirituality did not arise from Christianity, even though as early as 1518 Ndongo emissaries journeyed to Portugal requesting Christian missionaries in return, while pledging their conversion to Catholicism. Ndongo shrewdness should not be overlooked. In part, these overtures to the Portuguese crown stemmed from the Ndongo seeking diplomatic and political recognition as an independent polity apart from their Kongo overlords, and Portuguese military assistance in any coming conflicts against the Kongo kingdom. But Ndongo spirituality, as did most traditional African spiritual systems, possessed a remarkable flexibility and adaptability known as syncretism, whereby the rites, rituals, and symbols of a foreign spirituality were effortlessly incorporated without violence or displacement of Ndongo core beliefs.

Ndongo spirituality gave Anthony and Isabella, and those who came after them, strength when they needed it most. But that spirituality was a mixed blessing. It allowed Angolans to survive the horrors of capture and the Middle Passage. Then, on the other side of the Atlantic, it allowed them to survive the horrors and brutality of slavery. But it allowed them to survive, which also meant it allowed them to survive while creating a world whose riches and privileges they would never know. And, when Africans followed Anthony and Isabella from countries other than Angola, and also brought their native spirituality with them, their spirituality allowed them to survive in a similar way.

A good place to begin understanding the inner strength of men and women like Anthony and Isabella is by asking the questions: What happened to African societies where a husband or wife, a father or mother, a son or daughter, a good friend, suddenly disappeared in irons at the point of a weapon, never to be seen again? How did communities come to terms with such devastating losses? How did they heal?

Some years back, I was at work on a book about African mythology. Quite by accident, or perhaps by mythic design, I was one evening in the library of my local university thumbing through a book about African prophets when I stumbled upon a BaKongo myth pertaining precisely to these questions. In this myth, comrades ripped from the bosom of the BaKongo and whisked away by White men in ships were first conveyed to the realm of Mputu, and from there exiled "to an island where there was a forest with no food in it, and the sea on every side."[32]

Mputu is a reference both to the Portuguese (a contraction of *Mputoleezo*, a KiKingo word meaning "Portuguese") and to the mythical BaKongo realm of death, not of physical demise but an underground realm of unconscious energies and invisible powers; a realm that heroes and heroines in the myths of this region travel to, there engaging in battle with magical beings and bizarre forces.

And when the forces and powers of Mputu are bested, these heroes and heroines return with gifts and boons they bestow to the everyday world. *Mputu* is further a reference to the "agitated waters" of the Atlantic out of which White men appeared, into which Black men and women, boys and girls, disappeared. But the waters of Mputu separated the light world above from the darkness of the unconscious below, and the human soul, said the BaKongo, travels to Mputu after life, there to be reborn in a continuous cycle of birth, death, and rebirth.

Captured kinsmen and -women were heroes and heroines, the BaKongo myth relates, thrust unwillingly into the desolate landscape of Mputu to confront the dark forces and powers there. Ultimately, the myth tells of divine intervention to aid these beleaguered souls. "God gave them civilization . . . and food . . . and every needful thing." For the BaKongo, to this day, African Americans are considered to be the hero-souls of ancestors battling their way through Mputu, who will ultimately return home as all heroes and heroines must. "We're waiting for them," said an old BaKongo man, "this is nobody's country but theirs."[33]

This BaKongo myth is undated. But the Ndongo were subjects of the BaKongo, which means that Anthony and Isabella may have actually heard it, and, if not, surely they knew the myth of Sudika-mbambi, the Wonder Child, son of Kimanaueze the Younger, of the Kimanaueze cycle of myths, upon which this BaKongo myth may well have been based. Stories of Sudika-mbambi, predating the Portuguese, were prevalent throughout Ndongo native lands.

Sudika-mbambi came into the world through a miraculous birth befitting a mythic hero. He issued forth from his mother's womb talking, wielding a knife and sword, and asserting his right to be. Not long after birth, he went in search of the Makishi, forces that were terrorizing the land. Through alliance with magical beings known as the Kipalende, he vanquished the Makishi, only to have the Kipalende turn on him and capture him. They buried him deep in a hole, when magically a door opened and before Sudika-mbambi appeared a road leading to Kalunga-ngombe, king of Mputu, the underworld of souls.

A witch pointed the way to Kalunga-ngombe, who tested the hero a great many times, his ultimate trial being swallowed alive by a great underwater beast. But Sudika-mbambi was eventually released from the belly of the beast, resurrected, and went on to marry Kalunga-ngombe's beautiful daughter. And when Sudika-mbambi grew weary of the world, he headed into the eastern sky, becoming the sound of the thunderclap.[34]

Kalunga-ngombe is a mythical king presiding over the realm of Kalunga, viewed alternately as either underground or underwater. Kalunga is also the threshold, symbolized by the horizon over the ocean, that separates the ordinary world above from the mythical ground of Mputu below. So Sudika-mbambi's story—his struggles with the Makishi, capture by the Kipalende, and transit to Kalunga-ngombe—can also be read as a metaphor for the capture of African slaves and their transit to the Americas through the dreaded Middle Passage. And there is every reason to believe it was viewed just this way by Anthony and Isabella. "[T]he sea passage of slaves," observes ethnographer Wyatt MacGaffey, "is not fully distinguished from the passage of souls, the slave trader from the witch, the geographical America from the land of the dead."[35]

• • •

Records show the *São João Bautista* set sail from Luanda in early 1619 under the command of Captain Manuel Mendes da Cunha, carrying 350 captured Africans, 200 of whom had been loaded under a license, or *asiento*, held by investors in Seville to sell them in New Spain (Mexico). As a Dutch-built fluyt she was rated at 180 *tunnes* (a tunne in 1619 was the equivalent of a cask of Bordeaux wine).[36] The *Mayflower*, which anchored off Plymouth in 1620, was also a Dutch fluyt, carrying 102 pilgrims, thus allowing for approximately a four-foot-by-four-foot space for each passenger to move around. Three hundred and fifty humans in an equivalently sized vessel yields just a little over a two-foot-by-two-foot space, so in all likelihood these Ndongo captives were packed tightly on their backs like sardines in the ship's hold awaiting passage across Kalunga, and entry into Mputu, a realm ruled by the severe king Kalunga-ngombe.

And the Middle Passage, that transatlantic leg of the sea voyage between Africa and the New World, was severe, measured even by the parameters of brutality known in the modern world, like the Jewish Holocaust, the Cambodian killing fields, the ethnic cleansing in the Balkans, or the carnage in Rwanda. By some estimates, ten to twelve million Africans were captured; a third were killed in overland marches from their point of capture to coastal staging areas, like the steaming-hot verandas of Portuguese merchants above the beaches in Luanda, from where they were shipped; and another one-third died during or awaiting the Middle Passage. All told, a holocaust of unprecedented and unspeakable proportions.

Africans captured and marched to the coast, then packed into the holds of slave ships, gave Europeans their first taste of wealth and power built from the decimation of Black lives, a taste which gave rise to a hunger that over many centuries has never been fully sated. But these Africans, for the most part, viewed themselves as unwilling travelers on a journey into the Land of the Dead. Not easily appeased, Kalunga-ngombe, king of this land, lay waiting for Captain da Cunha, and the souls aboard the *São João Bautista*, on the far side of the Middle Passage. Only now, this mythical master and merchant of death and deprivation had donned the guise of a hungry British pirate.

2

PIRACY AND EUROPEAN WEALTH

On the yonder side of their passage into Mputu, Anthony and Isabella met the pirate of Death. Many possess a "shiver me timbers," romantic notion of pirates as swashbuckling, Zorro-like figures with wooden peg legs, head scarves, and missing teeth, roaming the high seas. Few would connect piracy with slavery. Even fewer still, with European monarchs and heads of state.

Power protects wealth. Nations project naval force to protect maritime trade. United under a dynastic union, from 1580 to 1640, Portugal and Spain presented to the world as one.[1] But within this Iberian Union, as it was known, Portugal ruled the transatlantic slave and spice trade, supplying African labor not only to her colony in Brazil but also to Spanish colonies throughout the Americas. Spain controlled the transatlantic trade in commodities and goods, extracted by these African slaves, such as silver, gold, other ores, and tobacco.

The English and the Dutch desperately wanted a portion of this lucrative international maritime commerce. Incapable, at first, of directly challenging the Iberian navies, or matching Portugal's 150-year trading relationship with West African societies, these European powers simply resorted to piracy. Under sanction from the crowns of England and the Netherlands, English and Dutch pirates, known euphemistically as privateers, raided Iberian ships or settlements, robbing them of their treasure. If the ships carried human cargo, their African captives were, at first, resold to Iberian colonies in the Caribbean and Central and South America. Later, they were taken to places like New Amsterdam (New York City) and the colony of Jamestown, Virginia, for sale.

In 1560, the "Virgin Queen," Elizabeth I, commissioned a special branch of her Royal Navy, outfitting them with letters of marque, which made legal under English law their charge, anywhere in the world, to plunder the Iberian fleet and raid their colonial settlements in the New World.[2]

Sir Francis Drake, Sir John Hawkins, Sir Walter Raleigh, and Sir Richard Hawkins, all well-known "Sea Dogs," as they were called, were simply pirates with permits, sanctioned by the Elizabethan crown to rob merchant vessels and pillage rival colonial villages for the purposes of establishing England as a merchant sea power. While minerals, ore, and spices formed much of the Portuguese trade with Africa, and the transatlantic trade, the heft of that trade was in humans captured in Africa, then sold as slaves in the Spanish and Portuguese colonies of the New World. Here, again, is an early example of slavery creating European power and wealth.

In 1586, Drake raided the Spanish colony at Cartagena, Colombia, boarding 250 Africans whom he carried up the eastern seaboard, dropping some of them off on the island of Roanoke, where he sought unsuccessfully to resuscitate the dying colony. While much is written of the "Lost Colony of Roanoke," established more than a year after Drake left the island, little is written about the "lost colony" of Africans he left behind.[3]

John Hawkins prowled the high seas contemporaneously with his cousin Francis Drake. Hawkins's father, William, is credited with establishing the "Triangular Trade," which took slaves from Africa, sold them in the Americas, then brought back products, such as rum, sold in England for a handsome profit. The younger Hawkins followed in the wake of his father. He chartered Royal

Navy ships, and sailed under the English flag. Referred to, inaccurately, as "England's first slave trader," for the thousands of slaves he captured and sold, in 1565, after returning from the second, and most successful of three slave runs, he was granted by Elizabeth I a coat of arms featuring a bound slave.[4]

Hawkins's first slaving run in 1562 was a modest affair, financed by a small coterie of London businessmen and mid-level government officials. But it turned a profit, and was enough to convince a powerful group of London merchants and high-level government officials to back his second expedition in 1564. As with his previous venture, for this second voyage, Hawkins turned to a then novel investment vehicle, a joint-stock, limited-liability company. Only this time it was much larger than before and he named it the Africa Company.[5]

Stated simply, a joint-stock company represents a way of raising capital for a venture in which each investor, or shareholder, is entitled to profits based on the value of their shares. A limited-liability company means that each investor is liable for the company's debts and losses only based on the value of their shares.

John Hawkins, a sixteenth-century entrepreneur with an innovative idea for making money, scoured England for venture capital much like a high-tech wunderkind with an innovative idea today scours Silicon Valley in search of venture capital. While joint-stock, limited-liability corporations are the most common means of raising equity capital (cash) in the modern world, they were wholly new in sixteenth-century Europe. The slave trade contributed to their enduring success. Even given the loss of two ships loaded with hides bound for Europe, Hawkins's second voyage turned a profit estimated to be between 40 and 60 percent.[6]

Our mental images of slavery center on Black men and women marched out of Africa in irons, packed head to toe in slave ships, sold at auction like cattle, then clothed in tatters, laboring in fields beneath the whip of masters and slave drivers. We would do well to enlarge that mental imagery to include well-dressed, powerful European aristocrats, sitting comfortably around highly polished wooden tables, enveloped in a cloud of blue-white cigar smoke, discussing the profitably of their investments in the slave trade.

Historian Robert Pollitt describes such an enlarged view of the slave trade. "[I]t is in the syndicates that supported the ventures, the hazy figures in London who had the gold to make them possible, rather than in smoking cannon, sinking ships and Hawkins's cries of treachery that the significance of England's first experience with slaving is to be found. Who were these men who were willing to risk large sums on such risky ventures? What were their motives? Did they have any idea of the possible impact of their investments?"[7]

These men included powerful merchants and political figures in London, and even more powerful figures associated with the royal court. Originally, they came from all over the English countryside but they converged on London, and Buckingham Palace, to secure their status, their power, their privilege, and their wealth. Their ranks included Sir Thomas Lodge, the preeminent London wool merchant born in Shropshire, who eventually succeeded in becoming lord mayor of London; Sir William Chester and Sir William Garrard, both at various times an alderman, sherriff, and lord mayor of the city; and the Queen's courtier and confidant, Robert Dudley, the Earl of Leicester, whom many believe was also her preferred paramour. The merchants associated with Hawkins's slave runs also invested heavily in real estate outside the City of London.[8]

Slavery spurred capitalism through creating wealth and political power in Europe. While the swashbuckling exploits of the Sea Dogs are thrilling, more important is that the traffic in human beings they accelerated brought together merchants, politicians, and real estate moguls in a "profit-oriented melting pot,"[9] a cauldron from which emerged enduring business, financial, and political institutions very much with us to this day. And what began in England soon spread throughout Europe before finding its way to America.

Dutch privateers equaled their English counterparts, raiding Iberian merchant ships, taking on slaves, then selling them to Spanish settlements in the New World, later even to the English. Dutch Jewish merchants, many of whom escaped the Portuguese Inquisition for safety in the Netherlands, also acquired and sold thousands of slaves during the latter part of the sixteenth century.[10] Nearly all of the slaves captured by Dutch and English privateers came from the Ndongo region of Angola, home to Anthony and Isabella.[11]

For both the English and the Dutch, elbowing their way into the transatlantic slave trade through piracy fed their simultaneous push to establish settlements in the New World. Until the beginning of the seventeenth century, the English and Dutch had few. Jamestown, Virginia, was founded by the English in 1607 and New Amsterdam (New York) in 1625 by the Dutch. Both nations had already in place a supply chain providing African labor, which they only needed to divert to their newly founded North American colonies.

At the beginning of the seventeenth century, legalized piracy, otherwise known as privateering, thus took on new urgency. With rising need, privateers could now sell their human cargo looted from the Portuguese, with less risk, to friendly English and Dutch colonies under whose marque they sailed. Then, slowly, what began as privateering turned into outright slave trading as the English and the Dutch sailed directly to Africa for slaves rather than plunder them from Portuguese ships on the high seas.[12]

By all accounts, Anthony and Isabella's transatlantic crossing through the Middle Passage was brutal. Aboard the *São João Bautista*, fresh water and supplies ran low, death and sickness among the malungu ran high.[13] The ship limped into port in Jamaica in the summer of 1619, where Captain da Cunha sold twenty-four younger children in exchange for water and supplies, allowed his crew, and maybe the rest of his human cargo, a short moment of respite ashore before casting off for Vera Cruz, Mexico. After tacking to port, while rounding the Yucatán Peninsula, the *São João Bautista* sailed southwest past Campeche.

Imagine standing watch on the deck of the *São João Bautista*. Squinting one eye to peer down the length of an extended brass telescope, when over the horizon you spy sails and soon after the hull of the privateer *White Lion*, followed by the sails and hull of her consort, *Treasurer*.

"*Piratas!*" you cry out in Portuguese, pointing toward the horizon ahead.

A cannon shot explodes not long after, crashing into the ocean before you, and a sea battle commences.

The *White Lion*, commanded by Captain John Colyn Jope, sailed under a Dutch marque, which is one reason Sir John Rolfe would later describe her as a "Dutch man of Warr."[14] John Colyn Jope (also Johan Jope, Jupe, Chope, or Choppe) was actually a Calvinist minister from Cornwall, England, whom some claim inspired the "Flying Dutchman" of Wagner's opera *Der Fliegende Holländer*,[15] and the ghost ship in Disney's hugely successful film series *Pirates of the Caribbean*. According to legend, the Flying Dutchman can never make port and is cursed to sail the oceans forever. According to the late Major Hugh Fred Jope, USAF (Ret.), a direct descendant of Captain John Colyn Jope, a Virginia newspaper article in March 1821 described a cunning maneuver employed by his ancestor:

Whenever the privateer Jope came within sight of a merchant ship, he dispatched a fast-moving pinnace (a tender or dinghy) under oar to reach his prey, loot it, and bring back the booty, then he made off under sail, leaving only the sparse remains of the merchant for any consorting vessels. This maneuver earned Jope the nickname "Flying Dutchman."[16]

But the Flying Dutchman can also be understood in terms of the mythic wisdom of Africans, like Anthony and Isabella, now as booty aboard Jope's ship. By sailing past the horizon, they had crossed over Kalunga, entered the realm of Kalunga-ngombe, where in Jope they had met their ferryman, carrying them to Mputu, the mythic Land of the Dead. And couldn't one say that for more than four hundred years, Africans on ships like the *White Lion* really were symbolically damned never to make port, for each time one set foot on land in the New World, ten more on African soil were packed into a slave ship's hold?

Whatever the origin of the mythical Flying Dutchman, Jope apparently employed his maneuver against the *Treasurer*, commanded by Captain Daniel Elfrith: sending a tender to loot the *São João Bautista*, then outracing his consort to Virginia, where he traded Anthony, Isabella, and the other eighteen and odd captured Africans for "victualls (whereof he was in greate need as he pretended) at the best and easyest rates they could," according to Rolfe.[17]

Three or four days after the *White Lion* arrived at Point Comfort, the *Treasurer* sailed in with approximately thirty more Angolans, then turned around to sail hastily away before Captain Elfrith had the chance to sell or trade most of his captured human treasure, even though Elfrith, according to Rolfe, also "was in greate want of victualls."[18]

Political intrigue roiling the Virginia colony hastened Elfrith's departure to Bermuda.[19] Then, in a bizarre, convoluted conclusion to the arrival of the first Africans in colonial America, a leaky *Treasurer* limped back into the James River in February 1620 carrying a handful of the original Africans captured from the *São João Bautista*, who were bartered, or sold, before she sank in a creek off the James River.

After many dismal months at sea, with a brief stop in Jamaica, Anthony and Isabella had a chance to reclaim their "land legs" in colonial Virginia, having been traded to colonists for food. Standing finally on terra firma, though firmly in the grip of Mputu, they could look back out to Kalunga, the horizon line over the Atlantic, as many malungu would, to know the Land of the Living was now as mythically out of reach for them as the Land of the Dead once was.

· · ·

What Anthony and Isabella could not have known is how the success of their delivery altered the fate of many Angolans who would follow them into Mputu. Guaranteed labor, from Portugal's war with the Ndongo, and the privateering that commandeered captured slaves, spurred English and Dutch settlements up and down the east coast of North America. International trade, centered in Europe, and critical to the success of the American colonies, was an industry established on the back of the transatlantic slave trade. So, too, was a European shipbuilding industry that supplied the vessels both for this trade and for capturing trading vessels, especially those with Black human cargo aboard.

In the years to come, trade and shipbuilding industries would cleave so that American centers for both emerged. But even more important, beneath trade and shipbuilding was a banking and finance industry centered in London that invested in, and secured handsome profits from, the trafficking of Anthony, Isabella, and their malungu.

The slave trade generated wealth in Europe. Profits from the slave trade fueled a European economic expansion, figuring critically in the Industrial Revolution.[20] The transatlantic slave trade stimulated the development of credit markets. Using slaves as collateral gave slave owners a competitive advantage over other entrepreneurs.[21] This trade in humans also helped to establish the widespread use of joint-stock, limited-liability companies, not only John Hawkins's Africa Company, but also the Royal African Company (set up by English royals for English merchants in 1660 to pursue direct slave trade), the Virginia Company (which initially founded and ran English settlements in both Virginia and Plymouth, Massachusetts), and the Dutch East India Company, known as the VOC (short for Vereenigde Oostindische Compagnie), which proved its worth making and distributing profits to shareholders based on success in the slave trade and exploitation of other African resources, such as ores and spices.

From 1672 to 1713, the Royal African Company (RAC), for example, dispatched 500 ships to Africa, bought 125,000 slaves, lost 25,000 in the dreaded Middle Passage, and sold the remainder to British planters in the Americas.[22] RAC also issued its own letters of marque not for the plunder of Spanish and Portuguese slave ships, but to allow the Company's ships to bypass British naval blockades.[23]

Prince Andrew, the currently disgraced third child and second son of Queen Elizabeth II of Britain and her husband, Prince Philip, Duke of Edinburgh, is the current Duke of York. But in 1633, when a son, named James, was born to King Charles I and Henrietta Maria, he was immediately designated the Duke of York. When that Duke of York sold his shares in the RAC in 1689, he racked up a handsome annual 12 percent return.[24]

"D.Y." was branded across the chests of many thousands of slaves, representing the initials of the Company's founding governor, the Duke of York, who ascended to the throne in 1685 as King James II.[25] "RAC" replaced the duke's brand on slaves after he became England's king.[26] The RAC provided West African gold to the Royal Mint, which named the "guinea" coin in honor of the region of Africa where the RAC took much gold, and stamped the coin with the RAC's elephant logo.[27] But most important, RAC profits from the exploitation of African human and natural resources enhanced the political clout of investors like the Duke of York, Sir Robert Clayton, Sir John Banks, Sir Edmund Andros, Baron Francis Hawley, and Sir Ferdinando Gorges; men who influenced the monarchy, dominated the politics of the City of London, controlled the early financial houses of the City of London (the equivalent of Wall Street),[28] and directly or indirectly administered the fate of English colonies in North America.

These were the Englishmen behind the clouds of blue-white cigar smoke, raising brandy snifters in plush boardrooms of wood and crushed velvet, dispensing the fate of hundreds of thousands of Africans captured and sold as slaves in order to increase their wealth and enhance their power.

• • •

Spain was not to be outdone by England. The English pioneered a novel financial institution, the joint-stock, limited-liability company, to enter the slave trade. But as discussed previously, the Spanish pioneered a novel financial instrument, the asiento (literally, a seat), as early as 1518 to supply their New World colonies with slave labor.[29] Through an asiento, the Spanish crown granted an annual contract to individuals or companies, like the Cadiz Slave Company, to supply Spanish colonies with a fixed number of *piezas de Indias*. These were standardized slave units with one *pieza* the equivalent of a prime, healthy male slave.[30] The *asientista* (holder of license) could make money buying slaves in Africa, then selling them in the Spanish colonies through the Portuguese traders who ran the slave ships plying the Atlantic.

Marranos (Iberian Jews forced underground throughout the Middle Ages but still practicing their faith in secret) within the so-called "New Christian" mercantile elite held many of the asientos in the seventeenth century.[31] Like British joint-stock, limited-liability companies, the Spanish asiento was a novel financial instrument against which Spain issued long-term bonds (*juros*) to finance governmental expenditures.[32]

Asientos were dispensed through free-market capitalism. Spain granted slavery asientos to whomever paid the highest price. This meant that much like a modern stock market (which also describes principal members as holding seats), ordinary citizens in the seventeenth and eighteenth centuries could invest in the slave trade. In 1713, by treaty, at the end of one of many Anglo-Spanish wars, the British government took over the exclusive asiento for Spain for a term of thirty years, which it then turned around and sold to the joint-stock South Sea Company (SSC), headquartered in London. The contract called for the SSC to deliver 4,800 slaves each year for thirty years to Spanish American colonies. It also called for the SSC to pay the Spanish crown a duty of 33.5 pesos (approximately $500 USD in the year 2020 value) per slave supplied on top of a 200,000 ($2.5 million USD) pesos advance. But ordinary citizen investors like Mary Baker or Abraham Elton of

Bristol also owned shares in the SSC.[33] Slavery made wealth for European nations and their citizens.

Insurance against loss was another important aspect of the European financial services industry birthed by the slave trade. A 2004 lawsuit filed by ten American descendants of slaves, in the US District Court for the Northern District of Illinois, alleged the involvement of many banks and insurance companies in profiting from the slave trade, Lloyd's of London among them. The plaintiffs unsuccessfully sought reparations, though they successfully exposed Lloyd's longtime and long-term involvement in insuring slaves and slave ships beginning in the seventeenth century.[34]

Profit margins, credit markets, financial instruments, and insurance are the key factors in the creation and maintenance of stable economies and in fueling economic growth. Slavery provided a means of establishing these sectors in Britain, the Netherlands, Spain, Portugal, and other European countries. Eventually, this huge financial services industry would travel across the Atlantic, like the slaves upon which it was built, finding an American home in places like Wall Street in New York City and the financial district of Boston. From here, these sectors would drive everything from the Westward Expansion, to the Industrial Revolution, to Silicon Valley in America, creating and redistributing trillions of dollars of wealth.

Black lives mattered in shaping this nascent European financial system, which, in turn, shaped the American financial system that many profit from to this day. In subsequent chapters, we will explore in much greater detail how Black lives created White wealth, which also gave rise to White power. But before any of this could happen, slavery would need to create wealth and power for American slaveholders, plantation and factory owners, which it did as they became stable producers and manufacturers of goods that Europe desired—goods based on tobacco, cotton, and sugarcane grown by slave labor. Agriculture was the route to that stability. Slavery was the route to successful American agriculture. And a European, mainly English financial services industry provided the liquidity (the cash) that the American agrarian economy needed. Still, even before slavery, agriculture, manufacturing, and financing could profitably wed, another crucial question demanded an answer.

Were Anthony, Isabella, and the other first Africans in America slaves, or were they servants?

SERVANTS OR SLAVES?

In February 2019, Virginia governor Ralph Northam, in the fight of his political life, after being caught on camera as a college student dressed in blackface, appeared across from Gayle King, the Black cohost of *CBS This Morning*. The embattled governor, attempting to offer an apology, said, "We are now at the 400-year anniversary—just 90 miles from here in 1619. The first indentured servants from Africa landed on our shores in Old Point Comfort, what we call now Fort Monroe, and while—"

An indignant King would have none of it. "Also known as slavery," she cut him off.[1]

And the media had a field day with yet another tone-deaf remark on race by the governor, who then suffered a well-deserved, on-screen drubbing by a sharp Black female journalist.

But history, it turns out, gets the last word, if not the last laugh. For both Northam and King were right—and both were wrong! Though so many Americans, Black and White, believe, as does Gayle King, that those first Africans came here as slaves, Anthony and Isabella, and the other first Africans to arrive in Virginia in 1619 aboard the *White Lion*, were sold, or bartered, into an ambiguous netherworld of bondage somewhere between indentured servitude and slavery; an indeterminate purgatory with implications that cut to the very quick of the founding of America and her institutions; a fluid yet dangerous limbo with ramifications that still confound us to this day.

Many feel that calling these Africans indentured servants somehow whitewashes slavery's legacy. Nothing could be further from the truth. In fact, calling them slaves obliterates a quintessential aspect of the legacy of slavery in America by removing a cornerstone from understanding where we began as a nation still divided by race. But, then, calling them indentured servants obliterates the legacy of the differential, unequal, brutal treatment singled out for Black Americans in this land of liberty, equality, and fraternity.

So, the truth, as it frequently does, lies somewhere in between; in between white and black; in between indentured servitude and slavery; in between eventual freedom and perpetual bondage. But determining that in-between line, that status of Africans in America, was an important first step in ordering the hierarchy of power and wealth in the colony and then in the nation.

• • •

A tidewater itself is an in-between place; a region of transition between rivers and the sea; a zone where saltwater ocean tides affect freshwater rivers. A casual glance at a chart of the Tidewater area of Virginia shows a confluence of rivers pouring into Chesapeake Bay. In the south bay, the James River has traveled 350 miles from the Appalachian Mountains to join the Elizabeth and Nansemond rivers, near Newport News Point, where they form Hampton Roads Harbor. Then, cutting a deep channel, the waters squeeze between the tip of the Virginia Peninsula to the north, and shallow Willoughby Spit to the south, before welcoming Chesapeake Bay, and a few miles farther east, emptying into the Atlantic.

A careful mariner, coming into the south part of Chesapeake Bay, would favor the peninsula's northern shore, thus avoiding its southern shoals. Looking for safe harbor from the winds and a tempestuous Atlantic, that mariner would recognize the small bight just to starboard around the tip of the peninsula and anchor a ship there. On April 28, 1607, when the crew of Christopher Newport's flagship, *Sarah Constant* (by some accounts the *Susan Constant*), found the channel around the peninsula's tip leading to safety it put them in "good comfort," and so they named the adjacent land Cape Comfort.[2] Long before these Englishmen, the Algonquian Chesepian people of the area used the word *Chesepiooc*, referring both to the "Great Water" of the Atlantic and a village at the mouth of the bay; in that village most likely the Kecoughtan tribe lived.[3]

Where a prudent sailor would see safety in Cape Comfort, a prudent soldier would see a fort on the long stretch of land sixty feet above the cape where the Kecoughtan made their village. Fort Algernon was the first fort built by the English at the tip of the cape in 1609, and this led to war with the neighboring Kecoughtan village. When the Kecoughtan captured and killed colonist Humphrey Blunt in July 1610, Sir Thomas Gates, who'd just made his way from England to be governor of the Virginia colony, used it as pretense to mount a vicious revenge attack, known as the Kikotan Massacre. Many natives were killed as Gates pushed the Kecoughtan inland, establishing two forts to secure and maintain the colonists' advantage. Fort Charles was built two miles inland from Cape Comfort; Fort Henry, a small garrison of fifteen, was built nearby.[4] A young, up-and-coming colonial merchant-planter named William Tucker was placed in charge of the garrison at Fort Charles, with orders to continue the war against the Kecoughtan.

William Tucker was a colonial, colloquial "man for all seasons." Though he had no naval or military background prior to his arrival in Virginia in 1610, he was put in charge of subduing local Native American tribes, which he did with often brutal and ruthless efficiency, such as offering wine laced with poison at peace talks with the Powhatan.[5] He was a prominent merchant in London, a shareholder in the Virginia Company, a colonial tobacco planter, a sassafras trader, and owner of the *Sea Flower*, a merchant vessel he used for annual trading runs to England, which may have earned him the honorific "Captain," by which he was referred.[6]

Tucker was also an "ancient planter," a colonial-era term used to describe those who'd arrived in the Virginia colony prior to 1616, entitling them to a share of profits of the Virginia Company. But the Virginia Company showed no profits, so land was distributed in lieu of hard cash. Through these land grants of one hundred acres to ancient planters, and through a number of real estate purchases and sales, William Tucker amassed an estate of more than 850 acres in Elizabeth City, where he grew tobacco on what has been referred to as "the first plantation" on colonial American soil.[7]

So, there is little surprise to learn the first plantation owner soon met the first Africans to arrive in bondage.

As commander of the garrison at Point Comfort, Tucker was there, right there in the late summer of 1619, as *White Lion* rounded Cape Comfort, lowered her sails, threw her anchor, and came to rest in a small bight below his fort. Rolfe tells us that those "20. and odd Negroes . . . the Governor [Sir George Yeardley] and Cape Marchant [Abraham Piersey] bought for victualls (whereof he [Capt. Jope] was in greate need as he pretended) at the best and easyest rates they could." Tucker obtained Anthony and Isabella, most likely for work on his plantation, either from Yeardley or Piersey, both of whom he knew well.[8]

Tucker acquired Anthony and Isabella not really as servants but, then, not quite as slaves.

Some point to underlying European racism to support their claims that colonial America was predisposed to view these first Africans as slaves, and treat them accordingly. Muslim-turned-Christian Johannes Leo Africanus, whose sixteenth-century travel accounts were widely read by educated Europeans, like William Tucker, spoke derisively of sub-Saharan Africans: "Negros likewise leade a beastly kinde of life, being vtterly destitute of the vse of reason, of dexteritie of wit, and of all artes. Yea they so behaue themselues, as if they had continually liued in a forrest among wilde beasts."[9] This thinking is further buttressed by citing the racism rampant in the centuries-long war of Catholics to drive North African Muslims from Portugal and Spain.[10] Furthermore, the reasoning goes, Christianity itself has deep, racist roots in the view that Africans descended from the cursed Ham of the Book of Genesis.[11] Racism came first, this school says, then came slavery.

Captain William Tucker's muster[12] recorded in the self-reported Virginia census of 1624/25, is used to back up these claims. The muster shows Tucker's family and beneath them his servants, and beneath them a native man, and beneath him, Anthony and Isabella and their child. The age of the servant, the ship that brought them to the colony, and the year they arrived, are shown for White Europeans but not for the native man, or for Anthony, Isabella, or their child. This, these observers note, is evidence that natives and Africans of that time did not have a status equal to Whites. Without ages, how were the lengths of their indentures known?

Not so fast, say others. While Tucker's muster is one of the larger, there are other musters where individual White servants are shown without a ship or without an age. The muster of Dr. John Potts (who supplied Tucker with the poison used at peace talks with the Powhatan) shows Ivie Banton, a maidservant arriving on the *Abigaile* in 1622, but does not show her age.[13] The muster of Edward Blany shows servant Randall Smallwood without an age or a ship.[14] It's doubtful that Banton or Smallwood were Africans, for Africans were almost always listed with a designation "Negro" or "Negroe" or "Negar" affixed.

This second group believes that "[s]lavery was not born of racism," as Eric Williams, prime minister of Trinidad and Tobago, famously said, "rather, racism was the consequence of slavery."[15] It's largely an economic argument applied to early English and Dutch colonies in America, where the first Africans had essentially the same worth to planters as indentured servants until it seemed clear that slavery gave a better profit margin.[16]

Furthermore, there were no laws in early colonial Virginia that distinguished African from European servants; hence, in all likelihood they were treated equally until those laws began to change somewhere around 1640. Of course, Indians and Africans had no age associated with their entries in colonial musters because they had no birth records. Finally, this second group might point out that Anthony, Isabella, and their child were not included with the real property Tucker possessed, shown at the very bottom of his muster, hence, they were not considered chattel slaves, as many after them would be considered and so listed.

Still, a third group says be wary of the other two. First, historians should be very cautious of bias, lest they bring modern prejudices and aspirations to bear on examining the past. Use of the word *negro* or its various derivatives, for example, should not be taken as a sign of racism, at least not in early colonial history. The word was merely descriptive of people with darker skins, although over time, as people with darker skins became the only ones enslaved, *negro* became the equivalent of *slave*.

Furthermore, this third group says, a distinction should be made between the first generation of Africans arriving in the American colonies and those who came after.[17] For the first group of Africans, English and Dutch colonists had the concept of indefinite but not inheritable servitude, while for those Africans who came after, colonists applied the concept of lifetime, inheritable slavery.

Religion also played a factor. These observers, looking at Tucker's muster, would point out the word *baptised* associated with William Crashaw, a native man, and William, the child of Anthony and Isabella. *Baptised* implies that some, if not all, of the early Africans were Christian, or had at least adopted Christianity in some form prior to, or during, their bonded service. This was known to be the case in Angola, from where Anthony, Isabella, and most of the first generation of Africans came, and where Christianity had been prevalent since the early 1500s. So, this third group stakes out a slightly different position from the other two: the first generation of Africans were regarded as slaves by the early colonists, but slavery had not yet been fully defined as it would be later.[18]

Is there that much difference between slavery, with the term undefined, and servitude, with the length undetermined? Furthermore, why does any of this matter?

Human systems—economic, political, legal, social, cultural—do not suffer uncertainty well. If the abbreviated discussion above shows anything, it is the uncertainty surrounding the status of the first Africans in America. If modern scholars, with the benefit of a greater knowledge than their predecessors, and, therefore, greater hindsight, are at odds in their designation of this first generation of Africans, imagine the confusion of early colonists. Human systems evolve to eliminate ambiguity and remove confusion. And, it is out of this movement to reduce the uncertainties surrounding the status of these first Africans that principal economic, political, legal, social, and cultural institutions and industries of power and wealth in America were born. Institutions and industries still with us today. Whether the first Africans in America were servants or slaves matters. How America evolved from the uncertainty of their status into a nation of certain slavery, for those Africans coming after them, matters even more.

In reading William Tucker's muster, my attention is drawn to something I've rarely seen reported by others—the hierarchical class arrangement of the groups beneath his family. In almost every muster reported in the 1624/25 census, a class hierarchy is set: White planters and their families on top, then White servants, followed by Indian servants, followed by African servants, followed by personal property. One historian who did pick up on this hierarchy was my friend and mentor Lerone Bennett, Jr. "Before the invention of the Negro or the white man or the words and concepts to describe them," Bennett wrote, "the Colonial population consisted largely of a great mass of white and black [and native] bondsmen, who occupied roughly the same economic category and were treated with equal contempt by the lords of the plantations and legislatures."[19] Bennett goes on to say,

> Curiously unconcerned about their color, these people worked together and relaxed together. They had essentially the same interests, the same aspirations, and the same grievances. They conspired together and waged a common struggle against their common enemy—the big planter apparatus and a social system that legalized terror against black and white bondsmen. No one says and no one believes that there was a Garden of Eden in Colonial America. But the available evidence, slight though it is, suggests that there were widening bonds of solidarity between the first generation of blacks and whites. And the same evidence indicates that it proved very difficult indeed to teach white people to worship their skin.[20]

Here, when Bennett talks of "white people" he does not mean the Tuckers, Yeardleys, and Pierseys of colonial Virginia, he means the ordinary White European indentured servants who worked for them.

Choice crafts character, whether for a person or a nation. Early American colonists, like the Tuckers, Yeardleys, and Pierseys, made fundamental choices that coalesced to craft the character of this nation. One choice, as Bennett points out, open at least for a while, was the road to universal justice. Though never seriously considered, this choice would have entailed engagement with the first Americans, Native Americans, in a partnership to mutually develop the vast resources of North America. Instead, Europeans arrived on this continent touting a legacy of manifest destiny, of papal bulls and religious convictions that anyone before them was not a partner to engage with diplomatically, but an adversary to conquer violently, through subterfuge, poison, or a gun.

Another choice, Bennett notes, also never seriously considered, was the road to universal equality, wherein all immigrants, Black and White, and Native Americans already in America, would be given the right to participate in a free and cooperative system of labor. But this would have required the abandonment of social and cultural notions of masters and servants, imported into early America with colonists as they stepped from their boats.

A third choice, though less robust than the other two, would have been the road to universal opportunity, wherein even in a system of masters and indentured servants, all servants, regardless of color, would be afforded the same opportunities to work off their indentures, then assisted to successfully strike out on their own. For a while, this road was actually taken until colonial masters encountered a roadblock: freedom dues.

• • •

For a moment, let us step back to remind ourselves what was at stake for men like William Tucker, John Rolfe, George Yeardley, Abraham Piersey, and the other planter-merchants of colonial Virginia. Many recall that in December 1606, some one hundred Englishmen set sail from London on a flotilla of three ships led by Captain Christopher Newport aboard the flagship *Sarah Constant*, bound for the coast of Virginia. They arrived at Cape Henry, the southern entrance to the Chesapeake Bay, on April 26, 1607, and from there made their way up the James River to Jamestown Island, where they determined to establish a settlement.

Few realize that the men on these ships were members of an elite group, most of them shareholders in the Virginia Company, a joint-stock, limited-liability company granted a charter by King James I for the settling of Virginia. In modern terms, we would call these men members of a start-up, whose purpose was making money for its investors or shareholders, which included, for the most part, them.

With survival their first goal, Jamestown Island proved a poor choice. On this swampy lowland, mosquitoes and malaria thrived, game ran low, and inhospitable soil made growing crops nearly impossible. But instead of finding ways to make peace with the local Algonquin tribes who'd long understood how to survive, colonists engaged in bloody contests with them, intent on displacing them from their homelands. William Tucker arrived on the *Mary & James* in 1610 near the tail end of the "Starving Time," a period that winter when three-quarters of Jamestown succumbed to disease brought on by starvation, and those left resorted to eating nearly anything— cats, dogs, horses, and even each other. For the first ten years of their existence, the colony relied on resupply ships from the Virginia Company in England to keep them going.

But in August 1619, when Anthony and Isabella stepped onto Virginian soil, they stepped into a colony beginning to move past survival. Colonists had gained the upper hand in pushing natives from lands so colonists could occupy them. They began growing crops, often copied from natives, more suitable for Virginia's soil. This meant they could turn their attention to the real business they'd come to Virginia for: making wealth for the Virginia Company, and for themselves. While the Company failed in 1624, and James I took direct control over the colony, the business of making wealth never ceased for men like William Tucker.

Colonial wealth had a formula: (a) a crop, from which to make a product; (b) a market for that product; (c) a means to get that product to market; (d) land to grow the crop; (e) investment to secure and expand the preceding; and, (f) most important, labor to grow and process the crop. By 1620, Virginia's colonists had nailed down most portions of this formula: tobacco was the crop; pipe tobacco, cigars, and snuff the products; Europe the market; ships plying the Atlantic a means to market; land could be taken from Native Americans; and, investment was supplied by shareholders of the Virginia Company. Which left only one, huge question: What about labor? The first answer was indentured servitude.

Said in the lofty terms of economics, indentured servitude collateralized debt financing for transporting Europeans across the Atlantic to work in British colonies. Said simply: the colonies needed labor, European workers couldn't get to the colonies, European banks couldn't lend workers because there was no way to enforce such transatlantic transactions, so the Virginia Company allowed workers to borrow against future wages to pay for their voyage to America.

The Company experimented with several variations on this theme. First, workers signed on with the Company, which transported them at Company expense to the colonies, where they continued to work for the Company for seven years in order to pay off their transportation costs, and actually accumulate a share in the Company at the end of their time of service. But in the early years of the Virginia colony, working conditions were harsh, food was scarce, disease and illness rampant. Many workers died or ran off for a better life with nearby Native American tribes, which meant a total loss of the Company's investment. The Company's initial response to runaways was punishment by death, but the realization soon set in that a better solution to the labor problem needed to be found.[21]

Next, the Company introduced a "rent a worker" program, whereby workers, still sent to the colony at the Company's expense, could be rented out for a year by the Company's planters. One problem with this new system was that some planters tried and succeeded in seducing rented workers away from other planters, leaving the original renters with the bill. Another problem concerned who was responsible for the upkeep and maintenance of the workers. When you rent a car, for example, other than returning it with a full tank of gas, you generally don't think about bringing the car in for maintenance— that's the company's problem and its expense passed on to you in the cost of the rental. But the workers were three thousand miles away from the Company, which had no means of enforcing contracts, so the Company demanded that planters be responsible for the health and welfare of the workers. If a worker fell ill or died, the planter would still be responsible for rental payments to the Company, though at a negotiated reduced rate. In short, the renters were responsible for protecting the Company's investment, which the Company soon realized was not sustainable.[22]

So, when a new group of Company officers were seated in London in 1619 with a realization that Virginia's population desperately needed to grow, they determined a new system of indentured servitude that served as the model for the next two hundred years. Workers were transported at Company expense from England to Virginia; the cost of the voyage was advanced to the workers, who were bound for a fixed term of years and sold outright to planters for this term, once they arrived in the colony. It was a huge success, with planters enthusiastically acquiring workers at what appeared to be a bargain. It was a huge success for the Company, which, once it received a lump sum from the planter, no longer had to concern itself with the worker's health or welfare.[23]

This refined version of indentured servitude also introduced the idea of derivatives into British capitalism. A derivative is a new financial product created on an underlying real asset. Indentured servants were the underlying real asset. Packaging and selling contracts for their supply to the colonies was the new financial product, which the Virginia Company then sold to individual investors in England and in the colonies. Purchasing bundled labor contracts increased the Company's revenue stream. In other words, indentured servitude created a labor market where workers were viewed as simply a commodity. And in a later chapter, we will see how exactly the same packaging of slave labor was used in the American stock market.

"They were worked hard, were dressed in the cast-off clothes of their owners, and might be flogged as often as the master or mistress thought necessary," said J. B. McMaster in a series of 1903 lectures on colonial America. "Father, mother and children could be sold to different buyers. Such remnants of cargoes as could not find purchasers within the time specified, were bought in lots of fifty or more by a class of speculators known as 'soul drivers,' who drove them through the country like so many cattle and sold them for what they would bring."[24]

No, not slaves!

A professor of American history at the University of Pennsylvania, McMaster depicted the lives of White indentured servants in colonial Virginia. But just as Anthony and Isabella's lives began in the recesses of Angola, the lives of colonial White indentured servants began in the recesses of England.

You're one of many homeless children wandering the streets of London, when a kindly woman stops you, and offers you food if you'll only follow her. Moments later, several men sweep you off your feet and toss you into a warehouse filled with other crying children. Or, perhaps you're simply poor, out of work, a beggar. Men step from the shadows, grab you, gag you, carry you off to the sounds of your muffled screams, then toss you into a depot where you await transport to a ship's hold.

That next morning, or a few mornings later, you find yourself trapped on a vessel, far out to sea, bound for the American colonies.

You have just been "spirited away" by men and women known throughout seventeenth-century England as "Spirits." In fact, merely calling out "Spirits!" in a seventeenth-century London crowd was enough to cause instant pandemonium as people scurried to safety for fear of being scooped up, and sent across the sea to America.

Spirits worked as agents on behalf of ship captains, merchants, politicians, English nobility, courtiers, and even members of the royal court. When caught, rarely were Spirits prosecuted. The court cases that do exist indicate how widespread the practice was. In 1643, the Middlesex County Court sentenced Elizabeth Hamlyn to jail and to be whipped "for taking of diverse little children in the street and selling them to be carried to Virginia." In 1655, Christian Chacrett was accused of being "one that taketh up men and women and children and sells them on a ship to be conveyed beyond the sea." Chacrett specialized in spiriting away families to Virginia. In 1671, John Stewart stood accused of spiriting away five hundred individuals a year for more than a decade, with a bounty paid to anyone who supplied him with victims. In the same year, William

Thiene, an East Smithfield cobbler, was accused of spiriting away 840 people in a year.[25]

But Spirits were not the only means to fill the coffers of a ship with White men, women, and children destined to be sold.

You could also have been a sex worker, trolling London's streets after dark, when the *clipetty-clop* of horses over cobblestone catches your ear. A fine carriage stops. Lace curtains part. A gentleman beckons you with a wink and the curl of his index finger. Alone with him in the cabin's soft crushed velvet, you're trapped. And, the next thing you know, he's seized you, gagged you, then tapped the outside of the carriage, as the horses trot off toward the wharf.

Or, you might be a woman inside London's notorious Clerkenwell House of Correction, there for no other reason than asking a well-stocked merchant for food for your starving young children. Your jailer slips a large skeleton key into the lock, tumblers click, and the door to your cell creaks open. A sailor appears, by leave of his captain, he says. You're terribly thirsty. He's carrying a large bottle of liquor. He pours you a glass. Then another. And another. And another. Until your legs feel like they're giving out from under you. And the last thing you remember as the sailor lifts you in his arms is passing a smiling warden who waves to the sailor as he carries you out of the prison.

Then, maybe, you're in front of a white-wigged magistrate, facing a death sentence for stealing a pail of milk from your employer, even though you accidentally kicked over the pail and spilled it instead. The magistrate offers you a stark choice: death by hanging or penal transportation to the Americas to work fourteen years as a servant. Is there any doubt which choice you would make?

Political prisoners, Irish Catholic priests, Quakers, captured soldiers, dissenters, and undesirables of any kind rounded out the ranks of those contracted, coerced, or connived into making the passage to America, and working there as indentured servants.

Most White indentured servants did not come to America through the polite exchange of contracts and signatures over a pint in a seaside pub. They came by way of skulduggery. And most perpetrators of crimes contributing to this trade in White servants were not prosecuted because White servitude fit neatly into a larger British plan: drive the poor and the undesirables from the kingdom's shores, into her colonies, if necessary. It's an idea with an old history in England. Sir Humphrey Gilbert, who unsuccessfully sought the Northwest Passage to Asia, wrote in 1576, "[a]lso we might inhabite some part of those Countreys, and settle there such needie people of our Countrie, which now trouble the common welth, and through want here at home, are inforced to commit outrageous offences, where they are dayly consumed with the Gallowes."[26]

In a letter to his king in 1611, Don Alonso de Velasco, the Spanish ambassador to England, put it succinctly, "Their principal reason for colonizing these parts is to give an outlet to so many idle, wretched people as they have in England, and thus prevent the dangers that might be feared of them."[27]

This system by which White landowners accrued wealth and power through the labors of others was enacted, even perfected, on Europeans, not Africans. Early on, when there were no Africans in the American colonies, poor White lives mattered in creating rich White wealth and power. Slowly, that changed. But Anthony and Isabella arrived at a colony where the vast majority of White colonists were servants living just beyond the reach of the manacle and chain.

FROM SERVITUDE TO SLAVERY

In 1624, White settler William Mutch had apparently worked off his indenture to Captain John Harvey. But master and former servant got into an altercation. Harvey demanded to see the contract ending Mutch's indenture, while Mutch demanded his freedom dues before showing Harvey the contract. The standoff ended with Harvey assaulting Mutch by truncheon—"ftrooke over ye pate wth his Trunchione" (*struck over the head with his truncheon*)—which prompted Mutch to sue Harvey. The case worked its way up to the colonial Virginia Supreme Court, where Dr. John Potts, a member of the court, affirmed the facts as Mutch stated. Still, the court did not rule in Mutch's favor.[1]

Why would they?

Harvey, known as an irascible sort, would later be knighted by Charles I and appointed governor of the colony. His case with Mutch was as much about status, privilege, and class in colonial America as it was about the law. Sir John Harvey was a member of the English aristocracy. William Mutch was not.

In beating Mutch with his truncheon, John Harvey was acting out a belief that *a servant shall never rise to my equal, and it is my right and privilege to keep him down.* Men, like Harvey, had come to Virginia seeking power and wealth. They also sought to retain the privileged social status they had known in England. They both needed and despised men like Mutch. They further recognized that in attempting to control such men, through indentured servitude, they were fostering a social underclass that would eventually rise as their competition once the indentures had been served.

A more permanent solution was required, and it would be found in the large numbers of Africans soon to be imported to the colony. But until that time, men like Harvey devised and refined a brutal, violent, oppressive regime to keep men like Mutch down. A template that ensured power and wealth would remain within the hands of a few, a template they could call upon when Africans arrived.

Meeting in Jamestown, the Virginia General Assembly, later the House of Burgesses, which served the American Founders as a model for the United States Congress and House of Representatives, was first called into session on July 30, 1619, by Governor Sir George Yeardley. Captain William Tucker, owner of the first-ever plantation and soon-to-be owner of Anthony and Isabella, was a member of that body when on August 3 and 4, just two weeks prior to the couple's arrival, that first-ever session of the first-ever White legislative body in America enacted the first-ever laws regulating servitude: White servants were bound by the contracts they entered into in England. White servants could not marry without the consent of their masters. And, White masters could publicly flog their servants, or employ such cruel punishment as nailing a servant's ears to a pillory.[2]

Why were such matters important then? Servants far outnumbered their planter-masters. At least three out of every four colonists in seventeenth-century Virginia was a servant.[3] So, planters had a vested interest in controlling the lives of their servants. But planters also viewed themselves as the New World aristocracy. "The system of indentured service," notes historian Philip A. Bruce, "in its social effects differed but little, if at all, from the system of slavery." Bruce continues, "It really accentuated the social divisions among the whites more distinctly than the presence of the institution of slavery itself did. The indentured servants were as much a legalized lowest class in Virginia as the noblemen were a legalized highest class in England. It gave purely class distinction a recognized standing in the Colonial Courts of Law."[4]

Why are such matters important now? In the growing debate over the intersection of race and class in America, particularly regarding which came first, the historical record, at least, seems clear. Class preceded race as the basis of inequality in the supposed land of equality. Both in the seventeenth century, and today, the American upper class (the 1 percent) was (and is) as concerned about class distinctions among Whites as it was (and is) about racial distinctions between Whites and Blacks.

While this intersection between class and race greatly influenced the development and codification of slavery in the seventeenth century, it continues its profound impact on our institutions today. Who can seriously look at Richard Nixon's "Southern Strategy," which peeled southern Whites away from the Democratic Party to build the modern Republican Party, without also seeing racial animosity used to trump class distinctions? Who can conscientiously examine the statistics showing increased segregation in schools since the 1960s as White families send their children to White private schools of their own creation (rather than to private academies frequented by the White upper class), and not see the impact of class and race? And, who can watch video after disgusting video of White police officers murdering young Black men and women, even inside their homes, then going scot-free for months without question or arrest, and not also be aware of the hand that class and race plays in criminal justice?

Racial distinctions have long been the basis of eugenic notions about the superiority of one race over another. That skin color conveys intelligence (the lighter the color, the smarter), for example, is one of many enduring pseudoscientific ideas about race that continues to crop up year after year, and which many Americans firmly believe. But even in the absence of race, class distinction also borders on eugenics.

As much as disease, severe weather, incompetent farming, and making constant wars with Native Americans, the absence of women as colonial wives bearing children threatened the survival of the Virginia colony. So, not long after Anthony and Isabella arrived in 1619, the Virginia Company sent about 100 mail-order brides to the colony, primarily for indentured servants, each purchased for somewhere between 120 and 150 pounds of tobacco. It proved a huge success and a second shipment of women soon followed. Often the women were former inmates of the ironically named Bridewell prison near London. The story of these "tobacco wives," as they were known, has been fictionalized, and immortalized, in the television show *Jamestown*. But writing about this situation, historian T. J. Wertenbaker raised the ugly head of eugenics, in voicing his belief that "[a]s years went on, the scarcity of women became a distinct blessing, for it made it impossible for the degraded laborer, even though he ultimately secured his freedom, to leave descendants to perpetuate his lowly instincts."[5]

As repugnant as Wertenbaker's thoughts about White servitude are, Abbott Emerson Smith went even further:

Essentially it was simply a workable means of supplying white settlers and cheap labor. Its social consequences were by no means altogether good, for it certainly tended to make the colonies "sinkes" into which the refuse of Europe could be thrown. Perhaps it was a fortunate thing that pioneer conditions were as difficult as they were, if there is any truth in theories of heredity, for the weak, diseased, and unenterprising were not preserved. The strong and competent survived, and if this manner of separating sheep from goats put too great a premium on sheer physical health, that at least was something well worth distinguishing and preserving. There was a speedy winnowing of the vast influx of riffraff which descended on the settlements; the residue, such as it was, became the American people.[6]

As modern as these distasteful views are, they were present when Anthony and Isabella arrived, if not articulated quite so clearly. Remember William Tucker's 1624/25 muster? It laid out class in colonial Virginia simply: planters first, White servants next, Native Americans to follow, and Blacks last.

• • •

In recent years, the internet has circulated a story that the Irish were the first slaves in colonial America. The story states that in colonial America Irish slaves outnumbered African slaves and endured worse treatment at the hands of their masters. Though it's undergone many iterations, and many have claimed authorship, the thrust of the story is contained in an article titled "Irish: The Forgotten White Slaves."[7]

White nationalist groups have adopted the story in an effort to minimize the effects of slavery on Black Americans, and to claim that Blacks are too vocal in seeking justice. "If the Irish can pull themselves up from slavery, so, too, can Blacks. You don't see the Irish asking for reparations," so the reasoning goes. Black advocacy groups have railed against the myth as debasing and diminishing the history and suffering of Black Americans. Meanwhile, Irish activists have used it to showcase Britain as an oppressor, and to downplay the Irish role in the transatlantic slave trade. Historians have come to debunk the myth in its entirety, in essence saying that it conflates White servitude with Black chattel slavery, when the two are vastly different systems of labor.

Seems many groups get a bite of this apple!

And, here might be a perfect opportunity to offer yet another view because White indentured servitude profoundly affected Black slavery. First, *myth* is entirely appropriate in this context, though not in the way most ordinarily think of the term. When people hear *myth* their immediate association is with a falsehood as opposed to a fact, even though that is not the original sense of the word. Facts are denotative truths. Myths are connotative truths. Facts are literal. Myths are metaphorical.

Myths always contain some essence, some essential kernel of truth, even if wrapped in an off-putting, bizarre package. This is the case with the myth of Irish slaves. The story usually begins with the reasonable-sounding statement: "The Irish slave trade began when James II sold 30,000 Irish prisoners as slaves to the New World. His Proclamation of 1625 required Irish political prisoners be sent overseas and sold to English settlers in the West Indies."[8] However, there is no such proclamation in any recorded history of the British monarchy.

So, where's the truth?

In 1688, after what is referred to as the "Glorious Revolution," the Catholic monarch James VII/II was deposed by his Protestant daughter Mary and her husband, William of Orange, who reigned as co-monarchs, she until her death in 1694, he until his death in 1702. Britons who wanted to see James VII/II restored to the throne were known as Jacobites (from Jacobus, the Latin rendering of James). Jacobites, Irish priests, and political prisoners were some of the frequent targets of unscrupulous English authorities who captured or coerced them into transport to American colonies as forced indentured servants.[9]

A second assertion is that Irish slaves outnumbered African slaves. In early colonial Virginia and Massachusetts, White indentured servants far outnumbered anyone else.[10] By 1640, there were fewer than one hundred Africans in Virginia, so there is every likelihood that Irish indentured servants did, indeed, outnumber Africans.

Of course, the major assertion of this myth is that White servitude is in some way equivalent to Black slavery. Here, the debunkers go too far to press their counterclaims.

The enslavement of Africans involved abductions, human sales at auctions, and lifelong forced labor in a system that defined humans as property and trapped the children of those slaves in the same bondage.[11]

Wait a minute! With the possible exception of hereditary status, White servitude, as I have shown above and continue to show below, involved abductions, human sales at auctions, and, in some cases, lifelong forced labor in a system that defined humans as property.

Those attempting to debunk the myth of Irish slavery paint an overly benign picture of White servitude, as did Shawn Pogatchnik, writing for the Associated Press recently: "Indentured servitude, while often accompanied by years of deprivation and exploitation, offered a usually voluntary means for impoverished British and Irish people to resettle in the Americas from the 17th century to the early 20th century. Contracts committed the servant to perform unpaid labor for a benefactor or employer for a fixed number of years in return for passage across the ocean, shelter and sustenance."[12]

This makes it sound as though indentured servitude was a benevolent immigration program for lower-class British and Irish citizens seeking a better life in America. It was anything but that. White servitude was a brutal system of labor that served as a dry run for chattel slavery.

J. B. McMaster, in his study of White servitude, wrote, "They became in the eyes of the law a slave and in both the civil and the criminal code were classified with the Negro and the Indian."[13]

Historian and philosopher John Fiske uses the language and imagery of myth to put forth the truths of White servitude:

Their lives were in theory protected by law, but where an indented servant came to his death from prolonged ill-usage, or from excessive punishment, or even from sudden violence, it was not easy to get a verdict against the master. In those days of frequent flogging, the lash was inflicted upon the indented servant with scarcely less compunction than upon the purchased slave; and in general the condition of the former seems to have been nearly as miserable as that of the latter, save that the servitude of the negro was perpetual, while that of the white man was pretty sure to come to an end. For him, Pandora's box had not quite spilled out the last of its contents.[14]

To say that the brutality of White servitude rivaled that of Black slavery does nothing to demean or diminish the experience of Black Americans; it does not, in any way, whitewash or minimize the impact of slavery. In fact, understanding that White servitude was the template for slavery forged in a crucible of violence and inhumanity indicts neither the servant nor the slave, but instead the perpetrators of both systems.[15]

White servitude was a colonial-era dress rehearsal for Black slavery. A "historic proving ground," wrote Lerone Bennett, Jr., for the monumental, and consequential, system to succeed it:

> The plantation pass system, the fugitive slave law, the use of the overseer and the house servant and the Uncle Tom, the forced separation of parents and children on the auction block and the sexual exploitation of servant women, the whipping post, the slave chains, and the branding iron: all these mechanisms were tried out and perfected *first* on white men and white women. Masters also developed a theory of internal white racism and used the traditional Sambo and minstrel stereotypes to characterize white servants who were said to be good natured and faithful but biologically inferior and subject to laziness, immorality, and crime.[16]

"Rule, Britannia!" That rousing patriotic anthem once sung by millions across a colonial empire upon which the "sun never set" contains the following refrain, bellowed to clenched, pumping fists: "Rule, Britannia! Rule the waves: 'Britons never, never, never will be slaves.'" Though sung without the slightest hint of irony, here in America, land of the free, home of the brave, Britons, and many fellow Europeans working as White indentured servants, were certainly treated as de facto slaves from the seventeenth to the early part of the nineteenth century.

In some instances, even the façade between White servitude and White slavery dissolved. In 1609, Captain John Smith, famed explorer of North America, and savior of Jamestown, bartered Henry Spelman, a White servant, to the Powhatan tribe, in exchange for the native village of Powhatan (near present-day Richmond), whose acquisition Smith hoped would yield provisions needed for Jamestown to survive the coming winter. After rescue a year later, Spelman reported, "I was carried by Capt. Smith, our President, to ye Fales [falls on the James River south of Richmond], to ye litell Powhatan [the Powhatan chief's son, also known as Parahunt], wher, vnknowne to me he sould me to him for a towne called Powhatan."[17]

North, in Massachusetts, also established by the London-based Virginia Company, slavery evolved as part of the local penal system. A Massachusetts court in 1636 decreed that Chousop, "the Indian of Black Island was adjudged to be sent to the island and there kept as a slave for life to worke, unless we see further cause."[18] Slavery sentences were handed down to White servants in a number of cases: In October 1638, to John Hazlewood for breaking and entry.[19] In December 1638, to William Andrews for assaulting his master.[20] On that same day, to Giles Player for breaking and entry, and theft.[21] In June 1640, to Thomas Savory for breaking and entry.[22] Later that same year to Jonathan Hatch.[23] And, in 1641, Marmaduke Barton, by some accounts a forebearer of philanthropist Clara Barton, was "condemned to slavery and to be branded."[24]

In 1659, a Massachusetts court, for the last time, attempted to impose a sentence of slavery, this time on the Southwicke family for being Quakers. The court empowered treasurers in the counties where the Southwickes resided, "to sell said persons to any of the English nation at Virginia or Barbadoes." But no one arose to carry them to Virginia or Barbados for sale.[25]

Notwithstanding the fascination and taboo surrounding White

slavery in America, the colonial world that Anthony and Isabella were thrust into in 1619 was, at best, in flux if not really in chaos. Slavery was not a fait accompli. Servitude was fast changing. The first plantations were just starting up. And, the Virginia Company, the ultimate lords of the manor, was failing. All of which did not bode well for our couple. Still, at the moment they arrived there was no colonial legal or social framework for slavery. That was yet to come. There was a legal and social framework for servitude. But it was still evolving, too.

Purchased by Captain William Tucker, put to work on his newly founded plantation, Anthony and Isabella, and their malungu aboard the *White Lion*, were dropped into the only social and legal status that existed at the time, indentured servitude, giving the laws and customs of the colony time to catch up to the demands and desires of the planters that came with the introduction of Africans into the labor market. It would take several decades for the laws of the land to align with the practices of the plantation.

In the meantime, plantations grew, and with them the amount of tobacco produced for export. Virginia growers had need for more than just field hands to plant, tend, and harvest the crop. Farm buildings for drying, curing, and storing tobacco were needed. So, too, the racks and other equipment located inside these buildings. Hogsheads, the large barrels used to transport and store tobacco, also needed construction. From making clothes for servants to making food for them, however meager the fabric or fare, the larger the plantation, the larger the support operation it required. Labor needs abounded, and many of those needs were for skilled labor.

Planters first looked to White indentured servants for skilled labor. And they were reluctant to let indentured servants go, even at the end of their indentures. Fraud by the planters was common. Trumped-up charges and false accusations leveled at indentured servants led to planters claiming the right to break contracts and unilaterally extend the length of a servant's term. Sometimes a year or two was added to an indenture. In the case of Black indentured servants, especially, many years might be added, and sometimes, indentures might be extended indefinitely. Indefinite indentures strayed just shy of slavery. Because the colonies operated under English common law, one right that separated even indefinite indentured servants from slaves was the right to petition a court for a ruling against their masters. A tricky matter, at best, because most judges were planters who also held servants or slaves, and most juries, if they were impaneled, were peopled not with peers but with planters, or at least property owners.

Indentured servants, White and Black, knew of these shifting demands of planters. Not only did they experience them firsthand while at work on the plantation, but also, they learned of these changes coming in county courts, where many of them, no doubt, received their legal education.

Those days when county courts met were considered holidays for all strata of colonial Virginian society. The following description, though tinged with gratuitous racism, captures the essence of "court-day," as it was known:

> The county courts were not only a training-school for statesmen, but were also incidentally an agency for the education of the people. Court-day was a holiday for all the country-side, especially in the fall and spring. From all directions came in the people on horseback, in wagons, and afoot. On the court-house green assembled, in indiscriminate confusion, people of all classes, the hunter from the backwoods, the owner of a few acres, the grand proprietor, and the grinning, needless negro.[26]

Some Black observers of court-day may well have been grinning, at least prior to the end of the seventeenth century, because they were learning how to mount a legal challenge to their bondage, knowing the court would likely entertain their plea. These were direct affronts to the colonial system of White power and wealth.

Take *Corven v. Lucas*, the June 1675 case of Black indentured servant Phillip Corven, cited earlier, who petitioned the Virginia General Court for his freedom dues as well as his freedom and won.[27]

In 1655, a twenty-five-year-old single mother, Elizabeth Key, engaged in an even tougher legal battle than Phillip Corven to win her freedom from permanent servitude and that of her infant son,[28] John. Her story, though long, is filled with drama and intrigue, and well worth the telling.

Elizabeth Key was born in 1630, to an Englishman, Thomas Key, and an African mother who worked for him as a servant. Elizabeth's mother, whose name has been lost, was one of the first Africans in Virginia.[29]

Thomas Key arrived in Virginia aboard the *Prosperous* in 1619, just a few weeks prior to Anthony and Isabella's arrival. His first wife, Sarah, died, not long after her arrival in Virginia aboard the *Truelove* in 1622. In 1628, he married a second time, to Martha, herself an ancient planter, vaulting Key into the ranks of prominent colonial Virginia families.[30] Key served one session, 1629 to 1630, in the Virginia General Assembly (House of Burgesses) as a representative from Denbigh (near Newport News). His relationship with Elizabeth's African mother began during the early years of his marriage to Martha. At age forty-one, in 1636, Thomas Key died in Isle of Wight County, Virginia, where Martha owned a substantial tract of land.[31]

Before his death and as part of his preparation to return to England with his wife, in 1636, Thomas Key wrote and signed a memorandum before prominent Northumberland County colonist Humphrey Higginson, that Elizabeth would be transferred as a servant to his care for a period of nine years, at which point she would be free.[32] The memorandum further stipulated that Higginson should clothe and feed Elizabeth during her nine years with him, and that should he travel back to England to live, he would pay for her passage, and carry Elizabeth with him as well. Finally, Higginson agreed he would not sell, barter, or transfer Elizabeth to anyone else.

At Elizabeth Key's first trial for her freedom before the Northumberland County Court jury, on January 20, 1656, Anne Clarke, thirty-nine, witness to the signing of the memorandum between Key and Higginson in 1636, testified that "mr Higginson promised to use her well as if shee were his own Child."[33]

As noted, Thomas Key died in 1636 before he could leave for England, and Elizabeth Key was transferred to Humphrey Higginson's custody. Anthony Lenton, forty-one, a servant to Higginson at the time and also a witness at the first trial, testified that "mr Higginson said that at the nine yeares end hee would carry the said Moletto [Elizabeth Key] to England and give her a portion [a part of the estate] and let her shift [assume responsibility] for her selfe. And it was a Common report amongst the Neighbours that the said Molletto was mr Kays Child begott by him."

Higginson did move back to England, only he did not take Elizabeth Key with him, and through a series of undocumented events, she passed into the possession and control of Colonel John Mottrom, a Northumberland County justice of the peace. Her nine years of service would have expired in 1645, but Mottrom did not release her; instead he appeared intent on keeping her under his authority for life (most likely for an indefinite period of indenture).

When Mottrom died in 1655, his estate inventory included "Elizabeth the Negro woman & her sonne." Sometime prior to Mottrom's death, Elizabeth Key had become romantically involved with William Greenstead (Greensted, Grinsted, Grimstead; the spelling varies in the records), a young lawyer apparently also under indenture to Mottrom as a servant, whom Mottrom used for legal representation. Together they had two children. One son, John, survived.

At Mottrom's death, William Greenstead took up Elizabeth Key's case in the Northumberland County Court against the administrators of Mottrom's estate, who'd classified her as a slave, and were prepared to dispose of her as such. Through her lover, Key pleaded three legal theories: (1) she was the daughter of a free Englishman, whose status she inherited; (2) she was a baptized and practicing

Christian, who could therefore not be held in perpetual servitude; and (3) she had been already held to a term of service beyond the initial nine years agreed upon in the memorandum between Key and Higginson. The third was a common pleading of indentured servants seeking remedy from their masters. Phillip Corven used it as part of his successful plea. The second had been tested with limited success in the case of other Africans seeking release from lifetime servitude. But the first pleading, Key's English parentage, had never been heard in a colonial Virginia court before. Combining all three was a masterful stroke, though some dispute whether William Greenstead was even educated,[34] much less an attorney at law, and the legal tactics may have been drawn up by Elizabeth Key herself, from time spent at court-days.

At any rate, testimony in the case began on January 19, 1656, and continued through the next day. A jury was impaneled by the Northumberland County Court to hear Elizabeth Key's pleadings, with Justice Nicholas Morris presiding.[35]

The plaintiffs called several witnesses, who, combined, testified that Thomas Key was Elizabeth Key's father; that a fine had been imposed on him for fathering her; and, that Thomas Key had made arrangements for only a nine-year period of servitude with Humphrey Higginson. The defense called only one or two witnesses. Nicholas Jurnew, fifty-three, swore under oath that "a Turke" had actually impregnated Elizabeth Key's mother. Elizabeth Newman, eighty, may have been recalled by the defense to testify that the plaintiff's counsel, William Greenstead, and the plaintiff had two children together, as a means of impugning Greenstead and his vigorous pursuit of this case. The jury returned its verdict that same day:

Wee whose names are underwritted being impannelled upon a Jury to try a difference between Elizabeth pretended Slave to the Estate of Col. John Mottrom deceased and the overseers of the said Estate doe finde that the said Elizabeth ought to be free as by several oaths might appeare which we desire might be Recorded and that the charges of Court be paid out of the said Estate.[36]

Key's victory, however, was short-lived, as the administrators of Mottrom's estate immediately appealed to the General Court in Jamestown. This appeals court heard the case on March 12, 1656, and though the records have been lost, the verdict was clear: the appellate court ruled against Elizabeth Key.

Elizabeth Key, however, did not give up. She appealed the appellate court's verdict to the colony's supreme court, in this case the Virginia General Assembly, which because of the significance of the matters at hand—progeny, religion, and the status of mixed-race offspring—agreed to hear her appeal. On July 21, 1656, a committee from the General Assembly issued its findings.

On the matter of whether Elizabeth Key was the daughter of Thomas Key, an Englishman, the General Assembly found, "[i]t appeareth to us that shee is the daughter of Thomas Key by several Evidences and by a fine imposed upon the said Thomas for getting her mother with Child of the said Thomas."[37]

On the matter of whether by virtue of being a child of Thomas Key, Elizabeth Key was herself free, the General Assembly found, "by the Comon Law the Child of a Woman slave begott by a freeman ought to bee free."[38]

This was the first bombshell finding.

The common law cited here by the General Assembly was English common law, upon which the colonial legal system rested. And within English common law, several centuries of rulings had established that the status of a child—whether villein (in bondage) or free—followed the status of the father. The General Assembly found in Elizabeth Key's favor, on that basis, since there were, at the time of her pleadings, no colonial laws to the contrary.

Just think about what this ruling meant for all of colonial America, in the middle of the seventeenth century, on the verge of establishing a system of slavery: any child born of a master forcing himself on a female slave would at birth be free. This would have completely disrupted the colonial system of power and wealth based on Black lives by offering mixed-race offspring a path beyond slavery.

On the matter of whether Elizabeth Key was a Christian, the General Assembly found, "shee hath bin long since Christened."[39]

This was the second bombshell finding.

A widespread belief at that time was that Christians holding other Christians in slavery went against core biblical teachings. Again, think about what this ruling meant for a system of slavery. Most slaves during the seventeenth century came from the Angola-Congo region of Africa, where Christianity had long been practiced, and most arrived in Virginia already baptized, already Christians. Those who were not Christian upon arrival mostly converted to Christianity, and many had their children baptized. This ruling also would have completely disrupted the colonial system of power and wealth based on Black lives by affording slaves freedom based on conversion to Christianity.

On the matter of whether Elizabeth Key was bound to Humphrey Higginson for only a term of nine years, the General Assembly found, "Thomas Key sould her only for nine years to Col. Higginson with several conditions to use her more Respectfully then a Comon servant or slave.

"For theise Reasons," the General Assembly concluded, "wee conceive that the said Elizabeth ought to be free and that her last Master should give her Corne and Cloathes [freedom dues] and give her satisfaction for the time shee hath served longer then Shee ought to have done."

But these conclusions were only the opinion of the General Assembly, which did not hand down a verdict. Instead, it referred the case back to the Northumberland County Court. This time the administrators of Mottrom's estate must have realized they stood little chance of satisfaction. They offered no further causes of action. So, on that same day, July 21, 1656, the Northumberland County Court ruled,

Whereas the whole business concerning Elizabeth Key by Order of Assembly [the Supreme Court] was Referred to this County Court. According to the Report of a Committee at an Assembly held at the same time which upon the Records of this County appears, It is the judgement of this Court that the Said Elizabeth Key ought to be free and forthwith have Corne Clothes and Satisfaction according to the said Report of the Committee.[40]

Also, on that day, Elizabeth Key and William Greenstead had the Northumberland County justice of the peace post a notice of their intention to marry.

While July 21, 1656, must have been a very good day for this couple, it was a jarring wake-up call for the colonial architects of slavery. English common law, as Elizabeth Key's case so clearly demonstrated, contained two major loopholes that demanded closure for slavery to take root as the basis of wealth and power in colonial America. If Black lives were to matter in creating White wealth, then a system of White power was also required to circumscribe and control those Black lives.

LEGISLATING FAITH, LOVE, AND LUST

Maryland, prior to 1632 considered part of Virginia, moved first. By modern-day standards, it should have been called "Elizabeth's Law," when, in 1664, Maryland slave owners, reacting to the fear of slaves becoming Christian, then suing for their freedom, convinced the lower chamber of the Maryland General Assembly to ask the upper chamber to close that loophole.

> Itt is desired by the lower howse that the vpper howse would be pleased to drawe vp an Act obligeing negros to serve durante vita they thinking itt very necessary for the prevencon of the damage Masters of such Slaves may susteyne by such Slaves prtending to be Christned And soe pleade the lawe of England Wherevpon was drawne vp an Act intituled An Act for Slaves, and ordered to be sent to the lower howse.[1]

Durante ("duration") *vita* ("lifetime") is a Latin phrase made popular during the beginnings of American slavery. So, when used in the context of slavery, it means "service for a lifetime."

The upper chamber responded immediately by drafting "An Act Concerning Negroes & other Slaues":

Bee itt Enacted by the Right Honble the Lord Proprietary by the aduice and Consent of the upper and lower house of this present Generall Assembly That all Negroes or other slaues already within the Prouince And all Negroes and other slaues to bee hereafter imported into the Prouince shall serue Durante Vita And all Children born of any Negro or other slaue shall be Slaues as their ffathers were for the terme of their Liues . . . [2]

But it wasn't enough for slave owners who wanted a specific exemption for religion. So, seven years later, in 1671, the upper house took another bite at the apple in drafting "An Act for the Encourageing the Importacon of Negros and Slaues into this Province" or "Elizabeth's Law II":

That where any Negro or Negroes Slave or Slaues being in Servitude or bondage is are or shall become Christian or Christians and hath or have Received or shall att any time Receive the Holy Sacrament of Babtizme before or after his her or their Importacon into this Prouince the same is not nor shall or ought the same be denyed adjudged Construed or taken to be or to amount vnto a manumicon or freeing Inlarging or discharging any such Negroe or Negroes Slaue or Slaues or any his or their Issue or Issues from his her their or any of their Servitude or Servitudes Bondage or bondages . . . becoming Christian or Christians or Receiveing the Sacrament of Babtizme Every such Negroe and Negroes slaue and slaues and all and every the Issue and Issues of every such Negroe and Negroes Slaue and Slaues Is are and be and shall att all tymes hereafter be adjudged Reputed deemed and taken to be and Remayne in Servitude and Bondage . . . [3]

And that is how a loophole is sealed shut!

What began in Maryland in 1664 and 1671 was much larger than these acts of a state legislature articulated in archaic language. One by one, colony after colony cleaved itself legally from English common law because that common law posed a threat to the establishment and perpetuation of slavery, a threat to White power and wealth. Freedom from slavery threatened the freedom of White planters. Said another way: white planters and slave owners realized their freedom was tied to the bondage of their slaves.

So, scrap the old legal system and create a new one. In reaction to the threat of freedom, a novel American system of jurisprudence was forged in the fires of slavery; a system that would perpetuate White power and wealth, even as it led to Black Americans being given short shrift in the great founding documents of the country and in major court decisions such as *Dred Scott*; a system that would give rise to great men like Thurgood Marshall waging war against its inequities; and a system whose threats in areas such as criminal sentencing and voting rights are very much with us today.

Popular history notes the American War of Independence beginning outside of Boston with the "shot heard round the world," on the night of April 18, 1775, commencing with the battles of Lexington and Concord. I date the beginning of that war a century earlier to the pleadings of Elizabeth Key in a Northumberland County Court, and the reaction of legislatures throughout the colonies to the loopholes she exposed in the colonial system of slavery.

This reactive formation of an independent American jurisprudence, based on wealth, privilege, and race, is yet another example of a "road not taken." Instead of affirming the results of the Key case, and constructing an independent jurisprudence around the results, colonial legislatures, and the planter-merchant aristocracy behind them, systematically worked to dismantle every aspect of the case that led to Key's freedom. Like the development of antibodies in response to a virus infecting the human body, colonial legislative bodies wanted to inoculate their colonies from infection by the virus of Black freedom, threatening their power and wealth.

Virginia soon followed Maryland to close slavery's religious loophole.

In 1667, a court in Lower Norfolk County, Virginia, heard a

freedom suit brought by a man named Fernando, held as a slave by Captain John Warner. Fernando asserted the "Elizabeth Key Doctrine," that as a Christian who'd lived for a period of time in England, he could not be held in lifetime bondage, and "therefore ought to serve noe longer than any other servant that came out of England according to the custome of the Country."[4]

With no witness testimony, Fernando relied on written documents attesting to his Christianity and life as a freeman. He asked the court to consider "serverall papers in Portugell or some other language which the court could not understand which he alledged were papers From serverall Governors where he had lived a freeman and where hee was home."[5]

Like Anthony and Isabella, Fernando was most likely from Angola, captured and transported from there by the Portuguese, captured a second time by a privateer who may have taken him to England, from where he was sold into slavery in America. And, also like Anthony and Isabella, there's every likelihood that Fernando was baptized at birth in Angola, since Catholicism had been present there for more than two hundred years by 1667.

The Lower Norfolk County Court handed down the following ruling: "Wherefore the Court could find noe Cause wherefore he should be free but Judge him a slave for his life time, From which Judgement the said Negro hath appealed to the fifth day of the next Generall Court."[6]

Sadly, we cannot follow Fernando's case any further because the records of the General Court for these years were destroyed.

Shortly after Fernando's case appeared before a lower court, the Virginia General Assembly passed "An act declaring that baptisme of slaves doth not exempt them from bondage."

WHEREAS some doubts have risen whether children that are slaves by birth, and by the charity and piety of their owners made pertakers of the blessed sacrament of baptisme, should by vertue of their baptisme be made ffree; It is enacted and declared by this grand assembly, and the authority thereof, that the conferring of baptisme doth not alter the condition of the person as to his bondage or ffreedome; that diverse masters, ffreed from this doubt, may more carefully endeavour the propagation of christianity by permitting children, though slaves, or those of greater growth if capable to be admitted to that sacrament.[7]

But a loophole still existed for Africans baptized prior to entering the country. So, like their sister colony to the north, in 1682 the Virginia General Assembly drafted a more comprehensive statute, which read, in part,

Negroes, Moors, Mollattoes or Indians, who and whose parentage and native country are not christian at the time of their first purchase of such servant by some christian, although afterwards, and before such their importation and bringing into this country, they shall be converted to the christian faith; and all Indians which shall hereafter be sold by our neighbouring Indians, or any other trafiqueing with us as for slaves are hereby adjudged, deemed and taken, and shall be adjudged, deemed and taken to be slaves to all intents.[8]

Of course, even this act left open the "Angolan loophole," whereby a country could be considered Christian, the parents of a person abducted from there could be Christian, and the abducted person, therefore, could be Christian. Since the records of the General Court of this time were destroyed, we don't know if Fernando employed this legal strategy. But surviving records beyond this time do not show circuit courts, or the General Court, ruling in favor of slaves suing for their freedom on the basis of baptism and conversion to Christianity.

Just as the overall effect of these laws demonstrates the reactive creation of American jurisprudence in response to slavery, within these laws regarding religion and slavery are the seeds of a reactive transformation of American Christianity, another instance of Black labor (slavery) giving rise to new American forms of traditional institutions. Prior to the enactment of such laws on religion and slavery, English common law, once again, dictated the status of individuals, whether bonded or free.

Christianity was a prime mover in the demise of the feudal system of serfs and lords, widespread throughout Europe. But religion has never prevented Christians from slaughtering and enslaving each other, though it has given them injunctions not to do so. In seventeenth-century Europe, while Christian-against-Christian carnage reigned, scholars debated whether a Christian could hold another Christian a slave. And in the American colonies, a few Africans, like Elizabeth Key, managed to slip through the cracks to freedom by asserting their Christianity, until laws like those above were enacted, sealing those cracks, and the fate of slaves forever.

Religion is yet another American institution where freedom became based on bondage. These laws sealing the fate of slaves also sealed the fate of Christians. For as slavery continued, and more slaves became baptized, and a Black anti-slavery Christianity emerged, many White Christians had to react, had to construct and reconstruct particularly tenuous and ludicrous defenses of their faith and its ongoing support for slavery. Out of these tortured scriptures rose an American Christianity, rooted in slavery and racism, still preaching its gospel today.

• • •

There are times when I close my eyes to imagine a White bishop addressing the faithful, only his flock are all Black slaves, in from a long day's toil in a plantation's fields. The bishop makes the sign of the cross over his heart while speaking in Latin. But where I'd expect to hear *"In nomine Patris, et Filii, et Spiritus Sancti,* amen" ("In the name of the Father, the Son, and the Holy Spirit, amen"), I hear, instead, *"In nomine Matris partus sequitus ventrem durante vita,* amen" ("In the name of the Mother, that which is brought forth from the womb follows the womb for life's duration, amen").

Partus sequitus ventrem and *durante vita,* more than any Latin phrases, capture the scope, the horrors, the brutality, and the essence of slavery in an uncannily blessed way. Found throughout colonial-era legal proceedings, these phrases served as cannon shots across the bow of British tradition, declaring an American war of independence on five hundred years of established English common law; common law which affirmed, to the contrary, *partus sequitur patrem* ("that which is brought forth follows the father").

The consequences were monumental.

Had Elizabeth Key's case been adjudicated on the basis of *sequitur ventrem* ("follows the mother"), she would not have been freed. But only English common law of *sequitur patrem* ("follows the father") was available to the justices, who, probably on that basis more than anything else, decided the case in her favor. Her father was a free Englishman, so Elizabeth was free.

It would have been exceedingly difficult for slavery to take hold under a "follows the father" rule. Masters regularly slept with their female slaves and servants, and free Black men regularly had wives who were enslaved. Under "follows the father," children of these unions would be free, and the number of free Blacks would have grown steadily. Planters and merchants, ever more dependent on slave labor, could not allow or afford for that to happen.

The Virginia General Assembly put an end to "follows the father" by enacting a law in December 1662, titled "Negro womens children to serve according to the condition of the mother." It read simply,

WHEREAS some doubts have arrisen whether children got by any Englishman upon a negro woman should be slave or ffree, *Be it therefore enacted and declared by this present grand assembly,* that all children borne in this country shalbe held bond or free only according to the condition of the mother, *And* that if any christian shall committ ffornication with a negro man or woman, hee or shee soe offending shall pay double the ffines imposed by the former act.[9]

Since Maryland led the way in closing the religious loophole to freedom, what about this question of "following the father" or "following the mother"? The 1664 Maryland law cited earlier contained this clause at the end: "all Children born of any Negro or other slaue *shall be Slaues as their ffathers were* for the terme of their Liues [italics added]."[10] In keeping with English common law, Maryland actually enacted, or at least experimented with, *sequitur patrem*. But it must not have gone well because the 1671 law, also cited above, essentially replaced the earlier statute, with the clause, "Every such Negroe and Negroes slaue and slaues *and all and every the Issue and Issues of every such Negroe and Negroes Slaue and slaues* Is are and be and shall att all tymes hereafter be adjudged Reputed deemed and taken to be and Remayne in Servitude and Bondage [italics added]."[11]

Buried in the new law's language to prevent the use of Christianity to escape slavery is an implicit transition from "following the father" to "following the mother" in Maryland.

While to this point, we've focused on the Chesapeake region of the colonies, Virginia and Maryland, as the epicenter of slavery, let's now, for a moment, turn our attention north, to New England, where slavery also took hold during the latter part of the seventeenth century.

Traveling south to north in America, one senses, even today, that racism and bigotry in the south is openly "in your face," while in the north, covertly "in their hearts." This was certainly the case with religion and slavery in seventeenth-century New England as compared to seventeenth-century Virginia and Maryland. Early southern religious support for slavery, as discussed above—the need to close the "Elizabeth Key" loophole—was forthright and direct, no doubt reflecting the presence of more people of African descent in southern colonies, and a stronger reliance on bonded Black labor for their economies.

In New England, infused from the beginning of European settlement with puritanical religious ideals, coming to terms with slavery and religion, and with the relatively few dark-skinned people in its midst, was a more tortuous affair. Puritans were Protestants seeking to purge the Anglican Church of its Catholic trappings. They emphasized a special, direct covenant between man and God, bypassing mediation through a priest. Where in Catholicism, a parishioner addressed a priest, who, in turn, addressed God, with a clerical hierarchy leading up to the pope, whereas in Puritanism, all human beings possessed a personal covenant (a compact or bond) with God, removing the need for such a tiered approach to the Divine.

Covenants bound individuals to God, congregations to a church, individuals to a congregation, individuals to a family, families to a community, and so forth. The social and political lifeblood of New England towns was based on covenants. For this, the Puritans held, was how Jesus's beloved community would be realized on earth. This is why, even today, the proliferation of small New England towns seems centered around their steeples and their spires.

But this orderly Puritan plan had not figured on African members of that beloved community, who did not look like them. Bonded Africans in colonial New England were simultaneously viewed as human beings, created in God's image, and as property, which Christians could own and sell. "Slaves were undoubtedly understood as personal property," notes historian Monica Reed, "but they were more than that because of the religious tradition in New England that maintained that all people, regardless of color or legal status, were children of the same God."[12]

"Render therefore unto Caesar the things that are Caesar's; and unto God the things that are God's."[13] God ordained that slaves were socially inferior to their masters, and to White men and women, this line of religious reasoning meant God also ordained that in his eyes slaves and masters were spiritual equals.

Judge Samuel Sewall, a colonial Boston businessman and prominent figure in the Salem witch trials, authored a famous essay, supposedly critiquing slavery, which stated, "*These Blackamores are of* the Posterity of Cham, *and therefore are under the Curse of Slavery.*" He continued, "*The* Nigers *are brought out of a Pagan Country, into places where the Gospel is Preached* . . . that good may come of it." Then, concluded, "These *Ethiopians*, as black as they are; seeing they are the Sons and Daughters of the First *Adam*, the Brethren and Sister of the Last ADAM, and the Offspring of GOD; They ought to be treated with a Respect agreeable."[14]

Which makes me want to press further the theological question: Are we to be seen as the children of Jesus (the last Adam) or the children of Ham (Cham), cursed by the color of our skin, and destined like the Flying Dutchman to forever sail the oceans of humanity without finding a welcoming human port?

Cotton Mather, Harvard graduate, prolific author, Puritan minister, and also prominent in the Salem witch trials, penned a pamphlet called "The Negro Christianized,"[15] in which he entreated slave owners, himself among them, to "*Show your selves Men*, and let *Rational Arguments* have their Force upon you, to make you treat, not as *Bruits* but as *Men*, those *Rational Creatures* whom God has made your *Servants*."[16]

But then, Mather concludes, "What *Law* is it, that Sets the *Baptised Slave* at *Liberty*? Not the *Law of Christianity*: that allows of *Slavery* . . . directs a *Slave*, upon his embracing the *Law of the Redeemer*, to satisfy himself, *That he is the Lords Free-man*, tho' he continues a *Slave*."[17]

More than a decade earlier, in 1694, a group of Christian ministers convened in Boston, where they prepared a resolution against polygamy, adultery, drinking, fortune-telling, sorcery, and the growing moral turpitude of the colony. The resolution, first delivered to the Commonwealth's General Assembly in 1694, then again in 1696, also included the following plank: "It is Desired That ye wel-knowne Discouragement upon ye endeavours of many masters [to] Christianize their slaues, may be removed by a Law which may take away all pre[text] to Release from just servidet, by receiuing Baptisme."[18] But the General Assembly never acted on the resolution.

Puritanism was not a rigid, inflexible system, which was good for its adherents, if not so good for the Africans in New England held as servants and slaves. By the middle of the seventeenth century, New England had already become a hub of commerce, supplying the other American colonies, and those as far away as the West Indies, with food and building materials. There was also New England prowess in shipbuilding, leading the powerful English merchant-politician Sir Josiah Child to warn in 1692:

> Of all the American plantations, His Majeſty has non ſo apt for the building of ſhipping as New England, nor none comparably ſo qualified for the breeding of ſeamen . . . and, in my poor opinion, there is nothing more prejudicial, and in proſpe&t more dangerous, to any mother-kingdom, than the increaſe of ſhipping in her colonies, plantations, and provinces.[19]

Within a decade of Child's warning, Massachusetts rivaled Britain as the shipbuilding capital of the English-speaking world[20] with Boston bankers on track to rival their London counterparts as financiers of the growth in New England shipbuilding and trade. All of this placed New England squarely in the center of the Atlantic slave trade, and of slavery within the colonies. So, much as it had earlier in England, slavery begot in New England the rise of these new institutions of power and wealth.

Puritanism adapted to provide religious cover for the enslavement of human beings at the core of these new American institutions and the jobs and wealth they generated within New England's beloved community. As children of the same God, African servants and slaves were once inferior members of this beloved community. Ultimately, they were theologically banished from it. As commerce eclipsed covenant, slaves became property, and slavery a means of accumulating temporal wealth, and a display of spiritual status.

As wealth accumulated to individuals and family, a concern over property rights also grew. English philosopher William Wollaston, whose thinking influenced the Founders, resulting in the phrase "the pursuit of happiness,"[21] incorporated into the Declaration of Independence, laid out the case for private property in a dense, compact tome finished shortly before his death in 1724.

> There is then ſuch a thing as property, founded in nature and truth: or, there are things, which one man only can, conſiſtently with nature and truth, call his. Thoſe things, which only one man can truly and properly call his, muſt remain his, till he agrees to part with them . . . or death extinguiſhes him and his title together, and he delivers the lamp to his, next man.[22]

By Wollaston's time, slaves in New England and throughout the American colonies were such things, "which one man only can, consistently with nature and truth, call his." And owning slaves was a self-evident truth for which the colonies declared independence and went to war.

Some preachers fretted. "We should Examine by the rules of God's Word, whether our Desire, Esteem and Trust be not inordinately plac'd on Worldly Riches," said Joseph Sewall in a 1717 sermon, "whether our hearts do not go out after them with too much Vehemency; and whether our pursuit of them be not too Eager and Earnest."[23]

Others simply reinterpreted the word of God, and the meaning of providence, in terms of financial success. Samuel Whitman, of Farmington, Connecticut, preached a gospel of "practical Godliness": "God usually indulges Religious Nations with much Outward Prosperity. The way to the Paradise of Temporal 'Prosperity, lieth thro' the Temple of Vertue. When there is much of Practical Religion among a People, God usually maketh them to Prosper in all that they set their hands to."[24]

This new religious outlook on the accumulation of property and wealth assuaged the consciences of New Englanders involved in slavery—either in the Atlantic slave trade or in the use of slaves in their local enterprises. "If slavery yielded more money, then by the turn of the seventeenth-century, it came to have a positive [e]ffect," observed Monica Reed. Similarly, if God ultimately determined how successful a community would be, then the success of the developing New England economy was good evidence that God approved of colonists accumulating wealth through their increased involvement in an Atlantic economy and consequently the slave trade.[25]

. . .

Sex is an inconvenient truth that can sweep away in one great tidal wave the tidy sandcastles of society and politics erected by men. Sex can propel humans to the brink of madness, or inject madness into human affairs. Sex knows no boundaries. Sex cannot be tamed by human rules and laws, by social norms and conventions, by race or creed, by religious beliefs or political convictions. Whether springing from lust or love, sex is a dangerous disruptor of social and political orders, which the architects of slavery sought to control.

Sex is also the route by which the important social institutions of family and community are created and propagated. Wealth flows through family inheritance, accumulating generation after generation. Ensuring family order enhances the accumulation of wealth. Disrupting family order diminishes such accumulation. The wealth gap so evident between Black and White Americans today has roots in colonial-era efforts to enhance White families while diminishing Black families. Black Americans' labor, particularly during slavery, enhanced the order and accumulation of wealth by southern and northern White families, in part, because slavery, by design, devastated the Black family. All of these developments, however, had their origins in colonial-era attempts to control sex.

The danger began even before Anthony and Isabella arrived in Virginia in August 1619. Named by Queen Elizabeth I, the supposed "Virgin Queen," who may not have married but was, by all accounts, no stranger to sex, Virginia was the only colony (is still the only state) so named after a woman.

Eastward Hoe, a satirical, scandalous play written by the English dramatist John Marston and two colleagues in 1605, tells the story of a group of adventurers heading off to Virginia. Performed several times before being banned until 1614, Act III, Scene 3 finds the adventurers in an English tavern, mulling over the sexual delights of colonizing Virginia. "Come, boys," says Captain Seagull, "Virginia longs till we share the rest of her maidenhead." When asked who's so delighted in that maidenhead before, Seagull replies, "A whole country of English is there, man, bred of those that were left there in '79; they have married with the Indians, and make 'hem bring forth as beautiful faces as any we have in England."[26]

So, female Native Americans were the basis of Virginia's sexualization, yet the "beautiful" children of these various unions were still English (*partus sequitur patrem*). With the ratio of women to men in Virginia very low, and the need for labor very high, the Virginia Company, and the colonial Founding Fathers, were very concerned about Englishmen breaking away from the colony in search of native women as wives. The tale of Pocahontas, John Rolfe, and John Smith is merely a popularized, sanitized version of this theme of sexualized native women available to satisfy the desires of needy Englishmen.

Early Virginian colonists lived under the draconian rules of Sir Thomas Dale, governor of the colony in 1611, then again from 1614 to 1616. "Dale's Code," as these measures were known, addressed homosexuality and other forms of what was, then, considered illicit sex.

No man shal commit the horrible, and detestable sins of Sodomie vpon pain of death; & he or she that can be lawfully conuict of Adultery shall be punished with death. No man shall rauish or force any woma[n], maid or Indian, or other, vpon pain of death, and know ye that he or shee, that shall commit fornication, and euident proofe made thereof, for their first fault shall be whipt, for their second they shall be whipt, and for their third they shall

be whipt three times a weeke for one month, and aske publique
forgiuenesse in the Assembly of the Congregation . . . [27]

Here, fornication meant sex outside of marriage. Dale also made
it clear that no one was to run away to nearby native villages for
love, or lust, or to escape from labor. "No man or woman, (vpon
paine of death) shall runne away from the Colonie, to Powhathan, or
any sauage Weroance else whatsoeuer."[28] Powhatan (the Powhatan
chief) led his people during Dale's tenure, and Weroance, although
the name of a particular Algonquin leader, was often used to describe Native American leaders in general.

Of course, colonists did run away, fornicate, and engage in sodomy
and adultery. If caught, especially if caught running away to native
villages, they were subject to Dale's particularly gruesome "paine of
death," according to Sir George Percy's eyewitness account:

[M]any of them beinge taken ageine Sr Thomas in A moste severe
mannor cawsed to be executed. Some he apointed to be hanged
Some burned Some to be broken upon wheles, other to be staked
and some to be shott to deathe all theis extreme and crewell tor-
ture he used and inflicted upon them To terrefy the reste for
Attempteinge the Lyke . . . [29]

Here *staked* meant impalement, in which a sharpened metal pole
was driven headward from the base of a person's torso, through the
length of their body, then the other end implanted in the ground.

Being mesmerized by the macabre is not the point. Rather it is
understanding the extreme, inhumane measures colonial authorities took to enforce the social order. And how, even before Anthony
and Isabella arrived in Virginia, a brutal system of enforcing social
order, through regulating sex, had been foisted on colonists. After
the arrival of Africans, the brutality of that system was simply di-
aled up for them.

Colonial authorities, and the colonial aristocracy, composed of planters and merchants, felt surrounded on all sides. Any stability that England might have offered was a perilous three months and three-thousand-mile sea crossing away. And even there, in England, property rights were changing, the ranks of the poor were swelling, and traditional family roles were morphing. Besides, planters and merchants were determined to create a social hierarchy here in America that kept them at the top. Colonists in Virginia were surrounded by a wilderness where Native Americans practiced strange family and social customs that the English viewed as coming from the devil. Polygamy, berdache,[30] and communal property were ideas practiced by Native Americans that were foreign to Englishmen. And then there was the colony itself, where Englishmen outnumbered Englishwomen four to one.

Then, as today, for the sake of social order and financial gain, groups of men conspired to traffic in, and control, the bodies of women. Recognizing this threat to the Virginia Company's long-term success, and therefore its long-term profits, in England in 1619, Sir Edwyn Sandys, then the Virginia Company's CEO, suggested,

> [T]he people thither transported, though seated there in their persons for some fewe yeares, are not settled in their minds to make it their place of rest and continuance, but hauing gotten some wealth there, to returne againe to England: ffor the remedying that mischief, and establishing of a perpetuitie to the Plantation . . . send them ouer One hundredth young Maides to become wifes; that wifes, children and familie might make them lesse moueable and settle them, together with their Posteritie in that Soile.[31]

Sandys's remarks underscore a simple message: steady families, steady profits. The Virginia Company sent 140 women to the colony within several years of Sandys's remarks. Seventeenth-century sea captains bartered women conscripted, coerced, or spirited from England for tobacco. Pennsylvania and Massachusetts offered "maid lotts," of as much as seventy-five acres, to unmarried women who paid their own transportation.[32]

Religious ministers were enlisted to enforce the colony's social and moral order. Women could not marry without the consent of their parents, or their masters or mistresses, and ministers needed to assure such consent on penalty of censure.[33] Marriage became an important regulatory tool. Sex outside of marriage was a punishable offense, even after colonial Virginia authorities put in place rules less draconian than Dale's Code.

There's the fascinating 1629 case of Thomas(ine) Hall, accused of fornication with a servant named "Great Besse." But soon questions of gender superseded questions of Hall's sexual transgression. When asked what gender s/he was, Hall said both. In England, Hall dressed as a man to join the military, but as a woman to do needlework after discharge, remaining as a woman until the opportunity arose for travel to Virginia, when Hall again dressed as a man. Hall was ordered to dress as a woman. This upset the "good wives" of the colony, who, under court order, gave Hall a physical examination and determined "hee was a man." Hall was then ordered to dress as a man. But this upset the men of the colony, who then searched Hall's body for female genitalia. Finding none, but finding an extremely small penis, they, too, determined Hall to be a man. Most likely, Hall suffered from severe micropenis. Splitting the difference, the General Court of Virginia ordered Hall to wear men's breeches but a woman's coif on his head (think, *The Handmaid's Tale*) and an apron around his waist.[34]

Add to Hall's case that of Joane (Goody) Wright in 1626, a left-handed woman and midwife accused of being a witch. Goody (a diminutive form of "Goodwife," often used in reference to witches) stood accused by the "good men" of the colony of sapping their masculinity—loss of the ability to hunt, plant, and provide. But the "good wives" of Virginia accused her of cursing their femininity—loss of the ability to do housework, have children, or maintain their sexually pristine reputations.[35]

Local authorities, investors, planters, merchants, judges, ministers, the "good people" of colonial Virginia all came together in support of family and social order, and against any ambiguities or threats.

On August 19, 1619, Sir Thomas Dale died halfway around the world in Machilipatnam, India, almost to the day when Anthony and Isabella and the other first Africans stepped foot on Virginian soil. Their arrival proved the latest threat to the social order of Virginia and confounded the problems for which Dale had offered such vicious solutions. Now, not only were there more non-Englishwomen whom Englishmen might desire, but also more non-Englishmen who might compete for the available few Englishwomen.

Englishmen were forbidden sex with African women. An act of the General Assembly on September 17, 1630, pronounced "Hugh Davis to be soundly whipped, before an assembly of Negroes and others for abusing himself to the dishonor of God and shame of Christians, by defiling his body in lying with a negro; which fault he is to acknowledge next Sabbath day."[36]

One wonders whether Thomas Key was present at Davis's public whipping. Key's African servant would have just given birth, or was about to give birth, to a baby girl named Elizabeth, which he fathered. But presumably Davis was a servant, which meant he was subject to harsher restrictions than the mere fine Key was ordered to pay for the same offense. Key had privilege and status, which by all appearances, he had married into rather than achieved on his own. Furthermore, in punishing Davis "before an assembly of Negroes and others," the penalty seemed directed at sending a message not just to White Englishmen, but also to Africans, particularly African women, about the dangers of interracial sex.

Sexuality is a unique institution of power, as any politician, male or female, who's been caught in a sexual scandal will attest.

In 1640, the Virginia General Assembly, probably acting in its role as the colonial supreme court, ordered "Robert Sweet to do penance in church according to the laws of England, for getting a negroe woman with child and the woman whipt."[37] Here, the White man's penalty, for the same crime, was less severe than the Black woman's.

In 1642/43[38] the House of Burgesses (General Assembly) passed another law targeting African women: *"Be it also enacted and confirmed That there be tenn pounds of tob'o. per poll & a bushell of corne per poll paid to the ministers within the severall parishes of the collony for all tithable persons, that is to say, as well for all youths of sixteen years of age as vpwards, as also for all negro women at the age of sixteen years."*[39]

"Tithable persons," those required to pay taxes, or in the case of slaves or servants their masters required to pay taxes on them, were defined in a 1629 act of the General Assembly as "all those that worke in the ground of what qualitie or condition soever."[40]

The importance of the act, and the meaning behind it, requires a brief explanation. Prior to 1619, when Anthony and Isabella arrived, survival was the primary concern for all Virginia colonists. Men, women, and servants toiled together in the fields ("in the ground") and in the home. But after the 1622 raid on Jamestown by Algonquin chief Opechancanough, which killed 347 colonists[41] (25 percent of the population), a new mindset emerged.

It appeared the colony would survive, and a ruthless, brutal campaign was mounted against neighboring tribes, led by men like Captain William Tucker, master of Anthony and Isabella. The colonial planter elite, like Tucker, dominated the General Assembly, where they also worked to establish a new social order, re-creating the patriarchal system they knew from England. Men were to work as planters, women to work in homes raising children and engaged in domestic chores. Hence, the intent of the 1629 act was to tax primarily adult men, not women, and the extension of that act in 1642/43 was to also tax Black women (White women only if they "worke in the ground").

Black women were not to be considered the equals of White women. Whether they worked in the field or in the home they were to be taxed. So, the act really stands as early legislative support for the power of White families, and a legislative assault on the power of Black families, by targeting only Black women in this way.

Maryland was not far behind. As part of "An Act Concerning Negroes & other Slaues" presented at the beginning of this chapter, the Maryland General Assembly added provisions meant to terrorize Englishwomen from marrying Black slaves.

[D]ivers freeborne English women forgettfull of their free Condicon and to the disgrace of our Nation doe intermarry with Negro Slaues by which alsoe diuers suites may arise touching the Issue of such woemen and a great damage doth befall the Masters of such Negros for preuention whereof for deterring such freeborne women from such shamefull Matches . . . That whatsoever free borne woman shall inter marry with any slaue . . . shall Serue the master of such slaue dureing the life of her husband And that all the Issue of such freeborne woemen soe marryed shall be Slaues as their fathers were And Bee itt further Enacted that all the Issues of English or other freeborne woemen that haue already marryed Negroes shall serve the Masters of their Parents till they be Thirty yeares of age . . . [42]

But this portion of the law also contained a loophole, exploited by unscrupulous masters who contrived to force their White female servants to marry Black men, reaping the benefit of these White women, and their children, becoming slaves. This was clearly not the intention of the legislature, which closed this particular loophole in 1681 by declaring the women and children of such contrived marriages free, and slapping a fine of ten thousand pounds of tobacco on the masters and mistresses involved.[43, 44]

In time, Massachusetts ran third to Virginia and Maryland with a 1705 act titled "An Act for the Better Preventing of a Spurious and Mixt Issue, &c."[45] In severity, Massachusetts surpassed them. Legislators, perhaps having learned from their southern counterparts, issued a sweeping, comprehensive, and vengeful law that contained none of the loopholes previously seen in the southern colonies.

If a Black man had sex with a Christian (White) woman, he was ordered severely whipped, then sold out of Massachusetts. The woman, meanwhile, was ordered to maintain any child of such union at her own expense, and if unable to do so, she was to be sold as a servant within Massachusetts in exchange for the maintenance of her child.

White men who had sex with Black women were also ordered severely whipped, then fined five pounds ($1,300 in 2020 terms) toward the maintenance of any child that came forth. But the Black woman of such an illicit liaison was ordered sold out of Massachusetts as was the case with Black men.

Blacks were permitted to marry other Blacks but interracial marriages were strictly forbidden with stiff fines of fifty pounds levied on anyone otherwise authorized to perform marriages in Massachusetts who presided over such an interracial union.

Based on laws, rules, and judgments regarding religion, family, and sex, from Virginia to Maryland to Massachusetts, the presence of Africans in the American colonies, whether slave or servant, created and supported new institutions of colonial power and wealth. Profits fattened. Class and racial boundaries were erected and tightened. A jurisprudence of inequity was jump-started. A religion appeasing slavery took shape. A shipbuilding industry took hold. A financial services sector was launched. The foundations of White families were established, while Black families were systematically destroyed.

While all of these roads taken reflect so many more that were not, they also demonstrate the extent to which colonial authorities went to control Black lives so they would facilitate, rather than disrupt, the creation of White power and wealth.

RUNAWAYS AND REBELS

The spring and summer of 1640 was a busy time for the Virginia General Council. Governor William Berkeley had appointed twelve men to the General Assembly's upper house as his advisers and as the colony's supreme judicial body, over which he ruled. Now, on their docket they found numerous reports from anxious planters of runaway servants and slaves. Among them, a report from one of their own, Colonel Hugh Gwynne, a member of the lower house representing Charles River County, soon to be renamed York County. Gwynne was entered into Council records as a "gentleman." Under English law, by which the Council operated, that meant he ranked as a noble granted permission to bear a coat of arms.

Gwynne reported three of his servants missing and run away to Maryland, where they were captured and currently being detained. He wanted to sell them in Maryland, which King Charles I had only recently separated from Virginia as a sovereign colony, but that sale required the approval of these twelve men. Considering the dangerous consequences that runaway servants posed to social order, and their desire not to relinquish authority to another colonial jurisdiction, on June 4, 1640, the General Council refused Gwynne's request, instead ordering the runaways extradited from Maryland to face punishment in Virginia.[1]

A month later, on July 9, 1640, with the men back in custody in Virginia, the General Council handed down its sentence. All three servants were to receive thirty lashes by whip. Victor, a Dutchman, and James Gregory, a Scotchman, were to serve out the remainder of their indentures to Gwynne, then one whole year additionally after that. But the third servant, the Council said, "being a negro named John Punch shall serve his master or his assigns for the time of his natural life, here or elsewhere."[2] For this reason, some consider John Punch the first slave in America.

In July 2012, a widely reported story linked President Barack Obama to John Punch. DNA testing and extensive genealogical research showed Obama was a descendant of Punch, not through his African father, but instead through his mother from Kansas, an unlikely twist in the remarkable story of this president's diverse roots.[3] The headlines were compelling, such as "First Black President is Descendant of First Black Slave."

But was Punch the first Black slave? Or was he one of the last Black indentured servants? In the colonial transition from indentured servitude to slavery, lifetime servitude, the sentence meted out to Punch, was a final stage prior to opening slavery's door of no return. The term *slave* is found nowhere in the court documents related to Punch, where he is referred to as a servant. Although the connection between Punch and future president Obama is remarkable, more important may be what his sentencing tells us about the institutions that runaway Black men like him helped to create. But first, we need to dig a little further into the Council's docket.

Also in front of the Council on July 22, 1640, was a complaint by Captain William Pierce, an ancient planter. Pierce was identified by the honorific "Efq" or "Esquire," which under English law ranked him above a "gentleman," like Hugh Gwynne, but below a knight, like Governor Sir William Berkeley. Pierce was also a member of the General Council from 1632 to 1643, so he was making his case in front of the same men he sat in judgment with all the time.

Pierce reported that six of his servants and "a negro of Mr Reginolds" had plotted to run away to New York ("unto the *Dutch* plantation") on the night of July 18. Andrew Noxe, Richard Hill, Richard Cookeson, John Williams, Christopher Miller, and Peter Wilcocke were owned by Pierce. Emanuel, a Black man, was owned by Mr. Reginolds.

At the appointed time that Saturday night, Emanuel took one of Pierce's skiffs along with corn flour, shot, and guns. The men sailed down the Elizabeth River, but they were ultimately apprehended and returned to Jamestown to face the judgment of the Council. Miller, a Dutchman considered to be the ringleader, was given a punishment of thirty lashes, and his cheek branded with the letter *R* (*runaway*). Furthermore, he was required to work in shackles for Pierce for at least one year, longer if Pierce thought necessary, then after fulfilling the terms of his indenture to Pierce, to serve the colony for seven years more. Wilcocke also received thirty lashes and branding, but his additional term of service was set at three years. Cookeson received no lashes, but his term of service was lengthened by two and a half years. Noxe received thirty lashes but nothing else. Hill, upon good behavior, received no punishment at all. Williams, also a surgeon, received no lashes but was required to serve the colony an additional seven years. Emanuel, the Black man, received thirty lashes, branding, and a year's work in shackles.

Emanuel's verdict came two weeks after Punch's verdict. It was, by far, much less severe and with no mention of lifetime servitude. In 1640, slavery for Blacks was still not fixed in the minds or verdicts of Virginia's colonial elite, even though the colony was heading in that direction.

A few things, however, surface as more important than a comparison of sentencing harshness: how runaway slaves, like illicit sex, threatened the colonial social order; why the colonial ruling class fretted over runaways and worked so hard to halt them; and, the institutions that emerged to recapture and punish these men and women. While complete records of many early cases, like those cited above, have not survived, other records of the time, and other laws of the American colonies, give us clues to answering these questions. Through these clues we can piece together the beginnings of yet another uniquely American institution—a constabulary force with roots in tracking down and returning runaway servants and slaves in support of the financial harm caused by runaways to their masters—in other words, the institutions of American policing and law enforcement.

By the summer of 1640, the Virginia General Assembly had already enacted a law that all Whites would be provided with guns and ammunition, but Blacks would not: "ALL persons except negroes to be provided with arms and ammunition or be fined at pleasure of the Governor and Council."[4]

On June 30, 1640, in between the time the Council ordered the return of John Punch from Maryland and issued his lifetime sentence, the twelve men and the governor created one of the first public forces to hunt down and retrieve escaped Black men. They granted John Mottrom[5] and Edward Fleet the authority to raise a party of fourteen armed men, more if needed, from the militia of Charles River County (York County) to go in pursuit of "certain runaway negroes and to bring them in to the governor."[6] The expense for this force was to be borne by the counties, "from whence fuch negroes are runaway."[7]

This police force was created by the Council, not enacted into law by the General Assembly. In their 1642/43 session, the Assembly passed a more general law regarding runaway servants, with no distinction given to race. The wealth and welfare of colonial planters was paramount:

> WHEREAS there are divers loytering runaways in the collony who very often absent themselves from their masters service, And sometimes in two or three monthes cannot be found, whereby their said masters are at great charge in finding them, And many times even to the loss of their year's labour before they be had, *Be it therefore enacted and confirmed* that all runaways that shall

absent themselves from their said masters service shall be lyable to make satisfaction by service at the end of their tymes by indenture [namely] double the tyme of service soe neglected.[8]

Furthermore, a second attempt garnered the runaway servant branding on the cheek with the letter *R*. If convicted of running away with weapons that wound up in the hands of native tribes, the runaway "shall suffer death as in the case of ffelony." Apparently, this did not deter runaway servants, Black or White. So, in 1661 the General Assembly enacted a law "that in case any English servant shall run away in company with any negroes who are incapable of makeing satisfaction by addition of time"[9] such English offenders would serve not only the additional time given them by the 1642/43 act, but the time that would have been given to the Black person under that previous act. The implicit assumption in this law is that Blacks under slavery or lifetime service were "incapable of makeing satisfaction by addition of time." The act was further amended a year later to say that "if the negroes be lost or dye in such time of their being run away, the christian servants in company with them shall by proportion among them, either pay fower thousand five hundred pounds of tobacco and caske or fower yeares service for every negroe soe lost or dead."[10]

But even with these revisions, the Council felt the 1662 act was not enough. So, in 1672, they issued a blanket "shoot to kill" exemption for anyone hunting runaway Black servants or slaves.

As I write these words, cities in the United States and around the world are flash points. Their citizens are angry. People of color, and of good conscience, are protesting the murder of George Floyd on May 25, 2020, by members of the Minneapolis, Minnesota, police.[11] More generally, they are protesting the callous use of force and wanton killing of Black men and women by US police who seem to know no bounds and no restraints.

Disregard for Black lives is not new. This violence against Blacks did not begin in recent times. It did not begin one hundred or two hundred or even three hundred years ago. The trope of the Black "super predator" lying in wait for Whites is found 350 years ago in the following act from 1672. Here, one reads of the allusion to Blacks roaming the colonial countryside, bent on terrorizing and threatening the lives and property, the wealth and well-being, of Whites. This, in turn, justifies the need for overwhelming force, in utter disregard of Black lives. Disregard for Black lives is found within the fibers of the American nation, woven tightly into the very fabric of this country, as this following act so clearly shows. The act is recounted here in its entirety and original wording, including sidebar summaries of its various sections as found in the source document. Given the continued worldwide unrest over police brutality and racial inequity, the following act is well worth the read, even with the need to spend a few moments longer deciphering its antiquated English. Remember it was put into law in colonial America in 1672.

LAWS OF VIRGINIA, SEPTEMBER, 1672 — 24th CHARLES II
ACT VIII.

An act for the apprehension and suppression of runawayes, negroes and slaves.

FORASMUCH as it hath beene manifested to this grand assembly that many negroes have lately beene, and now are out in rebellion in sundry parts of this country, and that noe meanes have yet beene found for the apprehension and suppression of them from whome many mischeifes of very dangerous consequence may arise to the country if either other negroes, Indians or servants should happen to fly forth and joyne with them; for the prevention of which, *Be it enacted by the governour, councell and burgesses of this grand assembly, and by the authority thereof,* that if any negroe, molatto, Indian slave, or servant for life, runaway and shalbe persued by warrant or hue and crye, it shall and may be lawfull for any person who shall endeavour to take them, upon the resistance of such negroe, mollatto, Indian slave, or servant for life, to kill or wound him or them soe resisting; *Provided alwayes*, and it is the true intent and meaning hereof, that such negroe, molatto, Indian slave, or servant for life, be named and described in the hue and crye which is alsoe to be signed by the master or owner of the said runaway. And if it happen that such negroe, molatto, Indian slave, or servant for life doe dye of any wound in such their resistance received the master or owner of such shall receive satisfaction from the publique for his negroe, molatto, Indian slave, or servant for life, soe killed or dyeing of such wounds; and the person who shall kill or wound by virtue of any such hugh and crye any such soe resisting in manner as aforesaid shall not be questioned for the same, he forthwith giveing notice thereof and returning the hue and crye or warrant to the master or owner of him or them soe killed or wounded or to the next justice of peace. *And it is further enacted* by the authority aforesaid that all such negroes and slaves shalbe valued at ffowre thousand five hundred pounds of tobacco and caske a peece, and Indians at three thousand pounds of tobacco and caske a peice, And further if it shall happen that any negroe, molatto, Indian slave, or servant for life, in such their resistance to receive any wound whereof they may not happen to dye, but shall lye any considerable tyme sick and disabled, then alsoe the master or owner of the same soe sick or disabled shall receive them from the publique a reasonable satisfaction for such damages as they shall make appeare they have susteyned thereby at the county court, who shall thereupon grant the master or owner a certificate to the next assembly of what damages they shall make appeare; *and it is further enacted* that the neighbouring Indians doe and hereby are required and enjoyned to seize and apprehend all runawayes whatsoever that shall happen to come amongst them, and to bring them before some justice of the peace whoe upon the receipt of such servants, slave, or slaves, from the Indians, shall pay unto the said Indians for a recompence twenty armes length of Roanoake [a type of tobacco] or the value thereof in goods as the Indians shall like of, for which the said justice of peace shall receive from the publique two hundred and fifty pounds of tobacco, and the said justice to proceed in conveying the runaway to his master according to the law in such cases already provided; This act to continue in force till the next assembly and noe longer unlesse it be thought fitt to continue.

Runaways either negro, mulatto, Indian slave or servants, resisting may be killed or wounded.

Proviso.

Master indemnified by the public, & person killing not to be questioned.

Value of such negroes, &c.

Negroes, &c. wounded and lingering, their owners to be paid.

Reward to neighbouring Indians for apprehending runaways.

It is not clear if, or how long, the act was extended. That may not matter, for the act successfully unleashed forces directed against Black lives that took centuries to rein in, and, in some cases, have not been reined in even today. The act promised the colonial planter elite compensation for the killing of a Black laborer, their financial loss equated to the value of a Black life. This was yet another step toward slavery, of treating Blacks as property and that property in financial rather than human terms. The act devalued the life of a Black servant or slave by declaring White masters and slaveholders, and those in pursuit of runaway slaves, immune to prosecution. If they killed a Black servant or slave, they would never face trial nor would they be liable for a crime.

In a subsequent chapter, we will return to this act in examining the roots of policing in America. But for now, this act of 1672 stands as a legislative milestone that protects the freedom of

White American colonists through creating institutions of law enforcement and criminal justice that insure the bondage of Blacks and, for that matter, Native Americans.

The act also sets Native Americans against Black Americans, giving the former financial reward for helping to apprehend runaway slaves. Throughout history, some tribes did track down and return Black runaways, while other tribes opened their communities to shelter them. There is a long, and sad, history of Native American and Black American communities misunderstanding each other. I live on a reservation, though to my knowledge I am not Native American. A few years ago, while working with the tribe, I had occasion to visit another tribe farther south, and there spend some time with their chief, who was a prominent member of several national organizations lobbying on behalf of Native American interests. The chief proceeded to lecture me on how native lands were stolen from tribes.

I stopped him. "Do my people look like they stole those lands from your people?"

"No. But they do look like the Buffalo Soldiers."

He was referring, of course, to the post–Civil War Black soldiers of the American West, who made their mark through wars against Native Americans. It's a complaint justly leveled by Native Americans against Blacks serving in the US Army then.

"And Native Americans were enlisted and paid to track down slaves for the most brutal and inhumane punishments," I said. "The point is not whose pain is greatest, nor who lost the most, nor who brutalized the other more. The point is how do we get beyond all of this that has been used to separate our communities and find common ground to bring us together to fight for the justice and equity we deserve?"

Throughout the 1990s, a friend with both Native American and African American ancestry ran a program in the northeast US called Broken Arrows, which was devoted to healing the wounds and the rifts between these two communities. But the wounds run deep. They were opened long ago, by acts like this one in 1672 from the

Virginia Assembly, which set the tenor and tone for future acts and actions, which would build on these precedents it set.

• • •

No single event in late-seventeenth-century colonial Virginia still captivates the imagination and fascination of historians, history lovers, and political junkies as Bacon's Rebellion. It is seen by some as the first rumblings of the American Revolution; by others as the first integrated movement for social and racial justice; and, still by others as a dark and tragic moment in Native American history. If one were to place a marker on the timeline of servitude bleeding into outright slavery for Africans imported into the colony, Bacon's Rebellion, from 1676 to 1677, would be a good place to press that pin. The rebellion showcased all of these elements, brought to a head in a contest between two aristocrats: Sir William Berkeley, seventy, the governor of the colony, and Nathaniel Bacon, Jr., thirty, his cousin by marriage. Bacon was no Robin Hood, but Berkeley was no king.[12]

Within a few days, or perhaps even a few hours, of Anthony and Isabella reclaiming their land legs, Captain William Tucker, of James City County, had claimed them as servants on his, the first plantation. Within a few years, Captain Tucker had also claimed command of the colony's response to the killing of 347 Jamestown residents by the Algonquin chief Opechancanough, in 1622. And that response? *"Ita dum singuli pugnant vniuersi vincuntur,"* recommended colonist Edward Waterhouse in a 1622 report to the Virginia Company, quoting the Roman politician Tacitus: *So long as they fight separately, the whole is conquered.* And Waterhouse in that same report went on to recommend that the Indians, whom the English had once "used as friends," should now be "compelled to servitude and drudgery" to supply the labor needs of the colony.[13]

Kill them. Set them at each other. Reap the rewards of Indian slaves as a result.

By the mid-seventeenth century, when William Tucker, the son of Anthony and Isabella, would have been in his twenties, it's not hard to imagine his parents, if they were still alive, warning him that what was happening around them bore ominous similarities to Angola when they were taken by the Imbangala. Only here, the English had replaced the Portuguese, and the Africans had been replaced by Indians. Before plunging headlong into the Atlantic slave trade, colonial Virginia had a thriving internal slave trade in Indians. In fact, in the years leading up to Bacon's Rebellion in 1676, Indian slaves outnumbered Africans (slaves, servant, and free) "up river" on the James.[14]

Despite its name, and depictions in recruiting brochures of the time, Virginia was anything but virgin wilderness when the English landed in 1607. Two hundred or more Indian villages existed in Tidewater Virginia with an extensive interconnecting system of "wide Indian highways" leading south to the Piedmont and to other tribes south and west.[15] Tribes as far away as the Iroquois, in mid-Atlantic North America, used these waterways for trading and for war.

William Byrd, invited to Virginia by his uncle, Thomas Stegge, in 1669 soon learned much about these Indian trading routes. Living on the edge of the colony, Byrd traveled by water and by land, working the extensive trading networks established by his uncle with Indian nations west and south. There Byrd learned Indian languages, like that of the Occaneechi, who inhabited an island at the confluence of the Dan and Roanoke rivers, and the Westo (or Richahecrian), a fearsome Iroquois band forced to migrate far from the shores of Lake Erie to southeastern Virginia because of the Beaver Wars of the early seventeenth century, pitting the Iroquois against the Algonquin and their French patrons.

The Occaneechi were middlemen, taking English arms, ammunition, and other manufactured goods supplied by men like Byrd, in exchange for furs, pelts, and Indian captives brought to them by tribes like the Westo, who raided Indian and Spanish encampments as far south as Florida for slaves. When Byrd got back to the colony, he'd sell or barter those goods. Furs and pelts would be packed in

hogshead barrels and shipped to England. Indians would be purchased outright, or exchanged for tobacco, then put to work as slaves
producing even more of the leafy crop. Out of fear that Indians in
their own land might easily slip off, many Indian slaves were sold to
sugar plantations in the West Indies. Not only Black labor created
White power and wealth—all enslaved labor did.

In 1675, William Byrd found himself with a new partner: Nathaniel
Bacon. Bacon, who'd arrived in Virginia in 1674, at twenty-eight, had
connections. One cousin, also named Nathaniel Bacon, was a well-off
planter and member of Governor Sir William Berkeley's Council. The
other cousin was Frances Berkeley, none other than the governor's
wife. Bacon stepped off the ship from England with enough money
to buy his way into the colonial planter elite, purchasing a remote
plantation upriver from Jamestown, not too far from Byrd's land.

Even if his wealth placed him above their ranks, Bacon possessed
a knack for tapping into the angst and fears of struggling planters: depressed tobacco prices, rising taxes, a shortage of land and
labor, and the ever-pressing need to assign blame. Affixing blame
was easy: "Indians!" cried the struggling planters. Indians were the
source of all their troubles. Indians occupied land they needed for
expansion to grow more tobacco. Indian raids made farming the
land they had, often on the edge of the colony, more precarious.

African slaves, poorer planters had to pay for, and African slaves
were often snapped up by the wealthy. "I understand there are some
Negro Ships expected into York now every day," wrote one planter
to another, "before I can have notice, they'll be all disposed of."[16]
Indian slaves, on the other hand, could be bartered for, or if caught
by planters themselves, pressed into slavery free of charge, as Waterhouse's report to the Virginia Company, cited above, suggested.

Bacon's solution foreshadowed Union general Philip Sheridan's
statement two hundred years later: "The only good Indians I ever
saw were dead."[17] Bacon participated in, or encouraged the killing of,
as many Indians as he could; and many of those killings seemed like
murders of convenience or sport.

Thomas Matthew, in 1675, had just cheated some Doegs, a Native American tribe in Maryland, out of payment, when the Indians paddled back across the Potomac to take some of Matthew's hogs. Chased by an English sailboat, the Indian party was cut off, then decimated, which led the Doegs to exact more revenge on the English, including the killing of one of Matthew's workers. Matthew went beserk. The Stafford County militia, under Colonel George Mason, was called out. Mason surrounded a band of Indians in a cabin, whom he thought were Doegs. And when they came out under the pretext of negotiation, most were slaughtered. One Indian called out to Mason, "*Susquehanougs Netough*" ("Susquehannock friends"), before disappearing into the surrounding forest. The militia had not killed the Doegs, they'd slaughtered innocent Susquehannock, supposedly the colony's friends, sparking a war between the Susquehannock and the colonists.

Bacon reveled in the mayhem, which horrified Governor Sir William Berkeley, who'd devoted the later part of his career toward peace with neighboring tribes so that the wealthy Virginia planter elite could thrive. When Berkeley attempted to rein in Bacon and the others out to hunt down and kill any Indians they could find, Bacon seized the moment to label Berkeley a traitor and Indian collaborator, who supplied the weapons that Indians used to kill colonists.

With an arrogant narcissism known to many pompous populists, Bacon declared his wealth and power demanded that he look after the welfare of the less fortunate Virginian planters, who, with the encouragement of his partner, William Byrd, rallied around him, begging that he lead them in an Indian war. Lead these men young Bacon did, to war with the Susquehannock and Occaneechi, shredding any hopes of peace between the Jamestown colony and neighboring tribes. But that was precisely what the tempestuous young aristocrat from the upper James wanted.

Bacon also wanted a confrontation with Berkeley, which he got on June 23, 1676, in front of the Virginia General Assembly chambers. Bacon, at the head of a rabble of several hundred armed planters, met the governor, demanding a commission for continuing his rampage against the Indians. Initially, the governor and the Council refused, leading to a tense standoff at which Berkeley bared his chest and dared Bacon to shoot him. The Council backed down, capitulating to Bacon, and forcing Berkeley to follow suit. With Bacon having promoted himself to general, and now in control of Jamestown, Berkeley fled across Chesapeake Bay to the safety of friends on Virginia's Eastern Shore.

Meanwhile, Bacon issued his "Declaration in the Name of the People," on July 30, 1676. The eight-point declaration upbraided Berkeley for unjust taxation, cronyism, and aiding and abetting the enemy; that is, the neighboring Indian nations. Nowhere in the document can one find even a phrase suggesting justice for servants, let alone for slaves, or democracy preferable to the rule of monarchy. Bacon firmly believed that once the truth about Berkeley was known, Charles II would send ships and troops to his aid.

But a shrewd Berkeley managed to enlist the help of a Loyalist ship captain, and soon the tide turned. While Bacon was out of Jamestown hunting Indians, and his forces searching for Berkeley, the governor, now in command of a fleet of ten vessels, sailed back to retake the town. Bacon's meager forces guarding Jamestown deserted during the night of September 7, 1676, and Berkeley took back Jamestown with only a handful of men.

Bacon, camped out at the head of the York River, remained unfazed. Though his squadron had dwindled from weeks of chasing and killing the Susquehannock through Virginia's backwaters and swamps, he gathered about 150 men for the several days' march on Jamestown, displaying their Indian prisoners as they marched. One might well imagine a band of desperate men emboldened by the certain knowledge of gallows awaiting their capture. Then, and only then, Bacon, in need of swelling his ranks by any means necessary, "proclaimed liberty to all Servants and negros" who would march on Jamestown with him. Some seventy Blacks, servants, and slaves did, joining an army of four hundred. But championing the rights of servants and slaves was not a part of Bacon's declaration, never central to his governance plan. Liberty for servants and slaves was merely a desperate gesture of last resort.

The Battle of Jamestown began on September 13, 1676, and lasted for several days. On September 18, with Bacon at the gates of the city, Berkeley's officers lost their resolve and abandoned their positions, forcing Berkeley's reluctant retreat to one of several ships in Jamestown's harbor. Berkeley's ship floated a few miles downstream, before setting anchor. As darkness fell, a powerless governor watched from the deck of his ship as Bacon burned down Jamestown. Bacon had again won a round.

But by mid October, Bacon was bedridden in the Gloucester County home of Major Thomas Pate, delirious with a debilitating headache and bloody diarrhea, symptoms, it appears, of typhus fever. Bacon died on October 26, 1676, succeeded by his lieutenant, John Ingram, who sought to continue the insurrection. Ultimately, Berkeley prevailed. The remaining rebels were captured and some, like Ingram, were hanged. William Byrd, on Bacon's side from the beginning, managed to talk his way back into the governor's good graces, and thus avoid the executioner's hand.

Still, Bacon's Rebellion did not end with his death or with Ingram's capture and subsequent execution. Nor did it end with Charles II recalling Sir William Berkeley, an old and sickly man, back from his post, then repudiating him as the real cause of late troubles in the king's colony. The rebellion did not even end with Berkeley's death in July 1677, less than a year after Nathaniel Bacon's.

Bacon's Rebellion sculpted the political, economic, social, and cultural landscape of Virginia, structuring a colony, then a country, so that coming events would flow into that structure, and be shaped, like hot lead poured into a mold.

In the end, Bacon's Native Americans strategy held sway. Francis Nicholson, Berkeley's successor and the longtime governor of Virginia and Maryland, would take no such diplomatic approach to the Indian "neighbours" of either colony. The Susquehannock, the Occaneechi, the Piscataway, the Westo, and many other nations were wiped out by colonists, now unleashed from governmental restraint. What little of the Indian nations that English munitions did not destroy, English microbes did.

Eviscerated by war and disease, by the end of the seventeenth century most eastern Indian nations north of Florida were diminished in size and reduced to continually fleeing, or recombining with other tribes, or enslavement by the English. This left the colonists, particularly the non-elite planters and farmers whom Bacon so greatly appealed to, exactly where they wanted. More land upon which to expand. More crops to plant on that land. More profits to be made. More safety from fewer Indians. There was, of course, the loss of Indian slave labor. But, also like the Spanish experience in Central and South America, that void was filled by an ever-increasing new source of labor, this time stolen from Africa.

However, the biggest winners of Bacon's Rebellion, by far, turned out to be the very group Bacon railed against. The planter-merchant elite, the colonial aristocracy, the landed gentry—call them what you will. But also call them the group from which the Founders arose. For them, Bacon's Rebellion, while shocking and threatening, was a wake-up call, a colonial-era 9/11. And how they responded shaped a colony and a nation so powerfully that we are still snagged in the talons of their response today.

Berkeley might be gone, but Virginia's colonial elite had inherited his fear of the "Poore Endebted Discontented and Armed," those who'd coalesced around Bacon. The planter elite saw in Bacon's "Rabble Crue" more, perhaps, than Bacon ever had. And what they saw, they did not like. Bacon, remember, only extended a hand to servants and slaves in a moment of desperation. One can well imagine, then, Arthur Allen, of Surry County, a wealthy merchant, planter, speaker of the House of Burgesses, and a former ardent supporter of Berkeley, whispering to his fellow burgesses, "But what if those common planters, those White servants, Indian slaves, and, my God, those Negroes; what if they did rise up together against us?" Tobacco prices were still low. Taxes still high. Labor still unavailable or out of reach for many common planters. What if the dispossessed in colonial Virginia awoke to their dispossessors and took steps to do something about it? The colonial elite determined they should remain asleep.

The overall plan was deceptively simple: White colonial Americans, regardless of status or station, would define themselves as a single people not based on shared politics, economics, or culture but rather in reaction to the presence of the Other within their midst. At first, that Other was Indians and Blacks; by the end of the seventeenth century that Other was just Blacks—free persons of color or slaves. Race was the key to ensuring social order, the key, really, to liberty and freedom.

Here, then, we find the first great compromise, preceding all the great compromises to come: the Declaration of Independence, the Constitution, the Bill of Rights, the Electoral College, the Emancipation Proclamation, "40 Acres and a Mule," the Compromise of 1877, Richard Nixon's Southern Strategy, George H. W. Bush's Willie Horton, Bill Clinton's "super predator," and the list goes on. White colonists (later White Americans) procured the privilege of greater liberty because Blacks bore the burden of less.

Historian Edmund S. Morgan captured the aftermath of Bacon's Rebellion succinctly.

> The fear of a servile insurrection alone was sufficient to make slave-owners court the favor of all other whites in a common contempt for persons of dark complexion. But as men tend to believe their own propaganda, Virginia's ruling class, having proclaimed that all white men were superior to black, went on to offer their social (but white) inferiors a number of benefits previously denied them.[18]

In the years after Bacon's Rebellion, the Virginia Assembly paid constant attention to lowering taxes, granting land after indentures, extending enfranchisement, and to laws clearly separating races in sex, marriage, religion, and penal codes as we have seen earlier. In competitive elections for the Virginia General Assembly, for example, White aristocratic candidates were forced to appeal for votes to other White men whom they considered socially inferior.

Historian James D. Rice notes:

The implications of this new social order penetrated into almost every part of life. Racial slavery and white populism—white tribalism, one might say—forced Indians and Africans to shoulder the burden of resolving the tensions and divisions within colonial society. Now, a slave's every gesture and word was examined by whites for signs that racial discipline was being observed. As the slave population increased, even the poorest, unhappiest white Virginians were lifted further from the bottom of society.[19]

Even women were touched by this new social order. As described earlier, Black women (slave or free) were taxed simply because they existed, while White women were not. And where once White women were categorized as "good wives" or "nasty wenches," with the onset of American slavery that category of "wenches" referred almost exclusively to Black women, known on auction blocks and runaway posters as "Negro wenches," implying their promiscuity and availability for sexual exploitation by White men.[20]

The presence of Blacks as slave labor in late-seventeenth-century colonial America, and the fears of the White ruling class that Blacks might rise up and demand their due, forced the creation of this new social order and the institutions of wealth and power that issued from it. One-hundred years before the writing of the US Constitution, in the years following Bacon's Rebellion, the fundamental equation of American liberty and equality was forged and enforced: liberty and equality are possible for a privileged few, because they are denied to a great many, based on the color of one's skin. That fundamental equation is as true today as it was in the late seventeenth century.

A HOUSE BUILT ON SMOKE

"Makaya! Makaya!"

You can almost hear Anthony's excited murmurs to Isabella; almost see him gaze off to one side, as the pair marched at the point of matchlock muskets through the fields of Captain William Tucker's Elizabeth City plantation, leading to his home. Around them, rows of the broadleaf green plants with thick stems shot from the ground, swayed under the oppressive humidity. In the distance, wooden racks held giant leaves turning golden brown in the late August sun. Here, in Kalunga's kingdom, the Land of the Dead, the surprise of finding a plant so familiar surely evoked long twinges of sadness mixed with short paroxysms of joy for a homeland they were torn from, a country they'd now left far behind. Makaya, it appeared, had made the journey into this underworld of death and white devils before them.

Into what kind of world had they been thrust? This new world where a black earth gave birth to the familiar, while White men bore guns and ships and chains.

Anthony and Isabella knew tobacco (makaya); the leaf formed a part of their Angola-Congo culture for a century before their birth, and, yet, here they were meeting these plants again, in Virginia, after their capture and perilous journey across the Atlantic.

They did not know that tobacco had made the transatlantic passage many times, but usually in the opposite direction, from west to east.

Upon succeeding his father, James, to the English throne in 1625, King Charles I proclaimed that only tobacco from his American colonies should be imported into his kingdom, while also lamenting that Virginia was a colony "wholly built on smoke that would easily turn to air." Beneath Charles's turn of phrase, befitting of William Shakespeare, lay an understanding of tobacco as Virginia's "cash crop," and further that the cultivation of tobacco was tenuous—both labor and land intensive.

Slavery won out over indentured servitude in colonial Virginia for the very reason that it supplied colonial planters with lifetime labor, and did not require of them relinquishing valuable land in the form of freedom dues to servants who'd worked off their indentures. Agriculture was the first institution of power and wealth in colonial America, which Black labor built directly without receiving a share of either that power or that wealth.

Tobacco is a nightshade, in the same family as potatoes, tomatoes, peppers, and eggplants. In the wild, it apparently started growing eighteen thousand years ago. Natives of the South American Andes range began cultivating tobacco some six thousand to eight thousand years ago, their domestication of the genus *Nicotiana* perhaps predating and even forming the basis of their farming of other food crops such as maize.[1, 2, 3]

Tobacco use spread throughout North American indigenous populations for thousands of years prior to Columbus's arrival. On October 15, 1492, Columbus first reported seeing "dried leaves"[4] among the items carried by a Taino canoeist. Though he knew they "must be a thing highly valued,"[5] Columbus did not immediately grasp how and why tobacco was used, so returned the leaves to the native, sending him on his way. That quickly changed when a month later a landing party, while searching for the king of Japan[6] on what was in reality the island of Cuba, returned to Columbus with reports of "men and women with a half-burnt weed in the hands, being the herbs they are accustomed to smoke."[7]

Legend tells of Rodrigo de Jerez, one of the crew members who went ashore in Cuba, returning to Spain with tobacco seeds and leaves, then walking the streets of his hometown, Ayamonte, smoking cigars, before being arrested and thrown in jail.[8] Whatever the truth of this story, in the years after Columbus's return, Spain started tobacco plantations throughout Central and South America, where they enslaved indigenous people; and the coffers of monarchies filled from taxing a highly addictive pastime that spread rapidly throughout Europe.

The West African coast, the East African coast, the Middle East, India, China, Japan: in the late fifteenth and early sixteenth centuries Portuguese explorers left tobacco leaves and the use of tobacco with native populations wherever their ships came to anchor, like animal carriers of disease leaving a new pestilence in their wake. In less than a hundred years, a crop native to the mountains of Peru and Ecuador had infused the far corners of the earth. Tobacco scurried past Christian sanctions, so that Jesuits, among many Catholic sects, ran tobacco plantations and exploited slave labor in South America.[9] Not explicitly listed in the Quran as haram ("forbidden"), fatwas (religious edicts) against tobacco have been issued since the beginning of the seventeenth century, but many Muslims simply ignored the mufti's pronouncements.[10] Baal Shem Tov, the founder of Hasidism, reportedly smoked a pipe throughout the day.[11]

The cultures tobacco spread from and to developed spiritual systems and mythologies around its use. For natives of the Americas, where it originated and first spread, tobacco was incorporated into sacred practices often associated with shamans and individual or collective healing.[12] Once tobacco was introduced into China, Chinese medicine and philosophy developed around its potent ability to disrupt, and sometimes restore, the balance of yin and yang in the body.[13]

In the Congo and Angola, tobacco was an important part of

minkisi, sacred medicinal and healing techniques practiced only by *nganga*, the healer-priests of this region.[14] Anthropologist Emil Torday has pointed to evidence that tobacco was incorporated into foundational myths of the people along the Kasai River, tributary of the Congo, which begins in central Angola. A version of one such myth, reported by tobacconist and entrepreneur Alfred Dunhill, has a prodigal son of the Bushongo, Lusana Lumunbala, returning home from a long absence to extol the virtues of smoking tobacco.[15]

Whether as medicine or myth, Anthony and Isabella knew tobacco. It was grown and smoked around them. Tobacco was introduced to the Angola-Congo region either directly by the Portuguese in the early sixteenth century, along with other agricultural crops such as maize and coffee,[16] or indirectly by Arab Trans-Saharan traders who themselves had been introduced to it by the Portuguese.[17] In either case, tobacco was well established by the time that Imbangala warriors, working on behalf of the Portuguese, captured Ndongo slaves.

How did the Portuguese pay the Imbangala for Anthony and Isabella? The Imbangla were not only fearsome mercenaries, they were also fearsome merchants who controlled the trade running through their territory near Kasanje.[18] They traded tobacco for slaves often through Brazilian merchants in Luanda. These Brazilian merchants, in turn, were frequently creoles—that is to say, mixed-race children of Africans previously brought to Brazil as slaves to work on tobacco plantations for their Portuguese colonizers. They were born in Brazil but returned back to Africa to work for the Portuguese in the tobacco and slave trades.[19]

Convoluted. Complex. Compelling. And maybe worth recapitulating. Anthony and Isabella were most likely sold in exchange for tobacco by a merchant who himself was the child of a slave brought to Brazil from Angola to grow tobacco, only to return to Angola to barter tobacco for them. Anthony and Isabella were originally captured for transport to Spanish colonies in the New World, where they would, more than likely, be put to work as slaves on a tobacco plantation. Instead, they were seized as booty by Englishmen, and sold or bartered in Virginia. Then, they were taken ashore in shackles and chains to step onto a strange, foreign land where the first crop they were greeted by was tobacco, the source of fond memories of their homeland but also the source of great pain. Like a python curling around its victim, or blue smoke curling around the head of a smoker, tobacco curled around the lives of Africans in the sixteenth century on both sides of the Atlantic.

• • •

Terror and confusion reign aboard a ship in the throes of a powerful storm.

The helmsman cries out, "Lay her a-hold, a-hold! Set her two courses off to sea again, lay her off."

Mariners drenched from the storm reply, "All lost! To prayers! All lost!"

"A most dreadfull Tempest (the manifold deaths whereof are here to the life described) . . ."

Shakespeare's *The Tempest*? The first two lines.

John Rolfe's actual life? The last.

In May 1609, Sir John Rolfe set out from England for Virginia on *Sea Venture*, with his wife, Sarah Hacker. Newly constructed, *Sea Venture* was the flagship of the Virginia Company sent on a third supply run to a desperate colony. In the early morning of July 25, 1609, William Strachey, aboard *Sea Venture*, tells us they experienced "the cloudes gathering thicke upon vs, and the windes singing, and whistling most vnusually."[20] The storm, probably a hurricane, battered *Sea Venture* for four days, until Sir George Somers, captain of the ailing craft, cried, "Land!"

Without an anchor, and leaking badly, Somers ran the ship aground, stranding all of the 150 people aboard on an island now part of Bermuda. In the nine months they were on the island, the survivors constructed two smaller ships, the *Patience* and the *Deliverance*, which they sailed to Jamestown in the spring of 1610. While still in Bermuda, Rolfe's wife gave birth to a daughter, Bermuda, who subsequently died. Rolfe's wife passed away not long after.

Colonial Virginia, at the time of Rolfe's arrival, was surrounded by Indian nations who cultivated tobacco. Like many English smokers, Rolfe, a dedicated smoker himself, felt the variety of tobacco cultivated by the Indians, *Nicotiana rustica*, was "poore and weake, and of a byting tast."[21] Using *Nicotiana tabacum* seeds, from plants grown by the Spanish in Trinidad and the Orinoco Valley of Venezuela, Rolfe experimented with growing, harvesting, drying, and curing his crop. He also enlisted other colonists in the enterprise, like William Tucker of Elizabeth City, master of Anthony and Isabella. In 1617, twenty thousand pounds of Virginia tobacco were shipped to England. In 1618, forty thousand pounds. And by 1629, with 1.5 million pounds, Virginia tobacco dominated the English market.[22]

A tobacco seed is miniscule. Depending upon the variety, there are about 300,000 to 500,000 seeds per ounce.[23] Imagine tobacco planter Captain William Tucker standing outside his garrison, on the banks above the James River, awaiting the arrival of the *São João Bautista*, with Anthony and Isabella aboard, holding an ounce of the seed. If each seed represented one person, he would have in his hand as many seeds as there were Black men and women in this country, slave and free, 150 years later, about the time of the American Revolution. With a pound of the seed, he would be holding about as many seeds as there were Blacks in the country 250 years later, before the Emancipation Proclamation.

• • •

Anthony clawed at the hard earth with a hoe.

She is a strange woman, he thought. Her body goes cold, and hardens. And it is then, when she is still cold and hard and barely starting to soften, these White men tear at her body using their wooden sticks with iron claws, mixing their seed with sand before pressing it into her. And when she is warmer, softer, and her seeds have begun to grow, when her green babies rise, we rip them from her and plant them in the body of her sister. This is not how we would treat the earth back home, where her body is warm and soft and moist and ready for our seed at any time.

Anthony had lived through five hardenings and softenings of the earth. He recalled a time three hardenings ago, when just as the earth was starting to soften, and they were pressing sand and seed into her, then, the men with darker skins came, grabbing the same tools used to tear into the earth. Some had guns. He thought they must be a band of Imbangala coming after him and Isabella once again. But, instead, they used the tools and clubs and guns on the men and women and children with White skins. One of these "Brown Imbangala," as Anthony called them, with his face painted, as the Imbangala back home had painted theirs, ran with a club raised high. All around him, people were screaming. Blood flowing. There was no place to run, to hide.

Anthony stood there, leaning on his hoe. Calm. Serene. He remembered thinking if this is how he was to leave the Kalunga-ngombe, the Land of the Dead, he was ready, tired of the time and toil under the hand and whip of the White men, ready to go home. Screaming, the Brown Imbangala ran up to him, stopped. They looked into each other's eyes. Anthony dropped his hoe and raised his arms palms up, waiting for the fatal blow to land.

The Brown Imbangala reached out. He rubbed his hand against Anthony's cheek as if trying to rub off his skin. Then he turned, screaming, and ran away. He was not at all like the Imbangala whom Anthony knew from home.

A stab in his back from a blunt instrument, and a screaming voice, startled Anthony from his musings. Still not fully understanding this strange new tongue, two words the White man spoke he'd come to know well, *work* and *Negar*. They always came as evil twins to Anthony's ears.

He shook his head then snapped back to hoeing the plot where the earth would then be seeded. Just a little over forty paces in each direction. Stakes marked the corners. Trees groaned, then cracked, then snapped. The ground beneath his feet rumbled as trees hit with a resounding thud. Smoke rose one hundred yards away. As he scraped away at his plot of earth, Anthony turned in the direction of the rising plumes of smoke above red-hot fires as other White men also toiled hard, clearing more forty-by-forty-paced plots of earth that he would have to hoe. Although he could not explain it, it pleased him to know that some White men made other White men work just as hard as he worked.

Anthony knew how to farm tobacco. Even if these White men did it differently from how his village did it back home. There, these tasks were the exclusive work of women, which only seemed right since women knew the body of another woman well. The thought of women cultivating crops reminded him to turn slightly to his left. Out of the corner of his eye he saw his Isabella also with a hoe, working a forty-by-forty-paced plot.

Five hardenings and softenings, that's the count of how many cycles he'd been through. In a few days, after the earth's body was broken, and neatly furrowed, a mixture of seed and sand would be lightly salted along each furrow. A blanket of pine boughs would be laid atop the seeded earth for warmth and protection. If it did not get to where his breath came out as smoke, and if the rains came, in a month, small green babies would sprout. If the rains did not come, he and Isabella might be forced to carry water from the river to pour over the beds. How strange, there was no rainy season here, as he had known back home.

Hundreds of seedlings poking through the pine needles meant thousands of tiny plants in each bed, which brought on "thinning time." Master Tucker had said that Master Rolfe, before his death, had advised separating each tiny shoot at least a hand's width apart, which meant each bed had ten rows of ten shoots each—a "hundred bed" was the phrase Anthony remembered hearing.

Thinning time meant hard work. What was that phrase the White men used? Anthony chuckled sarcastically to himself. "From can see, to can't see." Pine boughs must be lifted gently, so as not to damage the small shoots. Sometimes when Anthony was down on his hands and knees, his fingers would ache from plucking unwanted shoots. After thinning time came "bugging time," when he'd be back down on his knees inspecting each growing sprout, crushing the small brown beetles that loved the leaves as well. So much care given to tobacco, it felt like White men, like Master Tucker, loved the plant more so than he loved his children or his wife. That thought, Anthony would never dare share.

Sometime after checking for beetles in the morning, Anthony would spend the afternoon preparing hundreds and hundreds of knee-high mounds three to four feet apart. The White men called it "hilling." *Ocimu*[24] is the word Anthony thought they'd use at home. For these small mounds reminded him of anthills. This, too, was hard work. Even working as fast as possible he could prepare no more than a few hundred such hills a day, when thousands were needed.

Sometimes a White man would appear in the fields and other White men would gather around him, happy, slapping each other on the back. Usually, the man had a paper he pulled from his pocket. Usually, the others pointed excitedly to this paper. Surely, these White people have strange customs, Anthony thought. But they spoke a word that Anthony came to understand because after this ritual gathering the man would no longer be seen in the fields. He might visit the others but he would not be under the whip or the hand of the overseer. He would not be forced to work the tobacco. The White men also spoke of something they called "freedom" and Anthony knew it meant the same as *omonamani*[25] in his native tongue. He and Isabella had no papers. He feared he might never see the day when men slapped him on the back.

If there was not too much "smoke breath" and not too much damage from the beetles, when the earth was supple, and a few weeks before days and nights were equal, babies were taken from one mother and given to many others, as he worked to carefully dig out the shoots, now two hands high, and replant them in the bellies of the thousands of small hills. Several shoots were always left in the beds, particularly those planted last. Sometimes the earth-mother bellies did not take the babies, who would die. Then, the hills would need to be given new babies.

As they grew, the children needed constant attention. Cutworms crawled out overnight, feeding on the leaves, ready to hatch as moths. Anthony pinched the pale worms between his fingers, flicked them to the ground before crushing them beneath his feet. After hours of bending over to pluck weeds, his back ached.

Anthony tended to these green children daily for about two months, when "priming" and "topping" began. On each plant, several leaves closest to the bottom were cut away with a knife, while at the same time he removed a small, tightly growing bunch of leaves at the top of the plant, which would have yielded a bright yellow flower containing thousands of seeds.

After topping, the children reached higher than Anthony's chest, and still daily he moved through row after row removing sickly leaves, delicately cutting away the small shoots that grew from the wounds of topping, lest smaller leaves develop in their place.

It seemed Anthony's work was never done. If not topping or priming, then he was inspecting each leaf for the crawling worms called hornworms, picking them off and also crushing them under his feet. When plants had grown almost twice his height, and ladders were the only way to reach the leaves, harvesttime had arrived. By that time, light and dark slowly balanced in the sky.

Now, Master Tucker seemed more agitated than usual. Anthony, Isabella, even the other White servants had learned to stay as far away from him as they could during this time. Each morning he paced through the tobacco fields, peering through the plants, patting them down, squeezing them between his fingers.

"Cut this row now, Anthony!"

"Leave this one for tomorrow, Anthony!"

"Not ready for a few more days, Anthony!"

It was dangerous work. Sharp knives were used to cut the plants.

Some of the White men working alongside him simply leaned over and struck a blow between the bottom leaves and the ground. The first year he worked Master Tucker's tobacco fields, Anthony showed them a method he remembered from the women of his home. Grab the bottom of the stalk, between the leaves and the ground, pull it out of the ground slightly to expose a bright white area of the root, then cut it with a swift, decisive blow there. The White men shook their heads and walked off. Anthony continued using his method. When it came time to cure the leaves, Master Tucker saw that his were easier to hang. After that, Master Tucker insisted that everyone use Anthony's method of cutting.

After cutting the plants, if it wasn't raining, Anthony left them on the ground for a few hours to wilt. The leaves, it seemed, got heavier and moister that way. They used to hang the cut plants, called "hands," outside on lines or sticks or fences. But this year, Master Tucker had them doing something new. Over the time when the earth was too cold and hard for planting, they'd built two new buildings, in which the leaves would be hung on lines or sticks like clothes. That took another four to six weeks, during which Anthony found himself constantly checking for mold, notifying Master Tucker if any was found.

Finally, Anthony was ready to "sweat" the tobacco, removing the leaves from the lines or sticks and laying them on the barn's floor. Particularly, if it got colder than they'd expected, they used logs to press the tobacco and increase the temperature of the leaves, but when they did that, Anthony would be on duty at least twice a day, looking for mold.

You might think that by now, they'd be through with this year's crop, but they weren't. Sorting came after sweating, and the phrase the White men used when examining the greenish-yellow to light tan leaves was "in case," which seemed to mean that a batch of five to fourteen leaves, which they tied together into a "hand," was just right—not too damp, or they would rot once they got inside the wooden shipping barrels, but not to dry, or they would crumble and turn to dust. Anthony laid out the hands to sweat.

He shook his head. How strange. By now, the tobacco leaves had spent nearly as much time out of the ground as they had in the ground, and still they were not ready to go to market. For the first crops, Anthony removed the leaves from their lines a final time, then twisted them into ropes, and wound the ropes into balls, some of which weighed almost as much as a man.

Lately, Master Tucker had insisted on a new system with them as well, which the captains of the tobacco vessels seemed to prefer. During the cold season, he and the other men would spend many hours building barrels from oak trees felled while clearing tobacco land the previous year. So, after sweating, Anthony "pressed" or "prized" the leaves into these large barrels, which the White men called "hogsheads." A hogshead full of tobacco weighed as much as six men. It was extremely dangerous work rolling a hogshead off a wagon, down to the dock for loading onto a ship. It made Anthony wonder how strong the men on the other side of the ocean must have been to unload them and cart them away.

Another cycle of tobacco growing was beginning and Anthony did not look forward to all the hard work he'd just run through in his mind. His muscles would ache. His back would hurt. He would get little sleep. In a short time, the sharp, pungent, sweet smell of sweating tobacco would seem never to leave him. Occasionally, on a Sunday afternoon, Isabella would fill a tub with warm water for him to soak in. Afterward, the water was rusty brown, and it, too, smelled like tobacco.

But there was one thing he did look forward to, one thing that gave him hope. Isabella was fertile, like the earth he knew from home. And soon she would give birth.

● ● ●

As far as William Tucker's eye could see, row after row of green tobacco leaves swayed in the gentle summer breeze. An idyllic image of Virginian tranquility and freedom. Before leaving, Sir George

Yeardley had seen to it that the Assembly passed laws favorable to planters like him. The new governor, Francis Wyatt, had continued in that spirit, though there were rumors that, within a year, Wyatt might be gone, and Yeardley, now under service of the Crown rather than the Company, placed back in.

Tucker studied the pamphlet in his hand, which his good friend, John Rolfe, had given him shortly before his death, "An Advice Hovv To Plant Tobacco In England, And How To Bring It To The Colovr And Perfection, To Whom It May Bee Profitable, And To Whom Harmefull." Some thought the mysterious author, known only as "C.T.," might be none other than Rolfe himself, though he denied it. More important than the pamphlet were Rolfe's notes on adapting C.T.'s advice to planting and growing tobacco in Virginia. In search of a sweeter, more palatable smoke, he'd done everything Rolfe suggested, from leaving leaves on the ground right after cutting to curing them inside to using hogsheads instead of tobacco balls.

While a part of Tucker knew he should be happy, another part felt nothing but a pervasive sense of dread. Would there be an infestation of cutworms or hornworms this year? More than his servants could handle? Would he judge the cutting of the leaves correctly? Perhaps he'd cut them too soon last year, and that's why his tobacco garnered a slightly reduced price than the year before? Should he use logs? Would there be heat? What about the new hogsheads, how would he get them down to the riverside wharf? A thousand questions faced him farming tobacco. But many planters like him faced such questions, too.

He had a lovely wife, Mary, and a beautiful daughter, Elizabeth. So, why was it that he also felt an overwhelming sense of dread?

He looked out on the servants working in his fields, White, Black, native. If each man eventually worked through the term of his indenture, and was granted not only freedom but also his freedom dues, including land, that would mean the steady growth of small tobacco farmers, competing with him for available labor and land.

He shook his head. Where would they go? Already land was growing scarcer by the year. And what kind of world would they create for young Elizabeth? All these men, without enough women for wives? Wouldn't they be prone to promiscuity? Wouldn't they lure women like his Elizabeth, when she came of age, into dangerous liaisons instead of a Christian family life? Already, he and many of his friends feared that unwed pregnancies were on the rise in the colony and those bastard children would end up as wards of the colony, draining precious resources for their care. He sighed.

Then there was the question of land itself. Or maybe it was the question of too little land. He let his fist pound his thigh. Wasn't that the real reason Opechancanough had attacked and killed so many three years ago? Land. The Weroance said the White men had broken a promise to leave; they'd overstayed their visit and the welcome of the Indians who'd helped them survive the early brutal winters. And, Opechancanough said the English came more and more every year. Sure, we pushed him and other Indians off their land, Tucker mused, but we're Christian tobacco farmers. Our crops are only good for two or three years in a field. After that the soil is depleted. So, we must obtain more land, then clear it to plant more tobacco. Opechancanough, the Pamunkey, the Susquehannock, they do not understand the ways of the English, Tucker thought, which is why, as the colony's appointed commander, it fell to him to bring the war to savages, forcing them to cede more land.

He knew his friends, the other ancient planters, agreed. They'd said as much in Jamestown after the General Assembly met last. Sitting on benches, between sessions, overlooking the James River, puffs of pipe smoke punctuating serious deliberations, all talk was of their future and their tobacco.

They thanked him for his efforts, and wanted to hear again the story of him handing poisoned wine to the Powhatan at what the Indians presumed were peace talks. The ancient planters laughed and agreed that after the Massacre of '22 the Indians deserved whatever came their way. "The savages know well the challenges of growing tobacco," Nathaniel Bass said, "and yet they don't take well to being servants or slaves. And now, with the success of our war against them, their numbers are steadily falling."

"Nathaniel," Tucker recalled saying. "I'm sorry your wife and children were slain in the massacre. I'm glad you were away in England. But I'm also afraid there's another side to the story that none of us want to face."

Bass pulled out his pipe. "Seems pretty simple to me. Less Indians, more land. William, what would that other side be?" He waved the pipestem at Tucker.

"Less Indians, more land, more men needed in our fields."

"We've got the headright system for that," Henry Watkins said. "We pay the Company the costs of bringing them over, and get fifty acres for each person in return."

"And look who we get," Tucker said. "The poor. The wicked. Thieves. Criminals. Women of ill repute. They're not from our stations, not of our class. Then what? In seven years, we're going to pay them to be free only to compete with us in tobacco or to swell the ranks of the poor. Worse yet, give them back land? The system's broken. I can see it coming and it doesn't look good."

"So, what's the solution, William?" Watkins asked. "The Irish?"

Tucker remembered how they chuckled, and how at that point he, too, raised his pipe to his lips and took a long draw. "As if they're any better." He let out a thin blue stream of smoke. "May give them a longer term but eventually they'll be free."

To a man, their heads turned down, and a long silence befell them.

Nathaniel Bass broke the silence. "William, I do not like where this is heading . . .

"Neggars!" Bass whispered that dreaded word.

"Slaves?" another murmured.

"Also a problem," Watkins said. "Can you imagine if our White workers, and our Indians, and our Negroes got together? Decided it was time to throw off their indentures and their chains? Who'd be in trouble then?" He pointed around the circle. "All of us here."

"Slaves! I'm tellin' you," Bass said, "that's where this is all heading. Only solution I can see. Like it or not, gentlemen, all of us, or at least our children and their children, are going to have to buy 'em if we ever expect to turn a profit on the weed."

"And keep a profit in our families," Edward Blany said.

At that moment, Tucker recollected looking up to the cross above the church steeple, then lowering his head, through a cloud of smoke.

"Nathaniel's right," Tucker said. He jabbed the air with his pipe. "That's where this is all heading, mark my words. And that's where I'll be, bartering tobacco for slaves. Bet many a sea captain or merchant'd go for that trade."

"Bet many already have," Blany added.

"And, that, gentlemen, is why we're here," Tucker said.

"To buy slaves?" Bass asked. "There's none to buy. Though if there were, I might pick up a few."

The men chuckled.

"No, gentlemen, not to buy slaves," Tucker answered. "But to set this country on a firm tobacco footing."

"Build a house on smoke?" Bass asked. "You sound like the king, William, trying to blow smoke up our arses."

Smoke belched from the men and the laughter seemed to know no end.

Tucker also laughed, and that brought him back from sitting with the planters along the James. He walked over to one of his many plants. He reached out to grab a leaf. Then, he pinched it, folded it between his fingers.

"Anthony," he bellowed. He couldn't see him. "Anthony," he hollered again. "Time to cut this row."

● ● ●

Colonial planters sold their tobacco, in bulk, to English merchants, who, in turn, repackaged and sold tobacco to consumers, often through grocers, for use in pipes, as snuff, or in cigars. To market their tobacco, grocers hired engravers to create "tobacco cards," similar to modern-day business cards, they could hand out to potential customers.

There's a surviving tobacco card from London during the reign of King George, the iconography of which captures well the relationship among tobacco, the planters, and the English. Above the name band of the card and to the right there is a White planter, sitting on a hogshead puffing a pipe, while behind him, and to his right, lies a tobacco curing barn. In his left hand the planter holds a cane, or stick, in contact with another hogshead tipped toward him by a diminutive dark figure who appears to be wearing a headdress. Three such dark figures stand interspersed between the rows of tobacco plants, two with obvious feathered headdresses. Of those two, one is holding a smoking pipe out and over a tobacco plant, its bowl facing down. The third dark man appears to emerge from a hogshead holding tobacco leaves in each hand. Above the figures lie four hogsheads, and arising from them a dual-headed dragon, holding tobacco leaves in each mouth, one head pointing to a vessel coming into port, the other to a vessel that is leaving. The inbound ship, at the right, is flying the Cross of St. Patrick, a precursor of the British Union Jack.

While we can never know for certain the minds of "Rogers, London," the grocer, or the engraver, from comparison to many other, similar tobacco cards of the era a few motifs stand out. First, there is the dominance or power of the well-dressed tobacco planter over the smaller, scantily clad dark men through his stick or cane, which may, in reality, have been used to guide the rolling of the hogshead to a wharf, but here also serves the purpose of a baton of commanding authority (*bâton de commandement*).

One is then tempted to say the figures commanded by the White planter are Indians in headdress, who first cultivated tobacco in North America, but that assertion would be wrong. The figures are actually African slaves in Indian headdress, a common conflated image in England at the time, which may represent how Black and Indian slaves cultivated tobacco for wealthy White planters, or how British merchants attempted to "romanticize" tobacco production and "exoticize" or "sexualize" tobacco consumption for their clientele. Black men's bodies, in this case, were the stereotypical icons of sexuality, devoid of any hint of the brutality of the slave system that gave rise to the product in the first place. "Indeed the specific brand of tobacco that the white man presumably smokes," says historian Catherine Molineux, in studying these cards, "is an extension of the black man's body."[26]

Rising from the hogsheads at the top center of the image is a double-headed dragon, which is often called an amphisbaena. Though the amphisbaena originates in Chinese mythology, where dragons are benevolent signs of prosperity and health, in Western mythologies dragons are the guardians of virgins and wealth. Both virgin (Virginia) and wealth (tobacco) are appropriate to this scene. But this bicephalic dragon appears to be staring at both the inbound and outbound vessels; hence, it is also a guardian of trade. In this respect, the dragon represents royal proclamations that only tobacco from English colonies should be imported into England, and that colonial-grown tobacco should be traded nowhere else.

King James I, author of the famous *A Counterblaste to Tobacco*, hated the "golden weed," but also recognized how it plumped his royal coffers. In 1625, just weeks before his death he issued "A Proclamation for the utter prohibiting the importation and use of all Tobacco, which is not of the proper growth of the Colonies of Virginia and the Summer Islands."[27] The year before, the king had dissolved the Virginia Company, giving him direct control over the colony, and a monopoly over Virginian tobacco. Charles I, James's son and successor, who inherited his father's dislike for tobacco, complained that the Virginia colony was "wholly built on smoke." Though Charles continued to extract tobacco revenue in the form of taxes from the British colonies, and expanded his father's restrictions on the tobacco trade, forbidding any other country from trading directly with Virginia. From the late seventeenth century up to the Revolutionary War, a series of Navigation Acts, passed by the British Parliament, and agreed to by the monarchs, imposed further British control on the tobacco trade with the colonies. The king, here, taking on the role of a two-headed dragon guarding his lair of gold.

Whether this symbolism was intended by design, or buried deep within the English psyche, one interpretation of this tobacco card is clear: it depicts a White man's power, wealth, and freedom based on the Black men he enslaves.

The fears and hopes of ancient planters prevailed. Virginia was an appendage of England, even more so after James I took over direct control of the colony from the bankrupt Virginia Company in 1625. A simple system was in play: Virginia supplied England with raw materials. English industries turned those raw materials into finished products. Those finished products were then marketed to the rest of the world. By royal decree, only tobacco from Virginia could be imported into England, with a tax, of course, for the royal coffers. With Virginia, and the other American colonies, prevented from directly manufacturing or trading outside of this system, tobacco soon became not only a commodity but a currency in and of itself. Colonists, or rather Black slave labor, literally grew money.

Goods and merchandise were paid for with tobacco. "[A]ll goods and marchandise imported into this colony which shall be sould for tobacco shall be only sould and bartered at James Citty," the Virginia General Assembly decreed in 1633.[28]

So were slaves: "He figures in the Talbot record in an agreement, dated May 20, 1671, with certain Boston merchants, to purchase five male and five female negro slaves for 3,680 pounds of tobacco each, to be delivered to him in Wye River."[29]

Debts were made, and settled, with tobacco, "being once payable and due, of what valew soever, either in money or tobaccoe the debt shall be."[30]

Taxes were levied with tobacco: "It is therefore thought fitting that there shall be levyed uppon every tithable person sixty-fowre pounds of tobacco."[31]

Fines were paid with tobacco: "Ministers, and others, joining in

Marriage any Negro whatsoever, or Mulatto Slave, with any White Person, forfeit 5000 lb. Tobacco."[32]

And human worth and property value were calculated in terms of tobacco: "one Negro Woman appraised at Six Thousand five hundred pounds of Tobacco and one pair of Cart Wheels appraised at Six hundred and fifty pounds of tobacco by Joseph Bullet."[33]

In colonial America, tobacco was not just a means to wealth, tobacco *was* wealth; wealth created by the labor of Black men and women.

Throughout the 1660s and 1670s tobacco prices trended lower, for many reasons, not the least of which were English taxes, Dutch competition, large American crop yields, and the plague in Europe, so severe in 1665 that no tobacco ships sailed from England to the colonies. All of which led Thomas Culpeper, governor of Virginia, in 1680 to declare to the English Crown that "the low price of tobacco staggers him notwithstanding, the continuance of it will be the fatal and speedy ruin of this noble Colony."[34]

Colonial planters, bleeding money, responded by cutting their shipments with floor sweepings, leaves, and other organic refuse. While temporarily improving financial rewards, ultimately this "trash tobacco," as it was known, led not only to lower quality but higher quantities and a further reduction in tobacco prices. To preserve wealth, and their tax base, colonial authorities stepped in.

Over the next half century, in what is the first instance of wide-scale market regulation in America, Virginia and Maryland led the way in mandating the amount of tobacco produced, standardizing the size of hogsheads, and prohibiting unregulated shipments. Most important, colonial authorities established quality-control boards with the authority to break open hogsheads, grade the leaves, burn trash tobacco, and issue notes of certification, called "crop notes," to owners indicating the final weight and quality of the tobacco shipped.[35] That soon turned the tobacco market around, as middlemen in England, and their customers, now had standards for the quality of the tobacco they purchased and smoked.

Maryland, in 1730, took this regulatory process one step further, actually creating a paper currency based on tobacco, similar to the crop note but called the "transfer note." Loose tobacco, turned in by planters to inspection warehouses in bundles, or hands (rather than hogsheads), was graded by quality and kind. Their batch was thrown in with other loose tobacco of a similar quality and kind and they were then handed a transfer note. This note entitled the owner to the same quantity, quality, and kind of tobacco that had been turned in.

Transfer notes were then used to pay debts, fees, and taxes. They could be used to purchase goods. And the notes themselves could be sold.[36] Before a gold or silver standard backed American paper currency, a tobacco standard did.

Clergy, tavern-keeps, blacksmiths, and other members of the working class grew tobacco in small lots, in their spare time, unlike large planters, who cultivated tobacco full-time and shipped their product in 1,000-pound hogsheads. Like a mountain so domineering that it creates its own weather system, tobacco created its own economic system in colonial America. Were there consumers for the product? Yes, the citizens of England and ultimately the entire world, though many countries tightly controlled the tobacco that entered.

Were there middlemen? Yes, by law, English merchants could only order tobacco from Virginia, which they did by the hogshead, then unpackaged and repackaged it for English consumers and the rest of the world.

Were there brands? One brand of graded tobacco might be indistinguishable from another. So, John Rolfe took the savvy step of fixing a brand on the Virginia product, Oronoco, and that brand, more than anything, helped to set the value of the product in the minds of English smokers who then demanded it.

Were there reliable means of getting the product from producers to the middlemen? There were. Planters like William Tucker actually owned their own ships that once a year made a regular voyage to England to unload their hogsheads and those of other planters.

Ships owned by English merchants and English companies made voyages across the Atlantic to Virginia and the other colonies, where they would travel up navigable waterways, or send smaller craft, to pick up hogsheads waiting for them at docks. Together they were known as the "tobacco fleet."

Were there producers? Absolutely. Virginia colonists recognized quickly the value of the tobacco to the point that under Crown control, James I realized the promise and the peril of a colony "wholly built on smoke."

Were the producers able to access the capital to expand—both in terms of land and labor, servant or free? Yes, they were. Here, English bankers stepped in, lending money to colonial planters to allow them to buy the land and slaves they needed to produce more, and more, tobacco for the English market.

Was the market regulated? Yes. As we have seen, colonial authorities ultimately certified the quantity, quality, and kind of tobacco shipped to England.

Was there a speculative market? Yes. Crop notes and transfer notes, issued by colonial authorities, guaranteed the quantity, and quality, but not the price. As the value of the underlying tobacco rose, so did the value of the transfer note; as it fell, the value of the note fell with it.

Yet, beneath all of this—beneath the consumers, the middlemen, the shipping, the financing, the producers, the regulation, and the speculation—lay the labor of Black slaves. Slavery was the foundation of the tobacco economy. In all of the bizarre and complex ways we've examined here, and will examine in the next chapter, Black lives supplied the economies of the "Tobacco Coast" with steady labor to cultivate the crop and to sell more and more of it. Agriculture was the first institution of wealth in America. Tobacco was the first product of that institution. But the forced labor of Black men and women was the basis of it all.

Then, in 1776, tobacco, and the Black lives behind it, fueled a revolution.

FOUNDING DEBTORS, FOUNDING DOCUMENTS

For nearly three months, over the holiday season of 1826, the following ad ran in the pages of *The Richmond Enquirer* and the Charlottesville *Central Gazette*:

> On the fifteenth of January, at Monticello, in the county of Albemarle; the whole of the residue of the personal property of Thomas Jefferson, dec., consisting of 130 valuable negroes, stock, crop, &c. household and kitchen furniture. The attention of the public is earnestly invited to this property. The negroes are believed to be the most valuable for their number ever offered at one time in the State of Virginia.[1]

While one is certainly stunned by the advertisement and sale of human beings alongside livestock, crops, and furniture, there's an even larger story behind this sad ad. When US president Thomas Jefferson died on July 4, 1826, he was deeply in debt to the tune of between $1 million and $2 million by today's standards.

George Washington's Mount Vernon estate failed in the 1760s, and his debt lingered throughout the War of Independence into the founding of a new nation, and his presidency. In a pre-Revolutionary War letter to George Mason, dated April 5, 1769,

Washington, though speaking through the voice of an aloof third-person narrator, says of mounting debt in Virginia, and apparently his attempt to hide his own:

"For how can I," says he, "who have lived in such and such a manner, change my method? I am ashamed to do it, and besides, such an alteration in the system of my living will create suspicions of the decay of my fortune, and such a thought the world must not harbour."[2]

In whatever esteem, or ambivalence, we hold the Founders and their truths, we must also hold them as debtors, especially the men of Virginia, like Jefferson, Washington, and Richard Henry Lee, and all those they represented. That many of the Founders were slave owners is well-known and now little disputed. But an even more important understanding of these men, their accomplishments and failures, how slavery compelled and complicated their lives and their legacies, might be gathered from considering their debt.

At this point, it may be self-evident where the debt of the Founders came from; they were, after all, lords and masters of well-established, substantial Virginia plantations, along the rivers and channels of Chesapeake Bay. Up to, and even through, the Revolutionary War, wealth and power in Virginia were based not on simple landownership, but on the simple fact of land used to grow tobacco. It sounds preposterous, if not comical, that a cancerous, addictive plant first grown in the Andes eight thousand years ago would shape the fate of these men and the destiny of a nation but tobacco seduced the world, and America rose, in part, from the ashes of that seduction.

What also becomes clear is that debt, to these Founders, was far more than a simple business transaction. British merchants held much of the Founders' debt. So, that debt structured the Founders' social and political relationships with England. But at home, the Founders held much of the debt of the others, often incurred in trying to pay off British merchants while maintaining a certain refined lifestyle. And they also held the debt of smaller and less affluent White planters. So, the debt of the Founders lies beneath pre-Revolutionary social and political relationships here as well.

Debt, an inevitable part of cultivating tobacco, structured the psychology of these men. It was an integral part of colonial tobacco culture and mindset. The Founders judged their own worth, and the worth of fellow planters, by the fitness of their "croppe" and the amount of their "debte."

For merchants on the other side of the Atlantic, debt was a simple business transaction—you borrowed money, always at an interest rate, and at some point, you paid it back. Economic conditions in the middle eighteenth century squeezed British merchants, and they pushed back in the only way they could, by "dunning"—calling in outstanding loans—from colonial planters. This, in turn, squeezed Virginian planters, pushing some, like William Byrd, into bankruptcy, and others, like Jefferson and Washington, to the brink of financial ruin. Tobacco debt, while not the principal reason for the colonies breaking away from Britain, created fallow ground in which the seeds of revolution could take root and grow in the minds of the Founders.

Yet, in reading through the scholarship on debt, tobacco, and the Founders, one is struck again and again by how even modern historians gloss over slavery. Slaves are mentioned frequently, but it is as though these men and women were simply necessary commodities for cultivating tobacco, like the right tools or enough land. Certainly, the Founders felt they were—necessary commodities, that is. And one comes away feeling that many historians feel so, too.

The Founders, the principal southern Founders, at least, like Washington, Jefferson, and Lee, built their wealth and power on their "houses of smoke"—their tobacco plantations. In other words, they built their wealth and power on the backs of Black labor. Without slavery there would have been no tobacco crop for which debt was extended by British merchants for the Founders to buy English fineries, more land, and more slaves. Without the unpaid, forced labor of Black men and women, there would have been no economic basis for the Founders' debt squeezing British merchants, who in turn squeezed the Founders, who in turn squeezed each other, who in turn squeezed poorer White planters, and who together got tired of all of the squeezing, and, finally, rose up against the British.

Slavery is the oft-excluded, inconvenient truth of the American Revolution. When it is included, what springs into sharp relief is the pivotal role played by slaves and free Blacks in creating this country through its founding documents and institutions, and how these documents and institutions affirmed time and again the fundamental compromise of this nation: the soundness of sacrificing liberty, justice, and equality for Black people, as long as these truths were affirmed and established for Whites. Again, and again, we are witness to this self-evident truth of race in America: freedom is a privilege enjoyed by a few because bondage is a condition suffered by many.

Prior to the Revolutionary War, Virginia planters felt the tightening of financial screws by the British. In November 1763, for example, came the apparently unrelated case of the Reverend James Maury before the Hanover, Virginia, County Court. Maury, an Anglican and a local representative of the Church of England, was used to an annual salary paid by Virginian taxpayers in tobacco, sixteen thousand pounds to be exact. With tobacco prices fluctuating, the General Assembly in 1758 decided to fix Maury's salary at two pence per pound, through legislation that became known as the Two-Penny Act. Maury, also a mentor of Thomas Jefferson, was enraged, and so were other Anglican ministers, who protested to King George. The king vetoed the act, thus enraging many local Virginians who believed he'd usurped their taxing authority. Maury, because of the king's veto, sued for three years of back salary.

Colonel John Henry, before whom Maury argued his case, was Patrick Henry's father. Henry decided in Maury's favor, ruling the minister should be compensated. But when the trial proceeded to the damages phase it took an unexpected turn. The defense hired a newly minted young lawyer named Patrick Henry. Arguing before his father, Patrick bore into royal authority; a king, Henry said, by vetoing acts of this nature transforms into a monarch and "forfeits all rights to his subject's obedience."[3] Patrick Henry's brash oratory limited Maury's damages to a mere one penny, while vaulting his own career, and presaging arguments that Jefferson would insert into the Declaration of Independence, specifically the mention of usurpations by King George thrice in that great document. Tobacco, once again, had swirled its way into the political affairs of Englishmen. Actually, tobacco had been in the midst of colonial affairs for quite some time.

London and Glasgow merchants controlled the purchase of tobacco from the colonies. A few years prior to the war, in 1772, a panicked financial sector caused British stock prices to plummet and credit to tighten. London merchants and investors, then, put colonial planters in a vise, refusing to accept their notes of credit, only cash, and denying further credit. Tobacco prices were lowered and loans were dunned. Jefferson, Washington, and the other tobacco planters were not only squeezed, they were irritated.[4] Jefferson believed a conspiracy against colonial planters was afoot. As he said later:

This is to be ascribed to peculiarities in the tobacco trade. The advantages made by the British merchants on the tobaccos consigned to them were so enormous that they spared no means of increasing those consignments. A powerful engine for this purpose was the giving good prices & credit to the planter till they got him more immersed in debt than he could pay without selling his lands or slaves. They then reduced the prices given for his tobacco, so that, let his shipments be ever so great, and his demand of necessaries ever so economical, they never permitted him to clear off his debt. These debts had become hereditary from father to son for many generations, so that the planters were a species of property annexed to certain mercantile houses in London.[5]

Meanwhile, George Washington, up the Potomac at Mount Vernon, struggled with tobacco problems of his own. Washington's paternal great-grandfather, Colonel John Washington, patriarch of the family, played a role in the events leading up to Bacon's Rebellion.

In 1674, the older Washington, under commission from then governor Berkeley, led a military raid, against the governor's wishes, that slaughtered a Susquehannock village across the Potomac from the estate he was building, called Mount Vernon. George, now inheritor of the estate passed down to him, sold his tobacco each year in London through Robert Cary & Company, his agents. On September 20, 1765, Washington wrote to the company, unhappy with the price he'd received for his tobacco. "That the Sales are pitifully low, needs no words to demonstrate—and that they are worse than many of my Acquaintance upon this River—Potomac—have got . . . from Mr Russel and other Merchants of London for common Aronoko Tobo."[6]

Planters' unrest at their treatment by British tobacco agents was by no means limited to Jefferson and Washington. Robert Carter III, scion of the wealthy Carter family of slaveholders and tobacco planters, patriarch of the two-thousand-acre Nomini Hall plantation in the Northern Neck of Virginia, said to an English creditor in 1758, "I have experienced that the produce of my land and negroes will scarce pay the demand requisite to keep them. I have sold part to sink the debts due against me."[7]

Still, how does one get from tobacco pressed into hogsheads, to tea pushed overboard into Boston Harbor, to a declaration penned in Philadelphia, to shots fired on a Lexington green and a Concord bridge? Follow the money, of course, or at least follow the lack thereof. Washington, Jefferson, Lee, Byrd, all of the Chesapeake planters lived well beyond their means. They imagined themselves to be English patricians, reconstructing an American version of that aristocratic lifestyle. Monticello. Mount Vernon. Montpelier. Mount Airy. Oak Hill. Tuckahoe. Walnut Grove. Westover. Woodlawn. Sabine Hall. Nomini Hall. Gunston Hall. Stratford Hall. They built great Georgian estates along the banks of the Potomac, the York, the Rappahannock, and the James, which they outfitted with the finest European décor and furnishings. Their homes were the center of sprawling plantations, actually small cities, of thousands of acres filled with buildings and dwellings, and hundreds of smiths, and tanners, and curriers, and cobblers, and tradesmen, and slaves, who if they did not work in the rambling tobacco fields, worked in support of those who did.

Tobacco was a demanding mistress, even for the planters, let alone for their slaves. The planters' lives were bound to the cycle of the crop, as was the sense of their worthiness as adequate men. But to a man, the Founders perceived themselves in a blissful state of autonomy, independence, and freedom. "The public or political character of the Virginians corresponds with their private one," observed British travel writer Andrew Burnaby in 1759, "they are haughty and jealous of their liberties, impatient of restraint, and can scarcely bear the thought of being controuled by any superior power."[8]

These men really did think of themselves as "Fathers," or as one author put it, they "viewed themselves as Old Testament Patriarchs."[9] And the cities these patricians built around them only further supported that view. In truth, their world was a fiction, veritably a "house built on smoke." For everything from the land, to the buildings, to the furnishings, to the workers, slave and free, had been purchased on credit. And English merchants held those notes. But debt to the American masters of tobacco was not the same as debt to the British masters of trade. Debt was an expected part of the lifestyles of the rich and famous. They sent hogsheads of tobacco to British merchants, and they ordered linens, and drapes, and silver, and china, and carriages, and fine clothes in return. But rarely did the profits from the hogsheads meet the desires of the planters for those fine trappings of aristocracy, so the merchants extended them credit, and extended them credit, and extended them credit, until shortly before the Revolutionary War the merchants had no credit left to extend.

"There are but few of them that have a turn for business, and even those are by no means expert at it," said Burnaby of the Virginia patricians. "In matters of commerce they are ignorant of the necessary principles that must prevail between a colony and the mother country; they think it a hardship not to have an unlimited trade to every part of the world."[10]

For British merchants, on the other hand, debt was part of doing business. And when their credit ran dry in the eighteenth century, they had nowhere to turn except calling in their debts from the planters. The planters, then, with little "turn for business," saw this dunning not as business practice but as a breach of social etiquette. How dare British merchants cut off access to a lifestyle to which American planters had grown accustomed. Some planters, like Washington and Jefferson, preached greater frugality and thriftiness in response, even as they spent right up until their credit was maxed out. The Founders saw this "credit squeeze" as an affront not only to their tobacco trade but also to their view of themselves as autonomous, independent, free men.

Patriots were bred only from the ranks of those with "independent Circumstance," said Founder Richard Henry Lee. Independence was "the foundation on which liberty can alone be protected," said patrician planter Landon Carter, heir to his family's wealthy slave estate at Nomini Hall. And if those sound like sentiments that found their way into the call for independence and revolution, and the founding documents of this country, that's because they did.[11]

But the independence of the Founders was always hollow, for reasons which agitated them in the run-up to war. They were utterly and wholly beholden to the good graces and good credit of British merchants. Even more important, though rarely discussed, the Founders had the privilege of viewing themselves as independent precisely because they held hundreds on their plantations enslaved. Without slaves to produce tobacco, there was no basis for the Founders to consider themselves free. Without slaves, the Founders would not have had the luxury of time to pursue such lofty ideas of liberty and equality. They would have been bound to the land and the cycle of cultivating tobacco, just like the slaves whose labor allowed these men the fiction of seeing themselves as free.

It's surprising to hear these patricians talk of their fears of enslavement to British merchants, when they themselves held so many slaves. Writing in the *Virginia Gazette*, in 1771, an anonymous planter lamented, "it is not through any regard the merchant hath for the planter that he gives his note, or advanceth cash on his behalf, but in the end to serve himself, and enslave the other."[12]

Fear preceded war. Strapped for cash, some planters turned on each other, calling in their own debts. Others railed against the merchants. Still others simply begged. An association of planters attempted to stop importing the English goods they'd grown so accustomed to and fond of—that didn't last long. Another group tried to squeeze merchants by withholding shipments of tobacco—that didn't last long either. Many lost their estates and their fortunes. Washington, in crisis at Mount Vernon, switched from tobacco to wheat, which actually turned out to be an astute move. The General Assembly closed county courts to debtor suits brought by British merchants.[13] In the end, none of this worked. Debt ate away at the Founders' estates, but they didn't go to war over debt. Debt also ate away at the Founders' sense of autonomy, independence, liberty, nobility, honor, and freedom. And those principles were worth the fight.

• • •

Virginia's tobacco planters played an oversize role in drafting the Declaration of Independence. Jefferson chaired the committee. He worked on the Declaration while ensconced at the home of Jacob Graff, on the outskirts of Philadelphia, away from the Pennsylvania State House, now Independence Hall, where the Congress met. In drafting that foundational document, he used not only his own writing but also documents written by planters, and slaveholders, George Mason, George Washington, and Thomas Ludwell Lee.

The Declaration is, first and foremost, a document affirming the sanctity of certain self-evident principles—independence, life, liberty, and the pursuit of happiness—and the sacrilege of others: usurpation of those self-evident principals, taxation without representation, a capricious use of authority and law. While those principles resonated throughout the colonies, they held special significance for the men from Virginia. They were not only philosophical ideas, they represented a way of life. Beneath those vaunted principles lay the stench of debt, from which the Founders from Virginia recoiled. Beneath that debt lay the sweet aroma of prized tobacco and a way of life these Founders wished to reclaim. But beneath the debt and the tobacco lay the pungent odor of sweat from the bodies of thousands of Black slaves.

Tobacco, and the culture around it, was never far from these Founders' hearts or minds. Though research casts doubt on whether George Washington actually wrote, "If you can't send money, send tobacco,"[14] tobacco was used by the colonies to finance the Revolutionary War. French sympathizers, notably Beaumarchais, in 1775, set up a secretive shell company in Spain, Roderigue Hortalez and Company, to funnel French and Spanish arms to the American colonies in exchange for tobacco, all shipped through the ports in Santo Domingo (present-day Haiti).[15] The Revolutionary War was also known as the "Tobacco War," in part because tobacco, so valuable to the economic health of England and the royal treasury, made the colonies worth fighting for. But why stop there? If the Revolutionary War can be called the Tobacco War, then it can also be called the "First War Over Slavery," since tobacco and slavery were so inextricably linked.

• • •

Jeffersonian disingenuity lies beneath any ambivalence about slavery that might have worked its way into the Declaration of Independence. Some point to the Declaration's "missing clause" as proof of slaveholder Jefferson's anti-slavery desires. In enumerating King George's usurpations and offenses, Jefferson wrote,

> He has waged cruel war against human nature itself, violating its most sacred rights of life & liberty in the persons of a distant people who never offended him, captivating & carrying them into slavery in another hemisphere, or to incur miserable death

in their transportation thither. This piratical warfare, the op-
probrium of infidel powers, is the warfare of the Christian King
of Great Britain, determined to keep open a market where MEN
should be bought & sold, he has prostituted his negative for sup-
pressing every legislative attempt to prohibit or to restrain this
execrable commerce: and that this assemblage of horrors might
want no fact of distinguished die, he is now exciting those very
people to rise in arms against us, and to purchase that liberty of
which he has deprived them by murdering the people upon whom
he also obtruded them: thus paying off former crimes committed
against the liberties of one people, with crimes which he urges
them to commit against the lives of another.[16]

That clause did not survive the final edit; still the slaveholder
from Virginia "doth protest too much, methinks." Jefferson's protest is not really against slavery, but against the slave trade. The
Virginia Assembly sought to regulate the market in slaves by re-
stricting the importation of new Africans into the colony, so the
value of the slaves already there would rise. This way, men like Jefferson and Washington and the other planters could make more
profit from buying and selling slaves on a growing domestic market. King George, in ruling against American action to regulate
the slave trade, struck down those measures—i.e., "prostituted his
negative"—to prevent such restrictions. Finally, the closing lines of
this missing clause might possibly be the most disingenuous.

By the time the Declaration of Independence was written the
Revolutionary War was well underway. On November 7, 1775, John
Murray, the Fourth Earl of Dunmore, and royal governor of the Virginia colony, issued a proclamation, known as Dunmore's Proclamation,[17] declaring freedom to all slaves who left their owners and
aligned with the British royal forces. This enraged slave owners like
Jefferson, hence his words in the Declaration about the king "now
exciting those very people to rise in arms against us."[18] Fear of an
armed insurrection by slaves struck terror in the hearts of these

men, as it had in the hearts of their forefathers shortly after Bacon's Rebellion. Dunmore was soon forced from his post, and took three hundred former slaves with him.

In reading the Declaration of Independence, it takes some discernment to unearth the role Blacks played in preparing the firmament from which sprang Jefferson's lofty words and high-minded, self-evident ideals. But that effort brings with it the rewards of peering behind those words and ideals into the reasons why this document, and the war it wrought, came about. A similar discernment is necessary in approaching the other founding documents, especially the Constitution. Overt references to negroes, Blacks, or slaves are rarely used. But the presence of Blacks, free and slave, at the birth of the nation is keenly felt in how the documents were written, and from the institutions that arose as a result.

Biblical zeal attends discussions of constitutional interpretation. "Strict constructionists" contend that judges must focus solely on the text of the US Constitution as it was written 250 years ago, avoiding any interpretations, or inferences, from constitutional clauses, lest they be considered "judicial activists." But those labeled judicial activists bristle at the term, contending it is merely code for decisions that someone else does not like. They prefer to think of themselves as interpreters of a "living Constitution," a dynamic document whose meaning must grow and change over time. It's often a bitter fight breaking along a conservative and liberal divide, with strict constructionists on the conservative side and living constitutionalists occupying far more progressive ground.

In the days leading up to the 1987 bicentennial celebration of the US Constitution, esteemed Supreme Court Justice Thurgood Marshall spoke eloquently of this divide. Marshall, a Black man who, as a lawyer for the NAACP in 1954, had argued the seminal *Brown v. Board of Education* case, striking down "separate but equal" in front of the high court he now sat on, said to a meeting of lawyers in Hawaii, "I do not believe that the meaning of the Constitution was forever 'fixed' at the Philadelphia Convention. Nor do I find the wisdom, foresight and sense of justice exhibited by the Framers particularly profound."[19]

There is probably no person better suited than Marshall to speak of the role Black folks played, albeit *in absentia*, in the design and draft of that foundational document of the United States. Through his eyes, and brilliant legal mind, what comes across, once again, is that in this land of the free, some have the great privilege of freedom because many bear the great burden of bondage.

For Marshall, this privilege and this burden begin with the Constitution's opening three words, "We the People." "When the Founding Fathers used this phrase in 1787," he said, "they did not have in mind the majority of America's citizens."[20] Article 1, Section 2 makes clear whom they did have in mind.

> Representatives and direct Taxes shall be apportioned among the several States which may be included within this Union, according to their respective Numbers, which shall be determined by adding to the whole Number of free Persons, including those bound to Service for a Term of Years, and excluding Indians not taxed, *three fifths of all other Persons.*[21]

Further along in that esteemed document is a clause often referred to as the Fugitive Slave Clause, which affirmed the rights of slaveholders to have any state return their runaway slaves. On a sweltering July 4, 1854, William Lloyd Garrison spoke out against it. Garrison stood in front of a Framingham, Massachusetts, crowd of thousands, twenty miles from where the first shots of revolution were fired on Lexington's green. Above him hung an inverted US flag, draped in black. Beside him were Sojourner Truth and Henry David Thoreau. An abolitionist crowd had gathered to mark the birthday of a young nation—only seventy-eight years had passed since the Declaration of Independence, not even seventy years since the writing of the Constitution; it would be another ten years before the Emancipation Proclamation. Garrison spoke toward the end of the event, a copy of the US Constitution trembling in his hand. "A covenant with death," he declared it. "An agreement with hell." Then he set the Constitution ablaze, proclaiming, "So perish all compromises with tyranny!"[22]

The disingenuous words Marshall drew attention to, the compromises Garrison railed against, are many, evidence of the direct and indirect ways that the pillars of the Constitution, and hence of the nation, were erected on the unrepresented presence of Black slaves in the midst of White men who were unable and unwilling to forge a covenant with truth, so they opted instead for a covenant with death.

The word *slave* never appears in the body of the Constitution, but only once, in the Thirteenth Amendment, passed in 1865, when slavery was abolished after the Emancipation Proclamation. Even then with an exception for slavery as a punishment for crimes. The words *slave*, *negro*, and *Black* were not included in the Constitution in deference to the sensibilities of northern delegates, while allowing the objectives of southern states to be achieved.

It's hard to know how many of those who profess to carrying pocket-size copies of the Constitution with them have carefully read the document they carry around. If they have, then perhaps they already know that in the body of the Constitution, as it was drafted and ratified in 1788, there are six clauses dealing directly with slavery without ever mentioning the word:

Preamble. "We the People." Does not include a majority of American citizens.

Article I, Section 2, Paragraph 3. "Three-fifths clause," which Thurgood Marshall protested.

Article I, Section 9, Paragraph 1. "Import and export clause." Allows southern states to continue importing slaves, and northern states to continue shipping them.

Article I, Section 9, Paragraph 4. "Capital taxation clause." Any taxation based on the "three-fifths clause."

Article IV, Section 2, Paragraph 3. The "Fugitive Slave Clause," which Garrison protested.

Article V. Prohibits any changes to the importation or taxation clauses until 1808.

Seven clauses indirectly protecting slavery:

Article I, Section 8, Paragraph 15. "Domestic insurrections clause." Congress empowered to call out the militia to put down insurrections, including slave insurrections.

Article I, Section 9, Paragraph 5. Prohibits indirect taxation on slavery through taxing southern products such as tobacco and rice, later cotton.

Article I, Section 10, Paragraph 2. Prohibits indirect taxation on slavery through taxing imports or exports.

Article II, Section 1, Paragraph 2. "Electoral college clause." Incorporates the "three-fifths clause" into presidential elections.

Article IV, Section 3, Paragraph 1. "New states clause." Anticipates admission of new slave states to the Union.

Article I, Section 4. "Domestic violence clause." Requiring federal protection of states against domestic violence, including slave rebellions.

Article V. "Ratification clause." Requiring three-fourths majority to ratify amendments gives southern states an ongoing veto of constitutional changes.

And, an additional six clauses used to protect slavery:

Article I, Section 8, Paragraph 4. "Naturalization clause." Congress to prohibit the naturalization of nonwhites.

Article I, Section 8, Paragraph 17. "Federal district clause." Congress to regulate institutions, including slavery, in the federal district, Washington, DC.

Article III, Section 2, Paragraph 1. "Diversity jurisdiction clause." Allows only citizens of the states to sue in federal courts; slaves were considered property and not citizens.

Article IV, Section 1. "Full faith and credit clause." Requires states to recognize the laws of other states, thereby coercing free states to recognize the laws of slave states, which also supported the Fugitive Slave Clause.

Article IV, Section 2, Paragraph 1. "Privileges and immunity clause." Requires states to grant equal privileges and immunities to citizens of other states, but not applied to free Blacks.

Article IV, Section 3, Paragraph 2. "Territorial regulation clause." Allows Congress to regulate territories. But the Supreme Court ruled in its 1857 Dred Scott decision that this regulation of slavery did not extend to banning it.

The total number of clauses within the Constitution varies somewhere between 75 and 85, depending upon what is, or is not, considered a clause. That means a staggering amount of the Constitution, between 20 to 25 percent, is devoted directly or indirectly to supporting slavery, and excluding Black Americans from the benefits conferred to "We the People."[23]

How could this happen?

Nearly every major debate over the Constitution had slavery at its core, even though the word never found its way into the text. And, let us just take a moment to remind ourselves that by slavery, we are not just talking about holding a person against their will, but forcing that person to produce the goods, and deliver the services, that generate power and wealth for the slaveholder.

For most of the Revolutionary War, the thirteen original states united under a document called the Articles of Confederation. But with growing awareness of the limitations of those articles, a Constitutional Convention, for the purpose of amending them, was called for May 1787 in Philadelphia. Held, once again, in Philadelphia's Pennsylvania State House, where the Declaration of Independence had first been drafted. Delegates from every state in the fragile, new union, except Rhode Island, met from May 14 to September 17. After a little over one hundred days, what emerged was not an amended set of articles, but an entirely new constitution.

Within two weeks of the convening, the fate of Black Americans, slave and free, took center stage in the debates and deliberations.[24] The issue had to do with the nature of the new Congress and how representatives would be determined. Virginia's governor, Edmund Randolph, the scion of a well-established family of tobacco planters, proposed a legislative branch with two chambers, one composed of younger members to serve three years, the other composed of older members to serve seven years, both using a state's population to apportion the number of seats.

And the fight over slavery was on!

Northern delegates objected to using population as the basis for representation because southern delegates intended to count slaves as well, giving the south a big advantage in both the House of Representatives and the Senate. Southern delegates rejected the idea proposed by the north of counting only the number of "free" men because southern states, like Virginia, were more populous than, say, Pennsylvania precisely because of their slaves. From late May until early July 1787, the debate on representation ping-ponged back and forth between northern and southern delegates, with each side threatening, more than once, to scrap the Union rather than give in to the other's demands.

Slowly the shape of a compromise emerged; so, too, the shape of an unlikely alliance. The new nation would have two legislative bodies: a lower one, the House of Representatives, based on population count; and an upper one, the Senate, based on equal representation of two senators from each state. That still left an open question of how to count the population for representation in the House—by "quotas of contribution," the polite phrase the gentlemen in Philadelphia used to mean "include the slaves"; or by "numbers of free inhabitants," which meant to exclude slaves. In either case, both northern and southern camps were in agreement that Blacks, slave or free, would not have the vote, they just couldn't agree on whether slaves should be included in the count for the House of Representatives.

During the second week of June, James Wilson of Pennsylvania, soon to sit on the first Supreme Court, proposed a compromise that had first surfaced, years earlier, in debate around a formula for taxation in the amended Articles of Confederation: count slaves as three-fifths of a person. Of course, in that earlier debate, the south rejected the idea because it meant that southern states like Virginia and South Carolina, with the greatest number of slaves, would pay a larger share of taxes. As the basis for taxation, the formula failed, and the amendment was never passed. But the general idea of counting slaves as three-fifths of "free Whites" remained alive, only to surface again when the issue became representation, and the document the new Constitution. Charles Cotesworth Pinckney, slaveholder and delegate from South Carolina, seconded Wilson's motion.

On July 12, the issue came to a head. Delegates from Virginia, North Carolina, and South Carolina issued an ultimatum: count our slaves, or lose your Constitution. A vote was called. Results were tallied. The three-fifths formula prevailed. The south won a crucial battle, in the course picking up surprise support from New England delegates, which presaged a coming alliance between the "carrying trade" of the north and the "slave trade" of the south. A trade in which a New England–based shipping industry carried goods produced by slave labor in the south for markets around the world, and those same ships carried slaves from Africa, for sale on southern auction blocks.

With this first Faustian bargain consummated, other clauses in the "covenant with death" seemed to follow more easily. A three-fifths formula had been established for incorporating slaves into the Constitution, and that formula found its way into other important clauses such as taxation and the election of the Executive.

So what? It's a great story and a pity the Founders treated slaves so poorly. But that all happened long ago. Get over it! Slavery no longer exists. Black Americans are not counted as three-fifths of a person. They can vote. So can women. You're living in the past. How can any of this possibly affect us now?

These are popular refrains spoken by many, blind to the impact of the decisions this group of White men made over the course of one hundred days in Philadelphia in 1787. These men determined how the institutions of power and wealth in America would be shaped, for centuries to come, based on the presence of Black men and women, who could not vote but whose presence was still keenly felt.

Without the three-fifths compromise, there's a good chance we would not be facing the climate crisis. Without the three-fifths compromise, there's a good chance far fewer Americans would have died from complications of COVID-19. Without the three-fifths compromise, there's a good chance we would not be a country as divided by race now as we were when the Founders acquiesced to that compromise.

Of course, we cannot know any of this for sure. But what we can know for sure is that without the three-fifths compromise, every four years when we pull the levers at a polling station, or seal the envelope of a mail-in ballot and drop it in a mailbox, we would be electing a president based on "We the People," not based on "We the Electors," a group known as the Electoral College.

America does not hold popular democratic elections for a president. Since the ratification of the Constitution, the country never has. Instead, the country elects a president through an Electoral College, wherein each state is allocated a certain number of electors. This means, as we have seen far too often, a presidential candidate can lose the popular vote but still win the election in the Electoral College. The "will of the people" has no meaning. While the Electoral College is sometimes touted as a means of leveling the field between small states and large states, slavery was actually the complicating factor that brought the Electoral College into being.

Five days after the three-fifths compromise had been voted on, and approved, the Constitutional Convention took up the election of the president.[25] A debate unfolded on now familiar grounds. Direct election of the Executive by the people was flatly rejected by southern delegates because they had fewer White men to vote. James Madison, champion of the people, was concerned. Though Madison favored the idea of direct election of the president, he was troubled that it would weaken the power of southern states. So, the Electoral College was created, which allowed the three-fifths clause to increase the number of presidential electors the south held on to because the three-fifths clause determined the number of representatives they began with in the House.

Even White men, who could vote, had the value of their votes diminished. Southern states rejected the direct election of the president because they desired to hold on to slavery. As "We the People" became more inclusive, through amendments to the Constitution that expanded suffrage to people of color and to women, the inherently undemocratic Electoral College still remained as an enduring legacy of a racist past; a legacy that renders the true meaning of "by the people" null and void in terms of electing a person to the highest office in the land.

With the ratification of the Constitution in 1788, the die of a new nation had been cast, forged in battle, ripened with history, filled with promise, yet haunted by an unspoken, powerful dark presence. Black folks, the Founders' reliance on them and fear of them, were behind the creation of American institutions of governance and political power articulated in the Constitution, even though they were not allowed to vote, and the Founders never mentioned them in that hallowed document. Within this American die, the lives of Black men and women had been cast, and cast well; a cast given them ever since Anthony and Isabella first set foot on Virginian soil: work to ensure the creation of the institutions of power and wealth for White America, but never ask, and never expect, anything in return.

A GREAT WHITE HOPE

On January 27, 1938, in Marion, South Carolina, Josephine Bristow, a seventy-three-year-old Black woman, spoke with Works Progress Administration (WPA) field interviewer Annie Ruth Davis about her life as an ex-slave. Davis, thankfully, was employed to write down Bristow's story.

I don' know how long dey had to work, mam, but I hear dem say dat dey worked hard, cold or hot, rain or shine. Had to hoe cotton en' pick cotton en' all such as dat. I don' know, mam, but de white folks, I guess dey took it dat dey had plenty colored people en' dey Lord never meant for dem to do no work. You know, white folks in dem days, dey made de colored people do. De people used to spin en' weave, my Lord! Like today, it cloudy en' rainy, dey couldn' work in de field en' would have to spin dat day. Man, you would hear dat thing windin en' I remember, I would stand dere en' want to spin so bad, I never know what to do. Won' long fore I got to where I could use de shuttle en' weave, too. I had a grand-mother en' when she would get to dat wheel, she sho know what she been doin. White folks used to give de colored people task to spin en' I mean she could do dat spinnin. Yes'um, I here to tell you, dey would make de prettiest cloth in dat day en' time. Old time people used to have a kind of dye dey called indigo en' dey would color de cloth just as pretty as you ever did see.[1]

Josephine Bristow, both in what she said and what she didn't, depicted not only a post–Civil War south, but a post–Revolutionary War America, where the fault lines of wealth and power were shifting. By the time of the Constitutional Convention, in 1787, it was possible to speak of the "upper south" and the "deep south," of "old money" and "new money." Tobacco once reigned supreme in Virginia and the upper south. But by 1800, tobacco had been dethroned in the deep south, replaced by the cry of, "Cotton is King." The upper south, indeed, the northern part of the nation, migrated away from labor-intensive agriculture. The indigo-dyed cloth, "just as pretty as you ever did see," was primarily not for slave garments but for the profit of northern textile industries.

America is a country that prides itself on not looking to the past, instead always toward the future. With the exception of the mixed-race children of Thomas Jefferson, we hear little of the descendants of the "great planters" and Founders, though what wealth of theirs that remained was passed along, so even today we refer to it as old money. In Virginia, describing someone belonging to the FFV (First Families of Virginia) still lends them an aura of American aristocracy, even if that aristocracy no longer exists. For, once the country had severed its ties with Great Britain, there was new money to be made and "new power" to be had.

Many things once done exclusively in England now could be done at home. Though tobacco was waning, merchants were still needed for the international trade in southern products, such as cotton. New England answered that call. British shipping no longer exclusively transported colonial goods, so an American shipping industry needed to fill the void. New England stepped forward, again. And merchants and planters (now of cotton more so than tobacco) still needed credit to buy and sell land and slaves. Banking centers like New York City emerged to meet that need. There was also the rise of a "governing class" in America, no longer reliant on the politics of a British monarchy but the politics at home. Atop all of this, an Industrial Revolution was underway, bringing profound changes in the way raw materials were turned into finished goods.

Despite so much changing by the turn of the nineteenth century, one thing remained constant. Beneath these new American institutions of power and wealth, in fact fueling their rise, was the enduring presence of Black lives and Black labor, primarily slave labor.

• • •

A young man with an Ivy League education is destined to become a lawyer, when his life takes an unexpected turn. He finds himself in a basement, at work on a new technology, from which he emerges with a device in hand that revolutionizes the world. It's a story with a familiar ring.

From Apple to Microsoft to Google to Facebook, we know these young men and women who disrupt the world with a revolutionary new technology. Only this young man we're speaking of here was born in Massachusetts in 1765. He attended Yale University. He toiled in the basement of a Georgia plantation owned by Continental Army major general Nathanael Greene. He disrupted the world of southern agriculture and slavery. The year was 1793. The device he emerged with was the cotton gin. His name was Eli Whitney.

Prior to the gin (short for *engine*) cotton was easily as labor intensive as tobacco. Two different species of the plant occur naturally: long staple and short staple. Staple, or fiber length, is what gives cotton its texture and feel. The longer the staple, the silkier the feel. Egyptian and pima cotton, for example, are extra-long varieties of the long-staple-cotton species. But 95 percent of cotton produced in the United States is a short-staple variety known as upland cotton. It's strong but soft, requires low maintenance, and is used in everything from jeans to flannel clothing. The name *upland* refers to an area inland from the coast and closer to the Piedmont Mountains in the west of Georgia and South Carolina—the upland—where this cotton was grown.

Not all cotton is white. Cotton bolls, those fluffy clumps from the plant, also appear in naturally occurring hues such as green or brown or yellow. In the nineteenth-century deep south, slaves were allowed to grow only a bit of this harder-to-deal-with "colored cotton" for making their own clothes and goods. Plantation owners prevented them from growing the upland, white cotton, afraid they might sell it.

One can just imagine Josephine Bristow sitting on her rickety porch in Marion, South Carolina, while in front of her a White woman, pencil in hand, asks questions and writes on a lined pad. Josephine leans back in her chair and presses her lips together, back and forth, as though chewing on invisible memories. A low "ummmmm" is heard in response to a question about whether she remembers picking cotton. Tired eyes look out beyond the White woman, past the porch; look back in time fifty or sixty years. Compressing all those "can see to can't see" days laboring in the fields—sights of Black and brown bodies bending to caress fluffy bolls; the arthritic pain her fingers still harbored; the horrific sounds of leather tendrils teasing strips of skin off bloodied backs—Josephine, the memories flooding faster than her words, says softly, quietly, "Yes'um . . . Had to hoe cotton en' pick cotton en' all such as dat." Rocking in her chair, another "ummmmm" punctuates her reply.

The White woman does not know how to render the silence, or the well of pain and pride and wisdom hidden in this ex-slave's words, so she writes down simply, "En' all such as dat," trying, at least, to faithfully render the vernacular she hears.

What's there, beyond the threads of "en' all such as dat," spun tight like cotton yarn, are recollections of endless years of Black lives withering, so row after row of green plants, and their fluffy debris, could grow. "En' all such as dat" began sometime in late winter as the hard ground softened to admit penetration by a harrow and a plow. Each day the dreaded "Horn of Pain"[2] sounded, calling slaves from their slumber before first light. Black men and women cleared the detritus of last year's crop—cutting stalks by hand or plowing them under. Then, from behind a horse, harnessed to a harrow, the soil was worked, and worked, and worked again, into a fine loam. A horse or a mule pulled a man and a plow along the land; sometimes it was just a person with a shovel, digging deeper furrows, which were then fertilized with manure. After the danger of frost had passed, green seeds were carefully sprinkled into the trenches, like petals thrown before a bride, then covered over with dirt.

With rain and luck, and a successful wedding night, six weeks later the earth gave birth to thousands of small green shoots. Plants were thinned by hand and hoe, so a hoe would fit easily between them and now "En' all such as dat" meant, in Josephine's words, "hoe cotton" or "chopping time." Using tools that resembled weapons at the end of long wooden handles, weeds such as pigweed were cut at the root and delivered as fodder to the hogs. Then, over and over again, Black men and women and children moved through fields with hoes chopping away at the earth to remove smaller weeds, then back again, chopping again, to keep them at bay. There's a point at which the chopping stops and the field is declared "laid by."

By mid June, Josephine, her family, and others around her were witness to the foot-high plants producing a tiny pinkish "fruit" known as a "square," which opened into a white flower. Pollinated by wind or insects, the day after pollination the white flower turned pink, then red, then brown as it began to die. From the death of the flower, a green pod or boll formed on the plant. By now, Josephine would have seen daylight fading earlier and earlier each day, as the bolls popped open to reveal their fluffy white treasures.

Finally came the time for Josephine and the others to harvest or "pick cotton," which meant gathering the fluffy white fibers laboriously by hand. With different fields planted and ripening at different times, picking cotton extended well into the fall. Even then, Josephine's work was not over. For it came time to separate the cotton fibers from the cotton seed.

Josephine may have heard talk of "cotton-rollers," slaves whose main job it was to tease out fibers from long-staple cotton, grown on Georgia and South Carolina Sea Islands by the Gullah people, African slaves brought there to work on cotton plantations. They used a tool called a cotton roller, originally created in India. Long-staple cotton sold at a premium price because there was so much less of it, and because it produced a finer, silkier feel.

Josephine, like most ex-slaves, had heard stories of distant ancestors cleaning cotton by hand. The upland cotton that grew on the plantation enslaving her was full of sticky seeds, making it a far more difficult variety to winnow. It took one man, most often a slave, nearly a full day to clean a single pound of cotton lint by hand.

Enter Eli Whitney in 1793 and his new machine that separated cotton lint from seed.

At this point, the question I'd put to Josephine would have been: "Mother, did you ever hear that the cotton gin was meant to reduce slavery?" I can imagine what she'd say.

"Chile, hush yo' mouth! Reduce us numbers! Ain't never heard dem Old time peoples talk 'bout such mess. Why, I was dere. I seen 'em. Colored folks en' White folks all linin' up at the ginnies wid dey cotton. Money in dey pocket fo' White man. 'Nuther day's hard work for de colored folk 'cause dey ain't seein' none a de White man's money any time soon. Chile, I was dere. And I ain't seen no' heard nothing 'bout a ginny bringin' us numbers down. Wish dey woulda'. Lord, Lord, don' I wish dey woulda'. Near as I can figger it, ginny ain't done nothin' but bringin' us numbers up. Mo' colored folks under Massa's whip. Mo' colored folk in his fields. Mo' colored folk hoein' cotton en' pickin' cotton en' all such as dat."

Josephine would have been right. Despite all of the modern-day writers who claim, without attribution, that Eli Whitney invented the cotton gin believing it would reduce slavery, nothing in his letters suggests that's the case.

In a September 11, 1793, letter to his father, explaining the basic functioning of the cotton gin, and what he'd done with himself after graduating from Yale, Whitney says, "This machine may be turned by water or with a horse, with the greatest ease, and one man and a horse will do more than fifty men with the old machines. It makes the labor fifty times less, without throwing any class of People out of business."[3]

In search of a patent for his device, in a November 24 letter of the same year, Whitney wrote to then secretary of state Thomas Jefferson, "It is the stated task of one negro to clean fifty Wt. (I mean fifty pounds after it is separated from the seed) of the green-seed cotton Per Day."[4]

Mostly, Whitney's correspondence shows his obsession with establishing a New England factory to make the machines that he and his business partner and former Yale colleague, Phineas Miller, would ship to the deep south, and his concern at the outpouring of money in fending off others who claimed to have invented the cotton gin before him.[5]

Whitney was in it for the money, not for social justice.

But, for a final moment, let us return to our dear sister Josephine talking to Annie Ruth Davis on that porch in Marion, South Carolina. "En' all such as dat" concludes with the presentation of cotton to the intake tubes of a gin mill, which sucked it into the gin, then spit it out as bales of cotton, each weighing about five hundred pounds. Sometimes the bales were loaded onto ships or trains for transport to New England textile mills, or overseas to mills in Britain.

At other times, slave women like Josephine's grandmother worked at "jennys," whose wheels you can almost hear spinning in her granddaughter's words. Josephine's grandmother probably first spun cotton yarn from a portion of ginned cotton, then wove yard after yard of cloth sitting at a "spinning jenny," pushing the shuttle back and forth. Josephine reminds us that "Old time people used to have a kind of dye dey called indigo en' dey would color de cloth just as pretty as you ever did see." The "Old time people" grew indigo on the same plantation as cotton for this purpose. The blue in blue jeans comes from the indigo first used by the "Old time people" to dye the denim cloth they wove.

If Josephine's "Marster" followed *Affleck's Southern Rural Alma-*

nac, and Plantation and Garden Calendar, as many did, they would read the following under January's "The Cotton Plantation" section: "And the negroes, being refreshed by their holidays, and ready to enter with new spirit upon another year's labor, will press on briskly with the preparations for a new crop."[6]

Another cotton cycle began for enslaved Black men and women and children. "Dey worked hard, cold or hot, rain or shine"; Josephine doubtlessly emphasized *hard* from the depths of the pain and suffering and sorrow she knew, drawing the word out in ways the White woman could never imagine how to record. "Had to hoe cotton en' pick cotton en' all such as dat."

Whitney's portrayal as an anti-slavery champion may have come from those who thought his gin would be the "kill shot" for slavery. Hand cultivation of cotton, as the "Old time people" did, was time-consuming and unprofitable. The upkeep of slaves nearly equal the profit from hand-processed cotton. But the cotton gin turned that equation upside down.

Josephine and "dem people" must have experienced the gin's impact. With it, Whitney introduced yet another variable into the process of how Black labor creates White power and wealth—technology—and from 1793 onward, technology became a permanent fixture of the equation. With the cotton gin, Josephine's "Marster" and many other White planters recognized the tremendous wealth awaiting them. But that wealth was predicated upon filling the belly of the hungry new mechanized beast. And filling the beast's belly meant two things—acquiring more land and more slaves.

Even if they'd known, what could "dem people" have done? In many respects, the process resembled what had happened nearly two hundred years earlier with tobacco, only now with the force and the urgency of a new sovereign nation. Native Americans held the land that White men needed. So, in the first half of the nineteenth century, several treaties signed between the United States and Indian nations east of the Mississippi established Indian reservations west of the Mississippi, and forced Native Americans to migrate there. That, in turn, freed up land east of the Mississippi for White men and their cotton.

As far as slave labor, if the "Old time people" came to South Carolina before 1808, there's a chance they came directly from Africa, through the Middle Passage, to a slave market in Charleston, where they were bought by Josephine's "Marster" or some other plantation owner. After 1808, America banned the international slave trade but American ships still made runs to the West African coast for human cargo. Though a domestic market in breeding and selling human beings had begun to thrive, essentially Black men and women were treated not as human beings but as cattle, in a domestic slave trade some called the "Second Middle Passage."

"Mother," I want to ask Josephine. "Do you know what happened to that pretty dark blue cloth your grandmother wove, or the bales of white cotton your father wrestled into the back of a wagon?"

Would a crooked-tooth smile and a deep laugh signal the absurdity of my question?

"Chile, dat cotton's gon'. Sure as spring leaves wintuh, dat cotton's gon'. Afta' dem bales come out de gin mill dey piled high in a wagon. Den Massa or some White man call for a colored man come sit by 'em on da wagon. En' dey's off to Charleston. May be two deys, may be even mo' fo' I see 'em again. Heard tell of big ships takin' hundreds of dem cotton bales. All just like ours. Den pushin' off, letting dere sails drop, and slipping out to sea. Yes'um. Heard dat's a pretty sight. Ain't never seen de ocean best as I can 'member. But heard dem peoples up north like our cotton for dey bi'ness. En' dem peoples way 'cross the ocean in England likes it fo' dey bi'ness, too."

• • •

Resource rode her heavy lines at Gadsden's Wharf as Robert Mackay paced the docks. East, beyond Fort Moultrie, a red-orange sun slithered up from an Atlantic horizon. Charleston's wharfinger ordered vessels arranged by ports of origin and destination. Slave ships from

Africa at the head of the wharf, closest to open water. Ships destined up the coast to New England next. Finally, ships calling at southern ports. *Resource*, tucked at the back of this line of ships, awaited a cargo from *Montezuma*, now in quarantine on Sullivan's Island, just outside Charleston. After loading his cargo onto *Resource*, Mackay would ride her to Savannah, and unload the goods for his store.

He liked the dance animated before him. Waves tumbling into the harbor, slowed in passing the barrier islands, then touched each vessel in turn, causing the tall masts, dressed in off-white furled sails, to bow and curtsey to each other.

He did not like the stench. Yesterday's horse manure, washed from the wharf into the ocean, lay trapped between ships' hulls and the pier, raising a pungent aroma, even as horses were already busy dropping today's. Dawn brought life to the wharf. Wagon wheels whined as negroes worked under watchful eyes, hauling sacks of rice from squat white waterfront warehouses in wagons up to waiting ships. Other negroes rolled hogsheads of tobacco to loading planks. Some drove wagons piled high with cotton, stacking the bales along the wharf's edge.

Mackay had heard the *Montezuma* was due into port any day. And he'd also heard, with so many other vessels expected, her cargo and her sales would go fast. He needed to be here when she docked, or the best negroes would be sold first.

Mackay thought how much he loved the sea. He smiled. He also loved his wharf-side shop and his wife and daughter in Savannah. Then, he stiffened. Be that as it may, he left no opportunity unanswered to travel the southern coast, or to New England, or across the Atlantic to London, in search of the finest goods for sale by Meins & Mackay, Co. of Savannah, purveyors of "Woolens and other Fall Goods" from London and "Particular Madeira Wine" from Funchal, and, of course, slaves from the West African coast.

When last in England, he'd commiserated over a fine dinner with owners of the Lancashire textile mills. Prices for his cotton were low. Owners were concerned about the stability of a commodity based on slavery.

Mackay remembered picking up an embroidered napkin from the table, inspecting it closely, rubbing it between his fingers. "This napkin, I believe, comes from our fine cotton, gentlemen," he said. "Georgia will go to war again, with anyone who should so ever try to harm our beloved institution of slavery. For without it, we would have no cotton. And without cotton, America would have no standing in the world."

"But wasn't slavery set to be outlawed in 1808?" the Lancashire merchants asked. "What then? Our mills will go hungry without the fluffy food. Our purses will go even hungrier."

Mackay recalled laughing. "The international trade, dear friends, the international trade alone was banned. We raise and breed our slaves there, much as we do our cattle. Our domestic supply will only grow, and will last us well into the future. As our slavery goes, so goes our cotton. And so goes our nation."

For the first time, Mackay heard the merchants talk about a grumbling they'd heard among their workers that some might not touch raw cotton picked by American slaves.

"Gentlemen." He tapped his glass. "Gentlemen. Simply order them away from such thoughts." The gentlemen stopped eating, looked up from their plates. "We treat our slaves as the mindless, simple children they are," he remembered saying. "You should treat your workers the same."

Wood rumbled over wood, calling Mackay back from his thoughts, as Black men rolled the wooden hogsheads down the docks. Mackay shook his head. Sidestepped a pile of horse manure and continued his pacing and pondering. He'd also dined with textile merchants in New England, and heard much the same as from their colleagues in Liverpool. With them he was not so polite.

Mackay remembered pounding his fist at dinner, startling the merchants. "My friends," he said. "The success of Meins & Mackay, Co. has made me captain of the artillery, alderman, church warden, justice of the court, bank director, and I could go on. All in Savannah. I cannot imagine any privileged civic position to which I could not accede should I so desire. Are not each of you in similar positions within your towns and cities? Are not the bankers of Boston and the tontine your friends, as they are most certainly mine? Business, gentlemen, business is the key to all other success. My south will fight anyone denying you cotton or denying us slaves."

A great commotion arose on the wharf, rousing Mackay again from his thoughts. He turned to see masts gliding in from the ocean. *Montezuma* had arrived. He walked with others swiftly toward the masts, toward the head of the wharf. There Mackay stopped to watch a waterborne ballet. *Montezuma* had been released from quarantine. In the middle of the fairway, her crew turned the ship within her length, dropped her lower sails while keeping her topsails set in opposite directions, effortlessly heaving-to, then waiting, leaning over the cap rails waving as though without a care, as the wind blew them slowly, steadily into a space just longer than their ship, between two other vessels on the wharf.

No sooner had *Montezuma*'s gangway been lowered, when merchants clambered around it, anxiously awaiting the ship's cargo. But the master appeared first, with the vessel's papers in hand, ready for the wharfinger. On the captain's way down the gangway, Mackay called out, "Sir, Captain Anley." Upon reaching the dock, the captain turned toward Mackay, who reached an outstretched hand through the mob. "Robert Mackay, sir, merchant from Georg—"

"Mr. Mackay," the captain said, interrupting. He smiled, nodded. His legs buckled slightly beneath him as he stood but he returned the handshake nonetheless. Then, the captain made a sweeping gesture toward the ship. "Mr. Mackay, you'll be pleased to know I have set aside, for your pleasure, a cargo of only the finest negroes obtained by me directly from Africa."[7]

• • •

Between 1783 and 1808, when the transatlantic slave trade was officially banned, Gadsden's Wharf in Charleston was the first stop in

America for an estimated 100,000 West African slaves. Many were purchased by lowland rice planters. Upland cotton farmers bought others. And, for some, Gadsden's Wharf was just a way station on a journey ending in slavery in the cotton and sugar plantations near New Orleans. What the "Old time people" sensed but could not have known was that in 1791, the US produced only two million pounds of cotton annually and the population of slaves was approximately 700,000. But by 1801, thanks to the Cotton Gin, cotton yield had jumped exponentially to 48.5 million pounds, and the number of slaves to over one million. South Carolina alone, that year, accounted for eight million pounds of cotton exported primarily to Liverpool textile miles. And by 1860, a country producing 1.6 billion pounds of cotton per year held over four million souls in perpetual bondage.[8,9,10]

Slavery grew cotton. Cotton grew slavery. And both grew White power and wealth.

James Henry Hammond married into the South Carolina planter class, through his wife, Catherine Elizabeth Fitzsimons, who delivered to him twenty-two square miles of land, multiple plantations, and more than three hundred slaves. An early member of the pro-states' rights, pro-slavery, anti-federal-government Nullifier Party, Hammond possessed wealth, like that of merchant Robert Mackay, which fueled his rise through the ranks of South Carolina's political class. He bounced between Washington and Columbia, first as a member of the House, then as governor, and finally as a US senator.[11]

Scandal did not halt Hammond's rise. The politician Thomas Jefferson Withers, in two sexually explicit letters, described his 1826 homosexual affair with Hammond. Hammond, himself, in diaries he called "secret and sacred," and not published until 125 years after his death, unabashedly described his "familiarities and dalliances" with four nieces. As was the prerogative of White slave owners, like Thomas Jefferson, Hammond repeatedly raped two of his female slaves, one of them possibly his daughter, who bore a number of his mixed-race children. After the public airing of many of these brutal transgressions, Hammond's wife left him, only to return once he went to Washington as a senator.[12]

As governor, Hammond declared, "I firmly believe that American slavery is not only not a sin, but especially commanded by God through Moses, and approved by Christ through his apostles . . . Slavery is the corner-stone of our republican edifice," he said. "I repudiate, as ridiculously absurd, that much lauded but nowhere accredited dogma of Mr. Jefferson that 'all men are born equal.'"[13]

As senator, in March 1858, Hammond confronted his colleague from New York, Senator William Seward, with these words,

> Without firing a gun, without drawing a sword, should they make war on us we could bring the whole world to our feet . . . What would happen if no cotton was furnished for three years? I will not stop to depict what every one can imagine, but this is certain: England would topple headlong and carry the whole civilized world with her, save the South. No, you dare not make war on cotton. No power on earth dares to make war upon it. Cotton is king.[14]

Hammond, through his hubris, coined the phrase "Cotton is king." When the south seceded, and America descended into civil war, southern international diplomacy coalesced around this notion that the world could not survive without cotton, and hence without slavery. Using this "King Cotton Diplomacy," the Confederacy attempted to coerce England and France into alliances by withholding cotton. But the effort failed and a Union blockade on cotton succeeded. This disruption in raw cotton shipped to England, however, helped to plunge the Lancashire textile industry into what has been called the "Cotton Famine."

Still, British textile workers stood with Black American slaves, often against their industrial masters. Writing to Abraham Lincoln on New Year's Eve in 1862, the day before the Emancipation Proclamation was to go into effect, Mayor Abel Heywood of Manchester, then within the ancient county boundaries of Lancashire, expressed the views of several thousand working-class men, who unanimously approved his correspondence. The long letter reads, in part,

> As citizens of Manchester, assembled at the Free-trade Hall, we beg to express our fraternal sentiments towards you and your country . . . One thing alone has, in the past, lessened our sympathy with your country and our confidence in it—we mean the ascendancy of politicians who not merely maintained negro slavery, but desired to extend and root it more firmly. Since we have discerned, however, that the victory of the free North, in the war which has so sorely distressed us as well as afflicted you, will strike off the fetters of the slave, you have attracted our warm and earnest sympathy . . . [15]

In places like Lancashire, merchants and manufacturers rose to become the bankers and financiers of the industrialization begun with cotton.[16] A similar arrangement took place in New England, where the mercantile houses marketing a cotton mill's output were also the source of a mill's credit. Both in England and New England, merchants depended on mills. Without textiles to sell there was no profit to make. Many of the large mercantile firms on both sides of the Atlantic did international business in more than just textile goods. But they depended on cotton to support their other trade in sugar, rice, and tobacco.

Francis Cabot Lowell, Samuel Slater, Eli Whitney, all good New England men, the first Captains of Industry, were at the helm of the Industrial Revolution, as it docked in America. Amoskeag, Naumkeag, Wamsutta, a few of the New England textile mills they fostered, household names in the nineteenth century, known then worldwide for quality cotton apparel, known now only to the whispers of history as mill names these good New England men, and their many brethren, stole from Native Americans along with the riverine land their sprawling campuses occupied. Both mills and tribes ultimately succumbed to powerful forces beyond their control before being catapulted into bankruptcy or compelled into extinction.

For millennia, Amoskeag Falls was a sacred place for the Amoskeag, who'd returned there each year to fish. They stopped returning in 1848. One writer recalled a visit toward the end of one of these annual pilgrimages when a native couple were married at the falls. While the White man described it as "a picturesque contrast to the more modern business of the mill,"[17] one can imagine the Native Americans, their fish and their sacred river now polluted by the mill's effluent, feeling it a grotesque contrast and affront to the ancient spirituality of their tribe.

Before the mills went bankrupt in the twentieth century, though, they generated wealth and power; power, of course, both politically and literally, as they were most often located at the bottom of falls so rushing water could drive the turbines creating cotton fibers on jennys, forcing the fibers to fit onto thousands of spindles, drawing them through shuttles and looms. These "power mills," as they were called, manufactured dresses and shirts and pants to wear, sheets to sleep on, napkins to dab at the corners of one's mouth, and thousands of cotton products New England merchants hawked worldwide as "made in the USA."

Before the mills' bankruptcy, and with his last heave-to, a captain, finally at home from the sea and not looking for a big-city job transcribing ship manifests, might find a fledgling mill just the right kind of vessel. After all, he'd made money bringing slaves from Africa to Charleston, then cotton from Charleston to Boston and on to Manchester, New Hampshire; or from Charleston to Liverpool, then on to Manchester, England. He understood trade, so, of course, he understood the value of investing in a mill that took cotton and turned it into textiles for sale worldwide.

So, too, a merchant who'd traded in cotton, slaves, tobacco, rice, and indigo might also find investing in a mill appealing. In the late eighteenth and early nineteenth centuries this is where the money to put up the brick walls of a textile mill came from. This is how the waterwheels dammed once sacred rivers. This is how jennys and looms and their spindles got running. This is how small community banks were begun in New England mill towns. This is how wealth made in the slave trade, or the products of slavery, was laundered, transferred, and passed from one generation of White Americans to the next.

Mills occupied rivers for more than just power. From the factory warehouse, textiles were delivered to barges, pulled by ox teams along smaller rivers or man-made canals, to waiting scows. Scows moved product along larger waterways to ships at docks up and down the New England coast, in towns like New Bedford. Ships moved product directly overseas to merchants and consumers, or to even larger seaports like Boston or New York, from where the products were then moved internationally.

The owner's search for money followed the flow of the textiles. When local funds were exhausted or insufficient for their needs, New England owners, most of them in the northern parts of the region, went downstream to Boston, or even farther to budding banks and a stock market in New York City. Robert Mackay knew this. When in New York City, he stayed at the Tontine Coffee House, an elegant, exclusive Wall Street establishment founded by a group of stockbrokers in 1793 as a place to meet over trade—trade in commodities such as sugar, cotton, and tobacco, but also in enslaved human beings.[18]

Sitting on her porch, with a child in her lap, Josephine Bristow could not know this: that her sore, aching fingers, hands, and back, and the labor of the "Old time people," built towns like Manchester, New Hampshire, and Lowell, Massachusetts, and Biddeford, Maine; an entire New England textile industry and other essential and supportive industries like shipping and merchandizing; and a banking and financial services industry that greased the gears of this vast trading empire. She did not know that without the cotton which she and the "Old time people" picked, it's questionable whether those towns would have come into existence, those mills would have been built, and those banking and financial institutions created. Josephine spoke for a generation of "Old time people" whose lives and labor built White power and wealth.

I CAN'T BREATHE

I watched police officer Derek Chauvin choking the life from George Floyd as he lay facedown gasping, "I can't breathe," and I thought, I've heard this before; I've seen this before, too. Not in the similar tragedies from police choking to death Eric Garner or Anton Black or Javier Ambler or Derrick Scott or Manuel Ellis or Byron Williams. Not in the stories of how police forces emerged from "slave patrols," as they did. Not in the callous disregard for Black lives enacted in the laws of colonial America. Nor even in the brutality against Black men and women enshrined in the US Constitution and unleashed on city streets almost daily today.

But I had seen this before. I had heard this before. And then I remembered where: the Bible.

In the Old Testament, Joshua 10:24-25 says,

So it was, when they brought out those kings to Joshua, that Joshua called for all the men of Israel, and said to the captains of the men of war who went with him, "Come near, put your feet on the necks of these kings." And they drew near and put their feet on their necks.

Joshua said to them, "Do not be afraid; do not be discouraged. Be strong and courageous. This is what the Lord will do to all the enemies you are going to fight."

The five kings to which these two biblical verses make reference are the heathen kings of Canaan, purportedly arrayed in battle against the Israelites. Joshua, on the side of the Israelites, defeats these kings, and in a display of their preeminence and victory, commands his officers to place their feet on the kings' necks, as is God's desire they do.

Assyrian king Tiglath-Pileser III, in the eighth century BCE, may have been the inspiration for these verses, as a gypsum bas-relief, now in the British Museum, shows him with his foot on the neck of a defeated enemy, possibly an Egyptian warrior-king.[1]

"Canaanite kings" in these biblical verses refers to the tribes supposedly descended from Ham, and therefore descended from the "curse of Canaan" (known more widely as the "curse of Ham"), which conferred upon them servitude. Since Africans were considered descended from Ham and cursed by him, this curse was long viewed as a biblical justification for slavery.[2]

There is certainly a connection to be made between the Old Testament and English colonists enacting laws in colonial America justifying the use of extreme force against runaways and the creation of slave patrols leading to the establishment of police forces. But to fully appreciate this connection recognize that in the late sixteenth century, prior to the establishment of a permanent English settlement in Jamestown, Britain and the Iberians (Spain and Portugal) were locked in a bitter contest over Christianity, played out in the Americas with the help of the first-ever runaway African slaves, the Cimarrons.

Britain, surprisingly, viewed herself as a great liberator of the oppressed, in this case the native peoples of the Americas and African slaves, yes, African slaves, both forced by Spaniards into service their New World plantations and in their mines.[3] John Ponet, at one time the bishop of Winchester, a highly esteemed position within the Anglican Church, used the Bible as the basis of prolonged, complex arguments against the divine right of kings, citing, among many examples, the Canaanite prince Eglon, who is, most likely, one of the kings referenced in the verses from Joshua above.[4] In the sixteenth century, Englishmen saw their struggles against Spain and a Spanish pope in these biblical terms, and they saw anyone aligned against the Spanish as an ally and a friend.[5]

Throughout the sixteenth century, Spanish colonies in the New World purchased African slaves, many from Angola, brought to them by the Portuguese, to work their tobacco and sugar plantations and their mines. From Cuba to Chile, slaves rebelled and ran away. One group of runaway slaves fought their way to freedom then settled as an outlawed community of some three thousand near the city of Nombre de Dios, in Panama, and the surrounding inhospitable mountains. The Spanish called them the Cimarrons, from the Spanish word *cimarrón*, meaning "wild" or "untamed," from which also comes the English word *maroon*, meaning a fugitive Black slave.[6] Another suggested derivation of Cimarrons comes from the indigenous Taino word *si'maran*, meaning "the flight of an arrow."[7]

Throughout the 1500s, the Spanish worried that runaway slaves, perhaps in combination with enslaved Indians or other mixed-raced individuals, would rise up against them, threatening Spain's hold on her colonies. In 1573, those fears were confirmed. Sir Francis Drake, the Sea Dog, on a plundering trip to the Spanish Main (the waters surrounding Spanish colonies in Mexico, the Caribbean, Central and northern South America), combined forces with the Cimarrons to intercept a land caravan carrying silver and gold from Peru through the Isthmus of Panama. Four years later, Drake's lieutenant, John Oxenham, returned from England to Panama to join forces with the Cimarrons to pillage Spanish encampments along the South American west coast.

Drake referred to the Cimarron as "certaine valiant Negros fled from their cruel masters the Spaniards."[8] Spain's reaction was further legislation throughout her colonies, begun as early as 1571, known as *Ordenanzas para los Negros* (Black Codes)[9] that specified harsh penalties: hanging for returned slaves who'd run away to join with the Cimarrons, and similar brutal sentences for Indians or Spaniards who helped such slaves escape. The *ordenanzas* ("codes") were enforced by the Spanish military, and local militias like the *ran-cheadores* in Cuba, expert slave hunters who were paid for each slave captured and returned.[10] Three hundred years before Jim Crow, two hundred years before the US Constitution, Europeans, especially in New Spain, had in-place patrols to search for, and intercept, African slaves seeking freedom, and the accompanying penalties. The roots of police brutality run deeper than American slavery.

Englishmen like Drake played a surprising role. England hated Spain, and the oppression of a Catholic pope. Ponet's polemic against the divine right of kings was as much about the Spanish monarchs, descended from God and blessed by the pope, as it was about the English Crown. Anyone ready to rebel against the Spanish was a friend. When it came to Cimarrons, Spain was well aware "this league between the English and the Negroes is very detrimental to this kingdom, because, being so thoroughly acquainted with the region and so expert in the bush, the Negroes will show them methods and means to accomplish any evil design they may wish to carry out."[11]

But Drake and other Sea Dogs were also captains of the English slave trade, begun through their piracy and looting of African slaves from Portuguese vessels, whom they then sold to Spanish colonies in the New World before the English had established colonies of their own.[12] On one hand, Britain claimed to be liberators of Africans enslaved by Spain, while on the other hand, Britain assisted in providing Africans to be enslaved by Spain.

Slavery in the midst of freedom? What an English, and truly American, contradiction that did not start with Jefferson's opening words in the Declaration of Independence but at least two hundred years earlier; a contradiction that held to protect freedom, protect slavery; to protect slavery, protect freedom. The Cimarrons, and this fundamental contradiction, were not far from the minds of the English as they established a colony at Jamestown.

English colonization, in general, and Jamestown, in particular, was built on ideas inherited from the alliance of Drake and the Cimarrons. Such a preposterous idea is worth repeating: Sir Francis Drake's alliance with a community of liberated African slaves in Panama laid the foundation for the colonial exploits of the British Empire, specifically the colonial settlement of America.

Richard Hakluyt, adviser to the royal court and to Drake, authored a highly influential manuscript in 1560, *The Principal Navigations*, which not only described the major navigations of early English explorers, like Drake and Sir Walter Raleigh, but also delved into the mythic exploits of King Arthur and the Chaucerian knightly tales to claim Britain's manifest destiny to rule the seas, and the world.[13]

Spain stood in the way of Britain conquering the world. So, Britain, according to Hakluyt, writing in 1580, needed to establish colonies where it would be most advantageous to challenge the Spanish. The Straits of Magellan, that interisland route from the Atlantic to the Pacific at the southern part of South America that avoided Cape Horn, was Hakluyt's first choice.[14]

With whom should Britain populate this colony? Liberated African slaves. "For the Symerones," said Hakluyt, "a people detesting the prowde governance of the Spanyards, will easely be transported by Drake or others of our nation to the Straights, and there may be planted by hundreds or thowsands, how many as we shal require." Here, observed Hakluyt, the Cimarrons would "easily be induced to live subject to the gentle government of the English and to be planted there for the defense of the Straights." Whom else? "To these Symerons we may add condemned Englise men and women, in whom there may be founde hope of amendement." By "condemned Englise men and women,"[15] Hakluyt meant not only those convicted of crimes, but the wretched and poor of English society, whose ranks were growing steadily by the late sixteenth and early seventeenth centuries.

Cimarrons and "condemned Englise men and women" would find freedom from the tyranny of Spanish rule and Catholicism, through the "gentle government of the English," and the Christianity of the Anglican Church.

Spain had essentially ceded most of the lands north of Florida to the English, Dutch, and French. As talk of New World glory reached a crescendo in the English royal court, and the Virginia Company was founded in 1606, Richard Hakluyt was brought in as a consultant. There were no Cimarrons in North America, but there were Indians. So, Hakluyt advised,

> Nothing is more to be indevoured with the Inland people then familiaritie. For so may you best discover al the naturall commodities of their countrey, and also all their wantes, all their strengthes, all their weaknesse, and with whom they are in warre, and with whom confiderate in peace and amitie, &c. which knowen, you may woorke many great effectes of greatest consequence.[16]

For early English colonization efforts, race was not as important as power. Aligning with the "good" local population, who would be grateful for the help of the English, and their God, in fighting the "bad" local population, was the route to that colonial power. Find the "good" Indians, and with them fight the "bad" Indians. Bring in poorer Englishmen (Hakluyt's "condemned Englise men and women") to fill out the colonists' ranks. All of this controlled, of course, by the directors and investors of the Virginia Company.

Only it didn't turn out that way. Lower-class Englishmen, and a precious few women, did come to Virginia. Half-hearted attempts at good relations with local tribes were sought. But after Opechancanough's raid of Jamestown in March 1622, all Indians were "bad." In early colonial Virginia, the English prided themselves on being "free men," when, in reality, they knew little about situating new settlements in the most advantageous places, relying almost exclusively on local Indian tribes for food, and frequently decimated the very tribes that had given them much-needed assistance.

Native Americans, who lived in a sustainable relationship with the land and the environment, had more leisure time, and by objective measures more freedom, than the English. Yet, an Englishman running away to local tribes risked capital punishment found in Dale's Code—"Paine of death" by the most brutal means as described earlier.[17] So, even the English poor, at the lowest rungs of colonial society though considered redeemable through harsh work for the English gentry, were now also on the "bad" side of the colonial ledger, along with those "bad" Indians. By the 1670s, as outright slavery eclipsed indentured servitude, Africans imported into Virginia as slaves were injected into the lowest rungs of colonial society, and, of course, were on the "bad" side of this ledger as well.

Colonial Virginia was a society where freedom was predicated on the existence of bondage. The planter aristocracy could claim they were "free," precisely because there were others they had exterminated or enslaved, and even the poorest White farmer or planter could claim being "free" by comparing his fate to that of the enslaved Africans around him. But bondage was also predicated on the existence of freedom. The planter aristocracy had the freedom to exterminate Indians, enslave Africans, and entrap poor English out of fear. Should these downtrodden rise up to claim their freedom, let alone join together in this claim, the freedom enjoyed by the planter aristocracy would be demolished by those in bondage seeking freedom of their own.

In this environment, a servant or slave running away was far more than just a crime, it was an affront to a well-established social order. We have already described how, after Bacon's Rebellion in 1676, the planter aristocracy of colonial Virginia enacted laws prohibiting English running away with Africans, punished Africans running away with English more severely than their English comrades, and provided English impunity for killing Africans in the process of attempting to recapture them.[18]

Well into the Revolutionary War, Dunmore's Proclamation, as

noted earlier, offered freedom to slaves who would leave their masters and join with British forces. As many as two thousand slaves may have directly reached Lord Dunmore in this way. By 1776, British general Sir Henry Clinton had a policy of offering freedom to slaves crossing over to British lines, officially issued in 1779 as the Philipsburg Proclamation. As many as 100,000 slaves in total may have attempted to secure their freedom by becoming Black Loyalists, though many died of disease once they did.[19]

On December 14, 1775, an outraged Virginia Convention, having replaced the colonial General Assembly, issued a counter-proclamation, declaring "that all negro or other slaves, conspiring to rebel or make insurrection, shall suffer death, and be excluded all benefit of clergy" (i.e., these runaways could not avoid the death sentence if tried) and ordering their surrender to any commander of revolutionary troops. While not as extensive as the *Ordenanzas para los Negros* of the Spanish in South America, this proclamation is the first instance of an American legislative body, as opposed to a colonial legislative body, sanctioning the use of extreme force against fugitive slaves seeking freedom.

It should come as no surprise, then, that a new nation, which led the way in freedom, also led the way in bondage. As previously noted, the Fugitive Slave Clause found its way into the US Constitution as Article IV, Section 2, Paragraph 3: "No person held to service or labour in one state, under the laws thereof, escaping into another, shall, in consequence of any law or regulation therein, be discharged from such service or labor, but shall be delivered up on claim of the party to whom such service or labour may be due."

As usual, there was no reference to slaves or slavery in the clause, but there was also no mistake about its intent. The first order of business on August 28, 1787, was the Privileges and Immunities Clause of the Constitution, guaranteeing citizens of each state the privileges and immunities of citizens of any other state. Cotton planter Charles Cotesworth Pinckney, one of the delegates from South Carolina, raised an objection that the clause might prevent a slave owner from traveling with his slave from one state to another state that had already outlawed slavery. Many states already had exemptions for slaves transported as property, so Pinckney's weak objections were easily overcome, and the Convention moved on to the Fugitive Slave Clause. Here, Pinckney, and Pierce Butler, the other South Carolina delegate, would not be stymied. They proposed that in the US Constitution fugitive slaves should be "delivered up like criminals." A brief, tepid challenge was mounted by Roger Sherman of Connecticut, and James Wilson of Pennsylvania, before the Constitutional Convention caved to the south, once again.[20]

A ruling in an English court set a precedent for this constitutional clause. James Somerset was born in West Africa, then captured and brought to Virginia in 1749, where he was purchased by Charles Stewart. Stewart, then relocated to Massachusetts, stationed there as a colonial customs officer, then traveled back to England on business in 1769, taking James Somerset with him. Somerset fled from his master in England. Stewart later recaptured Somerset, then consigned him to Captain John Knowles, master of the *Ann & Mary*, for sale in Jamaica.

Prior to his departure, Somerset was baptized, and in 1772 his godparents petitioned the Court of King's Bench, comparably Britain's supreme court, to hear Somerset's plea challenging his imprisonment by Stewart and his imminent removal from England. The court agreed. The stakes were high, involving not only Somerset but famed British abolitionist Granville Sharp. The attorneys on both sides were some of the most prominent British legal minds of the time. The arguments were intricate. The case was heard before Chief Justice William Murray, the 1st Earl of Mansfield.[21]

Somerset argued that colonial laws might allow slavery, but no English laws did. Stewart countered that slaves were property, that property was paramount under English common law, and that a dangerous precedent would be set if all Blacks in England, approximately fifteen thousand at the time, were released.[22] After hearing arguments, Mansfield delayed his decision for a year, freeing Somerset on his own recognizance.[23]

Somerset v. Stewart drew international attention, and a global public anxiously awaited Mansfield's ruling. Mansfield, a conservative jurist, first ruled that the contract for sale of a slave was valid in England, which appeared to tip the scales in Stewart's favor. This allowed Mansfield to reduce the issue before him to the question of whether a slave under American law could be coerced (forced imprisonment) under British law. Mansfield ruled that where a slave was held did not force a determination of the slave's status in England—in other words, just because Somerset was a slave in America did not necessarily mean he was a slave in England. Then Mansfield dropped a bombshell:

> The state of slavery is of such a nature, that it is incapable of now being introduced by Courts of Justice upon mere reasoning or inferences from any principles, natural or political . . . in a case so odious . . . no master ever was allowed here to take a slave by force to be sold abroad because he had deserted from his service, or for any other reason whatever; we cannot say the cause set forth . . . is allowed or approved of by the laws of this kingdom, *therefore the black must be discharged.*[24]

Sixteen years later, and an ocean away in Philadelphia, *Somerset v. Stewart* still sent shivers through the south. Pinckney and Butler wanted the right to have slaves, and travel with them, enshrined in the US Constitution. The Privileges and Immunities Clause would place a slaveholder, and his slaves, under the authority of any state they traveled to. If that state did not recognize slavery, that slaveholder's slaves might be declared free. Pinckney and Butler got their way with the Fugitive Slave Clause. Even though the Thirteenth Amendment, ratified in 1865, abolished slavery, it did not render the entire Fugitive Slave Clause moot. The clause has never been repealed, or specifically amended, and so stands as a reminder of the Founders' commitment to slavery and to the south.[25]

Furthermore, the Fugitive Slave Clause served as legal justification both for slave patrols, which attempted to prevent slaves from leaving their masters, and for "slave hunters," who sought to track down runaway slaves and return them. To the Second Amendment (the right to bear arms) add the Fugitive Slave Clause (the requirement to return runaways) and there came into being a number of enterprising vigilantes who went to work for slaveholders, and became the progenitors of modern-day police forces.

Then again, even the Second Amendment is intimately linked to slavery and slave patrols. Patrick Henry, a Virginia slaveholder, opposed ratification of the US Constitution because he believed, among other deficiencies, the Constitution gave the federal government the right to control state militias. This, Henry was afraid, would allow the federal government to control the use of slave patrols by southern states. In debate with James Madison over whether Virginia should ratify the Constitution, Henry said, "If the country be invaded, a state may go to war, but cannot suppress insurrection. If there should happen an insurrection of slaves, the country cannot be said to be invaded. They cannot, therefore, suppress it without the interposition of Congress."[26]

Ultimately, Madison won the debate but Henry and other slaveholding Founders exacted their revenge, through language in the Bill of Rights that guaranteed southern control over slave patrols, or the polite word of the Bill of Rights, *militias*: "A well-regulated Militia, being necessary to the security of a free State, the right of the people to keep and bear Arms, shall not be infringed."[27]

Slaves could definitely not be part of southern militias. Free Blacks sometimes could, but only as unarmed drummers or buglers. To the south, the phrase "well-regulated Militia" was a dog whistle for "slave patrols." It's popular to point to North Carolina, in 1704, as having the first organized slave patrol, but it may also be misleading.[28] As noted in previous chapters, the system that ultimately became slavery in the US was first enacted and perfected on White colonists in Virginia. In fact, the Virginia Company used paramilitary force as early as 1612 to enforce a broad set of martial laws, which colonists lived under; Dale's Code, as described above, reserved the harshest penalties for runaways.

In both the previously cited 1640 cases of John Punch, Barack Obama's ancestor, who ran away with a group of servants, and Emanuel, who also ran away with a group of servants, court records indicate the runaways were "Brought back."[29] It is possible that the slave owners in each case, by themselves, went after the runaways to bring them back. More likely is that the slave owners either hired others to bring the runaways back, or they asked the local sheriff or marshal of the county court to search for and return the fugitives, which meant organizing a group of local citizens, a militia, for that purpose.

"An act for the apprehension and suppression of runawayes, negroes and slaves," passed in September 1672 by the Virginia Assembly, and cited in full previously,[30] most clearly demonstrates the official sanctioning of paramilitary slave patrols by colonial authorities. The term "slave patrol" is not mentioned anywhere in the act, but the phrase "hugh and crye" is found throughout. "Hue and cry" derives from English common law, where it is found in the Statute of Winchester of 1285, which requires that either sheriffs, or private citizens, witnessing a crime raise and sustain a "hue and cry" while chasing an alleged criminal from town to town until that person is apprehended.[31]

"Hue and cry" implies the Statute of Winchester of 1285 was in effect, or at least acknowledged, by the Virginia Assembly as the basis of colonial-era law enforcement of runaway slaves. After all, Virginia in 1672 was a British colony, where English common law applied. The Statute of Winchester of 1285, originally written in French under the reign of Edward I, created a "watch and ward" system manned by armed citizens between the ages of fifteen and sixty.

And the king commandeth . . . in every city by six men at every gate; in every borough, by twelve men; in every town, by six or four, according to the number of inhabitants of the town, and they shall keep the watch continually all night from the sun-setting unto the sun-rising. And if any stranger do pass by them he shall be arrested until morning; and if no suspicion be found he shall go quit; and if they find cause of suspicion, they shall forthwith deliver him to the sheriff.[32]

If the suspected criminal did not stop, the statute required those in pursuit to raise a "hue and cry" until he was caught. And the statute also assigned collective punishment for a crime: "the people in the country, shall be answerable for felonies and robberies done among them."[33]

Modern policing textbooks considered this statute a milestone in the history of policing. The Statute of Winchester of 1285 remained in effect, essentially unchanged, in England for six hundred years, and fundamentally shaped criminal justice and law enforcement in the American colonies, and the United States.[34]

Jonathon A. Cooper, assistant professor of criminology and criminal justice at Indiana University of Pennsylvania, observes "the Statute [of Winchester] set up a system of justice administration that would cross the Atlantic and form the basic framework of American colonial and post-colonial policing."[35]

By applying key elements of the statute to the pursuit and apprehension of runaway slaves, the Virginia Assembly in 1672 tied the development of American policing directly to slavery. Colonial need for the unpaid labor of Black slaves helped shape and define American law enforcement for centuries to come. Slave patrols that later came into existence in the eighteenth and nineteenth centuries; police forces that emerged from these patrols in the nineteenth and twentieth centuries; and the excessive use of force against individuals and communities of color by police with impunity, throughout the history of America—all can trace their origins to this medieval statute.

Slave patrols in colonies south of Virginia, such as South Carolina, can also trace roots to Spanish law influenced by the long-term use of slaves in Spanish colonies. From 1566 to 1587, Santa Elena, now Parris Island, South Carolina, was the capital of La Florida, Spanish Florida. By 1571, the Cimarrons and other rebellious slaves had precipitated Black Codes (*Ordenanzas para los Negros*) throughout New Spain, from South America to the Caribbean Islands. Spanish and Portuguese colonizers "used a combination of former slaves, paid slave catchers, and the militia as apprehenders, all of them forerunners of patrols."[36] South Carolina attempted to use Native Americans to hunt fugitive slaves but that backfired because colonists wanted to sell those same Indians into slavery.

Town bells announced curfew, slaves carried passes or wore identification buttons, and patrollers were required to work after dark, during church, or over holidays, those times when White slaveholders perceived the greatest risk. Slave patrols enforced the criminalization of being Black. Even meager slave cabins were not safe. Patrols had the right of "no knock" entry to search for weapons and contraband, or to rape slave women. Free Blacks were forced to pay taxes for patrols. Prisons, called "cages," were built to house slaves apprehended by patrollers. From the colonial era until the Civil War, slave patrols protected White wealth accumulated through Black labor—the very labor that made possible that wealth. They were never intended, nor did they ever operate, to guard the safety of Blacks.[37]

Participation in slave patrols was, at first, compulsory, frequently without pay but with fines levied for noncompliance. White men were required to report for regular service and training. Some colonies, like South Carolina, even required female slaveholders to provide a male substitute for their patrol service. But after the Revolutionary Way, membership in slave patrols was often considered beneath the dignity of the wealthy, who were ready to pay for someone else to protect their wealth.[38]

After the Revolutionary War, American society was changing.

Plantations grew, slave populations exploded, little towns became large cities. Some slaves even lived off of plantations in urban areas at night, commuting by foot to fields and plantation houses each day. All of this meant more Blacks in motion and more churning angst for Whites. The "night watch" of the country became the "neighborhood watch" of the city. Voluntary participation of White residents was not enough. Town councils sought permanent patrols, petitioning state legislatures for the necessary funds. When overburdened legislatures refused, towns turned creative. One township might attempt to annex another, preventing jurisdictional disputes between slave patrols, and spreading the burden for paying patrols over a larger tax base. As patrols in urban areas grew, and patrols, in general, were becoming less private and more public, they were beginning to be called "police," and their members took oaths, often administered by justices of the peace: "I, [patroller's name], do swear, that I will as searcher for guns, swords and other weapons among the slaves in my district, faithfully, and as privately as I can, discharge the trust reposed in me as the law directs, to the best of my power. So help me, God."[39]

Taking an oath like this made the slave patroller a "sworn officer" and that's a huge, significant distinction in law enforcement and judicial circles. Sworn officers have a greater degree of public trust than non-sworn officers; in the performance of their duties, sworn officers are allowed to carry firearms, make arrests, be shielded from certain forms of prosecution, and wear or carry a badge attesting to this superior status.

The advent of civil war only heightened southern Whites' fear of slave revolts and insurrections, now they were fighting a battle to preserve slavery on two fronts: externally, against the north, and internally, against the Black men and women they had so long held in bondage. From ages eighteen to thirty-five, as war conscripted men for the front lines, slave patrols were depleted, leaving southern Whites even more jittery of reprisals from slaves. Many called for buttressing slave patrols in any way possible. Boys too young for war, and men too old, were recruited into the patrols. Injured soldiers returned from battle to join the ranks of the slave patrols. As White plantation owners left their slaves to fight, vigilante groups took over from patrols to keep those slaves in their place. Owners that stayed sought exemptions for their overseers, now needed not only for the harvesting and planting but for the depleted ranks of the patrols.[40]

Then, on January 1, 1863, Lincoln signed the Emancipation Proclamation, and with it unleashed the south's worst nightmare: slaves would be set free. At the time of the Emancipation, North Carolina had in place a twenty-slave exemption—own twenty or more slaves, and you were exempt from reporting to the Confederate Army. This way slaveholders remained home to protect their property and their wealth. Archibald Arrington, running for reelection to the North Carolina Congress, regretted he'd voted for the law: "At the time I thought it absolutely necessary for our safety, and more especially for the safety of the families of our soldiers, that the most vigilant and efficient police should be kept over our slaves."[41]

Some panicked owners, off to war, hired their own private patrollers. And many slaves, without owners present to protect their property, fared worse under the brutal reign of unrestrained private patrollers. In more urban areas, such as Richmond and Charleston, the depletion of slave patrols meant that more and more of their responsibilities were handed over to local police forces. Toward the end of the war, the south forced conscription of all White men between seventeen and fifty, which decimated the ranks of the slave patrols. Now, with Union troops advancing throughout the south, Confederate soldiers were on double duty, fighting against northern soldiers and patrolling against southern slaves crossing over to Union lines. Southern towns, on the verge of being overrun by northern troops, decreed that every able-bodied resident defend the town, and keep the peace, as slave patrols, police, and home guard duties were fused.[42]

Many slaves did cross over to the Union, bringing plantations to a grinding halt and swelling urban areas, and Union camps, with freed Black men and women. With the war over, a new normal set in, in the south, and reinvigorated and revamped slave patrols soon rose again. Slavery may have ended in name, but the policing of Blacks by Whites had not. Sometimes, Union commanders furnished men to work with local patrols. At other times, the presence of so many newly freed men and women in urban centers overwhelmed the ability of Union commanders. Richmond, for example, went from twelve thousand slaves in 1860 to thirty thousand free men and women in 1865.[43]

Taking a playbook from the old south, the post-war federal government then reimplemented a pass system. Although Whites were also required to carry a pass, the system disproportionately affected Blacks. Blacks, whether free for generations or newly freed, were required to have passes available only from Whites. Union forces often gave the job of enforcing this pass system to local police forces, or helped them, which meant Blacks experienced little difference between the new pass system and the old.[44]

Still, even in this climate of renewed White fear, Black citizens of the south had a brief window of hope. Even before the Civil War's end, northern control of some southern cities, like Portsmouth, Virginia, in 1861, brought the first-ever Black policemen, chief of police, and justice of the peace. That ended abruptly in 1866, when elections returned the city to all-White law enforcement.[45]

Admitting defeat, southern states passed laws ending slavery. But that only meant they then doubled down on ways to subjugate Blacks. New Black Codes, and anti-vagrancy laws, were enacted, along the lines of a *Lynchburg Virginian* editorial, which suggested that,

The most stringent police regulations may be necessary to keep [freedmen] from overburdening the towns and depleting the agricultural regions of labor . . . The magistrates and municipal officers everywhere should be permitted to hold a rod *in terrorem* over these wandering, idle, creatures. Nothing short of the most efficient police system will prevent strolling, vagrancy, theft, and the utter destruction of or serious injury to our industrial system.[46]

In terrorem is a Latin term, meaning a threat issued to compel a party to act without resorting to a lawsuit, or to criminal prosecution. Basically, *in terrorem* is rule by fear, or rule by terror. And by the late 1870s, as Union troops left the south, such rule by terror emerged as the de facto norm for policing. During the day, White men in police uniforms enforced draconian anti-vagrancy laws and Black Codes. At night, or sometimes brazenly during the day, many of those same men donned white robes and white hoods, or simply attacked Black communities in their official capacity as police, exacting retribution from Black men and women, whose very existence and freedom affronted the social order these police were sworn to protect.

Slaves called them patrollers, patty rollers, or paddy rollers,[47] long before the racist association between the Irish and "paddy wagons" found its way into the lexicon of law enforcement. The "beat," originally a term used to describe how slave patrols in South Carolina organized themselves, is now a common phrase to describe the geographic area supervised by a single police officer. And, even the notion that a police force "patrols" has been handed down from the era of slave "patrols."[48]

Tactics, not just language, bind slave patrols to modern-day policing. Slave patrols used systematic surveillance methods to monitor a specific population—a tactic carried over to stakeouts, informants, drones, and facial recognition technology in modern times. Slave patrols immunized their members from prosecution for excessive use of force against people of color, much as police have been similarly immunized from prosecution in recent times. "Excessive use of force," "racial profiling," "no knock" searches, "stop and frisk" policing, differential enforcement of the law—these are just some of the ways that modern policing practices echo the problematic racist practices of the past.

• • •

Black lives and labor shaped American policing. But as demands for changes in American policing grow stronger, the question remains whether American policing can be reformed. Prior to writing this chapter, I would have answered, unequivocally, yes! After finishing this chapter I'm much less certain or sanguine.

For a number of weeks in the spring and summer of 2020, protestors marched in the streets of cities, large and small, around the world in the wake of George Floyd's death at the hands of White Minneapolis police officers. The protestors called for sweeping changes to policing, under the banner of "Defund the Police." It's a slogan which strikes fear in many, similar to the fear that gave rise to slave patrols in the past. But for communities and individuals of color, modern-day policing has failed, and short of rethinking how to keep communities safe, it's doubtful that policing, as we know it, can ever be reformed.

Many police forces have been operating under consent decrees from federal courts for decades, put in place to stop practices such as excessive use of force and racial profiling. Clearly, those consent decrees and the reforms that came with them have not worked. Police officers continue to use excessive force, and Black people continue to die as a result. Weeding out so-called "bad apples" and bringing in more people of color as police officers seem like reasonable policies. Yet we now learn that a 2006 FBI report showed White supremacist groups recommending their members join police forces.[49] Getting police out of schools, demilitarizing the police, training police forces in de-escalation not confrontation, sending mental health professionals rather than police on many emergency calls, all seem like rational policies.

Yet, in looking back over the long history of policing and law enforcement, one cannot help being struck how a seven-hundred-year-old system has survived as the basis for policing in the modern era. Would this be accepted in any other realm? Can you imagine if our communication technology had not evolved over seven hundred years? We would have no internet, no computers, no cell phones, no satellite communications. We would be stuck in the Middle Ages, which is where policing is stuck now. To be sure, police forces have modernized through technology. Computers predict. Drones surveil. Military weapons are employed. But the underlying basis of policing remains little changed from the "hue and cry" of the Statute of Winchester of 1285, only that "hue and cry" is now delivered through a 911 call, and augmented by the arrival of a SWAT team.

All sworn officers take an oath that usually makes reference to them supporting the US Constitution, and upholding its laws. Herein lies both the problem and the path toward change. The Constitution was built on the Founders' appeasement of the slave-holding south. It is an inherently racist document. To swear to uphold the Constitution is to swear to uphold that racism. A reckoning is needed with the past.

Statutes as well as statues must be toppled. The racism inherent in the Constitution must be addressed, and it must be eliminated. Only then will reenvisioning American policing truly be possible. Short of that, reforms may be proposed and they may be implemented but they will never correct the underlying problems that give rise to police violence against communities of color. There are three constitutional issues prerequisite for wide-scale reimagining of public safety:

1. **Amend the Constitution by repealing the Fugitive Slave Clause.** Though an attempt at repeal was made shortly after the Emancipation Proclamation, it never succeeded. The clause remains in effect, and under some limited circumstances is still problematic, as a 1988 case in Kansas (*United States v.*

Kozminski) showed.[50] A preamble to the amendment should state its intention to correct the damage done by the original clause, which appeased the slaveholding south. This is probably the easiest step to take and it would also remove from the oath of a sworn officer this ugly reminder of policing's racist roots.

2. **Eliminate vestiges of the three-fifths clause.** From the election of local sheriffs to the election of the president of the United States, America needs to be a true, popular democracy. The only way to do this is to make the popular vote the basis for the election of the president and to eliminate the Electoral College, which is another holdover from the Founders' appeasement of the slaveholding south. As with the Fugitive Slave Clause, any legislation to address the three-fifths clause should begin with a preamble about the need to redress this clause's extremely racist past, and the benefit to popular democracy the legislation would confer. Eliminating the vestiges of the three-fifths clause will not be easy. Representation in the House of Representatives is dependent upon it; so, too, is electoral politics. But as long as the vestiges remain, especially the Electoral College, America will never be a popular democracy, only a representative one, and the will of the people will never be enforced. Sworn officers will be pledging to uphold a Constitution wrapped in the eighteenth-century racism of the Founders.

3. **Amend the Second Amendment.** By far, this will be the most challenging. Not even the brutal murder of children is enough to pry Americans away from their love affair with guns, or their erroneous belief that owning them is a God-ordained right. Gun manufacturers and the NRA have a stranglehold on politicians on both sides of the aisle. But, just like the Fugitive Slave Clause and the three-fifths clause, the Second Amendment is rooted in the racism of the northern Founders' appeasing of the slaveholding south. Southern delegates understood this

amendment as the north giving tacit approval to their slave patrols, the racist patrols that became the basis of policing. Furthermore, by taking military-grade weapons out of the hands of the public, everyone will be safer, and the need for police in schools would be removed. Short of amending the Second Amendment, every few months more Americans will needlessly die because lawmakers fail to muster the necessary will to prevent that from happening by strong gun control legislation.

Talk of police reform in America is no longer sufficient. An antiquated model of American policing based on seven-hundred-year-old ideas about "us" versus "them" should no longer stand. The history of this country demonstrates that Black lives, and Black labor, mattered only in creating a system of policing designed to suppress those lives, and to control that labor. The continued deaths of Black men and women like George Floyd, Breonna Taylor, and Ahmaud Arbery at the hands of police call us to rethink and refashion policing and public safety so that not only do Black lives matter but those lives are protected as well.

Derek Chauvin's conviction for the murder of George Floyd did not, and will not, usher in a change in American policing, just as the election of Barak Obama did not usher in a change in racism or racial violence in America, even though some suggested Obama marked the beginning of a post-racial America. In fact, after Obama was elected, violent White racism increased in America. And, just a few miles down the road from the courthouse where Chauvin would be convicted just a few days later, police officer Kimberly Potter shot and killed an unarmed, young Black man, Daunte Wright, during a routine traffic stop.

Demilitarization, better training, greater accountability and transparency, civilian control of police, banning choke-holds and no-knock warrants. After George Floyd's death, legislatures around the country sought to institute police reforms. But these reforms are mere tinkering in an effort to solve the more pervasive problem of American policing. They remind me of the first century Greek astronomer, Ptolemy, trying to account for the aberrant motions of the planets.

Ptolemy, like most others of the day, believed the Earth was the center of the solar system, around which the Sun and the other planets orbited. When he observed the planets moving with wildly irregular orbits, he called the orbits "epicycles," and went about proving the existence of these fictitious planetary motions. Science believed in a geocentric solar system. Society believed in a geocentric solar system. And the Catholic Church founded its core beliefs on a geocentric solar system. Epicycles made merely modest alterations to this prevailing dogma without overthrowing it.

Legislation to reform policing is evidence not of progress but of resistance to confronting the foundational issues of American policing; tinkering with the current system and hoping everything will still work. But tinkering didn't work for Ptolemy, and it won't work for American policing.

Ultimately, in the sixteenth century, Copernicus proposed a radical new heliocentric theory that the Earth and the planets revolved around the Sun. We need a Copernican revolution in public safety—one that would redefine the foundations of modern policing as Copernicus redefined the foundations of modern astronomy; a Copernican revolution that would reestablish American policing on a foundation far removed from the outdated Statute of Winchester of 1285, and even the ideas proposed in the US Constitution.

The Statute of Winchester of 1285 separated society into "us" versus "them," with police forces empowered to protect the "us" from the "them." In thirteenth-century England, the "us" were inhabitants of English towns and villages. The "them" were people out after dark, whether or not they were criminals. In colonial America, the "us" were slaveholders, the "them" were slaves, hence the passing of laws like the act of 1672 in Virginia, granting any White person immunity from killing or wounding a runaway slave. After slavery, the "us" became White Americans and the "them" became

Black Americans. Police formed the backbone of the Ku Klux Klan and the violence wrought against Black people in the Jim Crow era of post–Civil War America.

Police are a key aspect of maintaining social hierarchy and order, especially between Blacks and Whites in America. But as cities grew in nineteenth- and twentieth-century America, police even enforced the social order among Whites.

Harvard historian Khalil Gibran Muhammad observes, "The Anglo-Saxons are policing the Irish. The Irish are policing the Poles. And so this dynamic that's playing out is that police officers are a critical feature of establishing a racial hierarchy, even among white people."[51]

But eventually the Irish and the Poles were assimilated into White American society to become part of the dominant "us," leaving marginalized groups such as Blacks, Asians, Native Americans, and Latinos to remain forever "them."

Shortly after George Floyd's murder, Betsy Hodges, a former mayor of Minneapolis, the city where Floyd was killed by police, issued a broad indictment, not of the police but of the society from which the police emerge. Even those who consider themselves progressives were ultimately part of the problem, Hodges opined.

"Whether we know it or not, white liberal people in blue cities implicitly ask police officers to politely stand guard in predominantly white parts of town (where the downside of bad policing is usually inconvenience) and to aggressively patrol the parts of town where people of color live—where the consequences of bad policing are fear, violent abuse, mass incarceration and, far too often, death. Underlying these requests are the flawed beliefs that aggressive patrolling of Black communities provides a wall of protection around white people and their property."[52]

Police, Hodges is saying, are meant to protect White power and wealth.

With the police, politicians, and the public, including those who would otherwise consider themselves progressive, arrayed against fundamental changes in policing the prospects for meaningful change in American policing are not good.

"I'm always such a pessimist with police reform," says Yanilda González, assistant professor of public policy at the Harvard Kennedy School, "we have to distinguish what works with what can last, what can actually endure without coming under the typical strain of police resistance and politicians' incentives to undermine police reform."[53]

Still, those advocating for a change in policing should not stop. It took a century, the work of Galileo, Newton, and others, and the acquiescence of the Catholic Church to overturn deeply entrenched social and religious beliefs allowing Copernicus's heliocentric solar system to be accepted as the foundation of modern astronomy. So, too, it will take overturning deeply entrenched social and political beliefs, and perhaps a century as well, to bring about widespread acceptance of a new foundation for modern American policing.[54]

BEFORE THE MAST

A dusting of snow overnight reflected the light, making it appear much brighter than it should have been this early in the morning. My breath frosted the metal oil lamp I carried. A small flame flickered in my hand. I didn't really need it to see. But the warmth felt good. I crept from my cold room off the kitchen toward the roar of the reading room fireplace. Underneath me a floorboard creaked.

"Briton?"

I stopped. Sucked in a breath.

"Briton, that you?"

"Why, yessir, Master Winslow. It's me."

"Come in here. Come. And be smart about it."

I finally exhaled.

In the darkness of the reading room, gold leaf titles glittered orange on book spines. A chandelier in the center seemed to sway back and forth in the heat, tiny fire rainbows leaping from the cut glass. Had I not known Master Winslow was sitting in his high back chair, reading, I would have thought the room empty, since the chair hid him from view. His disembodied voice called out.

"Briton, do you know what day this is?"

"December, sir, the twenty-fifth day of December. Baby Jesus's birthday, sir."

Master Winslow's arm shot out. He tapped the seat to his right. "Briton. Here." He tapped the seat again. "Have a seat."

I started toward the front door. "But, sir, I'd just gotten up to fetch more wood for your fire."

"Nonsense, Briton. I've all the wood I need; besides, it's Christmas today, Briton, Christmas."

Master Winslow tapped the seat again. "Sit, Briton, you're a good Christian."

"I try, sir."

I set my oil lamp on the mantel above the fireplace, then took a brass snuffer to the flames. When I sat down, I looked over to Master Winslow. He had on no wig nor powder. But a ruffle-top blouse bound his neck tightly, and his cheeks, always too crimson for me, matched the color of the reading robe he wore. The hook of his nose pointed down to thin lips, and beneath them a double chin that ought to belong to a portly body instead of a thin one like his. He'd crossed one leg over the other. An unlit long-stem white pipe rested on the table to his other side. The gilded pages of his Bible lay open in his lap.

"It's Christmas, Briton. Just think of it. The miracle of it all. That Christ was born today. Soon to die. Then to be resurrected to new life again."

"A miracle, sir. Can that happen to anyone, sir? I mean dying and then being reborn."

"Briton, I do believe it can happen to anyone. Even to your kind. If you pray often, obey, and have faith, real faith in Jesus. Even to men of Ham's curse, like you."

"To Black men, sir?"

"Yes, Briton, to negroes."

"Sir, there's something I've been meaning to ask."

"You certainly picked a good day."

"Well, sir, I've an intention some time now. Intention to go a voyage to sea."

Master Winslow shut his Bible. He just stared into the flames.

"I mean, sir, of course, sir, I'd give you most of whatever I made. Nine out of every ten pence of my wages, sir, since I'm yours."

Master Winslow still said nothing. So, I thought it best if I joined him in silence. I just stared at the flames. Maybe I'd have the same vision as his. Maybe he was searching the flames for an answer. Maybe he was getting hotter in front of the fire, like I was. Maybe he'd get up, in a fit, grab one of the two swords hanging crisscross above the fireplace, and run me through. But I'd said it. I didn't know what would happen. But I'd said it and there was no taking it back now. Whatever Master Winslow did.

It seemed like hours but I supposed it was just minutes that passed, when Master Winslow stroked the side of his face with his fingers.

"Go a voyage to sea, eh, Briton?"

"Yessir."

"Ever been on the ocean?"

"No sir, but I know boats. Worked on them at Plymouth, during the cold months when nothing grows."

"Yes, you do know boats. I'll give you that. You'd make a fine addition to any crew. But do you think you'd like the sea?"

"Don't know, sir, but I think I'd like to find out."

Master Winslow picked up his Bible, thumbed through several pages. His head popped up; fire danced in his eyes.

"You know Jonah?"

I started singing the gospel, real low. "Oh, Jonah! Oh, Jonah! Go down to Nineveh, said the Lord—"

But Master cut me off.

"But Jonah didn't want to do the Lord's work, did he? So, he got on a ship to run away. There was a terrible storm and Jonah was thrown overboard. Swallowed by a great fish, he spent three days and three nights in its belly before that fish spit him out. And, finally, Jonah repented. He preached the gospel to the men of Nineveh, and they repented, too."

"It's like Jesus," I said.

"How so?"

"Well, sir, Jonah gettin' swallowed by that fish an' all is like Jesus getting nailed to the cross. Fish spitting him out's like Jesus being resurrected."

"You think of that yourself, Briton?"

"Yessir."

"I like that, Briton. I like that a lot. You ready to follow him, Briton?"

"Who, sir, Jesus?"

"No, Briton, Jonah."

"Don't know about that fish an' all, sir. But if my fish ain't nothing but a ship, then I'm ready to go a voyage to sea and have that ship spit me back out on land."

Master Winslow chuckled. He closed his Good Book, and took to staring at me. Just like he was staring at the fire. After a while he blinked. "Well, that settles it." He slapped his thigh. "Briton, a voyage to sea you shall go. *Good Fortune* is in Plymouth. You will ask for the sloop's master, John Howland. Known the Howland family for many years. She is bound for Jamaica. There to pick up a load of logwood, I hear. John tells me the mills need it for dye. But tomorrow, Briton, she's leaving tomorrow."

"Which means, sir, I must leave today."

I often walked into Plymouth, which only took me three or four hours. After departing from Master Winslow, I knew I was near to town when the road started downhill and I caught a glimpse of the vast ocean. As far as I could see, a dark blue line drawn on a light blue canvas. I stopped by the livery stable before heading to the harbor. There, I knocked on the stable-keep's door. David, a Black man, tall like me, opened the door.

"Your master that cruel?" David asked. "Send you to town for a couple of days on Christmas." He whistled low. Shook his head.

I shook mine back. "Ain't cruel at all. Gettin' born again this

Christmas, thanks to Master. Just like Jesus. I'm shipping out on *Good Fortune* and gettin' born again. Just like that baby was born on Christmas Day."

David smiled. "Must be what freedom's like," he said. "Like gettin' born again."

"Don't know. But I'll tell you all 'bout freedom when I return in a few months from Jamaica."

David and I hugged, then I grabbed my cloth satchel from the ground, slung it over my shoulder, and walked down the empty streets, heading toward the docks. Gulls cackled overhead. My breath left me like steam, then came back in cold, but smelling of salt air mixed with manure. Ahead of me only one ship showed any signs of life. Sailors rolled wooden barrels upon a gangplank where they slapped down hard on the ship's deck. *Good Fortune* was not long. Maybe forty feet would be my guess. A single tall mast rose from her center. Halyards fastened fore and aft had sails furled up around them.

As I approached the ship, a sharp voice cut through the chilled air. "That barrel goes below on the larboard. Damn you, Walters, I don't care if it is Christmas Day. Look lively, man, or you'll have no Christmas supper today and eat nothing but salt water. That's salted pork for the galley, not silk dresses for the girlies. Take it there, man, and be quick about you. We still have half the ship to load."

I figured the voice, and the burly man to whom it belonged, must be Captain John Howland. So, I walked toward him. He held a paper in one hand, blew his warm breath through the other, then alternated the hands he used for the paper and his breathing.

"Captain Howland," I said.

He looked up from his paper. His eyes ran the length of my body several times. "Not taking on any more loads, boy. No space in the holds." He turned back to his paper.

"Not here with a load, sir."

He grumbled, "Then what the hell you here for?"

"Reporting for ship's duty under your command, sir."

"Hell you are, boy. We got us a Black Jack aboard already, and that's already one too many."

"My master, John Winslow, said you were bound for Jamaica, and told me I should ask you to sign on as crew. That it'd be a personal favor to him."

"Well, did he say all that, now?"

"Yessir, he did."

"You get the hell outta here, boy."

He kicked me to the ground. My satchel flew from my hands, my clothes scattered on the hard earth. I looked up at a heavily bearded face, the snarl of yellowed teeth.

"And you don't come back to my ship ever again."

I scrambled to collect my clothes.

"Mr. Samuels," another voice boomed from the ship. "What's this commotion all about?"

The man in front of me snapped to attention.

"Sir, Captain, sir, this . . . this negro says he wants aboard as crew. And I told him we already got one Black Jack, and we ain't taking any more."

I looked over to a gentleman wearing white pants beneath a blue long-tailed coat, with a white blouse and silver buttons, and a matching three-point hat. He strolled the deck of the *Good Fortune* toward the gangway. The man in front of me bellowed.

"Captain coming ashore. Clear the gangway, you damned salty fools. Clear the gangway. Make way. Captain coming ashore."

Captain John Howland reminded me a lot of Master. Ruddy cheeks. A similar hooked nose and thin lips but no double chin. The captain, unlike Master, was shorter than me by a few inches. He strutted over to me, clasping one hand in the other behind his back. I stood up from gathering my clothes, stood at attention as I'd seen the others do. The captain wore gloves, and he jabbed me hard with an index finger to my chest.

"You want on board my ship?" He jabbed me in the chest again.

"Yessir."

"Like my first mate said, we already got our share of Black Jacks as crew."

"Yessir. I understand that, sir. But my master, John Winslow, said you might do him the great favor of having me ship aboard as crew to Jamaica."

"John Winslow?"

"Yessir."

"Your master?"

"Yessir."

"The John Winslow of Marshfield?"

"Yessir."

"Wants me to take you as crew to Jamaica?" His finger came at me again but I didn't flinch.

"Yessir."

"Hmmmm." Captain Howland paced around me. "Hmmmm."

Then he stopped walking in circles and walked over to the man he'd called Samuels.

"Mr. Samuels. You will show this . . . this . . ." The captain turned to me. "What's your name, boy?"

"Hammon, sir, Briton Hammon."

"You will show Hammon his berth."

"But, sir, we don't—"

The captain snapped, "That'll be all, Samuels. The Winslows are longtime friends of the Howlands. Not another word from you, Mr. Samuels. You will . . . show . . . Hammon . . . a berth."

Samuels growled, "Yessir."

I gathered the remainder of my clothes, and just like that I had the top bunk of a small wooden berth belowdecks in the fo'c'sle. No sooner had I thrown my satchel onto the berth, when Samuels was barking at me. I didn't dare smile.

"Hammon, damn you, man. Don't fancy Black Jacks. But if you're on my ship, you're under my orders. So, you help Walters load that next barrel."

We left Plymouth Harbor the day after Christmas. We were not long out to sea, when I first met the other Black Jack aboard. Moses Newmock, a man so light you'd almost swear he was White, hailed from Jamaica. He and I became fast friends. He'd been to sea for twenty years. He taught me all I needed to know about life before the mast—the ropes, and the sails, and the chores a sailor needed to do. And, once, when Little, and Doty, and Webb, and the other boys threatened me harm, Newmock grabbed a belaying pin, jumped 'tween me and the others, and said anyone touch me, they'd have to touch him first. That was the last I had of any trouble from the crew.

On the main, before the mast, brought me great comfort, even when in rough seas with waves taller than any tree I'd ever seen on land. Something about that motion made me sleep better, though it made some of the others vomit. When our quarters reeked badly, I'd stick my head out in the fresh air, careful not to let the captain or the watch officer see me. Looked like I could reach out and touch the stars. On calm nights, looking up at the heavens, I talked to my friend David, back in Plymouth. Talked to him about what it felt like being free.

I think we must have been out on the main for nearly a month, when one day, from the crow's nest high above us, I heard Collymore shout, "Land, ho!" He pointed off to his right. Every man ran to the rails. The helmsman leaned hard left into the tiller and the *Good Fortune* swung in the direction of land.

"You ever been with a woman?" Newmock asked.

"No."

He whistled low. "Got lots and lots of pretty colored gals in Jamaica. 'Bout all of them love sailors." He laughed. "Ham," he said. That's what he'd taken to calling me. "This is really going to be your maiden voyage." He slapped me on the back.

The next day, we tied up in Jamaica. And that night, with Newmock's expert guidance, I did enjoy my first maiden voyage. In fact, I enjoyed it for each of the four nights we were there. After that, we were off to Campeche. It took us ten days to get there, and each night along the way seemed like I thought of more and more to tell David about this thing called freedom. After tying up in Campeche, Captain Howland called for Newmock to accompany him and Samuels ashore, since Newmock was the only man who spoke Spanish. A few hours later, Newmock was back onboard the *Good Fortune* smiling, and for the next several days the crew did nothing but load logwood. After bringing ten tons aboard, my hands, my face, even my sweat turned red. But I was smiling, too, 'cause Newmock said we picked up a full load, and that meant money in our pockets once back in Plymouth. Master had never said if he agreed to him getting nine pence to my one, so I didn't know how much that would mean for me, but truth is, I didn't really care. So far, I liked a sailor's life, and if Master allowed me, I'd turn around and do it again.

Loaded heavy, the *Good Fortune* showed her weaknesses. We must have been in port for six or eight weeks, replacing planks, pitching the space between them. I even got to dive under the ship with Newmock, take a scraper, or a hammer and chisel, and go at the barnacles growing along the hull. In the evenings, I also got to sample Campeche's style of maiden voyages.

When it came time to leave, Captain Howland said we were headed straight across the Spanish Main to Cape Florida, turn to the larboard there, and up the coast to Plymouth. No stopping. No provisioning. No dallying. Every man aboard liked what they heard. Fifteen days later, it was me up in the crow's nest who hollered out, "Land, ho!" and pointed ahead to the larboard. I stayed in the nest as the helmsman, following the captain's orders, swung the boat to the larboard.

About an hour later, the deep blue of the ocean turned light, light green. I blinked several times, then rubbed my eyes to make sure the sunlight dancing off the water hadn't blinded me. But the light green was coming up fast, too fast. "To starboard! To starboard!" I sang out.

"Steady on the helm," cried the captain. "He's a lubber. Pay him no mind."

"Aye, Captain," the helmsman called back. "Steady as she goes."

"But, Captain, ahead . . ." I called down from the nest.

"Hammon, man, be still, or so help me God, I'll have you whipped before the mast."

"You can whip me all you want, sir."

The captain raised his head, and his fist, in my direction.

"But, sir, there's a reef dead ahead."

Good Fortune made an ungodly scraping sound as she skipped over the reef. Then with a huge thump, and a crash, came to a dead stop. As she careened to one side, I lurched for the netting above me and held on.

"Reeeef."

I heard the helmsman's feeble cry before the boat finally came to rest. Being barefoot made it easier for me to climb through the rigging descended around me, then shimmy down the high side of the mast. At the bottom, I lay on my back, sliding across the deck to the low side where the crew and the captain had gathered.

Webb came at me with a belaying pin. "God damn it," he spit. "It's what you get for having a lubber, and a Black lubber at that, in the nest."

Newmock held him back.

"Not his fault," said the helmsman. "He saw it. Called it with plenty of time."

The crew's eyes turned to the captain, who seemed to be muttering oaths and imprecations to himself.

"Captain," Webb said. "If we lessen our load, and get a pinnace with a line on the mast, when the tide comes in, we can right her, and be gone from this godforsaken point."

And a cheer from the men rose, "Dump the wood!"

"Never," said the captain. "Never. It's a half-year's wages there for everyone. Dump the wood, we might as well be dumping our wages, too."

Doty, with his thick Irish accent, spoke up. "Captain, better the wood than our lives. 'Sides, what's wages if you're too dead to spend 'em. Everything in Davy Jones's locker is free."

"We will not dump the wood, and that's an order. We will wait here for high tide to clear the reef, then use a pinnace to pull us out to sea."

Our galley was flooded. So, too, our quarters. We had little to eat and nowhere to sleep. Nerves had worn thin. Talk of mutiny floated among the crew. On the second day, the captain announced a new plan. The pinnace would ferry most of the crew ashore, while the captain and one hand would stay onboard waiting for the tide to right the ship. Onshore we would make a camp, forage for food, and cook, until a more suitable rescue could take place.

But as I rowed back to shore with the second group of men, we spied what first seemed to be more rocks exposed by the tide, but soon turned into Indians in canoes.

"Indians! Indians!"

We shouted to the captain, but it was hard to determine if he heard us, and by now we had problems of our own. Sixty of them, several to a canoe, paddled quickly and soon overtook our pinnace. Two canoes, each carrying three men with loaded weapons, stayed to guard us, as we floated adrift. The rest of their party made for the *Good Fortune*. We watched, in horror, as they boarded the ship and shot the captain, and all aboard, to death. They dumped the bodies overboard, then got back in their canoes and headed for us.

"Lads," said Samuel. "We are all dead men."

The canoes were soon upon us. We watched as they reloaded their weapons, then took aim, unleashing a volley that killed three men around me. I do not know why a bullet did not pierce my heart but at the sight of Young, and Little, and Doty covered in blood and slumped over, I dove into the water, preferring sharks or drowning to lead. Three or four minutes later, the crack of another volley sounded. I looked back to see my friend Moses Newmock slumped over the side of the pinnace, blood dripping in the water from his lips.

In a moment, I expected to see fins. But, instead, I saw canoes and the business ends of many rifles pointed in my face. Sopping wet, I was hauled into a canoe and beaten senseless with the handle of a cutlass. The Indians paddled back out to the *Good Fortune*, where one of them leapt aboard, set a fire, then retreated to a canoe. We bobbed in the water, waited, and watched, to the whooping and hollering of the natives, till *Good Fortune* burned to the waterline.

My captors kept me five days in their village. Each day I thought of Jonah in the belly of that big fish, and I wondered if I'd ever be spit out. On the fifth day, the *Tesoro del Señor*, a Spanish schooner, arrived from St. Augustine. As fate, or God's hand, would have it, I knew the master of this ship, whom I'd met in Campeche, where we both found the company of the same lady appealed to our maiden voyages there.

The natives appeared to have great respect for Capitán Ramon. They talked back and forth with him. While I did not understand what either of them said, Capitán Ramon's English was excellent.

"They agreed to release you to my custody," he said. "To travel to Cuba."

And, just like that, within a day's time, I stepped off the *Tesoro del Señor* in the port of Havana. But after four days there, my captors were there, too. I do not know if they paddled from Florida, or managed passage on another Spanish ship. They demanded me released to them, as I was their captive.

"Do not worry, señor," Ramon said. "We shall take up this matter with the governor."

Felipe de Fondesviela y Ondeano, marqués de la Torre, spoke abruptly to the natives.

"He is not happy," Ramon said. "That they killed everyone aboard the English ship except you."

There was more back-and-forth between the marqués de la Torre and the natives. Ramon turned to me.

"The Indians said they kept you alive because they know that 'men with burned skins' are more valuable. The governor said that from now on he will pay the Indians ten silver pieces a head for English brought to him alive, and agreed to twelve silver pieces for men like you with 'burned skins.'"

After their intercourse with the governor, the natives seemed pleased, and I never saw them again. For a year, I lived in the governor's castle and worked for him. I freely roamed the streets of Havana. I even came to speak passable Spanish. One evening, though, while out walking, a Spanish press-gang grabbed me, threw me into prison, and that next morning informed me I'd been pressed into service aboard the *San Pablo*, bound that day to Madrid. I refused to go, and was then thrown into a dungeon. There I stayed for almost five years. I knew no bleaker, darker belly than that of this iron and brick fish I'd been swallowed by. I appealed to anyone who came into that thankless pit to bring my name up to the governor, but it was not until an English merchant vessel sailing out of Boston stopped in Havana for repairs that I received any relief. One Betty Howard, the wife of the captain, at dinner with the governor, interceded on my behalf, and the next day I was ordered released to resume my stay at the governor's castle. I vowed then to escape this island prison, even with the pleasantries I now enjoyed again.

When an English twenty-gun warship pulled into Havana harbor, I snuck aboard and hid, revealing myself only as we left port for open water. I pleaded with the captain to take me, but he insisted he would not, and sent me back ashore in a pinnace. My attempted escape displeased de la Torre, who now had me closely guarded. In a year's time, however, perceiving a lapse in my guard's schedule, I slipped out of the castle and headed toward the harbor, where I knew a sloop bound for Jamaica was ready to cast off. But de la Torre's guards stopped me before I could get to the sloop.

Now, I was ordered to be one of six chair-bearers for Cuba's head bishop, who traveled around the country blessing and baptizing natives from a chair carried on our shoulders. I actually was paid for my service, and I lived quite well, though I continually searched for a way out. That way finally came in the form of the *Beaver*, an English man-of-war that stopped into port. With the intercession of a kindly benefactor, the lieutenant of the *Beaver* agreed to take me on board, and refused to hand me over to the Spanish who boarded his vessel, demanding my release.

Finally, I was heading away from Cuba. We stopped at Jamaica for only a few days, though long enough for me to renew my skills at captaining maiden voyages. Then, the *Beaver* set sail for England, as consort to a convoy of merchantmen. We arrived safely just north of Dover. I thought I might finally find some respite, but apparently my seamanship skills had grown to the point where I was now in high demand. I was passed between several man-of-wars until landing on the seventy-four-gun *Hercules*, which immediately left port. But before getting away from the Channel we were engaged in a smart battle with an eighty-four-gun French warship.

Captain John Porter, master of the *Hercules*, lost his leg in the fight, and seventy of our crew were killed. I myself received a head wound from being grazed by a bullet, and an arm wound where I'd been cut by a saber. But I recovered quickly. Seemed now that seamanship was all I knew. I shipped out on another warship but was discharged for my arm injuries. But land wasn't for me. Not long after that discharge, I got a severe fever which landed me in a small London apartment to recover. Lying in bed, close to death, again the image of Jonah and that big fish came to mind. I had no work, and I'd spent all my money, so I was now nearly destitute.

I felt compelled to sign on to a slaver bound for West Africa. The thought of manning a ship that would pick up people who looked like me, treat them like cattle, then deliver them for sale made me queasy, but lack of money made me even more ill. No other ship would have me now, especially with my arm injury.

The night before shipping off on the slaver, I overheard some men in a tavern talking about rigging a ship bound for Plymouth, captained by a man named Wyatt. So, I approached Captain Wyatt, explained to him my circumstances, and my years before the mast. For the next three months I re-planked and re-caulked his ship, mended sails, and generally got her ready to sail.

One day, while working in a hold, I heard a voice that sounded very familiar. I walked out on deck and saw Captain Wyatt speaking to another man. I shook my head. Rubbed my eyes. But before approaching I asked the ship's mate who was it that the captain was conversing with.

"Why, that's General Winslow," the mate said.

By this time, I was bursting at the seams, and I determined to take my chances even if I was wrong. I walked down the gangway toward Captain Wyatt and this other man. About twenty yards away I said, "Master Winslow?"

Both men swung around to me. But the cheeks of the man on the right flushed dark red. Then, I knew for certain.

"Briton? Briton, is that you?"

"Yessir, Master Winslow, it's me."

We rushed to each other and hugged each other. Tears came before any words.

"I thought you were lost at sea," Winslow said. "Thought I'd never see you again."

"Not lost, sir. Just in the belly of the fish for three very long days and three longer nights. But I finally got spit onto land."

Master Winslow and I sailed back to Plymouth with Captain Wyatt. Seemed we were all talked out by the time the ship docked. Master Winslow let me stay in Plymouth for as long as I wanted. He left for Marshfield in a wagon sent to pick him up. I walked over to the livery stable, knocked on David's door.

The door swung open. David's eyes flashed wide. "Briton, my friend." He patted me on the back. "Heard the *Good Fortune* and all aboard were lost off the Florida coast. Thought I'd never see you again."

"David," I said. "Let's find a place we can sit. I want to tell you all about freedom."

I never did go a voyage to sea again. But whenever I pass along the ocean, on my way into Plymouth, I look out to sea, I take a deep breath, and I give thanks that I once did.[1]

• • •

Briton Hammon was a Black Jack, a Black seaman in the Age of Sail, and he wasn't alone. By the early 1800s, Black men worked at 18 percent of all American seafaring jobs,[2] a remarkable number when the 1800 census also recorded Blacks as just over 18 percent of the total American population.[3] Black Jacks like Hammon endured the owners, the captains, the whips, the fears, and the general privations and hardships of being sailors, while also enduring the brutality and racism they encountered being Black and being at sea. In exchange, they enjoyed the adventure, the relative freedom, and the autonomy of a sailor's life. Aboard ships, they worked as cooks and deckhands, as first mates, and, in some cases, even as captains. Some Black Jacks were free. Others were slaves, like Hammon, hired out to the benefit of their owners.

Southern plantation slaves are popularly thought of as being either "field slaves" or "house slaves." Field slaves, the common wisdom goes, worked a hard life outside. House slaves worked an easier life inside. From there, many stereotypical images of slavery evolved, none more famous than Malcolm X's contrasting distinction between the "house Negro" and the "field Negro."

You have to read the history of slavery to understand this. There were two kinds of Negroes. There was that old house Negro and the field Negro. And the house Negro always looked out for his master. When the field Negroes got too much out of line, he held them back in check. He put 'em back on the plantation. The house Negro could afford to do that because he lived better than the field Negro. He ate better, he dressed better, and he lived in a better house. He lived right up next to his master—in the attic or the basement. He ate the same food his master ate and wore his same clothes. And he could talk just like his master—good diction. And he loved his master more than his master loved himself. That's why he didn't want his master hurt. If the master got sick, he'd say, "What's the matter, boss, we sick?" When the master's house caught afire, he'd try and put the fire out. That was the house Negro.

But then you had some field Negroes, who lived in huts, had nothing to lose. They wore the worst kind of clothes. They ate the worst food. And they caught hell. They felt the sting of the lash. They hated their master. Oh yes, they did. If the master got sick, they'd pray that the master died. If the master's house caught afire, they'd pray for a strong wind to come along. This was the difference between the two. And today you still have house Negroes and field Negroes. I'm a field Negro.[4]

As a charismatic orator, Malcolm with this two-minute riff brought audiences to their feet, laughing and shouting encouragement. After first debuting this sketch in 1963, it became a staple of many of his talks until his assassination in 1965. Unfortunately, he failed at the very homework he urged of others. Malcolm had not read the history of slavery well enough to know that not only was his a false and often baseless dichotomy, but also that he'd left out at least one important category of slave. Had Malcolm done his homework, perhaps the "boat Negro" would have been incorporated into his routine. Plantation owners feared boat Negroes more than they feared either house Negroes or field Negroes.

"Dont let the Boat Negroes go amongst the Plantation Slaves," South Carolina plantation owner Henry Laurens cautioned his overseers in 1764.[5]

Slaveholders like Laurens called boat Negroes *patroons*, a strange title given the earlier Dutch usage of the word for owners of large manors and slaves in and around New York City, and up and down the Hudson River.

"Load the boat as well as you can & take care to prevent any intercourse between Boat and Plantation Negroes and let me know how Abram the Patroon of the Boat behaves," Laurens asked his overseers in a 1765 letter.[6]

Throughout the coastal southeastern colonies in the nineteenth-century United States, the small workboats run by patroons went by many similar names—*periaguas, petty-augers, pereaugers, periaugers, petiaugers, pettiaugers, peteaugers, petteaugers, piraguas* (Spanish), *pirogues* (French)—all tracing their origin to a Galibi (Carib language) word of first contact, *piraua*, meaning "canoe."

Irish medical doctor and naturalist John Brickell, who traveled through Virginia and North Carolina in the early eighteenth century, wrote,

> And Laſtly, the large and Navigable Rivers and Creeks that are to be met with watering and adorning this Country, well ſtored with vaſt quantities of Fiſh and Water Fowl . . . They make very neceſſary Veſſels for carriage of their Commodities by Water, which are called in theſe parts *Periaugers* and *Canoes*, which are the Boats made uſe of in this Country . . . [7]

Periaguas were inexpensive boats, built on plantation grounds rather than in shipyards, from age-old techniques first developed by Native Americans. Brickell goes on to say the boats were "generally made out of one peice of large Timber, and that moſt commonly of the *Cypreſs* kind, which they make hollow and ſhaped like a Boat, with Maſts, Oars, and Padles, according to their ſize and bigneſs."

Fire or chisels hollowed out the boats, which ranged in length between thirty and forty feet. Some were monohulls. Others were like catamarans made by joining each half of a split log with planking. Paddles, sails, and long ferrymen poles were used for propulsion and steerage. Periaguas weighed anywhere from 3 to 20 tons with a volume of up to 4,200 gallons. Consider an average bathtub has a volume of forty-two gallons. Periaguas were typically manned by crews of five or more. Patroons commanded periaguas, and patroons were frequently Black men, slave or free.

Working the rivers was dangerous, and exciting, said "Look-Up" Jones, an ex-slave from South Carolina, and a patroon. Richard

Jones had earned the nickname "Look-Up" from his constant skyward gaze. He said, "I run on Broad River fer over 24 years as boatman, carrying Marse Jim's cotton to Columbia fer him. Us had de excitement on dem trips. Lots times water was deeper dan a tree is high. Sometimes I was throwed and fell in de water. I rise up every time, though, and float and swim back to de boat and git on again."[8]

Owners often outfitted periagua crews with special uniforms unique to each plantation. Henry Laurens dressed his boatmen in "Jack Robbins blue pea jackets, trousers of brown cloth, and a 'blanket Surtout' [overcoat]." Boatmen slaves on the Elliot plantation in Charleston, according to British journalist William Howard Russell, wore "red flannel jackets and white straw hats with broad ribands."[9] Like horses at a racetrack, these slave crews from different plantations would often race their periaguas against each other for entertainment, and gambling, of their owners.[10]

But the real business of patroons and their periaguas was making money for plantation owners. Shipping was the lifeblood of the American colonies and the early United States. Without ships, no colonists would ever have arrived. Without ships, no colonists would ever have survived. Without ships, no colonists would ever have thrived. The reason the Virginia Tidewater, the South Carolina Lowcountry, and the North Carolina lowlands prospered was because of their river systems. Natives had used these extensive waterways for millennia to trade, to travel, and to make war. As Europeans forcibly evicted these natives, the river systems remained a means to explore deeper into native-held territory, to conduct war against them, and then to claim their lands.

But rivers were also the means to ship products out. On periaguas of all sizes, manned by patroons and their slave crews, boats on these networks of rivers carried tobacco, sugar, rice, and cotton to larger ports where they could be injected into the international trade heading north along the coast, or east across the Atlantic, creating power and wealth for the White men who lived remotely, far upstream. And on other legs of this trade, products from Europe or the Caribbean might travel on large ships only as far as ports at Norfolk, or Charleston, or Savannah; from there the final miles to consumers meant travel by periaguas upriver. Goods circulated this way.

Briton Hammon and Moses Newmock went "a voyage to sea" to pick up logwood, a tree with a bloodred heartwood used by New England textile mills to dye the cotton that patroons like "Look-Up" Jones ferried from plantations to ships waiting in coastal harbors, frequently with Black Jacks as crew. Hammon and Newmock and Jones, and countless of thousands of Black Jacks, were essential links in the chain of trade that created wealth for, and conferred power to, plantation owners, ship owners, ship captains, mill owners, and slaveholders, like John Winslow.

Henry Laurens presided over the Continental Congress meeting in Philadelphia. Thomas Jefferson and George Washington relied on periaguas and their crews to bring their tobacco to market. Families like the Winslows, Laurenses, Jeffersons, Washingtons, and the generations of their descendants reaped the financial and political rewards that Hammon and Newmock and Jones, and their descendants, never did.

With slaveholders deriving such great benefit from their Black Jacks, what did they have to fear? What is it that Malcolm did not know?

Anyone who's ever been at the wheel of a boat knows how unpredictably it steers. Boats are subject to the vagaries of wind, weather, and water. For those who pilot them, the elements are their masters more so than men. Slaves knew this. Slaveholders did, too, and they feared the freedom experienced by these Black Jacks even as they reaped the rewards of their bondage.

When a slave revolt placed ex-slave Toussaint L'Ouverture in charge of Haiti, the US Congress, in 1799, debated the merits of recognizing the L'Ouverture government. Jefferson, writing to James Madison, who was out of office at the time, expressed his concerns. "We may expect therefore black crews, supercargoes & missionaries thence into the Southern states," he said. "[I]f this combustion can be introduced among us under any veil whatever, we have to fear it."[11]

Black Jacks were not only in the midst of trafficking in goods, but trafficking in ideas. "Worldly and often multilingual slave sailors regularly subverted plantation discipline," notes nautical historian W. Jeffrey Bolster.[12] A Black seafaring captain, Paul Cuffee, helped foment the largest slave rebellion in South Carolina history, led by Denmark Vesey. Frederick Douglass used his skill as an enslaved ship's caulker, and his extensive maritime knowledge, to deck out in sailor's garb and borrow a Seamen's Protection Certificate from a free Black sailor. Then on September 3, 1838, he slipped away from Baltimore to Philadelphia by train, blending in unnoticed among other free Black Jacks. From Philadelphia he traveled to New York City and, as a freeman, to the shipbuilding town of New Bedford, Massachusetts.[13] Blacks also filled the ranks of pirates, led by men like Edward Teach, also known as Blackbeard, and William Lewis of the Flying Gang.[14]

Many held tightly to their Seamen's Protection Certificate, issued by the United States beginning in 1796, which identified them as citizens under the protection of America both abroad and at home, regardless of race. An anomaly to be sure, yet this was one of the first official documents declaring free Blacks to be citizens of this country. Black Jacks returned from sea not only with these documents, but with good news and good hope. Black seamen, slaves and free, saw a world of promise beyond slavery, and they returned to Black communities throughout the United States with just such news, helping to agitate and organize for change.

When they were paid, or if they ran a black market beyond the watchful eyes of their owners, Black Jacks often made good money for their travails. They provided for families on land and helped build institutions such as churches, which became the pillars of Black communities across the nation. More than one Black sailor slipped effortlessly from the pulpit of a ship to the pulpit of a church, where they could preach and teach from real-world experience.

Black Jacks played a crucial role in creating and maintaining the extensive international mercantile system that generated White power and wealth throughout colonial and early America. But they also planted seeds that would one day flower into the loud, sustained calls for justice and equality, challenging these same American institutions of power and wealth.

OVER COFFEE

It happened over coffee.

London

In the latter part of the seventeenth century, groups of men in tall or triangular hats, in powdered wigs or none, with painted faces or ruddy natural cheeks, gathered daily at London coffeehouses, such as Lloyd's Coffee House on Tower Street. Over that "Newfangled, Abominable, Heathenish Liquor,"[1] they talked. Somewhat tongue-in-cheek, women, or perhaps those seeking to thwart the rise of these coffeehouses, bemoaned that men came away from such establishments with "nothing moist but their snotty Noses, nothing stiffe but their Joints, or standing but their Ears."[2] Not to be outdone, coffee-drinking British men defended their honor and virility with a counterpetition of their own.[3]

Battle of the sexes aside, in 1652, Pasqua Rosée, credited with opening the first coffeehouse outside of Constantinople (Istanbul), promoted coffee—called by one reviewer that *"Soot-colour'd Ninny-Broth"*[4]—as making one "fit for business."[5] Not surprisingly, Rosée's coffeehouse was located a stone's throw from London's fledgling stock market, the Royal Exchange.

And it was business—maritime business, to be precise—that brought men to Edward Lloyd's coffeehouse, which, not long after first opening, moved to Lombard Street, in the center of the City of London's burgeoning maritime business district. Edward Lloyd supplied these men with their daily doses of his "Mahometan gruel"[6] and with the latest shipping news—vessels arriving and departing, vessels expected, vessels lost, what cargo these vessels carried, and what cargo they were after. Tobacco from Virginia, cotton, rice, and indigo from South Carolina and Georgia, sugar from the West Indies, spices from the Far East, and, of course, that most important and prized cargo of all, human slaves from West Africa.

Many of Lloyd's customers had invested in these ships and their cargo, had particularly invested in slaves, so their risk and protection became matters of constant conversation. Coffee-fueled contemplations and tobacco-induced insights led some to offer services shouldering portions of that risk, at a fee, of course, and others to take them up on those offers. Eventually, this dickering over coffee and slaves became haggling over written contracts, which produced men specializing in maritime insurance.

In 1783, the Court of King's Bench, the British high court, heard a case on appeal of an insurance claim filed by a Liverpool syndicate operating slave ships between Africa and the Americas. Chief Justice Lord Mansfield, of fame in the *Somerset v. Stewart* case ("the black must be discharged") presided. Two years earlier in the Caribbean, the master of an imperiled slave ship, the *Zong*, owned by the Gerson syndicate, had willingly thrown overboard to their deaths 142 African men, women, and children. The merchants had their human cargo insured for loss at the standard maritime insurance rate of £30 per slave (adjusted for inflation, approximately $7,500 USD in 2020 terms). They contended the master of the *Zong* had acted according to standard maritime insurance covering "perils at sea" and jettisoned the slaves in order to save the other slaves, the crew, and the ship.[7]

"Perils at sea" were defined in the standard Lloyd's maritime insurance contract at the time, the result of a group leaving Lloyd's Coffee House to move over to the Royal Exchange as the Society of Lloyd's, then ultimately as Lloyd's of London.[8]

Zong was insured not by Lloyd's but by a group of Liverpool merchants. Though the insurance contract for the *Zong* has not survived, most contracts followed Lloyd's template with exemptions from liability for losses due to natural death, wastage, or spoilage but not for willfully jettisoning slaves with the hope of recovering losses. A lower court ruled in favor of the merchants. The insurance syndicate appealed. Mansfield's court overturned the initial ruling. But no records survive of the case's disposition after that.[9]

Lloyd's had insured the voyage of many slavers prior to the *Zong*, and went on to insure many slavers after the case.[10]

Philadelphia

A coffeehouse in Philadelphia became a favorite of the Founders. First opened on Front and Market streets as the London Coffee House in 1754, prior to the American Revolution, the coffeehouse was relocated to a larger space at 2nd and Walnut streets, once there called the City Tavern. Jefferson's Declaration of Independence was read there in 1776. Washington met Lafayette there in 1777. Franklin, Adams, and Paul Revere ate there often.

London Coffee House was near the docks. And, like its counterpart in London, the movement of ships and their cargo were daily recorded, especially the movement of slaves. Auction blocks stood outside of the coffeehouse where Africans could be inspected, bought, and sold by wealthier Philadelphians. The Second Continental Congress met at a room in City Tavern. Here the racist passions of southerners like Charles Cotesworth Pinckney and Pierce Butler were argued to shape the founding documents. while other, cooler, but still sympathetic ears, like those of Jefferson and Mason, listened for ways to appease them, which they ultimately did.

New York City

Legend tells in May 1792, twenty-four New York City stockbrokers met outside of 68 Wall Street, under a sycamore locals called a buttonwood tree, at the foot of Manhattan to sign the most important document in US financial history—the Buttonwood Agreement—which ultimately grew into the New York Stock Exchange. Financial markets have long been driven by psychology, and a compelling legend plays particularly well as just such a driver. An agreement among brokers was signed, that much of is well-documented.[11] But under a buttonwood tree? Probably not. And whether it grew into the New York Stock Exchange has also been convincingly refuted.[12] A less frequently told part of the tale is that this group of brokers, tired of meeting outdoors, took up business inside the nearby Tontine Coffee House.

Whether it was only this group that moved to the coffeehouse could be argued, for neither legend nor fact provides an answer. But after the Boston Tea Party, coffee, not tea, became the American "power drink," and brokers and merchants and businessmen did regularly meet at the Tontine Coffee House over an "Antichristian dose"[13] of their favored "Mahometan Loblolly."[14] The New York Stock Exchange did have its first offices on the second floor there.

A tontine is a "death pool" insurance annuity where subscribers pay into a common fund. Each year they receive their share of the interest accumulated by the investments of that fund. As subscribers die, survivors receive a greater share of the income, until the last survivor enjoys it all. Tontines are named after Naples banker Lorenzo de Tonti, who popularized the plan in France in the middle seventeenth century.

The Tontine Coffee House was organized as a tontine among its founding members, who met and mingled with the other investors popularizing this establishment in the eighteenth and nineteenth centuries. When questions of where to secure the best profits from investing arose, patrons of the coffeehouse needed look no farther than out the window, down the street from where they sat sipping or smoking.

In April 1731, the New York City Council passed "A Law Appointing A Place for the More Convenient Hiring of Slaves,"

> That all Negro Mulatto and Indian slaves that are lett out to Hire within this City do take up their Standing, in Order to Be Hired, at the Markett House at the Wall Street Slip untill such time as they are hired, whereby all Persons may know where to hire slaves as their Occasions shall require, and also Owners of Slaves discover when their Slaves are so hired.[15]

Francis Guy, an English-born American artist, created a famous 1797 painting of the Tontine Coffee House at the intersection of Wall and Water Streets.[16] The market house at the Wall Street slip, for the auctioning of slave labor, operated until 1762 just down Wall Street from the Tontine Coffee House toward the masts seen in the painting along the East River.

Guy's painting is a classic example of early-nineteenth-century art representing human domination of nature. The scene is framed, right and left, by the two most prominent and powerful coffeehouses of the era—the Tontine Coffee House (left) and the Merchant's Coffee House (right). But, instead of focusing on either establishment, Guy focuses the viewer's attention on the intersection of Wall and Water streets, actually on "Coffee House Slip," implied in the foreground, from where lines of an invisible ship's rope draw the eye to workers toiling and men inspecting barrels, possibly puncheons of rum.

Nature, dominated by humans, is both implied and expressed. Products processed from natural resources, such as coffee and rum, are implicit based on the location chosen and the men inspecting the barrels. However, closer inspection reveals three Black figures—two men and one woman—as expressions of the human resources also under domination. The two Black men, probably slaves, in the center of the painting are the only ones engaged in manual labor, while the Black woman just above them is trailing behind two White women, as though she were their servant, or perhaps their slave.

At the time of the 1731 law, cited above, an estimated 42 percent of White New York City residents owned slaves, a higher proportion than any city other than Charleston. By 1790, that figure had fallen to 20 percent of the city's population, but by 1800, closer to when Guy rendered his painting, it had risen to 25 percent.

Unlike the south, where slave ownership was confined, almost exclusively, to wealthy planters and landholders, in New York City slaveholding penetrated all rungs of society. "Widows from the lowest decile of the wealth distribution, struggling shopkeepers, artisans, and even sailors owned slaves."[17] With little or no cotton to pick or tobacco to harvest, having a few slaves was an investment for New Yorkers, like owning one or two apartments. Slavery was a moneymaking scheme even for average New Yorkers, who rented out their slave's labor by the day, which is precisely why the city council enacted the 1731 law to fix the Wall Street "Markett House" as the location where slave rentals would take place.

The Tontine Coffee House's redbrick edifice is painted by Guy in prominent detail above those toiling below; so, too, the other buildings at this corner and the affluent men and women congregating on the Tontine's porch. One message conveyed in this painting is clear: *this corner is where the domination of natural and human resources in America begins and this is also where it ends, in the profit, power, and pleasure of the privileged few.*

Even a casual glance through the laws enacted by the New York City Council during the seventeenth and eighteenth centuries reveals how obsessed the council was in regulating every aspect of the lives of slaves, and free Blacks, in the city. A palpable sense of fear, comparable to that demonstrated by the laws of the southern colonies, then states, permeates the city's codes, too, like this 1731 "Law for Regulating the Burial of Slaves."

For the Prevention of Great Numbers of slaves Assembling & Meeting together at their Funerals, under pretext whereof they have great Opportunities of Plotting and Confederating together to do Mischief, as well as Neglecting their Masters service. Be it further Ordained by the Authority aforesaid that not above twelve slaves Shall Assemble or meet together at the funeral of any Slave.[18]

But a 1991 excavation for the 475-foot-tall Ted Weiss Federal Building, at 290 Broadway in lower Manhattan, in the northwest corner of the Financial District, uncovered a burial site for tens of thousands of slaves. This cemetery is first seen on a map by city surveyor Francis W. Maerschalck in 1755. Just outside the man-made northern walls of the settlement, called "palisades" on Maerschalck's map, and just before a large freshwater pond, Maerschalck laid out with a dotted line an area labeled, "Negro Buriel Ground," clearly abutting Broadway at the site of the new federal building. Twenty-five feet deep, beneath several layers of previous building rubble, the remains of 419 Black men and women and children were discovered.

At first, the federal government simply removed the human remains and the artifacts, but continued the construction. The government rejected a request from the city's first Black mayor, David Dinkins, to stop construction until a suitable plan for the site was devised. This caused an uproar of protest and an upswelling of community support, which finally brought construction to a halt. Some wanted the entire burial grounds excavated and preserved. Others wanted a marker to denote the sacredness of the grounds. In the end, a compromise was agreed to: the human remains left in the ground were sealed, the human remains removed from the ground were reinterred, and a national monument, the African Burial Ground National Monument, run by the National Park Service, was established in the shadow of the new federal building.

Steps lead down to an underground black granite "Ancestral Chamber," with these words inscribed upon the walls:

For all those who were lost
For all those who were stolen
For all those who were left behind
For all those who are not forgotten[19]

It's powerful to realize New York's Financial District as a final resting place for thousands of Black Americans, slave and free. But it may be even more powerful to describe the financial market capital of the world as literally, and figuratively, built atop Black Americans, their bodies and their labor. Literally, slaves built the wall that became Wall Street. Figuratively, slavery created the foundation of much of the Street's early financial dealings.[20]

Imagine a cotton plantation circa 1800, owned by a man we'll call Marse. Cotton is planted and picked by men and women, like Josephine Bristow, who earlier told us how she and the "Old time people" had to "hoe en' pick cotton en' all such as dat."[21] It is loaded onto wagons by slaves, then transported to large gin mills, where it is run through those newfangled machines to produce seedless fluffy bales. Slaves load those bales back onto wagons for transport down to periaguas waiting at nearby river docks. Patroons, like "Look-Up" Jones, run slave boat crews to get Marse's cotton to Charleston and other port cities.[22] From there, other slaves load the bales onto larger ships, many with Black Jacks as crew, which sail north to ports like New York, Boston, and New Bedford. There, more slaves unload the bales, then reload them, again, for transport to textile mills in England or New England. Mills spin cotton into yarn, and turn the yarn into fabulous textiles, such as that for shirts and dresses, shipped and sold to waiting consumers in faraway places overseas.

Now, imagine that a five-hundred-acre plot next to Marse comes up for sale. Marse knows that if he can acquire it, he can make even more money growing and shipping more cotton. But Marse has two problems. First, he doesn't have the cash to buy the land; and, second, if he gets the land, he'll need more slaves, and he doesn't have the money to buy slaves either. So, what's he to do?

Turns out, after Eli Whitney's gin, Marse knows a lot of plantation owners in the same predicament. There's money to be made in cotton but first they need to acquire more land and more slaves. So, together they come up with a creative solution: start a bank, sell bonds, bring in money. Starting a bank is the easiest part. Together these plantation owners draw up a charter for a bank called the Southern Planters Bank. The charter is approved by the state of South Carolina, and Marse is named secretary.

But Southern Planters Bank has no money to lend—in fact, no money at all—and money is what these planters need. So, they write debt notes, or mortgages, to the Southern Planters Bank for the amount they need to purchase more land and more slaves. And they promise to repay those mortgages over time at a given interest rate. That's right, they ask a bank they've created for money they know that bank does not have.

Now, this sounds like a magician's trick that pulls money out of thin air, but it's a mortgage, and mortgages need to be backed by collateral—some tangible asset that can be seized and sold if a planter fails to repay. The planters know their land is probably not worth enough to serve as collateral, but they also know they each have assets that are worth plenty—their slaves—and those slaves, as property, can easily be resold, if they default, given the current need for labor throughout the south. So, they pledge their slaves as collateral for their mortgages. Now the planters have a bank without money, but a lot of mortgages backed by slaves.

These cotton planters also know that trying to sell a cotton plant or two is ridiculous, even run through a mill. No one in their right mind would buy them. But bundle several hundred cotton plants together, run them through a mill, and then you have enough to make a bale. Lots of people buy bales of cotton; after all, that's how these planters make a living. Similarly, they reason, no one would buy a mortgage or two, but bundle many of them together and then you have a bale of mortgages. Only don't call them bales, call them bonds. So, Southern Planters Bank packages groups of mortgages into bonds. And, mind your language, they don't create bonds, they issue them. The bonds represent mortgages backed by slaves.

Next, Marse, representing Southern Planters Bank, goes back to the state of South Carolina. "We have some bonds we'd like you to consider purchasing," he says.

A bank examiner studies the paper. "You boys mean these bonds are based on mortgages backed by slaves?"

"Yessir."

The bank examiner smiles. "Well, South Carolina does know something about slaves. I will tell you that. Charleston's the largest slave port on the east coast. One of these mortgages goes sideways, Southern Planters Bank grabs the slaves, sells 'em, we still get our money." Shakes his head. "Slaves?"

"Yessir."

"Damn, if you boys didn't come up with one helluva good idea. Good interest rate, too. Sure, we'll buy some bonds. Maybe start with several million dollars' worth. That sound okay?"

"Yessir."

And that's how the Southern Planters Bank got up and running with the money to give to White planters seeking to purchase more land and more slaves.

In the 1830s, powerful Southern slave owners wanted to import capital into their states so that they could buy more slaves. They came up with a new, two-part idea: mortgaging slaves, and then turning the mortgages into bonds that could be marketed all over the world.[23]

While packaging slave-backed mortgages into bonds was new, slave-backed mortgages had been around for a while. To climb out from under mounting debt, in 1796, Thomas Jefferson mortgaged fifty-two slaves to Henderson, McCaul & Company, merchants in Great Britain.

[T]hat for the purpose of securing to the said Henderson McCaul & Co. several sums of money due to them from the said Thomas by several bonds amounting to about fifteen hundred pounds with interest, and in consideration that the said Henderson Mc-Caul & Co. will forbear to demand by process in law, one third of the said debt till July 1797. one other third till July 1798. and one other third till July 1799, and for the further consideration of five shillings in hand paid to the said Thomas on their part, the said Thomas hath given, granted and conveyed to the said Henderson McCaul & Co. the following slaves to wit, Jame Hubbard and Cate his wife . . . [24]

Jefferson, who listed each slave by name, essentially asked his creditors not to take him to court; set up a payment plan allowing him three years to pay back the money owed; and backed this plan by offering as collateral fifty-two of the hundreds of men, women, and children he enslaved, should he fail to repay as promised. It was not the first nor the last time Jefferson would mortgage his slaves.

On the very same day, Jefferson sought similar relief from Van Staphorst & Hubbard, Amsterdam bankers, to whom he owed $1,900. He backed this request by mortgaging seventeen additional slaves.[25]

All told, in November 1796, Jefferson reported all of the slaves he had similarly mortgaged,

fifty seven negro slaves to William Short, fifty two other negro slaves to Henderson McCaul & Co., sixteen other slaves to Wake-lyn Welsh, eight other slaves to Philip Mazzei, and seventeen other slaves to the said Van Staphorsts & Hubbard making in the whole one hundred and fifty slaves[26]

Many real banks joined with actual planters, not just our hypo-thetical Southern Planters Bank, in a feeding frenzy around the profit potential of slave-backed securities, mortgages, and bonds. Between 1831 and 1865, Citizens' Bank and Canal Bank of Louisiana, both of which ultimately merged into JP Morgan in the 1930s, accepted slaves as collateral for loans. Some of those loans defaulted, and the bank ended up owning 1,250 slaves.[27]

The Georgia Railroad and Banking Company, and the Bank of Charleston, both acquired by Wachovia, which was ultimately acquired by Wells Fargo, owned slaves during this same period. Moreover, the Bank of Charleston accepted slaves as collateral on loans.[28]

At the time, the largest financial institution in the world, the Second Bank of the United States, a private corporation chartered in 1816, handled all financial transactions of the US government, its largest stockholder. A few hundred wealthy Americans held most of the bank's stock. A successor to Alexander Hamilton's First Bank of the United States, the Second Bank, also known as BUS or SBUS, was embroiled in controversy throughout its twenty-year existence. Virginia senators John Taylor and John Randolph, slave owners and staunch supporters of a rural, agrarian America, like their predecessor Thomas Jefferson, feared the bank threatened their southern way of life. "[I]f Congress could incorporate a bank," Taylor's reported to have said, "it might emancipate a slave."[29]

Taylor and Randolph failed to understand the country had moved on from Jefferson's pastoral vision of a nation of plantation owners and slaves to one based on industrialization and financial services backed by slavery. SBUS took the lead, investing heavily in cotton. State-chartered banks soon followed, leading to what historian Edward E. Baptist called an "orgy of bank-creation," by investing in cotton and providing slave-backed loans.[30]

The Commonwealth Bank of Kentucky was one such state bank born amid this orgy. In 1826, slave owner David Shipman of Kentucky conveyed a slave named Milly as collateral for a loan from Stephen Smith for Shipman's indebtedness to the Bank of Kentucky and other creditors, including Smith. Shipman could not repay his debt, so he left Kentucky to travel to Missouri, a free state at the time, and there he granted Milly her manumission. But, in 1827, Smith tracked down Shipman and made off with Milly, against her wishes or Shipman's, bringing her back to Kentucky. Milly sued Smith for her freedom, and the case wound up in the Missouri Supreme Court.

A decision turned simply on whether Milly, as property, belonged to Shipman or to Smith. At first, the court ruled that Shipman owned Milly, and returned the case to a lower circuit court for reconsideration. But when the case wound up back at the Missouri Supreme Court a second time, the justices agreed that Milly was free, pending enforcement of the contract between Smith and Shipman. Smith could not kidnap Milly, but he could foreclose on Shipman's loan and claim her as property. So, Milly was free, but not really.[31]

But back to Marse and the Southern Planters Bank, where the principals involved realize they have a "tiger by the tail," a tiger they want to turn loose on the world. How do they go about that? There were many ways a southern planter had of connecting to a worldwide market, but two of the most common, in the nineteenth century, were through a factor, or a broker. Both are terms for financial middlemen. Technically, brokers connect buyers and sellers of assets, for a percentage of the sale. Factors immediately pay a company the amount owed to it by a second company, before that second company has paid its invoice from the first company, also for a percentage of the invoice. The line between the two can get blurred, particularly if a commodity is involved, and that commodity is used like cash—tobacco and sometimes cotton were often used that way.

Southern planters had dealt with factors and brokers for decades. While some factors were located in the south, the largest factors and brokers were located in the north. Wealthy plantation owners, like Robert Mackay, whom we met earlier, often made regular trips north to accompany their shipments of cotton, tobacco, and sugar. Once there, they met with factors or brokers capable of selling their products around the world.

When Marse was in New York City, he stayed at the Tontine Coffee House, like plantation owner Robert Mackay did on his regular visits to the city.[32] It was conveniently located near the cotton docks, it had well-appointed rooms at a good rate, and it also had that intoxicating, thick "Mahometan gruel."

Over a cup, more likely a handleless bowl in those days, Marse savors the conversation with four other gentlemen around a table downstairs from his room.

"Sir, where are you from?" a gentleman asks.

"South Carolina," Marse replies.

"Interesting. Your accent sounds Irish."

"Grandparents came from the old country."

"And your line of business, sir?"

"Cotton."

"God bless you," says another, raising his head from a steaming bowl. "What would we do without men like you?"

"Actually, I have several thousand bales to sell, and I'm looking for—"

A man wearing a dark blue tricorne with gold trim cuts Marse off. "I'll take them at seven per pound."

"I was actually looking for ten."

The point of the hat facing Marse twists from side to side. "This market? Ten? No one in England'll buy it at that price. No one in New England either."

A man with horn-rimmed glasses nods, points out the window. "You can try Merchant's, across the street, but you probably won't find anyone on the Street buying at that price."

"Nine," Marse says.

"Seven!" says the man in the tricorne.

Marse pushes back from his chair, stands. "Gentlemen, thank you for your time." He starts to walk out.

The man in the tricorne calls out, "Eight!"

Marse stops, turns back. "Eight?"

"Eight."

"Gentlemen." Marse walks back. Retakes his seat. "I believe my coffee is still warm. And I also believe—how do you good gentlemen here in this great city say it?—I believe we have a deal."

He reaches across the table to shake each man's hand. A round of slurping and laughing begins. After several minutes, Marse clears his throat. "Truth of the matter is, gentlemen, I have other business to discuss."

The man with the horn-rimmed glasses sets down his bowl. "Other than cotton?"

"Related to cotton."

The man wearing the tricorne also sets down his bowl. "We already set the price at eight cents per pound. What's more than that?"

"Bonds."

A muffled cry rises from the table. "Bonds!"

"Yes, gentlemen, bonds. The Southern Planters Bank has issued a series of mortgage-backed bonds, which we would like to sell to investors in Europe."

"Bonds backed by what? Land? Livestock?" A man in a powdered wig waves Marse off. "They're junk, worth nothing."

"No, gentlemen, the mortgages are backed by our negroes."

The man in the powdered wig rears back. "Your slaves?"

"Yes, our slaves!"

The tricorne hat bends closer to Marse. Almost in a whisper, he asks, "How does it work?"

Marse whispers back, "Simple. Our most reputable planters take out mortgages with the bank for the money they need to purchase land, and the slaves to work it. They pledge their slaves—the ones they have, and the ones they'll purchase—as collateral for the mortgages. The bank then bundles a number of mortgages together into a bond. It then issues the bonds to investors."

"Brilliant," says the man in the tricorne.

"You see, that's what I was telling you about," says the man in the horn-rimmed glasses. "Derivatives. These bonds and the mortgages they're based on are derivatives of a solid asset, slaves. Derivatives, I'm telling you, that's where this is all heading."

"Don't mind Robert," the man in the tricorne says. "He gets carried away sometimes, but he's great with figures. I want to hear more about these slave-backed mortgages."

"There's really nothing more to them, except we'd like to sell them in Europe, and I thought you gentlemen might know someone who could help."

"Let me make sure I understand you," says the man in the tricorne. "Investor buys the paper. Bank holds the paper. Bank pays the investor when the bond comes due. Bank deals with any defaults."

"Of course, whoever sells a bond to an investor makes a fee based on the bond's worth."

"Five percent," says the man in the tricorne.

Marse shakes his head. "Gentlemen, my partners would be offended. We were thinking of one."

"Three!"

"One and a half," says Marse.

"Deal!"

Four hands reach across the table to shake Marse's.

"How many bonds can you get us?" asks Robert.

"How many can you sell?" asks Marse.

"London, Amsterdam, Paris," the man in the tricorne ticks off city names on his fingers. "Hell, maybe even Berlin. Why not? We'll take as many as you can get us."

"I'll let my partners know."

"Slave-backed bonds," says Robert. "Hmmm." He muses. Then he suddenly springs to life, snaps his fingers. "Own a piece of slavery, without ever owning a slave."

"Love it!" says the man in the tricorne. "We'll sell lots."

"And make lots more," another voice chimes in.

Edward E. Baptist and Lewis Hyman, in writing about the history of American finance, observe:

American planters organized new banks, usually in new states like Mississippi and Louisiana. Drawing up lists of slaves for collateral, the planters then mortgaged them to the banks they had created, enabling themselves to buy additional slaves to expand cotton production. To provide capital for those loans, the banks sold bonds to investors from around the globe—London, New York, Amsterdam, Paris. The bond buyers, many of whom lived in countries where slavery was illegal, didn't own individual slaves—just bonds backed by their value.[33]

Back at the Tontine Coffee House, a man who's not yet spoken clears his throat. "Gentlemen, gentlemen. I do not want to be the lone voice pouring cold water onto this celebration but these bonds are backed by slaves. Slaves are humans. They might get sick, or ill, or die. Then what? What's the value of each mortgage then?"

Robert is silent. He takes a gulp of coffee. Pauses. Takes another gulp. "Of course, why didn't we think of that before?"

"What?" the man in the tricorne murmurs. "What do you do if you're worried about your crop spoiling before it's shipped to market, or your cargo being damaged on a voyage from Europe, or the ship going down at sea? What do you do?"

He makes silent eye contact with each man around the table.

He taps the air in Robert's direction. "Insurance." He turns to Marse. "Can you ask each of the mortgagees to take out an insurance policy on their slaves?"

"Well," says Marse. "We haven't required it but I guess we could."

"Do that," says the man in the tricorne, "and we'll take as many bonds as you can get us by courier or by ship."

For Aetna, AIG (US Life), New York Life, Baltimore Life, and others, slave insurance was a huge market in the middle nineteenth century. Slave owners could purchase policies protecting them against the death, or loss of full use, of their slaves. "Slave insurance was one of the earliest forms of industrial risk management," said Michael Ralph, author of a recent study on the subject, "providing an important source of revenue for some of today's largest multinational insurance companies."[34]

Collateralized debt may be the most widely used financial service in the world today. If you have ever purchased a home, you have bound yourself to collateralized debt like the debt agreed to between the planters and the Southern Planters Bank. If you have ever purchased a car with the help of a lending institution, you have bound yourself to a collateralized debt. In these cases, the collateral is your home or your car but the principle is the same: You pledge the home or the car you are buying to the lender (investor). You agree to pay that lender a certain amount periodically until the entire amount you borrowed plus interest is repaid. If you default on paying the lender, your collateral will be seized.

Collateralized debt backed by slaves, bundled and repackaged as bonds, requiring insurance to protect both borrower and lender from the loss of collateral, built the banks and financial institutions named above, which are common household names today. It built the wealth of the American families behind these institutions. It also built the wealth of individuals and institutions around the world, far removed from the brutality and violence of the everyday life of a slave. About the only ones who did not benefit from collateralized debt were the enslaved people held as collateral, upon whose bodies and backs this financial system was constructed.

News of collateralized debt spread, probably over coffee in places like the Tontine Coffee House, where one person explained to another how money could be made using enslaved human beings as collateral. Even the word we use for this kind of financial instrument speaks to its inhumane roots. A "bond" binds borrowers to lenders, but the entire system was based on the bonds binding slaves to their masters and their labor.

It's not hard to imagine that when Marse left the table at the Tontine Coffee House, the men at the table continued to talk. Not only had they just been shown a new way of making money, but they'd closed a deal for selling cotton to their buyers in England or New England. It's also not hard to imagine where all of this was heading. If the demand for cotton rises and falls, so do the prices these brokers charge their sellers and buyers. Why not speculate on cotton prices?

If a broker believes in six weeks the price of cotton will rise, he can buy more than his sellers need at the moment, store it, sell it in six weeks to his buyers at a higher price, and then pocket the difference as well as his normal commissions. If a broker believes in six weeks the price of cotton will fall, he can sell an order to a buyer now, even if he doesn't have the actual cotton. Six weeks later, he can buy the quantity to fill the order at a lower price, then pocket the difference as well as his normal commissions. Of course, the price of cotton could move in the opposite direction but that's part of the risk and the thrill of speculation. And the brokers sitting around that table at the Tontine Coffee House were in the middle of the trade in cotton, tobacco, sugar, coffee, rice, and slaves—all commodities backed by slave labor. They were in the best position to know, or guess, which direction a market was heading. And sometimes, they could combine their buying power to force the market in a direction they desired.

The frenzy of exchanging shares, selling bonds, speculating on prices, making money, and creating fortunes soon grew too big for a coffeehouse table. So, a room was rented on the second floor of the Tontine Coffee House, where men who once sat at tables downstairs now sat at an even larger table upstairs; a table they called the New York Stock Exchange. If you wanted a seat at their table, you paid for the privilege. If you wanted your company listed with them, you paid for that privilege, too.

"The infant American financial industry," observed economic historian Edward E. Baptist, "nourished itself on profits taken from financing slave traders, cotton brokers and underwriting slave-backed bonds."[35]

But all of the slave-backed money flowing into traders and banks and brokers and underwriters had to go somewhere, and it didn't go under mattresses or floorboards. That money, like water, flowed.

It flowed from White American institutions and people that had it to White American institutions and people that wanted it, conveniently, tragically bypassing the Black Americans who'd created it. And, as the nineteenth century wore on, and the Civil War came and went, it became pretty clear where that money was headed. America was in the throes of an industrial revolution, and that slave-backed money was destined to build the industries that came to define American industrial prowess—steel, railroads, automobiles, mining, oil, energy, and eventually high technology. Yet, even here, far removed from plantations and cotton fields, the lives of Black men and women, and their labor, built the new mechanized corridors of power and wealth, whose riches and rewards they still did not share.

HELL ON WHEELS

With a plaintiff voice, elegant finger work, and immense dignity, Elizabeth "Libba" Cotten, a Black woman and her guitar, became a cornerstone of the American folk music revival in the 1950s and 1960s.

> Freight train, freight train, run so fast
> Freight train, freight train, run so fast
> Please don't tell what train I'm on
> They won't know what route I'm going[1]

Cotten wrote "Freight Train," her most famous song, at age eleven. Through the steady rhythm of her fingers plucking the strings of her upside-down guitar—a signature style called "Cotten picking"—you can hear a train's wheels rolling over joint after joint of track.

"We used to watch the freight train," Cotten said. "We knew the fireman and the brakeman . . . and the conductor . . . They'd let us ride in the engine."[2]

Cotten wasn't the only Black woman to sing about freight trains. Blues singer Clara Smith, no relation to Bessie Smith, recorded "Freight Train Blues" in 1924:

I asked the brakeman, let me ride the blinds,
I asked the brakeman, please let me ride the blinds.
The brakeman said, "Clara, you know this train ain't mine."[3]

"Riding the blinds" is a reference to the practice of riding in the dangerous space between two coupled railcars.

It's hard to listen to Elizabeth Cotten or Clara Smith without thinking of another Black woman named Rose, a slave, riding in the baggage cars of trains between Rock Hill, South Carolina, and Charleston, while her owner, Frederick Nims, relaxed in a first-class coach. Nims, a New England–bred civil engineer, had come south to work as a railroad surveyor. In 1857, he secured a contract to build a section of the Charleston & Savannah Railroad across thirteen rivers, and through malaria-ridden, snake-infested swamps, connecting the two port cities along the coastal lowlands. He brought Rose with him from Rock Hill as a cook.[4]

Work was divided between the malarial months of late June through mid-fall and the remainder of the year. Nims hired Irish workmen but he preferred slaves, particularly the "acclimated negroes" of the Lowcountry coast, many of whom had developed immunity to malaria and other tropical diseases. "Upcountry Black hands," like Rose, were sent into the interior come June, where she cooked for the men, who cut crossties for trestles until late October, when they could return to working on the coast.

Slaves and free Blacks—who would become known as "Gandy dancers,"[5] for the work songs and physical movements that accompanied their tasks—built, and maintained, the 8,800-mile southern railway system prior to the Civil War. Nims brought his own slaves with him, for example. When he needed more labor, he rented more slaves from local planters, who derived attractive profits. Some railway lines owned their own slaves for construction. When a line under construction crossed a "right of way" through a plantation, it was not uncommon for plantation owners to contract on their own with the railway to build that section using surplus slave labor. Even after slavery, railroads preferred Black labor, and states supported that preference through exploitative "convict lease" systems that lined government coffers and the pockets of railroad owners at the expense of Black men who laid and repaired the tracks.

A typical southern railroad profile is given in the report to stockholders of the Chattanooga & Nashville Railroad Company, known as the N&C, for the Civil War years 1860–1865. The company listed among its assets:[6]

Slaves owned at Nashville		7,230 54
Slaves owned in Georgia		121,542 75
—bales cotton, cost	$484,886 26	
Less for cotton sold	202,695 00	282,191 26

And gave further accounting of the slaves the company owned and sold, which they now considered a total loss.[7]

Buried in the list of N&C stockholders is the name G. B. Lamar, holding a large portion of N&C shares:[8]

Name.	Residence.	No. votes.	No. shares.
Lamar, G. B.	New York city	123	1,175 $^3/_4$
Lamar, G. B., in trust	. . . . . . do	26	206

Gazaway Bugg Lamar was a slaveholder, a cotton and shipping magnate, and a steamboat pioneer, operating out of Savannah, who moved to New York City in 1846 to found the Bank of the Republic of New York on Wall Street. Lamar, whom a contemporary called one of the "aristocratic money kings of the cotton states,"[9] speculated in buying and selling cotton, wheat, apples, and pig iron; in other words, he and his bank made money from slave-backed assets.[10] Through his bank, Lamar provided southern states and cotton planters access to New York credit markets. His bank traded in slave-backed securities such as bonds to provide the cash needed for southern plantations to expand, and for southern industries, like the N&C Railroad, to grow.

Along with his young friend Richard Lathers, who established the New York–based Great Western Marine Insurance Company, the two men and their companies pushed to restart an illegal transatlantic slave trade, and supported the antebellum south, from their Wall Street offices. Lamar and Lathers understood Wall Street's economic dependency on, and interrelationship with, the south. It was Lathers who on December 15, 1860, with Lamar in attendance, convened a meeting at his offices of two hundred of the "venerable and distinguished statesmen, the enterprising merchants, and the substantial citizens" of New York. By some reports not two hundred but two thousand men arrived, and the meeting, moved to another room, endorsed Lathers's support of slavery, and the south's concerns about its abolition.[11]

Lamar's son Charles owned the infamous yacht *Wanderer*, which brought the last large cargo of slaves directly from Africa to America in 1858, landing some four hundred kidnapped men and women at Jekyll Island, Georgia (the distinction of being the very last slave ship to America belongs to the *Clotilda*, which in 1860 brought between 110 to 160 Africans from present-day Ghana to Alabama).

Working with a syndicate of the most famous national and international businessmen at the time, Lamar provided a conduit for

American and European money to fund the secessionist south. He helped to secure and ship weapons made in Europe to the Confederacy. And Lamar was arrested and held as a suspect in the assassination of President Abraham Lincoln, though never convicted. Lamar settled with the US government in 1874 for a sum of nearly $580,000 for cotton confiscated by Union general William Tecumseh Sherman's troops on their march through Savannah.

In 1865, the Bank of the Republic of New York became the National Bank of the Republic of New York City.[12] In 1901, the National Bank of the Republic of New York City was merged into the First National Bank of the City of New York.[13] First National eventually became part of Citibank.[14]

A railroad built by slaves, which also bought and sold them. A railroad carrying cotton, and also owning this commodity whose value was based on slave labor. A railroad with access to New York City credit markets through banks trading slave-backed securities. The N&C along with shareholder G. B. Lamar offers a prime example of the intricate web of wealth and power erected on the backs, and at the expense of, Black lives and Black labor.

But the N&C was not alone.

In 1837, Holden Rhodes, president of the Richmond and Petersburg Railroad Company, told the General Assembly of Virginia the expenses his company expected in the following year. "The disbursements of the month of January will, from a variety of causes, be heavy. The hire of negroes is to be paid, and their clothing provided . . ."[15] Company books show the railroad paid anywhere from $80 to $140 per year to slave owners for the hiring of their slaves.[16] The Richmond and Petersburg Railroad Company merged into the Atlantic Coast Line Railroad, then the Seaboard Coast Line, which ultimately became part of the Amtrak and CSX systems.[17, 18]

In 1841, Alexander Mazyck, chairman of the Louisville, Cincinnati and Charleston Railroad Company, clearly expressed the intentions of many southern railways, at the time, in a resolution to his board which unanimously approved that he "be authorized as soon as the means and credit of the Company will permit, to purchase for the service of the Rail-road, from fifty to sixty male Slaves between the ages of sixteen and thirty."[19] The Louisville, Cincinnati and Charleston Railroad through merger became part of the South Carolina Railroad Company, which then became the Southern Railway, today's Norfolk Southern Railway.[20]

The Norfolk and Petersburg Railroad, the N&P, ran eighty-five miles between the two cities. Construction began in 1853 and was completed in 1858, under the supervision of slaveholder and civil engineer William Mahone. N&P, and many other railroads, ran newspaper ads for slaveholders wishing to hire out their slaves to the company. Most of the original track bed is still in service, though N&P is now part of the Norfolk Southern Railway.

Prior to the Civil War, 15,000 Black men, women, and children worked to build America's rail infrastructure,[21] and nearly all of those railways owned or hired out for slave labor.[22] By 1860, one-third of them employed 100 or more slaves. Twelve hundred slaves helped build the Atlantic & Gulf Railroad in Georgia; 500 constructed the Vicksburg, Shreveport & Texas Railroad; 1,493 men and 425 boys worked on the North Carolina Railroad in 1852.[23]

Little difference existed between the fields and the rails. The work was dangerous. Enslaved laborers, men and women, lost their limbs, and their lives, for the sake of railroad construction.[24] The owners and overseers were brutal. A rule book for the Tallahassee Railroad and the Pensacola & Georgia Railroad gave instructions for handling slave labor. "When a negro requires correction, his hands must be tied by the overseer and he will whip him with an ordinary switch or leather strap not exceeding thirty-nine lashes at one time, nor more than sixty in one day, or for one offense, unless ordered to do so by the supervisor and his presence."[25]

In 1844, the Alabama legislature approved a loan of $42,176 (approximately $1.5 million in 2020 US dollars) for the Montgomery & West Point Railroad line, which went to the purchase of eighty-four enslaved men, women, and children. Children under the age of ten drove carts. Some women cleared and graded roadbeds alongside of the men. Those women not on the tracks were forced to work as cooks.[26]

The Atlantic & Gulf, the Pensacola & Georgia, and the Montgomery & West Point railroads are now within the CSX system. The Vicksburg, Shreveport & Texas Railroad is split between the Kansas City Southern and Canadian National railroads. Passenger service along the old North Carolina Railroad is currently handled by Amtrak, with freight handled by Norfolk Southern. And the Tallahassee Railroad, originally financed by wealthy cotton planters to get their cotton to textile mills in England and New England, abandoned its roadbed in 1983.[27] It's now being maintained as a historical railroad trail.[28]

Every major railway in existence today is the product of dozens of name changes, acquisitions, mergers, and other transactions that engulfed smaller lines. But the unpaid labor of enslaved Black people created the wealth and power that rolled, and still rolls, along these rails. Along with the turnpikes, bridges, and canals, enslaved Black labor built significant portions of transportation infrastructure in America, particularly in the south.

● ● ●

As such a dominant force, railroads make it easy to forget that other public works and infrastructure projects were also underway in nineteenth-century America.

Originally, sharp wooden or metal poles (pikes) were assembled on a frame and could be swung (turned) across a road, barring an enemy's access by horse or by foot. Eventually, toll collectors inside booths replaced guards, and horizontal logs or other barriers replaced pikes, but the idea of turnpikes remained. The earliest turnpikes in the United States were constructed, often along old Native American trails, in the late 1700s by private corporations with the blessings and support of states. Turnpikes were built for wagons, horse-drawn coaches, and pedestrians.

In the early part of the nineteenth century, particularly in the south, turnpikes were built by enslaved Blacks. While railroads eclipsed them, many of the slave-labor practices used by railway companies were employed by those building turnpikes. Privately owned corporations, composed primarily of local stockholders, oversaw construction, and often received substantial funds from states. Enslaved labor was hired from local slaveholders, though sometimes slaves were bought outright.

Why buy slaves when you could hire them? "[T]he nature of the work will expose them to dangers which are not compensated by the terms," said George Washington, reluctant to hire out his slaves.[29] So, companies bought their own.

Construction of the thirty-four-mile-long Little River Turnpike, from Alexandria to the ford of the Little River, near present-day Aldie, Virginia, began in 1802 and finished in 1811. Under the supervision of plantation owner, slaveholder, and slave patroller Richard Ratcliffe,[30] the turnpike was one of the few macadamized roads in the country at the time. Macadamization, named after John Loudon McAdam, placed a convex layer of compacted crushed stone over a binding layer of stone dust.[31] Little River Turnpike was built to help farmers in the western part of the state bring their slave-grown tobacco and other crops to the port of Alexandria.[32] Once a route was selected, land was cleared and graded, and stones were quarried, crushed, then laid. It was hard work, for which Ratcliffe preferred slaves, hired from local plantation owners. From 1803 to 1808, he repeatedly ran an advertisement seeking to hire out enslaved Black men. Running along a similar route, today, Virginia State Route 236 is a multilane highway, without tolls, still known as the Little River Turnpike.

The Swift Run Gap Turnpike Company, in their books for 1829, showed an amount due, "To sundry persons, for negroes hired to work upon the road the present year," of $225. The next year, under the same entry it showed a debt of $365.[33]

One group, intending to bid on a Tennessee turnpike project

in 1838, reasoned they could "buy 300 Negroes, who would be able to build the road in one year. When the road was completed, they would be able to sell the Negroes at an advance of $100 each thereby turning a sizable profit."[34]

James Hays Piper, civil engineer and superintendent of the Southwestern Turnpike Company in Virginia, notes that his work force, in 1850, consisted of "36 men and boys, 7 horses, 6 carts." Though Piper does not specify whether these men and boys were enslaved, in the same note, he appeals to the Board of Public Works for rules that "may also be adopted with regard to the negro clothing," strongly suggesting that they were.[35]

Although railway construction overtook road construction until the height of the automotive era, enslaved Blacks involved in turnpike labor contributed to a new general ledger asset account, called in books of pre–Civil War America the "negro account," shorthand for the balance of slaves bought and sold. Caitlin Rosenthal describes modern-day business accounting practices such as asset valuation—appreciation and depreciation—as innovations first developed and widely used by slaveholders in accounting for their human labor.[36]

The "negro account" for the Upper Appomattox Company in 1831 showed a balance of $6,859, which meant the company owned enslaved Blacks, whom they accounted for as property. The Upper Appomattox Company, later known as the Upper Appomattox Canal Company, was responsible for constructing and maintaining the hundred-mile Upper Appomattox Canal Navigation System that allowed farmers from as far away as Farmville, Virginia, to ship tobacco, cotton, salt, lime, and wheat and corn flour to Petersburg, Virginia. In an addendum to its 1831 books, the company described for the Board of Public Works the difficulties in building and maintaining the canal. That year, they had replaced an aqueduct with "hired labourers," most likely hired slaves. "Previous to that, all our works were executed by slaves, purchased by the company, which, in this country, we find much cheaper than to hire labourers."[37]

James River bateaux (singular *bateau*) were the shallow draft boats that moved down the Upper Appomattox Canal, operated by Black Jacks, called boatmen. Once they unloaded their cargo in Petersburg, they used long poles to push their boats upstream against the current. A round-trip from Farmville could take two weeks or longer.

The Roanoke Navigation Company, chartered by the Virginia Assembly in 1804, performed a similar service along the 470 miles of tributaries to the Roanoke River. Here, too, bateaux operated by Black Jacks plied the waters. The company bought and sold slaves. In 1830, it reported "42 negroes belonging to the Company"; seven years later, company books showed, "Received for negroes sold . . . $7,043.58" and as property, "Thirty-three negroes, estimated to be worth . . . $14,025.00."[38]

In 1827, the Slate River Company, created by the Virginia Assembly in 1819 to make the James River more navigable and, where needed, to build canals, lists, "Amount expended in the purchase of five negro men . . . $1,900.00" and as income, "Amount received for the hire of four negro men . . . $235.00."[39]

The president of the Lynchburg and Salem Turnpike Company wrote to auditors of the Board of Public Works in Virginia in 1833, "The board of directors deemed it expedient to purchase three negro men, for the purpose of keeping the road in repair, instead of hiring hands, which was formerly done. This will account for the dividend's being so much less than usual."[40]

Canal companies favored enslaved Black labor over hired White labor, as the following report of the James River and Kanawha Canal Company noted: "The summer of 1838 was unusually hot and some of the Irish died of prostration. At this, a sort of panic seized the Irish and about two hundred of them quit work and migrated north. In the autumn the force became more stable and manageable, two-thirds of them now being tractable negroes."[41]

Another official observed, "The negroes being your own (or hired) you can command their service when you please—when your work is completed, if you have not further occasion for them, they can be sold for nearly as much, or probably more than they cost you."[42]

As early as 1793, South Carolina's Santee Canal Company hired nearly one thousand slaves to complete the twenty-two-mile-long canal, at times fighting with planters and with other public works projects to retain their enslaved labor force, even petitioning the state for special dispensation to import slaves during a ban on the transatlantic slave trade. Something the state had done for another canal company, the Catawba Company. The canal, connecting Charleston and Columbia, was completed in 1800 using almost entirely enslaved labor.[43]

Georgia's Brunswick Canal Company and North Carolina's Cape Fear & Deep River Navigation Company also employed slave labor.[44]

"I don't think people think of bridges and seawalls and forts as being constructed by slaves," said Jane Landers, a scholar of Florida's history. "But from the very beginning, slaves were responsible for building all of the major forts, the main public works, bridges and seawalls. All of those were constructed by enslaved Africans."[45]

Throughout early America, especially in the south, enslaved Black labor built the nation's transportation and public works infrastructure, to the profit and power of the individuals and companies that used them. Some of the infrastructure built by Black labor is still in use today, like "the Conduit," which delivers drinking water from the Potomac River to Washington, DC.[46]

• • •

More than trains rolled down the tracks. Modernity rumbled across America. Beyond a new way of moving people and goods, the railroad ushered in a new experience of the world. Railroads were early disruptors.

In the 1741 satirical book *Memoirs of Martinus Scriblerus*, Alexander Pope, who went by the nom de plume Martinus Scriblerus, proposed that the "modest request of two absent lovers" is "Ye Gods! Annihilate but Space and Time."[47] Though Pope wrote these lines in the eighteenth century, nineteenth-century philosophers, economists, and social theorists seized on the notion of the Industrial Revolution's "annihilation of space and time," and this phrase has been with us ever since to describe the disruptive effects of new technologies.

Even traveling at twenty to thirty miles per hour, a trip that once took several days by wagon now took several hours by train. Places which once seemed too far away now seemed too close to ignore. Railroads "annihilated space and time," as Constantin Pecqueur said in 1839, "Lille suddenly finds itself transported to Louvres; Marseilles to Nemours,"[48] or, in the case of America, Philadelphia transported to Baltimore or New York City to Richmond.

This annihilation of space and time was a hallmark of modernity delivered by the railroad—that miraculous, disruptive technology of the Industrial Revolution. Many believed that old systems could not survive the onslaught of modernity, and new systems would emerge in their place. For some, this meant supporting the growth and expansion of the railroad was a means of bringing an end to slavery. Surely, there were signs to suggest they were right.

Follow the tracks to freedom. Interconnected railroad tracks provided a cleared and graded path out of slavery. Some slaves who built the tracks also took them, to the consternation of the early railroad companies.

Ellen Craft was so fair skinned, she could pass for White. In fact, on December 21, 1848, she did, but not as a White woman, instead as an ailing young White man. With her husband, William, posing as her personal slave, the couple took "a desperate leap for liberty," setting off on a nearly thousand-mile journey from Macon, Georgia, to Philadelphia. He rode in the "negro car," she in first-class. From train to steamboat to train, the couple dined with the steamboat captain and barely escaped detection by those who suspected their ruse. They made it to Philadelphia and then on to Boston, where

William worked as a cabinetmaker and Ellen as a seamstress. But in 1850, slave hunters arrived in Boston looking to return the pair. They fled again, this time by ship to England, where they raised a family and wrote a book about their escape. In 1870, they finally returned to Georgia, setting up a school for newly freed slaves.[49]

Frederick Douglass also used the railroad. In his escape from Baltimore in the guise of a Black Jack, Douglass boarded a train to Philadelphia. He, too, narrowly escaped detection but his daring, and the newly shortened time between Baltimore and Philadelphia because of the rails, made his flight to freedom a success.

By the middle of the nineteenth century, several hundred enslaved Blacks a year escaped to the north, some, like the Crafts or Frederick Douglass, using railroads.[50, 51] In an effort to enforce the Fugitive Slave Clause of the US Constitution (Article IV, Section 2, Clause 3), a Fugitive Slave Act was passed by Congress in 1793, and a second in 1850. The Fugitive Slave Act of 1850 represented yet another capitulation to the south: northern officials who did not arrest fugitive slaves were fined, fugitives were denied habeas corpus (i.e., they were not allowed their day in court), and law enforcement officers who captured fugitives were entitled to a bonus. Slave owners needed only to supply an affidavit for fugitive apprehension to a US Marshal, a process which itself was abused to illegally capture free Blacks. Railroads were not immune to enforcement of the 1850 Fugitive Slave Act.[52] The Missouri legislature, in 1855, passed a law doubling the fines to railroads for transporting a fugitive slave.[53]

On May 28, 1855, Solomon Digges, a Black man owned by Elias Scholl, crossed the Mason-Dixon Line from Maryland into Hanover, Pennsylvania, calmly walked up to North Central Railway ticket agent Joseph Leib, and bought a ticket to York, Pennsylvania.[54] From there Digges escaped into the vastness of a northern abolitionist network. But the City of Baltimore sued the North Central Railway on behalf of Elias Scholl's estate, seeking to recover the value of Digges. In superior court, the city won. North Central Railway, however, filed with the Maryland Court of Appeals, which heard arguments in June 1860. The Appellate Court, citing the plaintiff's "right of property in his negro slaves is recognized by the Constitution of the United States, which is the supreme law of the country," let stand the lower court's ruling of $813.40 in favor of the slaveholder's estate.[55]

Fugitives were "passengers." Guides, like Harriet Tubman, were "conductors." "Agents" helped slaves find the railroad. Hiding places were known as "stations." "Stationmasters" hid slaves in their homes. Financial backers were called "stockholders." And slaves got on board the "freedom train" by obtaining a "ticket." From a railroad system built by enslaved Black labor, the Underground Railroad became a metaphor of escape to freedom. And from 1860 to 1865 that "railroad" helped somewhere between 40,000 and 100,000 slaves make their way north as far as Nova Scotia, south as far as Mexico, west all the way to British Columbia, and even east on the "Saltwater Underground Railway," to places like Bermuda or England.

"Slavery," said Frederick Douglass, "has no means within itself of perpetuation or permanence . . . It is against nature, against improvement . . . It cannot stand. It has an enemy in every bar of railroad iron . . ."[56]

But with slavery, modernity presented a double-edged sword. For Douglass, and northern abolitionists, modernity excluded slavery. For the south, modernity was rooted in slavery. The roads and railroads and canals built by slaves to enhance southern planters' access to markets were also being used to enhance slavery itself.

Railroads made it easier for cotton planters to get their cotton to market, which made cotton a more valuable crop. Planters, then, wanted to make more money, which meant more land to grow cotton, which also meant they wanted more slaves. But the international slave trade had been shut down, by law, in 1808. Outside of an illegal slave trade to America, which continued until shortly before the Civil War, the internal, domestic slave trade began to boom. Slaves, like human livestock, were bred for sale.

With a shift away from tobacco to cotton, tobacco planters from the upper south—Delaware, Maryland, Virginia, North Carolina—began selling their slaves to cotton planters in the deep south, and railroads provided ready access to this new market. Railroads made possible a transition from selling slaves at coastal port cities to inland towns that grew up around southern railroad stations. Thanks to railroads, these new slave markets brought together distant sellers and local buyers. Improved roadways and canals also helped. Now overland slave caravans had better routes to get their human cargo to market.

Railroads, as described earlier, also became major players in the domestic slave market. At first, many hired slaves, then later many purchased them outright. In some areas of the antebellum south, railroads owned more slaves then the largest plantations. A tighter slave market, with greater demand, meant that railroads helped to drive the price of slaves up, and this, in turn, attracted the interest of slave merchants and brokers, like Gazaway Bugg Lamar, and other Wall Street investors and banks, who saw a chance of garnering even more wealth.

Of course, this was not the first time a technology thought initially to bring an end to slavery contributed to its proliferation. The cotton gin had also dashed such hopes a generation prior to the railroad. While not annihilating both space and time, the gin had certainly annihilated the time it took to separate cotton lint from cotton seed. But no lessening in demand for slaves followed. Instead came an explosive rise, which helped, in large measure, to fuel the need to move more cotton more rapidly to market, and more slaves more rapidly to cotton plantations. Railroads, roads, and canals filled that need, railroads most of all.

Then, into this frenzied growth of wealth and power based on Black labor, feeding on itself to generate more wealth and power based on Black labor, a wild card entered, a second disruptor that did not annihilate space and time; instead, it was a technology predicated on the assumption that for all practical purposes, space and time did not exist.

● ● ●

On page 3 of the February 7, 1844, issue of *The Daily Madisonian*, then a Washington, DC, newspaper, sandwiched between a report on the first session of the 28th Congress, and an announcement for the last performance, that season, of the Hutchinson Family Singers, who sang anti-slavery songs at their concerts and toured with Frederick Douglass, was an advertisement seeking sealed proposals to supply seven hundred poles made from chestnut trees. The specifications were given: 680 poles to be 24 feet long, 20 poles to be 30 feet long, delivered in a month to the Baltimore & Ohio Railroad Depot in the city.[57]

Samuel Morse had laid twenty miles of copper wire underground before failing insulation caused him to rip it all out. With money running low and time running short, Morse's last best hope lay in erecting telephone poles aboveground along the B&O's right-of-way, approximately every 225 feet, spanning the distance between the US Supreme Court chambers (at the time in the basement of the US Capitol) and the B&O's Mount Clare station in Baltimore, thirty miles away, then stringing uninsulated wires from pole to pole.

With his wires strung, and members of Congress watching, on May 24 of that year, Morse tapped out a message from the court's chambers to his business partner, Alfred Vail, waiting at the B&O station: "What hath God wrought." The telegraph had come of age.

Morse did not invent the telegraph. The idea of sending encoded signals electrically over wires had been around for some time. But he did invent a way of reducing signal loss, the relay repeater. Prior to Morse's repeater, a single copper wire could not reliably carry a telegraph signal for more than twenty miles before the signal died out. So, Morse injected a relay and a battery into the lines, which boosted the signal as it traveled forward to the next repeater, and the next. Thus, the telegraph was not only a telecommunication system, it was the first wide-scale digital telecommunication system. The telegraph was digital, or binary, in two respects. Relays were either open or closed. Also, the characters of Morse code were composed of either long (dash) or short (dot) electrical impulses.

Telegraphs and railroads had long been intertwined. Before Morse, European inventors had even considered sending telegraphic signals through any conductive body such as water or railroad tracks, ideas Morse toyed with himself. Morse started the Magnetic Telegraph Company a year after his congressional success, and many small telegraph companies soon followed. All had the same question: Where to find the "right-of-way" to erect their poles, and string their wires? Railroads seemed the perfect answer. Railroad companies had either cleared and graded roadbeds throughout the nation, or they were in the process of doing just that. Only accidents and liability concerns made railroads initially resistant to provide such right-of-way. But through the first half of the nineteenth century, railroad networks grew in size and distance, chipping away at that resistance. For trains to run on schedule or for two trains running in opposite directions to use a single track, management and coordination at a distance was needed, something the telegraph provided.

For those prospering from the business of slavery, railroads and telegraphs offered something else: a more efficient way to make money off Black lives and their labor.

E. H. Stokes, of Richmond, Virginia, made his money that way. Wrote one female customer in March 1863,

> *Mr. E. H. Stokes*
> *I am anxious to buy a small healthy negro girl—ten or twelve years old, and would like to know if you could let me have one—I will pay you cash in State money (Confederate money)—and you allowing the per centage on it—I will take her on trial of a few weeks—please let me hear from you as soon as possible (—I would like a dark Mulatto).*[58]

It was as though she was shopping through the pages of an in-home catalog, selecting both the size and color of an item.

Dr. J. H. Burnett of North Carolina inquired of Stokes, "A friend of yours informs me that you were now selling negroes. I have a boy about 16 years old . . . and a cotton hand & another about 25 black hand. What can you get for them?" To which Stokes replied, $1,900 for the sixteen-year-old and $1,000 for the other.[59]

Stokes also had "drummers" throughout the south—as salesmen who'd "drum up" business were called.[60] A. J. Rux was a drummer in Alabama, who wrote to Stokes in 1860 and 1861, informing him of the dismal market in slaves.[61] Winbush Young, another drummer in Virginia, apparently understood the power of new technology; instead of writing, on June 24, 1862, Young sent Stokes a telegraph from Boston, Virginia: "I sent you by train three (3) negroes cash Eighteen Hundred (1800) Dollars."[62]

Those three Black folks did not ride in first-class. They rode in "slave cars" or "negro cars." "I have seen slave-pens and slave-cars filled with the unhappy victims of this internal and infernal trade," James Redpath said in 1859.[63]

It's a haunting image: train cars filled with unhappy people rolling toward uncertain fates. Though slavery ended by proclamation in 1863, that image lingered, surfacing seventy years later in Nazi Germany, when, once again, train cars filled with unhappy people rolled to uncertain fates. There, too, the telegraph and digital communication were involved, though it is a story for a later time.

When Frederick Douglass said that slavery had "an enemy in every bar of railroad iron," he added, "in every electric wire."[64] His beliefs may have been more aspirational than factual, for railroad iron and electric wire also contributed to slavery's proliferation, lining the pockets and increasing the power of many.

To the amazement of White Kentucky WPA writer Carl Hall, one of the unnamed ex-slaves he interviewed was careful "to avoid all telegraph poles, as that he thought the wire could detect and betray him, the telegraph was a mystery to his innorant [sic] mind.

He succeeded in making his way to Canada and freedom where he stayed until after the war, when it was safe to return."[65] Other than Hall's misspelling of "ignorant" in the original source, this ex-slave's fears may not have been so unfounded. Telegraphs often transmitted information about runaway slaves, so that masters and patrollers were waiting for them up ahead, along the path of their escape.

But Samuel Morse may have summed up the promises and paradoxes of these new technologies best. Morse, a virulent racist, who believed slavery was ordained by God, and those against slavery were sinners, compared enslaved Black people to orangutans.[66] He borrowed a passage from Numbers 23:23 when he sent that first message, more an exclamation than a question: "What hath God wrought!"

Yes. What hath God wrought? New technologies, like the railroad and telegraph, whose ultimate success was guaranteed by the lives and labor of Black people. Yet technologies that, like the cotton gin, were used to suppress Black lives, and make more efficient a brutal system of slavery; new technologies for which Black lives paved the way, but never reaped the rewards.

THE ONLY COWARDLY BLOOD

Baton Rouge had fallen.

While it seemed such a long time ago, only three months ear-lier New Orleans had fallen, too. What now kept Major General Benjamin Franklin Butler awake through the sweltering Louisiana nights, that summer of 1862, was protecting the gains his Union troops had made. Threatening from his north were the forces of the cunning Confederate general Meriwether Jeff Thompson, known also as the "Swamp Fox." To make the area Butler controlled more defensible, he ordered a wide swath of forest cleared—from the Mississippi River to Lake Pontchartrain around New Orleans. An order he gave to General John W. Phelps. After all, Butler rea-soned, Phelps could use the large number of runaway slaves at his camp ("contraband," they were called) as labor for accomplishing the task.[1]

But Phelps refused.

For the past several weeks, Phelps, a Vermont native and gradu-ate of West Point, had been training ex-slaves and free Black men as a fighting force. He'd requested of Butler not axes but arms for them.

Butler tried reason. President Lincoln forbade using negro troops, even disbanding the 1st South Carolina Volunteer Infantry

Regiment (Colored) organized by General David ("Black David") Hunter. Butler had ordered runaways returned to their masters. Besides, Butler told Phelps, the arms and equipment sent him were specifically reserved for White men; or, as General William T. Sherman would say, a year later, "I would prefer to have this a white man's war."[2]

Phelps would not back down. He trained men to fight. "[W]hile I am willing to prepare African regiments for the defense of the Government against its assailants I am not willing to become the mere slave-driver you propose . . ." Phelps then resigned. Butler denied it. So, Phelps returned his commission to President Abraham Lincoln. At one point, Butler described Phelps as "mad as a March Hare on the 'nigger question.'"[3]

While Lincoln brooded over Phelps, Butler's need grew. He impressed former Confederate soldiers into the Union's ranks. He requested reinforcements from the war department. When they refused, he threatened, "if they could not do anything for me by sending troops, I would call on Africa for assistance."

Call on Africa he did.

The 1st Louisiana Native Guard of the Confederate States of America was a militia of free Blacks, formed in New Orleans in 1861, to fight on the side of the Confederacy. When the Louisiana legislature passed a law in early 1862 that militias were to be composed only of "free white males capable of bearing arms" the Native Guard was forced to disband. But as Union troops, and the Union Navy under Admiral David G. Farragut, trained an assault on New Orleans, the Native Guard was briefly reinstated as a last-ditch effort before finally being disbanded when the city fell in the spring of 1862.

Butler, in the fall of that year, ordered the officers of the Native Guard rounded up. It surprised him that mostly light-skinned men stood before him, yet they had chosen as their spokesman a man he described "as dark as the ace of spades."

"My officers, most of them, believe that negroes won't fight," Butler said.

"Oh, but we will," said the group.

"Then tell me why some negroes have not in this war struck a good blow somewhere for their freedom?" Butler asked the spokesman. "All over the south the men have been conscripted and driven away to the armies, leaving ten negroes in some districts to one White man, and the colored men have simply gone on raising crops and taking care of their women and children."

The spokesman admitted his fear of answering the general's question.

Butler assured him that "whatever the answer may be it shall harm no one of you."

"General, will you permit a question?" the spokesman asked.

"Yes."

"If we colored men had risen to make war on our masters, would not it have been our duty to ourselves, they being our enemies, to kill the enemy wherever we could find them, and all the White men would have been our enemies to be killed?"

"I don't know but what you are right," Butler said. "I think that would be a logical necessity of insurrection."

"If the colored men had begun such a war as that, General, which general of the United States Army should we have called on to help us fight our battles?"

That, Butler admitted, was unanswerable.

"Well," Butler said, "why do you think your men will fight?"

"General, we come of a fighting race. Our fathers were brought here as slaves because they were captured in war, and in hand-to-hand fights, too. We are willing to fight. Pardon me, General, but the only cowardly blood we have got in our veins is the White blood."

The 1st Regiment of the 1st Louisiana Native Guard of the United States of America "became soldiers of the United States on the 22d day of August, 1862. In a very short time three regiments of infantry and two batteries of artillery were equipped, drilled, and ready for service. Better soldiers never shouldered a musket," Butler said.[4]

Their first test under fire was almost a year away.

• • •

Instead of accepting his resignation, Lincoln offered Phelps a promotion to major general, placing him at the same rank as Butler. Phelps agreed, but only if the commission was postdated to the day of his resignation. That, Lincoln could not agree to because it would have legitimized Phelps's contravention of Butler's order. So, Lincoln refused. Phelps returned to his Vermont farm. Butler was recalled to Washington. And Major General Nathaniel Banks took Butler's place.

In the summer and autumn of 1862, as this intrigue unfolded, Lincoln put the final touches on the Emancipation Proclamation. Following the advice of Edwin M. Stanton, his secretary of war, Lincoln would not announce his intention to free slaves until after the Union's next victory, which came on September 17 in Maryland at Antietam, where Union major general George B. McClellan repulsed the troops of Confederate general Robert E. Lee.

For Black leaders at the time, those hundred days between when Lincoln informed the south and when emancipation took effect were filled with apprehension. Was it a bluff, or would Lincoln actually sign the order? And what exactly would the order say? Lincoln himself equivocated. The chaplain of the Senate, Byron Sunderland, urged Lincoln to keep his promise.

"'Well, Doctor,'" Sunderland reported Lincoln saying, "'you know Peter was going to do it, but when the time came he didn't.'"[5]

Lincoln was, of course, referring to the biblical account of Jesus at the Last Supper foretelling the Apostle Peter's denial. Peter declared he would never disavow Jesus. But that next day, after Jesus's arrest, Peter did deny knowing him, denied it three times.

With all the gloss heaped on the proclamation, many facts remain conveniently overlooked. Lincoln did not issue the Emancipation Proclamation out of a desire to end slavery. Like the Founders before him, who appeased the south at almost every turn in crafting the Declaration of Independence, the Constitution, and the Bill of Rights, Lincoln's overarching concern was preserving the Union. He said as much in response to abolitionist and editor of the *New-York Tribune*, Horace Greeley:

> If there be those who would not save the Union, unless they could at the same time save slavery, I do not agree with them. If there be those who would not save the Union unless they could at the same time destroy slavery, I do not agree with them. *My paramount object in this struggle is to save the Union, and is not either to save or to destroy slavery.* If I could save the Union without freeing any slave I would do it, and if I could save it by freeing all the slaves I would do it; and if I could save it by freeing some and leaving others alone I would also do that. What I do about slavery, and the colored race, I do because I believe it helps to save the Union; and what I forbear, I forbear because I do not believe it would help to save the Union . . . I have here stated my purpose according to my view of official duty; and I intend no modification of my oft-expressed personal wish that all men everywhere could be free.[6]

Wednesday, December 31, 1862, was tense with hope and fear. At a Washington, DC, "contraband camp," where the federal government gave fugitive slaves temporary quarters, George Payne, a former slave, counted down the minutes. "Friends, don't you see de han' of God in dis?" he asked. "I have a right to rejoice; an' so have you; for we shall be free in jus' about five minutes."[7]

Another ex-slave stood before the crowd to welcome in "the Year of Jubilee."

Now, no more dat! no more dat! no more dat! When I tink what de Lord's done for us, an' brot us thro' de trubbles, I feel dat I ought go inter his service. We'se free now, bress de Lord! (Amens! were vociferated all over the building.) Dey can't sell my wife an' child any more, bress de Lord! (Glory, glory! from the audience.) No more dat! no more dat! no more dat, now! (Glory!)[8]

In Boston, on December 31, 1862, abolitionist William Lloyd Garrison delayed printing of *The Liberator*, hoping for word from Washington before going to press. By the next morning, the Emancipation Proclamation still had not been signed. Later that evening, Frederick Douglass and others gathered at Boston's Tremont Temple, voiced their hopes and aired their doubts. A line of messengers had been set up between the telegraph office and the temple. Eight p.m. came and went. Nine o'clock, then ten. Still no word. A cloud of despair began settling over the hall.[9]

Douglass recalled it might have been Judge Thomas B. Russell who then burst into the hall screaming, "It is coming! It is on the wires!"

When the initial tears and shouts of jubilation subsided, Douglass led the assembly.[10]

Blow ye the trumpet, blow!
The gladly solemn sound
let all the nations know,
to earth's remotest bound:
The year of jubilee is come!
The year of jubilee is come!

Then, his old friend, a Black preacher named Rue, picked up[11]

Sound the loud timbrel o'er Egypt's dark sea;
Jehovah has triumphed; his people are free.
Sing for the pride of the tyrant is broken,
His chariots, his horsemen, all splendid and brave;
How vain was their boasting! the Lord hath but spoken,
And chariots and horsemen are sunk in the wave.

The celebration moved from the temple to Twelfth Baptist Church in Roxbury, where an overflowing crowd lasted through the night.

But upon examining the proclamation in the cold light of a new day, a heavy veil of disappointment descended. It was brief and dry. Gone was Lincoln's typical grandiloquence. Military necessity was repeated throughout, with nothing said of human or moral responsibility. And a question remained as to whom, exactly, the proclamation emancipated.

The proclamation only freed slaves in ten Confederate states. But those were states that did not recognize Lincoln's authority anyway, and were in open rebellion precisely because they desired to maintain slavery. Some slaveholding border states, such as Delaware, Maryland, Kentucky, and Missouri, were excluded from the proclamation, which meant slavery could continue there. Nor did the proclamation apply to Tennessee, Louisiana, or the western counties of Virginia, which would go on to be West Virginia. Finally, some regions of the south already under the control of Union forces were excluded as well. Lincoln was, at least, true to his word: he issued a proclamation which freed some slaves, and left many still in chains.

Other forces also worked on Lincoln to issue the Emancipation Proclamation. A Union victory was not certain, even after Antietam. So, the proclamation offered freed slaves the opportunity to take up arms against their former masters. "I further declare and make known," the proclamation reads, "that such persons of suitable condition, will be received into the armed service of the United States to garrison forts, positions, stations, and other places, and to man vessels of all sorts in said service."[12]

Even with its obvious flaws, Douglass and others comforted themselves with the knowledge that the Emancipation Proclamation made clear this was not merely a war for the abstract notion of national unity, but a war for the concrete ideal of freedom. And freedom was a cause for which men would fight, and die.

• • •

In New Orleans, with the exception of Butler, no generals wished to be in command of Black troops. Two months prior to his recall to Washington, Butler assigned the 1st Louisiana Native Guard to Brigadier Godfrey (Gottfried) Weitzel. Weitzel refused the command. "I cannot command those negro regiments," he said.

> Since the arrival of the negro regiments symptoms of servile insurrection are becoming apparent. I could not, without breaking my brigade all up, put a force in every part of this district to keep down such an insurrection. I cannot assume the command of such a force, and thus be responsible for its conduct . . . I have no confidence in the organization. Its moral effect in this community, which is stripped of nearly all its able-bodied men and will be stripped of a great many of its arms, is terrible. Women and children, and even men, are in terror. It is heart-rending, and I cannot make myself responsible for it. I will gladly go anywhere with my own brigade that you see fit to order me. I beg you therefore to keep the negro brigade directly under your own command or place some one over both mine and it.[13]

Black troops caused enslaved Blacks to leave plantations, join the Union, or in other ways advocate for their freedom ("servile insurrection"), and this was causing consternation among the White citizens of New Orleans, whom Weitzel was more interested in protecting. Weitzel followed up with another communication to Butler.

> I have the honor to inform you that on the plantation of Mr. David Pugh, a short distance above here, the negroes who have returned under the terms fixed upon by Major-General Butler, without provocation or cause of any kind, refused this morning to work, and assaulted the overseer and Mr. Pugh, injuring them severely, also a gentleman who came to the assistance of Mr. Pugh. Upon the

plantation also of Mr. W. J. Miner, on the Terre Bonne road, about sixteen miles from here, an outbreak has already occurred, and the entire community thereabout are in hourly expectation and terror of a general rising.[14]

Soon, Butler would be recalled to Washington, and his replacement, Nathaniel Banks, felt much the same as Weitzel did about Black troops. Banks purged most of the Black line officers from the Native Guard. But Weitzel, still saddled with them, assigned the Native Guard to building bridges and acting as sentries. Then, in May 1863, Banks received orders that Port Hudson was to be taken, a Confederate stronghold north of Baton Rouge, along the banks of the Mississippi. Grant had been charged with operations against the Confederacy at Vicksburg. The success of Grant and Banks would mean the Mississippi River was effectively in Union hands.[15]

The infantry attack on Port Hudson began in the early morning hours of May 22, 1862. Despite a night of naval fire to soften the Confederate forces, Weitzel's troops, under the field command of Brigadier General William Dwight, were soon pinned down in a ravine. Bullets whined from a fortified ridge on one side of the ravine, called the Bull Pen; from a small dome-shaped pillbox on another ridge, known as Fort Desperate; and from an artillery battery on Commissary Hill. The Confederacy held the high ground, and their sharpshooters seemed to pick off Union soldiers at will. Poorly aimed "friendly fire" from the 1st Maine battery landed on Union troops as well.[16]

Into the slaughter, Dwight ordered the 1st and 3rd Regiments of the Louisiana Native Guard. They'd been working on a nearby pontoon bridge over the Mississippi, north of the main battle, which placed them in the worst possible position of attack. The remainder of the Union forces were to the northeast of Port Hudson, which meant the Native Guard had no backup or support as they approached the Confederate guns at the fort of Port Hudson.[17]

Six times, the Guard, under command of one of the few remaining

Black line officers, Captain André Cailloux, charged the parapets protecting the fort. Some soldiers leapt into the waters of a bayou leading to the fortification and attempted to swim across. Nearly every man was killed. Again and again, they tried. Some managed to engage the enemy, but with no backup they were soon repulsed.

Perhaps it was the adrenaline coursing through Cailloux's veins from a serious gunshot wound to his arm, but on May 27, he rallied his men for a final charge. Now berserk, in the original sense of that word,[18] with his wounded arm flailing wildly, Cailloux led the charge. His voice could be heard above the din of battle:

"*Suivez-moi.* Follow me. *Suivez-moi!*"

He alternated between French and English, yelling like a wild man.[19]

Cailloux fell fifty yards before the fort. His Native Guard was ordered to withdraw. Cailloux's body remained on the battlefield until July 9, when the forty-eight-day siege of Port Hudson ended. Grant had conquered Vicksburg, which led to the surrender of the port. On July 29, trumpets and trombones blared, in typical New Orleans style, leading the hearse that carried Cailloux on his final journey.[20]

Because of Port Hudson, and Cailloux, Banks had a change of heart. When reporting to the war department on the Siege of Port Hudson, he said of the Native Guard,

In many respects their conduct was heroic. No troops could be more determined or more daring . . . The highest commendation is bestowed upon them by all the officers in command . . . Whatever doubt may have existed heretofore . . . the history of this day proves conclusively to those who were in condition to observe the conduct of these regiments that the Government will find in this class of troops effective supporters and defenders. The severe test to which they were subjected, and the determined manner in which they encountered the enemy, leaves upon my mind no doubt of their ultimate success.[21]

Contrary to popular opinion, and the Hollywood movie *Glory*, starring Denzel Washington and Morgan Freeman, the 54th Massachusetts Infantry Regiment was not the first official Black regiment in the Union Army, the Louisiana Native Guard was. The 54th went into battle, leading the charge against Fort Wagner in South Carolina on July 18, 1863. But that was two months after André Cailloux led his men, and lost his life, against the Confederate garrison at Port Hudson.

Many Black soldiers and sailors followed. About 179,000 Black soldiers served in the Union Army, another 19,000 in the Union Navy. Roughly 40,000 Black members of the military died during the years of conflict, 75 percent of those from disease, and from the refusal of field hospitals to treat soldiers of color. Early in the conflict, Black soldiers received $7 per month serving in the US military, while White soldiers received $13 per month. The 54th and 55th Massachusetts Infantry Regiments spearheaded the fight for equal pay, refusing to accept anything less than what White soldiers received. After a nationwide outcry, which included a number of White soldiers, Congress passed an act in 1864 that granted equal pay. While that may have brought pay equity to Blacks and Whites serving in the armed forces, problems of unequal promotion and prejudice plagued Blacks in the military during the Civil War, and still plague Blacks in the military today.

This refusal of Union hospitals to treat Black soldiers, leading to their deaths, highlighted the medical disparities of the time, though these disparities began well before the end of the Civil War. In 1716, Onesimus, a slave to Cotton Mather, had proposed a means of inoculation against smallpox, but was cast aside in favor of White doctor Zabdiel Boylston, who then used Onesimus's skin prick method to prevent a serious 1721 outbreak in Boston.[22] After Edward Jenner's creation of a smallpox vaccine, Jefferson, in the late eighteenth century, experimented by inoculating his slaves, then challenging them with live smallpox virus. Only once they showed no symptoms, did he give the vaccine to his family.[23] And, perhaps, most infamously, by the end of the Civil War, J. Marion Sims had used Black slave women for painful experiments in gynecological surgery without anesthesia, in an effort to make them more productive "breeders" for White slave owners, earning him the title, "the father of modern gynecology."[24]

The Tuskegee Syphilis Study,[25] where the disease was allowed to run its full course untreated in Black men, had not taken place yet. Henrietta Lacks's cells had not yet been culled for medical experimentation.[26] The Influenza Outbreak of 1918, disproportionately affecting Black Americans, had not happened.[27] COVID-19 deaths ravaging Black communities were almost 150 years in the future.[28] Pulse oximetry, the ability to read oxygen levels through the skin, was an unheard-of technology. So, its importance in diagnosing diseases like COVID-19 coupled with its inaccuracy when reading through dark skin was unknown.[29]

Yes, the Civil War settled the question of whether the United States would remain united, but opened up so many more questions of how Black Americans would be treated in these United States, in medical care and beyond. Still, Black soldiers were there at the end.

When Grant crossed the Rapidan River to engage Lee's forces in the battles of his Overland Campaign, he had with him a division of Black troops, numbering about 8,000. At the same time, attacking Richmond, Benjamin F. Butler, long since returned from lessons learned in Louisiana, brought with him 5,000 Black infantrymen and 1,800 Black cavalries. As Grant outflanked Lee, heading into some of the war's most bloody hand-to-hand combat at Virginia's Spotsylvania Courthouse and Cold Harbor, he ordered General W. F. ("Baldy") Smith south of Richmond to advance on Petersburg. On June 15, 1864, Black troops, then called the United States Colored Troops (USCT), led the attack and succeeded in punching a mile-wide hole through the Confederacy's defenses, capturing six big guns and two hundred prisoners.[30]

But Smith did not press his advantage (Butler later accused him of "dilatoriness"), giving Confederate forces time for reinforcement.[31] This led to a ten-month siege of the city, participated in by thirty-four USCT regiments, battling at Darbytown Road, Fair Oaks, Deep Bottom, Hatcher's Run, New Market Heights, and Fort Gilmer. Black troops sustained heavy losses.

In early April 1865, Lee abandoned both Petersburg and Richmond, fleeing west toward Appomattox with the USCT 2nd Division in hot pursuit. It ended there, with Black troops "moving forward at double quick" and Confederate soldiers "retreating in confusion."[32]

On land and sea, Black troops were involved in every theater of the Civil War. They served with distinction, and died with honor. The Medal of Honor was created by the US Congress during the Civil War. Over fourteen hundred Union troops received the award; of those twenty-five were Black. General Benjamin Butler, at his own expense, created a medal officially known as the Army of the James Medal, but popularly known as the Butler Medal or as the Colored Troops Medal, which he issued to two hundred Black Union soldiers for their bravery and heroism in the Richmond and Petersburg campaign. But after Butler's removal from command, Black troops were forbidden to pin this "unofficial" medal on their uniforms.[33]

During these years of national strife, Black men and women helped shape the military, one of the principal institutions of America. Military service in America has long translated into political power and wealth, from the time of George Washington until the present day. Ulysses S. Grant, of course, became the eighteenth president of the United States; Benjamen Butler, the governor of Massachusetts; George B. McClellan, the governor of New Jersey; Nathaniel Banks, the twenty-first Speaker of the House of Representatives; "Baldy" Smith, the president of both the International Telegraph Company and the board of police commissioners for New York City; and the list is long. For a time, a very brief time, at that, Black men who'd fought against the Confederacy also experienced a similar rise in power and wealth, as we shall see in the next chapter.

• • •

For years, I lived in Richmond, Virginia, the capital of the Confederacy. My office was just off the north end of Monument Avenue, where the statues of Civil War generals rode high atop their horses. I'd always heard there was a secret code. Depending upon which direction the horse was facing, north or south, and whether the horse's head was sculpted up or down, you were supposed to be able to tell whether that general was killed in battle by Union troops or died of some other cause. I never committed the code to memory. I found the monuments distasteful, and avoided the avenue whenever I could. So, I rejoiced when after a yearlong legal battle, Lee's statue was taken down. My barbershop in Richmond was atop a former slave auction site. And I got an eerie feeling whenever I sat down for a cut. One of the main Confederate cemeteries in Richmond had a rather large pyramid modeled after the one at Giza, Egypt, which I passed each day as I drove into work. I don't know the backstory, but I always believed it had something to do with Antoine Bovis, the Frenchman who in the 1930s claimed that pyramids had the power to preserve the dead.

Richmond was particularly good at preserving the past. In the 1980s, one of the city's newspapers still referred to the Civil War as "the War of Northern Aggression" or "the late hostilities." As though the Spanish-American War, the First World War, the Second World War, the Korean War, and the Vietnam War were merely insignificant blips.

I have long wondered why the south seems never to have gotten over the Civil War; why the Confederate flag remains such a potent and powerful symbol; why Civil War generals are still revered as heroes; why it is still debated whether the war was fought over slavery.

Historians have offered many explanations, but, perhaps, there is none more powerful than the one chiseled into the marble memorial for the Confederate soldiers of South Carolina at the Gettysburg National Military Park: "That men of honor might forever know the responsibilities of freedom. Dedicated South Carolinians stood and were counted for their heritage and convictions. Abiding faith in the sacredness of States Rights provided their creed. Here many earned eternal glory."[34]

"Responsibilities of freedom"? What responsibilities of freedom exist that seek to enslave and hold enslaved human beings? "Abiding faith in the sacredness of States Rights"? By what moral creed does States Rights extend to the buying, selling, and ownership of human beings? It seems not only a civil war but a civil delusion. The only way an inscription like this makes any sense is if looked at as another instance of American freedom built atop the horrors of American slavery.

Yet, the Union had delusions of its own. With the issuance of the Emancipation Proclamation, the north finally had a principle behind its cause. And, while the proclamation is read primarily as a document freeing enslaved Black citizens, it can equally, and perhaps more powerfully, be read as a document clarifying the "responsibilities of freedom" for White citizens, north and south. The primary responsibility being that a nation cannot hold another human being in bondage and still call itself the land of the free.

In this regard, the Emancipation Proclamation is a statement of "freedom dues" both to those who claim to have "freedom" and to those who most assuredly do not. The Civil War, then, by this reckoning, represented a third opportunity for America to take "the road not taken." The first opportunity came not long after Anthony and Isabella, and their malungu, set foot on American soil. The second opportunity came when the Founders broke from England, and set about creating a new society based on new ideas about liberty, equality, and justice. The third now came after a blood-soaked conflict pitting the country against itself.

The results of the first two opportunities are well-known. By 1660, slavery was clearly established in the colonies, and by the Second Constitutional Convention in 1787, slavery was clearly encoded in the great founding documents of America. But with the end of the Civil War, a question remained: How would America respond given this third chance to pay freedom dues?

One major problem with the Union's response was that Lincoln had no plan. It's probably not a great idea to release four to five million enslaved people simply on a wing and a prayer, but that's exactly what Lincoln did: "And I hereby enjoin upon the people so declared to be free to abstain from all violence, unless in necessary self-defence; and I recommend to them that, in all cases when allowed, they labor faithfully for reasonable wages."[35]

Recommending that formerly enslaved people find work "for reasonable wages" is not a plan, it's a prayer.

The south, in contrast, actually did have a plan for what to do with slaves if they prevailed in the war. In March 1865, near the end of the Confederacy, President Jefferson Davis, an ardent slaveholder, and the Confederate Congress advanced a policy of arming and emancipating slaves. Davis was authorized to recruit up to 300,000 slaves for the Confederate forces, with no more than 25 percent of male slaves between 18 and 45 drawn from any given state.[36] Black Confederates, as they were known, trained in segregated regiments, though the war was over before they ever saw battle. Many more slaves populated the Confederate ranks as bound servants to White officers, as cooks, and on the staff of field hospitals.

Confederate secretary of state Judah Benjamin laid out what would happen after the south won its independence and had to deal with Black soldiers who helped bring about that victory.

The next step will then be that the States, each for itself, shall act upon the question of the proper status of the families of the men so manumitted. Cautious legislation providing for their ultimate emancipation after an intermediate state of serfage or peonage would soon find advocates in different States. We might then be able, while vindicating our faith in the doctrine that the negro is an inferior race and unfitted for social or political equality with the white man, yet so modify and ameliorate the existing condition of that inferior race by providing for it certain rights of property, a certain degree of personal liberty, and legal protection for the marital and parental relations, as to relieve our institutions from much that is not only unjust and impolitic in itself, but calculated to draw down upon us the odium and reprobation of civilized man.[37]

The south's plan was simple: *maintain White supremacy and slavery under the guise of serfage and peonage*. The north won the war. The emancipation of slaves took place. But what plan for ex-slaves would rule the peace?

At least Union general William T. Sherman and Secretary of War Edwin M. Stanton seemed to know that Lincoln needed a plan. And on the evening of January 12, 1865, before the Civil War was officially over, Sherman and Stanton addressed a gathering of Black Baptist and Methodist ministers, some former slaves, some formerly free, who'd climbed to the second floor of Sherman's headquarters in a private mansion bordering a lush tropical square in Savannah. The meeting began at 8:00 p.m. with Major General Edward Davis Townsend, one of Lincoln's military advisers, recording the affair.[38]

Garrison Frazier had been selected to speak for the group of Black ministers. Frazier, at sixty-seven years old, was born in North Carolina, and had been a slave until he bought his freedom, and his wife's, in 1857, for one thousand dollars in silver and gold. He'd been an ordained Baptist minister for thirty-five years. Though he no longer had a church, he did have the support of the assembled delegation.[39]

Sherman questioned Frazier on his understanding of Lincoln's actions and the goals of the United States at war. Frazier matched each question with a sophisticated answer. Sherman, then, got around to the most urgent matter—the need for a plan.

"State in what manner you think you can take care of yourselves, and how can you best assist the Government in maintaining your freedom," Townsend records Sherman saying,[40]

The way we can best take care of ourselves is to have land and turn in and it by our labor—that is, by the labor of the women, and children, and old men—and we can soon maintain ourselves and have something to spare; and to assist the Government the young men should enlist in the service of the Government, and serve in such manner as they may be wanted. (The rebels told us that they piled them up and made batteries of them, sold them to Cuba, but we don't believe that.) We want to be placed on land until we are able to buy it and make it our own.[41]

"State in what manner you would rather live, whether scattered among the whites or in colonies by yourselves?" asked Sherman.[42]

Frazier answered, "I would prefer to live by ourselves, for there is a prejudice against us in South that will take years to get over, but I do not know that I can answer for my brethren."[43]

Townsend notes, when polled, every minister agreed with "Brother Frazier."[44]

Finally, two years after the Emancipation Proclamation, Lincoln had the makings of a plan. Four days after this meeting, from the self-expressed desires of Black men long held in bondage, came General Sherman's Special Field Orders No. 15, accepted by Abraham Lincoln and otherwise known as "40 acres and a mule." Mules were not actually in Sherman's original order. He later requisitioned the US Army to lend them to newly freed Black landholders.

The scope of this post-emancipation plan was nothing short of breathtaking: distribute 400,000 acres of coastline stretching from Charleston to the St. John's River in Florida, and extending some thirty miles inland, to newly emancipated slaves—land formerly belonging to southern White slaveholders, and the most agriculturally productive land in those states. Furthermore, in this area, allow African Americans to organize and govern their own communities. In Special Field Orders No. 15, "freedom dues" had been accepted, allocated, and acted upon by the federal government. "40 acres and a mule" showcased the American government at its finest regarding her citizens of color. Reparations were the order. Sweeping promises were made. The country, it seemed, had risen to the challenge and taken "the road not taken" before.

Brigadier General Rufus Saxton commanded the Union fort at Port Royal, South Carolina. A West Pointer, born in Massachusetts, and an abolitionist, Saxton immediately began processing thousands of requests for land. By June 1865, 40,000 Black Americans had settled on the first 400,000 acres of land, called derisively by Sherman's critics "Sherman's Reservation." Six weeks before Lincoln's assassination, Congress passed the first Freedmen's Bureau Act of 1865, placing General Oliver O. Howard (for whom Howard University is named) in charge of land grants. Howard ordered Saxton to continue the land redistribution program, and another 500,000 acres of land were under consideration, to be taken from slaveholders and redistributed to slaves. Nearly one million acres of land, one million acres of wealth, were up for redistribution in this way.

• • •

Ex-slave William Colbert recalled the feeling of leaving slavery behind. He was ninety-three years old when he spoke with John Morgan Smith, a WPA writer, in 1937.

"Sho, I remember de slavery days. How could I forgits?"

"Was your master good to you?" Smith asked.

"[H]e was so mean. When he wuz too tired te whup us he had de oberseer do it; and the oberseer was meaner dan de massa . . . So when brother January he come home, de massa took down his long mule skinner and tied him wid a rope to a pine tree. He strip' his shirt off and said:

"'Now, nigger, I'm goin' to teach you some sense.'

"Wid dat he started layin' on de lashes. January was a big, fine lookin' nigger, finest I ever seed. He wuz jus' four years older dan me, an' when de massa begin a beatin' him, January neber said a word. De massa got madder and madder kaze he couldn't make January holla.

"Den," Colbert continued, "de war came. De massa had three boys to go to war, but dere wuzn't one to come home. All the chillun he had wuz killed. Massa, he los' all his money and de house soon begin droppin' away to nothin' . . . de las' time I seed de home plantation I wuz a standin' on a hill. I looked back on it for de las' time through a patch of scrub pines and it look so lonely. Dere warn't but one person in sight, de massa. He was a-settin' in a wicker chair in de yard lookin' out ober a small field of cotton and cawn. Dere wuz fo' crosses in de graveyard in de side lawn where he wuz a-settin'. De fo'th one wuz his wife."

Although 150 years premature, one cannot help but hear in the opening stanza of John Legend's stirring anthem "Glory" (theme song for the film *Selma*) a soundtrack also for William Colbert's vision looking back at Massa through a patch of scrub pines. *When that day comes, the glory will be ours.*[45]

The war was won. Black men and women had proved their mettle, laid down their fire along with their lives; lives that mattered in bringing forth a new American military, a new American union, a final decisive blow against slavery. Many were sure that in wresting their freedom, they would finally secure their freedom dues. "So sure America," as rapper Common ad-libs to Legend, that some whispered of a second American Revolution coming on the heels of victory at Appomattox. Oh glory!

A SECOND AMERICAN REVOLUTION

Hope rose with the sun in Charleston.

On the morning of January 14, 1868, Black people from all over South Carolina, many ex-slaves and some formerly free, circled the city block around the old Clubhouse, in a pilgrimage to this new seat of power. Down King they walked, turning right at Broad Street, turning left at Meeting Street, then right a final time at Tradd Street to wind up back on King. Some circled in the opposite direction, while overhead, seagulls cawed, and the smell of salt air wafted in from the ocean.

In downtown Charleston, once the heart of the Confederacy, an African market met the Champs-Élysées that morning. Gullah, spoken in the Sea Islands, mixed with patois, from those prevented by law from formal education, and with the refined English of Black men educated at the finest colleges in America and England. Passersby purchased and ate hoppin' John made from Sea Island field peas; benne cakes, from ancient African recipes; and fresh shrimp from the nearby sea.

Sunday best was in order. Black women in flowing hats twirled parasols, and dressed in long colorful pink, white, and chartreuse cotton and silk. Other women donned the simpler, less colorful dresses they'd retained from long, hard years on plantations. Some

Black men wore dark long-tailed frocks, with bushy, aristocratic muttonchops springing from their cheeks and walking canes dangling from their hands. Other men dressed in the scratchy, ragged-edged suits worn to church meetings, whenever their former masters and overseers allowed. Beneath many of their suits lay skin etched and welted from the lash.

From rich dark chocolate to buttery caramel to creamy café au lait, every conceivable skin tone could be found among the men and women circling the block that morning. Although only a few White men and women were present.

The Clubhouse they circled had once been home to the White denizens of South Carolina's cotton and rice plantations, where they met to sip bourbon, check newspapers for the latest market prices in New York and London, and discuss the rigors of owning slaves. From the Clubhouse on April 12, seven years earlier, no doubt these men raised glasses to toast the cannon fire reigning on Fort Sumter. Or, perhaps like so many other White citizens of Charleston, they casually strolled, partially drunk, a few blocks down to the harbor, there enjoying the opening rounds of a war, and a way of life, they could never imagine losing. And now, these men sat in the darkness of shuttered homes behind the palmetto-lined streets of the city, reading sympathetic newspapers, bitter with hatred, drunk with anger, brooding over revenge.

By late morning, the Black crowd circling the block began slowly drifting into the inner courtyard, inspecting trees and flowers and shrubbery as they took the brick paths between buildings and greenways forbidden to them before. Curiosity, fascination, and hope surely mixed with disbelief as they lined up on the steps of the old Clubhouse, now turned into a meeting hall for the South Carolina Constitutional Convention. Some gathered around a side entrance only for delegates. All wanted the opportunity to see the seventy-six Black men and forty-eight White men their votes had sent here. All over the south, similar conventions were taking place to allow former Confederate states back into the Union. But those gathered here in Charleston understood their convention was different; understood this moment was history in the making, when for the first time in America, Black men outnumbered White men at a constitutional convention that would determine the laws by which all men and women in the state lived.

Swells of pride, swoons of excitement, and cheers of admiration arose as twenty-eight-year-old war hero Robert Smalls made his way through the crowd to the side entrance. Born a slave, with a White father, as a teenager Smalls worked Charleston Harbor as a deckhand, then wheelman, aboard ships plying the harbor and the spiderweb of waterways leading inland. When war broke out, he was bound to the *CSS Planter*, a Confederate ship assigned to deliver messages, troops, and supplies, and to survey and mine Charleston Harbor and nearby channels.

But Robert Smalls had other plans. On the evening of May 12, 1862, with the White crew on land, Smalls left dock with the *Planter*, stopped in Charleston to pick up his family and other slaves, then headed across the harbor in command. Smalls was a Black Jack through and through. He dressed the part of a Confederate sea captain, he knew the whistles to sound passing Confederate checkpoints, and he navigated the *Planter* to safety, delivering her, her all-Black crew, and their families to Union naval forces.

A similar round of *oohs* and *aahs* arose as Robert Brown Elliott made his way through the crowd, shaking hands with those who'd delivered him here. Born in England, Elliott went to Eton then served in the British Navy, which brought him to Boston in 1867. At twenty-five, clean-shaven, with only a mustache, and by all reports commanding, Elliott sat quietly for the first two weeks of the convention. Upon finally speaking, he soon became one of the south's greatest orators.

Though in the minority, Franklin J. Moses, Jr., the son of a prominent Jewish family of Charleston, parts the sea of Black faces. Raised as an Episcopalian not a Jew, he does not seem the least ill at ease around Black men and women. In fact, Moses is known to keep the company of Charleston's beautiful Black belles. While Moses helped lower the Union's colors at Fort Sumter, he also jumped adroitly to the side of freedmen by the time of the war's end. Glad-handing Blacks for votes, kissing Black babies, always with an eye on the governor's mansion. *Don't take your eyes off Moses,* say his opponents, *he's charming, and unscrupulous; all in all, the consummate politician.*

Born of a Charleston Jewish economist and a Black woman, Francis Lewis Cardozo, thirty, also makes his entrance into the hall. A graduate of the University of Glasgow, Cardozo is a fair-skinned Presbyterian minister. The other notable minister who pushes through the crowd is Richard Harvey Cain. Older than most delegates, Cain, in his forties, leads the powerhouse Mother Emanuel AME Church in Charleston, where almost 150 years later, a young White man will execute nine parishioners. But today, oblivious of the history that will be made, he's aware of the history he and the others are making at this convention.

The second floor of the Clubhouse is well appointed, with high ceilings and plenty of space. It has been cordoned off with a wooden railing, separating the room into unequal parts, two-thirds of the space reserved for the delegates, one-third reserved for the public, most of whom are Black. Chairs without desks have been arranged for the delegates, benches for the public. A dais with a pine desk backed by American flags has been provided for the president of the convention. Sitting at separate tables, off to the side, are members of the press. Rooms on the ground and third floors make perfect places for committees to meet.[1]

Excitement and anticipation are buzzing through the hall, coursing through delegates and gallery alike. Although Blacks are far in the majority, northern advisers have suggested that, in the name of unity, they select a White man as chair. Perhaps unwisely, they do. At twelve o'clock noon, former slaveholder Thomas J. Robertson, one of the wealthiest men in South Carolina, rises. The hall quiets. Robertson gavels the convention to order with these words:

"We, the delegates of the loyal people of South Carolina, are assembled here for the purpose of restoring our State to her proper relations in the Federal Union. It becomes us to frame a just and liberal Constitution, that will guarantee equal rights to all, regardless of race, color or previous condition . . ."[2]

And that is precisely the constitution framed by this majority Black convention in South Carolina in 1868, and by many similar constitutional conventions across the south at that time; constitutions the citizens of southern states then approved.

From halls where slave owners once luxuriated, former slaves created institutions of wealth and power unlike those ever seen before in America, and never seen since; institutions that nourished the orphaned, hungry words of the Founders and spread the foundations of wealth and power across Americans regardless of race or class. Some called it a "Second American Revolution."

From the moment Anthony and Isabella first set foot on Virginian soil, events led America to this point. But what actually brought about the conventions in South Carolina, and Virginia and Mississippi and other southern states? And why did this Second American Revolution ultimately shrivel and wither away? To answer these grave questions, we have to step back several years from that sunny day in Charleston; step back, at least, to the start of the Civil War.

● ● ●

The Civil War might well be called the "War of Northern Confusion," pitting northern uncertainty of purpose against a clarity of purpose expressed by the south. Confederates were fighting to preserve slavery, or as expressed by the Confederacy, for "states' rights" and a "southern way of life." It was, at best, a vision of Jeffersonian utopia that never really existed. But that didn't matter; a southern way of life stood clearly enough in the minds of southerners to go to war over fear that northerners would wrest this neverland away.

Against this, the north fought, but for what? To preserve the Union, as Lincoln so often said? It's at best an abstract notion when compared to, say, "fighting for a way of life." Anyway, how do you preserve a Union in which one group of people desire to keep forever in bondage another group of people, who desire forever their freedom? It's a simple answer: you do not, or better yet, you cannot. In drafting the founding documents, the framers of the Constitution knew this, which is why they capitulated to the slaveholding south. Lincoln, deep down, probably knew this as well, which is why the Emancipation Proclamation was such a tepid document that, as noted earlier, only freed slaves in the areas of the country not under his control, and left them enslaved in the areas of the country under his control.

British newspapers were quick to point out the hypocrisy. The London *Spectator* decried the Emancipation Proclamation as "half consciously pressing along a road which ends in emancipation," then continued, the "principle asserted is not that a human being cannot justly own another but that he cannot own him unless he is loyal to the United States."[3]

If Lincoln was ambivalent, some Union forces were clearly not. Union troops, under the command of General Benjamin F. Butler, assisted Confederate general Braxton Bragg (a West Point graduate, after whom Fort Bragg was named) from a feared slave insurrection. Butler wrote, "General Bragg is at liberty to ravage the houses of our brethren of Kentucky because the Union army of Louisiana is protecting his wife and his home against his negroes. Without that protection he would have to come back to take care of his wife, his home, and his negroes."[4]

In light of efforts in 2020 to rename Fort Bragg, led by senior members of the US military who rightly point out that Confederate officers were traitors to their oaths to protect the Constitution, it's worth restating what General Butler said. Union soldiers, not Confederates, protected the home of Confederate general Braxton Bragg from slaves, while he was out killing Union soldiers. Even the freedom of the Confederacy to wage war, in this case, was more important to the Union than the freedom of slaves.

It has been said that soldiers fight for either a noble cause or from clarity of purpose; the Confederacy had both, the Union had neither at the beginning of the conflict. Freedom could have been the standard Lincoln raised as a counterpoint to slavery. But even when he finally did, with the Emancipation Proclamation, Lincoln only raised freedom's flag to half-mast.

Ambivalence has consequences.

Lincoln's ambivalence about the aims of war carried over into his aims for peace, which were tentative and lacking vision. In his State of the Union message to Congress on December 1, 1862, Lincoln handed over to Time the responsibility for bringing about racial equality after emancipation. "Time," he said, "spares both races from the evils of sudden derangement."[5] Even Shakespeare knew that Time did not spare, nor wait, for men. Time would not spare the races, nor did Time spare Lincoln, assassinated a month before the war's end.

So, the problem facing Lincoln's successor, Andrew Johnson—in fact, the problem facing the nation at the end of the war—was a classic "Humpty-Dumpty" problem. Now that the Union had fallen off the wall, could all the president's horses and all the president's men put Humpty-Dumpty back together again? How do you bring the rebellious Confederate states back into the Union? And what do you do with four to five million newly freed slaves?

Once again, the stakes could not have been higher. In the answers to these three questions lay the fate and the future of America. And the answers turned around the latter of the two questions because what was done with ex-slaves would determine how the former slave states were brought back into the Union. And what was to be done with newly freed slaves came down to this: Do you give them the right to vote, so they have power? And do you redistribute land, so they have wealth?

The president and his men had one set of answers. The former

Confederate states had another. And the newly freed descendants of Africa, along with their advocates, inside and outside of government, had a third.

• • •

One of the president's men, Congressman John Winthrop Chanler, of New York, described Johnson this way:

> Of the poor whites of the southern States, Mr. Speaker . . . Andrew Johnson, the present Chief Magistrate of this Union, has the proud distinction of having risen from the poorest of the poor whites to be the ruler of this Union. And, sir, much of his mercy, wisdom, and patriotism is to be traced to the sympathy he deeply feels . . . for the poor and lowly of every section and every land or race.[6]

Sympathy for every race? "Damn the negroes," Johnson once reportedly said. "I am fighting these traitorous aristocrats, their masters."[7]

By the time Johnson ascended to the presidency, Sherman's plan for "40 acres and a mule," a redistribution of wealth, was well underway, ready to take nearly a million acres of prime farmland from former slave owners and give it to former slaves. Thousands of ex-slaves signed up through the Freedmen's Bureau. They were given that land. They started farming. They brought in cattle. They organized churches and public safety and legislative bodies.

John W. Chanler also read into House records a letter Sherman wrote to Andrew Johnson, describing Special Field Orders No. 15: "I knew of course we could not convey title and merely provided possessory titles, to be good as long as War and our Military Power lasted. I merely aimed to make provision for the Negroes who were absolutely dependent upon us, leaving the value of their possessions to be determined by after events or legislation."[8]

So, what appeared to be a plan was actually a ruse. Sherman

intended to redistribute land only while the war lasted, to relieve the burden on Union troops of slaves fleeing to their camps seeking freedom. And now, the war was over. Within seven weeks of Lincoln's assassination, Johnson, a slave owner himself, rescinded "40 acres and a mule," ordering any lands distributed to Blacks returned to their original landowners. Johnson wasn't fighting against southern White aristocrats; he was fighting for them.

It fell to Oliver Otis Howard, head of the Freedmen's Bureau, to deliver the news from Washington to ex-slaves on Edisto Island, South Carolina, that they would be evicted and their land returned to former slave owners. An old Gullah woman, in the back of the crowd that day, listened intently. As the general struggled for words, she found her voice in the Sea Islands' version of a spiritual,

> *Nobody knows de trouble I've had,*
> *Nobody knows but Jesus,*
> *Nobody knows de trouble I've had,*
> *(Sing) Glory hallelu!*
> *What makes ole Satan hate me so?*
> *Because he got me once and he let me go.*
> *Nobody knows de trouble I've had . . .*

Howard broke down and wept.[9]

· · ·

While granting land, then rescinding it, is surely another broken promise of freedom dues, it can also be seen, albeit through the eyes of southern White planters, as a moment of exquisite perfection, 250 years in the making. From the moment Anthony and Isabella stepped onto the shores of colonial Virginia, many generations of laws, punishments, and prohibitions had gone into constructing an American political and social system based on race.

Andrew Johnson was a product of that system: a poor White

who, presiding over the corridors of power, felt excluded by the White men who he felt considered themselves better than him.

> I know there are those here who profess to feel a contempt for me . . . I have always understood that there is a sort of exclusive aristocracy . . . which affects to contempt all who are not within its little circle. Let them enjoy their opinions. This aristocracy has been the bane of the Slave States, nor has the North been wholly free from its curse. It is a class which I have always forced to respect me, for I have ever set it at defiance.[10]

Johnson even embraced confiscating lands of southern aristocrats for redistribution to poor White farmers. "Treason must be made odious," he said, "and traitors must be punished and impoverished. Their great plantation must be seized and divided into small farms, and sold to honest, industrious men."[11]

But when the wealthiest White planters, and their northern backers, needed it most, the American system worked as designed: a poor White president turned against the interests of Black men and women, against even the interests of other poor Whites, and acted in the interests of the powerful and the wealthy.

Johnson, and many others, said that the Emancipation Proclamation freed more Whites than it did Blacks.[12] By which he meant the Emancipation Proclamation pulled the economic rug out from under the planter aristocracy, and they could no longer dominate Blacks or poor Whites. In redistributing confiscated land to poor Whites, Johnson would have further diminished the power and privilege of the southern aristocracy. But that, in turn, would have elevated the power of all poor people—White and Black. In the end, that's something he'd been trained not to abide.

Instead, Johnson insisted on only three principal measures for a Confederate state to rejoin the Union: ratify the Thirteenth Amendment, which abolished slavery; swear loyalty to the United States; and pay off any war debts. With these conditions met, Confederate states could hold new constitutional conventions, new elections, and send new senators and congressmen to Washington.

The south followed the letter of Johnson's law, even if they rejected the spirit of northern rule, sending to the 39th Congress the vice president of the Confederacy, four Confederate generals, five Confederate colonels, six Confederate cabinet members, and fifty-eight Confederate congressmen.

Under Johnson's plan, Confederate leaders would have to apply directly to him requesting pardons. Some said that Johnson, though he despised the southern aristocracy, secretly yearned for their acceptance. Ironically, Johnson could have been speaking about himself when he lamented, "[w]e get men in command who, under the influence of flattery, fawning and caressing, grant protection to the rich traitor."[13] Not only did he roll back land redistribution, he issued over fourteen thousand pardons to wealthy Confederates, the very class he once railed against, including a sweeping pardon to Confederate president Jefferson Davis.

Chickens had come home to roost.

● ● ●

The former Confederate states were starting to like how Reconstruction was proceeding. With one problem—land—now behind them, southern politicians held state constitutional conventions, like the South Carolina Convention of 1865, in which they ratified the Thirteenth Amendment and elected new representatives. But that still left another problem looming—labor. War, and the Emancipation Proclamation, had created a class of people never seen before in the south, four to five million newly freed slaves. Southern farmers and planters had been stripped of their unpaid workforce, and the question then became how to regenerate the wealth that war and emancipation had destroyed.

Andrew Johnson said that prior to a state's readmission to the Union, and a withdrawal of Union forces, he wanted freed slaves granted protection. And protection is just what South Carolina gave freedmen—protection southern-style. The south reverted to the very system they'd just sworn to abolish, slavery, only now they called it, in the words of the South Carolina senate, "a code for the regulation of labor and the protection and government of the colored population of the State."[14]

The *Edgefield Advertiser*, in South Carolina, published "the Code" on page 1 of the January 3, 1866, issue. Most simply called them the "Black Codes."

Black Codes were not new. As noted previously, Spain had implemented *Ordenanzas para los Negros* three hundred years earlier to control African slaves brought into their New World colonies, who they feared might join forces with the British. Only the Black Codes introduced into law in the south, in the two years following the Civil War, went beyond mere control. They were aimed specifically at reducing former slaves into de facto slavery.

South Carolina's Black Codes were representative of those passed throughout the south. No one was under any illusion why the Black Codes were needed: "essential for the preservation of our labor system, and, indeed, for our social system," said Edmund Rhett, an adviser on the South Carolina codes. Rhett continued, "The general interest of both the white man and the negro requires that he should be kept as near to his former condition as Law can keep him. That he should be kept as near to the condition of slavery as possible, as far from the condition of the white man as is practicable."[15]

Freedmen were granted the right to marry, hold property, and sue in courts. But separate courts, run by White South Carolinians, were set up for former slaves, and intermarriage was expressly prohibited. Ex-slaves were denied the right to vote. With the Thirteenth Amendment now preventing private ownership of human beings, southern states stepped into the void as regulators of human bodies and human beings. Vagrancy became the cloak under which free Blacks were reduced to slave status. In South Carolina, for example, conviction of vagrancy allowed the state to "hire out" convicts for no pay. Special taxes were imposed only on Blacks, with failure to pay resulting in an automatic vagrancy conviction. *Apprentice* or *servant* were now the preferred terms instead of *slave*, but those they worked for were still called masters. South Carolina could force children of impoverished parents into nonpaying apprenticeships on plantations.

Blacks could not bear arms. Blacks could be employed in the fields raising crops, even growing crops of their own, but they could not sell anything without the expressed written approval of their employer or a judge. A Black person could not seek work as an artisan, mechanic, or shopkeeper without paying an exorbitant fee. Any White person could arrest any Black person, but for an alleged offense committed by a White person, another citizen could only *complain* to the court. Freedmen were forced by law to work "sunrise to sunset." Freedmen traveling off a plantation, or visitors traveling on, were required to have prior approval of the plantation's owner. In Louisiana, Black Codes even mandated that freedmen enter into labor contracts that bound their entire family, including any unborn children.[16]

Louisiana's Black Codes were called "An Ordinance relative to the police of negroes recently emancipated within the Parish of St. Landry." Police, in fact, were used to enforce them and police violence soon followed. In Memphis, from May 1 through May 3, 1866, White mobs led by policemen rampaged through the Black neighborhoods. Federal troops were sent in to quell the uprising but were too late to stop the carnage: 46 Blacks dead, 2 Whites dead, 75 Blacks injured, 100 Blacks robbed, 5 Black women raped, every Black church and school burned to the ground.[17]

The massacre in Memphis had barely sunk in when another wave of violence erupted in New Orleans, again led by police. The New Orleans Riot of 1866 (also known as "St. Bartholomew's Day Massacre") occurred at the Mechanics Institute in the city on July 30, 1866, where an interracial group attempted to reconvene the Louisiana Constitutional Convention, specifically to right the wrongs of the Louisiana Black Codes, and the refusal to give Blacks the vote. Thirty-eight people were killed, 34 of them Black. One hundred nineteen of the 146 wounded were also freedmen or ex-slaves. General Philip H. Sheridan, military commander of Louisiana, said in his official report, "It was no riot—it was an absolute massacre by the police—a murder perpetrated by the mayor."[18]

• • •

Black citizens, and their supporters, both inside and outside of government, were the third force in this Second American Revolution, which took place from 1867 to 1877.

To understand the titanic egos and forces at work during this decade, one other important fact is required. For most of the nineteenth century, Republicans weren't Republicans and Democrats weren't Democrats. At least not in the way we think of these two political parties today. The only thing the party of Abraham Lincoln had in common with the party of Donald Trump was its name. In fact, it's easier to switch the policies of the two parties when thinking about them in modern terms. Nineteenth-century Republicans were more like twenty-first-century Democrats, and vice versa. Nineteenth-century Democrats, by and large, were the "Make the South Great Again" party. While nineteenth-century Republicans, by and large, were pushing for more sweeping social, political, and economic change. Furthermore, Black labor, slavery, helped build the power of both parties and the modern-day two-party system we've inherited in America. Republicans in the nineteenth century were the anti-slavery party, Democrats were the pro-slavery party of southern White former slave owners.

An eloquent former slave, a principled New England abolitionist, a stalwart senator from Massachusetts, and a pugnacious congressman from Pennsylvania, the Republican "Gang of Four" led the charge for the Second American Revolution.

Though few know his name, many are heir to the legacy of Wendell Phillips, a Harvard-trained lawyer and scion of an American family that emigrated from England to New England in the early seventeenth century. Phillips emigrated as well, leaving the ranks of Boston's privileged and powerful in the nineteenth century to lead a radical progressive movement that fought first for abolition, then for the rights of ex-slaves. Phillips broke with better-known William Lloyd Garrison over the goals of the abolitionist movement. Garrison was content with the emancipation of slaves. But Phillips would settle for nothing less than racial justice after the north's victory. "[A]ll the negro asks is *justice*," he demanded.[19] The right to vote. The right to an education. And, most of all, the right to land.

Take the land from vanquished slave owners, he argued, and redistribute that land wealth to poor Blacks and poor Whites. "Confiscation is mere, naked justice to the former slave," Phillips said. "Who brought the land into cultivation? Whose sweat and toil are mixed with it forever? Who cleared those forests? Who made those roads? Whose hand reared those houses? Whose wages are invested in those warehouses and towns? Of course, the Negro's. Why should he not have a share of the inheritance?"[20]

Phillips really understood freedom dues owed Black Americans, and he wanted to repay that debt. He wanted Black folks to share in the inheritance of power and wealth their labor had created. One hears in Phillips's words an urgency not heard for another century, when Dr. Martin Luther King, Jr. broke with so many in his "Beyond Vietnam" speech at Riverside Church in New York City in April 1967.

We are confronted with the fierce urgency of now. In this unfolding conundrum of life and history, there is such a thing as being too late. Procrastination is still the thief of time. Life often leaves us standing bare, naked, and dejected with a lost opportunity . . . Over the bleached bones and jumbled residues of numerous civilizations are written the pathetic words, "Too late."[21]

One hundred years earlier, Wendell Phillips spoke similar words: "Harmony purchased at any sacrifice of the absolute need of the hour is dangerous. To do nothing is infinitely better than to do half of what we need."[22]

Frederick Douglass was Wendell Phillips's longtime friend. In his late forties now, the ex-slave cut a striking figure—six feet tall, a lion's mane of salt-and-pepper natural hair, a matching beard and mustache. Intensity of purpose set in his eyes and in his words. Intelligent, articulate, passionately desirous of freedom for himself and for all Black men and women, Douglass embodied everything about a Black man rejected by a large swath of White America at the time.

Douglass was impatient with Lincoln's tepid approach to the Civil War. Where Lincoln claimed he was fighting for the Union, Douglass claimed the fight was for something infinitely superior.

What business, then, have we to fight for the old Union? We are not fighting for it. We are fighting for something incomparably better than the old Union. We are fighting for unity; unity of idea, unity of sentiment, unity of object, unity of institutions, in which there shall be no North, no South, no East, no West, no black, no white, but a solidarity of the nation, making every slave free, and every free man a voter.[23]

Douglass also understood the work before America through and after the Civil War was not "reconstruction" but "National regeneration,"[24] by which he meant "a radical revolution in all modes of thought which have flourished under the blighting slave system."[25]

Inside the US Congress, Douglass and Phillips found powerful allies in a group known as the Radical Republicans, led by Charles Sumner in the Senate and Thaddeus Stevens in the House of Representatives. Sumner was tall and handsome. Like Phillips, he was also Boston bred and Harvard trained. And also, like Phillips, Sumner was a principled man. Sounding, too, like Phillips, a century ahead of his time, Sumner declared there was no place for anything but equality in America: "It is not enough to provide separate accommodations for colored citizens, even if in all respects as good as those of other persons. Equality is not found in any pretended equivalent, but only in equality; in other words, there must be no discrimination on account of color."[26]

Thaddeus "Thad" Stevens powered this Gang of Four. Born into poverty in Vermont in 1792, Stevens wore a black wig atop a stern face and a clenched jaw. He was sixty-seven when he returned to Congress in 1859, after a six-year hiatus. Although he was never elected House Speaker, he was given the chair of the House Ways and Means Committee, long considered one of the most powerful committees in Congress. Stevens had a vision of the country after the Civil War, at odds with the visions of Lincoln and Johnson. Stevens, not surprisingly as chair of Ways and Means, placed his faith in the power of the purse—economics—and after the war that meant confiscation and redistribution of land to ex-slaves. In bringing the Fourteenth Amendment to the House floor—which granted all citizens of the United States, including former slaves, "equal protection of the laws"—Sumner reproached his colleagues,

> In my judgment, we shall not approach the measure of justice until we have given every adult freedman a homestead on the land where he was born and toiled and suffered. Forty acres of land and a hut would be more valuable to him than the immediate right to vote. Unless we give them this we shall receive the censure of mankind and the curse of Heaven.[27]

On the inside masthead page of the April 3, 1861, edition of the *New York Times*, the paper ran a story lamenting Lincoln's lack of decisiveness with regard to the events unfolding at Fort Sumter, and two columns over, a story about emancipation in Russia.[28] The story on Lincoln certainly caught the attention of the Gang of Four, but so, too, did the story on Russia. For Czar Alexander II had recently emancipated serfs, granting them both houses and land. If it could happen in Russia, it could happen in America. This is precisely what the Gang of Four envisioned for freed slaves, as part of reconstructing the nation after war. Although Andrew Johnson, congressional Democrats, and the former Confederate states were appalled by their notion of such a "Radical Reconstruction."

With battle lines drawn, Thad Stevens fired the first shot in the Second American Revolution on September 6, 1865, in a speech in his home state of Pennsylvania. "Is this great conquest to be in vain?" he asked. Then answered, "That will depend upon the virtue and intelligence of the next Congress. To Congress alone belongs the power of Reconstruction—of giving law to the vanquished."[29]

Stevens strong-armed Congress. He hit politicians where it hurt, their power. Did the gentlemen realize that the Emancipation Proclamation now nullified the three-fifths clause of the Constitution? Did they really want southern states to return to the Union more powerful than before, with a larger voting block? Was this to be the reward for secession? If the answers were no, then the gentlemen must join with him in passing the Freedmen's Bureau Act and the first-ever Civil Rights Act, which extended citizenship to Black Americans.

Congress passed those acts in 1866. Johnson met them with a veto. But Congress overrode Johnson's veto, and the Civil Rights Act of 1866 went into effect. Southern aristocrats may have had the president in their back pocket, but they didn't have the Radical Republicans in Congress. And it was out of this fear of losing control of Reconstruction that the first constitutional conventions were held across the south, the first Confederate representatives were sent to Congress, the Black Codes were enacted, and violence against Blacks and their supporters grew.

The Ku Klux Klan, for example, grew out of this same need for Whites to exercise physical power to keep Blacks in their place, and southern society frozen in time. All of this—the Black Codes, the disenfranchisement, the violence—may have been too much too soon. There would be more battles fought in this Second American Revolution; initially, southerners may have overplayed their hand.

Freedmen in South Carolina organized the Convention of Colored People in November 1865. An understandably solemn mood settled over fifty or so men meeting at the Zion Church on Calhoun Street in Charleston, among them some who would later be present at the Clubhouse for South Carolina's Second Constitutional Convention. Tickets to the first evening's event went on sale for twenty-five cents, and the spacious meeting hall of the church was filled to overflowing with Black women and men waiting for the band to play, and the guest speakers to rise to the podium.

After a stirring interlude from the band, Major Martin R. Delany, made an honorary member of the convention, rose to a thunderous ovation. A handsome man with dark skin and intense eyes, he had been one of the first three Black men admitted to Harvard Medical School in 1850, then dismissed after a few weeks over widespread protests by White students. During the war, Delany commanded United States Colored Troops, becoming the first Black man to hold the title of major in the United States Army. But this evening, Delany spoke on the need for people of color to follow just and noble laws, and to be assured of the victory that would follow.

In an open letter to the White citizens of the state of South Carolina, the convention appealed to their higher nature. "We trust the day will not be distant when you will acknowledge . . . that we are worthy, with you, to . . . realize the truth that 'all men are endowed by their Creator with inalienable rights.'"[30] In a "Declaration of Rights and Wrongs" and an open letter addressed to the South Carolina legislature, the convention, point by point, repudiated the state's Black Codes, and refuted the prohibitions the legislature had enacted upon them. And, in a letter to the US Congress, the convention called for Union forces to protect them, and congressional action to strike down the Black Codes of the state.[31]

The north soon picked up on the south's attempted end run around abolition. "South Carolina Re-establishing Slavery," read a headline in the *New-York Tribune*. The article went on to expose the hypocrisy of the state's Black Codes.[32] The *New York Times* described South Carolina's Black Codes as "a great blunder" and a "bloody code."[33] "Arrogance," decried the *Cleveland Leader*, "South Carolina, in her rebel legislature, is re-enacting the worst features of the old slave-code."[34]

"We tell the white men of Mississippi," said the influential *Chicago Tribune*, "that the men of the North will convert the State of Mississippi into a frog pond before they will allow any such law to disgrace one foot of soil in which the bones of our soldiers sleep and over which the flag of freedom waves."[35]

The north was fired up and Radical Republicans were swept into the House and Senate in the election of 1866, giving Thaddeus Stevens and Charles Sumner a mandate to continue legislatively prosecuting the Second American Revolution inside the halls of power, while Phillips and Douglass continued prosecuting the revolution outside in the court of public opinion. Their next battle was clear: give Blacks the power they needed to fight back against the onerous south; in other words, give them the right to vote. Blacks had died for the north during the war; those alive should now participate in the power of the peace.

"What doth it profit a nation," Douglass thundered, "if it gain the whole world but lose its honor? I hold that the American government has taken upon itself a solemn obligation of honor, to see . . . that this war shall not cease until every freedman at the South has the right to vote."[36]

"I argue it simply as a question of security, not of justice, or magnanimity," said Phillips. "For a nation to ask a man to fight for them and then leave him without full citizenship, is an infamy which would make a man forswear all part in such a nation."[37]

It helped also that public discourse on Black suffrage had expanded from politics to economics. The argument was pretty simple: If nothing changed in the south, it would be necessary for a continued military occupation, which would mean greater public debt borne by the north. Give Blacks the vote and they would ensure southern states were responsible partners to allow back into the Union with less burden to northern taxpayers. Abolitionist Elizur Wright said as much in a letter to the *Boston Daily Advertiser*,

> I think I could easily convince any man, who does not allow his prejudices to stand in the way of his interests, that it will probably make a difference of at least $1,000,000,000 in the development of the national debt, whether we reconstruct on the basis of loyal white and black votes, or on white votes exclusively, and that he can better afford to give the Government at least one-quarter of his estate than have it try the latter experiment.[38]

Some called it sheer will borne of passion, others less disposed to Stevens called it hate, but in constant pain, and daily expecting death, an ailing Stevens crawled by cane from desk to desk in Congress, holding together his caucus long enough to pass the Fourteenth Amendment and a series of Reconstruction acts that gave the Black populations in the south the right to vote, and loyal Blacks and Whites in the south the right to determine the course of regenerating the nation.

Johnson railed against Stevens and the Gang of Four in his State of the Union address in December 1867. "It is worse than madness," the president said, to consider allowing Blacks a voice in the governing of the country. "Of all the dangers which our nation has yet encountered, none are equal to those which must result from the success of the effort now making to Africanize the half of our country."[39]

The president, however, came up short. Stevens lived long enough to bring charges of impeachment against Johnson. Though he failed to secure Johnson's removal by a single vote, he did strip him of much of his presidential power and patronage. On the night of August 11, 1868, surrounded by his longtime housekeeper and companion, a Black woman named Lydia Hamilton Smith, and Black preachers who came to tell him he had the prayers of their people, Thaddeus Stevens died. The Second American Revolution had lost its champion but not its momentum.

Of all that Thaddeus Stevens and the Radical Republicans accomplished in the second session of the 39th Congress, and they accomplished a lot, the one thing that remained just beyond their grasp, and would eventually lead to the undoing of this revolution, was land reform. Land remained in the control of the lords of the plantations, and that meant the southern aristocrats still controlled the wealth.

Lerone Bennett, Jr., following W.E.B. Du Bois, observed, "[T]he allocation of forty acres of land to every adult freedman would have created a democratic infrastructure that would have changed the course of American democracy. Failure to allocate that land led inexorably to a totalitarian South which foreclosed the possibility of creating a democratic North."[40]

Still, freedom dues, almost delivered, left Black citizens in the south with power they'd never dreamed they would actually have, and that power led directly to a sunny January 14, 1868, at the Clubhouse in Charleston. The Reverend F. L. Cardozo opened the seventh day of the Second South Carolina Constitutional Convention by asking delegates to pray with him. After his benediction, the convention offered a prayer of their own to Anthony and Isabella, and all the Africans captured and enslaved, shipped and whipped, bought and sold over the last 250 years in America; a prayer in the form of a short ordinance: *"We, the People of the State of South Carolina, by our Delegates in Convention, do hereby ordain and declare,* That all contracts, whether under seal or not, the consideration of which were for the sale of slaves, are null and void and of non-effect."[41]

It would not be unjust to imagine that on some evening during the early days of the convention, the choir director at Mother Emanuel AME Church thumbed through his hymnal, then asked the men and women standing before him to lift their voices in song:

Yonder comes Sister Mary.
How do you know it is her?
With the palms of victory in her hand,
And the keys of Bethlehem.
And the keys of Bethlehem, O Lord,
The keys of Bethlehem.

●   ●   ●

James Shepherd Pike reported from Bethlehem in early 1873. What he saw there revolted and disgusted him. From Columbia, capitol of South Carolina, he wrote:

Yesterday, about 4 P. M., the assembled wisdom of the State, whose achievements are illustrated on that theatre, issued forth from the State House. About three-quarters of the crowd belonged to the African race. They were of every hue, from the light octoroon to the deep black . . . Here, then, is the outcome, the ripe, perfected fruit of the boasted civilization of the South, after two hundred years of experience. A white community, that had gradually risen from small beginnings, till it grew into wealth, culture, and refinement, and became accomplished in all the arts of civilization . . . It lies prostrate in the dust, ruled over by this strange conglomerate, gathered from the ranks of its own servile population. It is the spectacle of a society suddenly turned bottom side up.[42]

Pike, born in Maine, and a correspondent and editor for the *New York Herald*, began life as an outspoken Radical Republican, friend of Thaddeus Stevens and Charles Sumner. He was an early advocate for Black suffrage, who somewhere along the way became embittered and disenchanted with the failures of Reconstruction. His book, widely read and highly influential at the time, *The Prostrate*

State: South Carolina Under Negro Government,[43] is also repugnantly racist. Yet, his observations on southern society "suddenly turned bottom side up" are firsthand. What he reported, repulsed him. But at least he reported what he saw. "Seven years ago," Pike wrote, "these men were raising corn and cotton under the whip of the overseer. To-day they are raising points of order and questions of privilege."[44]

Everywhere Pike looked, he saw Blacks in control.

The Speaker is black, the Clerk is black, the door-keepers are black, the little pages are black, the chairman of the Ways and Means is black, and the chaplain is coal-black. At some of the desks sit colored men whose types it would be hard to find outside of Congo . . . [45]

In the executive government, to be sure, the Governor was white. He got his place by dancing at negro balls and speculating in negro delegates. But the Lieutenant-Governor was colored, and the President of the Senate, and the Speaker of the House, and the Treasurer of the State, and nearly all the rest of the officials. Here was Columbia. Half the population was white, but its Senator was colored, and its Representatives in the Legislature and in the city government were nearly all colored men. So were its policemen and its market-men. Everybody in office was a darkey.[46]

If these were scary times for some Whites, they were heady times for most Blacks. Across the south during Reconstruction, Blacks stepped into positions of political power from the statehouse to the US Congress. In 1872, P.B.S. Pinchback briefly served as governor of Louisiana, the first Black man to be governor of a US state. In 1870, Hiram Revels represented Mississippi as the first Black US senator. In 1875, Blanche K. Bruce served six years as a senator of the same state. In all, an estimated two thousand Black men held some kind of elected office during Reconstruction.[47] Pike only saw once-proud

White southerners "cowed and demoralized,"[48] suffering "with a stoicism that promises no reward here or hereafter. They are the types of a conquered race."[49]

Pike seemed at pain to admit that these ex-slaves and freed-man "have a wonderful aptness at legislative proceedings. They are 'quick as lightning' at detecting points of order, and they certainly make incessant and extraordinary use of their knowledge . . . They have a genuine interest and a genuine earnestness in the business of the assembly."[50]

In roundabout, racist tones, Pike even spoke to the legislature's agenda.

> When an appropriation bill is up to raise money to catch and punish the Ku-klux, they know exactly what it means. They feel it in their bones. So, too, with educational measures. The free school comes right home to them; then the business of arm-ing and drilling the black militia. They are eager on this point. Sambo can talk on these topics . . . [51]

Pike also makes important observations about the limitations of this frightening Black power, because while Black people now held political power, the old White guard still held the wealth: "There was an exodus [of White men] after the war, but it has stopped, and many have come back. The old slaveholders still hold their lands. The negroes were poor and unable to buy, even if the land-owners would sell. This was a powerful impediment to the development of the negro into a controlling force in the State."[52]

Pike's racist views of Blacks in power in the Reconstruction-era south were not out of keeping in the north, especially at his newspa-per, the *New York Herald*. On June 13, 1871, the *Herald* ran a special section titled "The Carolinas," which featured reporting from the south with headlines such as "The Colored Semiramis of the South," "The Gentle Cutthroat Ku Kluxes," "Poor Whites Miscegenating and Robbing Hen Roosts," and "Rich Niggers Running Legislatures."[53]

Pike was right about the sudden turning of southern society "bottom side up," and perhaps his Radical Republican roots allowed him to marvel at the speed with which Blacks rose to the legislative power and challenges set before them. What Pike saw in South Carolina was in evidence throughout the south. What was first resolved at constitutional conventions, like the one at the Clubhouse in Charleston in 1868, was later enacted in legislatures, like the one at Columbia in the 1870s, as Blacks, and their Republican cohort, were swept into power by newly enfranchised Black voters, and newly disillusioned White voters who stayed away from the polls.

Reconstruction began with the right to vote, the third right defined in the new state constitution drafted by the men at the Clubhouse in Charleston in 1868. "Therefore, no attempt shall ever be made to abridge or destroy the right of suffrage which is now enjoyed by any person or persons in this State, except as provided for in this Constitution."[54] The convention handed the constitution over to the people of South Carolina for a vote, with Black men now able to cast a ballot. On April 16, 1868, the electorate approved the constitution, though many White voters, disgusted with a document created by a majority Black convention, did not vote.

The new South Carolina constitution declared representation at the state level should be based on population only, not wealth. Debtors' prisons were eliminated. The right of women to acquire and possess real and personal property apart from their husbands was established. And, nothing in South Carolina's constitution, or in most other Reconstruction-era constitutions, prohibited intermarriage between the races.

On the twenty-fifth day of the convention meeting at the old Charleston Clubhouse, Niles G. Parker, a White delegate from Barnwell, offered a resolution that the head of the Union forces occupying South Carolina abolish the existing district courts of the state. That resolution was voted on and passed. This effectively eliminated the odious Black Codes of the state, which had been used by district courts to penalize ex-slaves.[55]

And it went this way in Charleston, and in similar constitutional conventions around the south. With Black people in attendance, if not in the majority, discriminatory clauses of previous state constitutions were struck down, and new clauses erected that addressed the pressing needs of the newly freed people of the state.

State legislatures during Reconstruction wrestled with political and economic power. Certainly, the two are deeply intertwined. One can give rise to the other. But as efforts at campaign finance reform have shown over many years, money appears to trump politics when it comes to power. President Barack Obama said in his 2014 State of the Union address that, "It should be the power of our vote, not the size of our bank account, that drives our democracy."[56] It should be, but it's not, and it has never been. It certainly was not the case in the Reconstruction era, when Blacks held political power through the vote, but Whites held economic power through ownership of land.

• • •

Sometimes political power can bring about economic power, or at least serve as a check against it. With slavery's dissolution, land-ownership by former slave owners led poor Blacks and poor Whites to sharecropping and tenancy farming—slavery in every other way but name. So, with power, what did Black-run Reconstruction political and legislative bodies do when faced with sharecropping?

On February 18, 1868, Solomon George Washington Dill, known as S.G.W. Dill, rose to offer a resolution that would protect share-croppers and tenant farmers from gouging by landowners. The resolution was tabled but when Dill, a White Radical Republican, was allowed to speak, he said, "I insist on giving the poor man justice and all that truly belongs to him . . . Numbers of them are oppressed; numbers are without homes, without shelter, and cannot obtain it unless they give more than one-half of their physical labor to their landlords for shelter . . . I am begged to do something for them towards keeping the landlords in check."[57]

In taking this strong stand, Dill put his life at risk. Elected to represent Kershaw County, he never got to serve in Columbia. On the night of June 4, 1868, Dill was executed by assailants who were never found, though many reported the men belonged to the Ku Klux Klan. Dill's killing fit the pattern of the Klan assassinating Whites who acted against the interests of wealthy landowners.[58]

But others in the South Carolina legislature, and around the south, took up this cause. State legislatures passed tenancy laws to protect sharecroppers and tenant farmers; passed bills making it easier for poor people to obtain credit; and created state agencies charged with looking out for the poor.[59] Reconstruction justices and juries, many of them Black, delivered verdicts in favor of poor farmers against wealthy landowners.[60] Across the south, Black men, such as Blanche K. Bruce,[61] a US senator from Mississippi, and James T. Rapier, a US representative from Alabama, owned and operated large plantations of a thousand acres or more.

Taxation was another means by which political power translated into economic power during Reconstruction. Prior to the Civil War, state taxation throughout the south was based on a combination of property and capitation taxes. Property taxes were assessed on the self-reported value of land by plantation owners and capitation taxes were assessed on the number of workers employed. Property owners continually underreported the value of their land. And capitation taxes were graded to encourage slavery and discourage a free labor market; for example, a slave was assessed at 75 cents, a free White at $1 or more, and a free Black at $3 or more.

During Reconstruction, state legislatures, like the one meeting in Columbia, South Carolina, had been charged by newly approved state constitutions to meet more of the public need in education and care of the poor, in hospitals and mental health facilities. A new tax structure followed this new set of public priorities. Combined with huge state deficits incurred during the war and a collapse in the credit market for the south, southern states moved aggressively to raise property taxes, in some cases by a factor of ten, when compared to the pre-war period.[62] Black-run legislatures believed this might be a market-driven solution for land redistribution. Owners of large plantations and huge tracts of land would either be forced to sell or have their land confiscated for failure to pay taxes. That land could then be redistributed to landless freedmen and poor Whites, but land redistribution by taxation rarely happened.[63]

Increased taxation did have the effect of sending plantation owners up in arms. It also gave them a way to shift the focus of their attack from race to taxes, even though race was very much beneath the taxation issue. Such anger on the part of wealthy Whites contributed to the rise of violent groups supported by them, such as the KKK, and ultimately to an organized, successful political effort to undo Reconstruction.

One goal of the men meeting at the Clubhouse in Charleston, and an enduring, successful legacy of Reconstruction throughout the south, was public education. Ex-slaves, and free Blacks denied one, knew how important an education was. The convention's committee on education reported,

> [W]e hold these statements as axioms: that education is knowledge; that knowledge is power; that knowledge rightly applied is the best and highest kind of power; that the general and universal diffusion of education and intelligence among the people is the surest guarantee of the enhancement, increase, purity and preservation of the great principles of republican liberty . . . [64]

The post of state superintendent of education was established and made an elected office. A state board of education was created, composed of elected representatives from each county. And the General Assembly was charged with creating "a liberal and uniform system of free public schools through the State."[65] All public schools were open to all state residents regardless of race.

Behind the exclusively male corridors of power and wealth, one could observe another change in the fabric of southern society.

Black women had stepped into roles previously occupied exclusively by White women—the role of the powerful socialite, or, as the *New York Herald* called them, "The Colored Semiramis of the South." Semiramis was the name of the mythical queen of Babylon, and more generally a reference to a woman of great power. Catherine the Great of Russia had been referred to by the French philosopher Voltaire as "the Semiramis of Russia" and Elizabeth I of England as the "the Semiramis of the North." But it was the beautiful, charming, intelligent, and powerful Rollin sisters of Columbia to whom the *Herald* was referring in its headline and accompanying article. Another New York newspaper, *The Sun*, referred to the women as "Catherine de Medici, Charlotte Corday, and Louisa Mulbach," through their reporter, also in South Carolina in 1871, vying for the same story of Frances, Katherine, Charlotte, Marie Louise, and Florence Rollin.[66]

Men dueling for their attentions and affections was nothing new to the sisters. In South Carolina during Reconstruction, few Republicans held power without first holding forth at their integrated Columbia salon, referred to as the "Republican headquarters" of the state.

William Rollin, the patriarch, had emigrated from the Dominican Republic, where he owned land and slaves and established himself as a lumber merchant. Though little is known about the sisters' mother, the family quickly rose to the pinnacle of South Carolina's "colored aristocracy." Light skinned and ravishing, the sisters preferred others think of them as "French" rather than Black. Still, they taught in schools for ex-slaves, sued in court for equal treatment in public accommodations, and spearheaded the movement in South Carolina for women's suffrage.

The sisters lived in a richly appointed home in Columbia, close to the state capital building. Well educated, well-read, refined, they conversed as easily about the lines of Byron as they did about the machinations of politicians. They counted among their friends Martin Delany, Wendell Phillips, William Lloyd Garrison, and Frederick Douglass.

Frances married William Whipper, a Black politician of the age. When he questioned her counsel, she once replied, "You may be a wiser and better politician, but I fancy my womanly intuition can read more accurately the signs of the coming storm than all your weatherwise experience."[67] The sisters frequented the Executive Mansion while Robert K. Scott was governor. Tongue-in-cheek, Charlotte (Lottie) even showed the *Herald* reporter a mock-up of a national Republican ticket for 1872, which read, "FOR PRESIDENT—-R.K. Scott of South Carolina, FOR Vice-President—Charlotte Rollin of South Carolina."[68]

• • •

One can easily hear the voice of a Black preacher standing before worshipers at Mother Emanuel AME Church in Charleston. He's chanting low, "Good news! Good news!" as the choir winds down from "Yonder Comes Sister Mary." Suddenly, all goes quiet. The preacher drops his head into his Bible as though completely spent. He lets the silence build to a point where the pews are pregnant with anticipation. Then, just as suddenly, his head shoots up from his Bible. His eyes sweep across the congregation as though he were capable of peering deeply into everyone's soul.

He waves his Bible overhead, then thunders in a tremulous tenor,

"And Mary said . . .

I am bursting with Good News. He knocked tyrants off their high horses, pulled victims out of the mud. The starving poor he sat down to a banquet; the callous rich he left out in the cold. He embraced his chosen children, and piled on the mercies high. He hath brought down the mighty from their seats, and hath exalted those of low degree. He has filled the hungry with good things, and sent away the rich empty-handed." (Luke 1:46–53)

Voting rights, civil rights, greater diversity in politics, wealth re-distribution, taxation reform, prison reform, universal free educa-tion, women's rights, care for the indigent, expansion of credit, social safety nets: Black lives not only mattered, they were essential in cre-ating, and enshrining into law, these new institutions of wealth and power and equity across America. One would not be faulted for be-lieving these the accomplishments of a progressive movement of the twenty-first century, rather than the efforts of ex-slaves, and their supporters, in the 1870s. Reconstruction was a unique moment in the history of America. For the first time in this country, Blacks were allowed a share of, and a say in, the institutions of American power and wealth they helped to create. Reconstruction was not perfect. Hidden within its broad accomplishments were also the seeds of its eventual demise. But for a decade, at least, America tentatively trod the road of true democracy.

BACK AGAIN TOWARD SLAVERY

"They intend to kill you."

"I don't know why they have anything against me," Alfred Richardson said.

"They say that you can control all the colored votes; that you are making too much money; that they do not allow any nigger to rise that way," James Thrasher said.

"I've always kept the peace between the colored and white people."

"I tell you, you had better keep your eyes open. For they are after you."

"They tried before."

"They intend to break you up, and then they can rule the balance of the niggers when they get you off."

"Seems you're taking a might big risk coming to see me."

"They said they wanted me to join their party, but I told them I did not want to do it. I never knew you to do anything wrong, and these are a parcel of low-down men, and I don't want to join any such business."

"I've told some in town that some men are coming to kill me or run me off. I don't know whether I can stay safely. They told me, 'No, don't move away. They are just talking that way to scare you.'"

For three or four hours, Alfred Richardson listened to James Thrasher speak of the Ku Klux Klan and their plans. At nine o'clock he went to bed, but not before reinforcing his door with long scantlings across the width and fasteners down the sides.

That night, Alfred Richardson did not sleep long nor sleep well. He reckoned it must have been just after midnight when the distant pounding of hooves drew closer, and closer. Then, when the braying and breathing of horses stopped, the battering of shoulders against his front door began. He stood behind it.

"Who's there?"

"Never mind. God damn you, we'll show you who it is. We'll have you tonight!"

From the other side of the door came the thwack! thwack! of an ax. Splinters flew. Through a widening gap, the cold air of that January night rushed in, and along with it the sight of a torch and the barrels of long guns. The door would not hold against the onslaught. Alf raced upstairs, to a garret, where he'd stashed some guns. The swarm of men barreled inside.

From an opened upstairs window, he heard the bloodcurdling screams. "Help!" His wife screamed again, "Help!" Her screams were answered with a hail of bullets from the outside, luckily all missing their mark. Alf could hear the cacophony of voices from a crowd outside. A voice called out.

"He's jumped out the window. Shoot on top of the roof!"

Hurriedly, all the Klansmen, except one, clattered outside.

Alf now squeezed into the garret, the cramped crawl space, just under his roof. He looked out into the darkness of his home and tried to hold his breath. Hoped the one man left behind would not come his way.

Suddenly, a hooded masked face appeared in the garret and a voice shouted with glee, "God damn you, I got you!"

Three shots rang out. One ball tore through Alf's right arm. Two balls lodged into his side. The man danced with joy. "I found him! I found him!"

The shooter whooped and hollered. He charged downstairs to meet the others.

"Come back up here! I've got 'im! And I've shot 'im! But he ain't quite dead. So, let's go up and finish 'im!"

His strength draining rapidly, Alf pulled himself from the garret to the head of the stairs just as the men began clambering their way up, one holding a light behind the others. As they reached the top step, a blast rang out. Only this time from Alf's double-barrel shotgun. A man crumpled, dead, into a mass of blood, robes, and a mask. The other Klansmen grabbed him by the legs, turned, and ran fast downstairs and outside to mount their horses. They rode back into the darkness. Alf had survived the Klan's second attack.[1]

Alfred Richardson left Watkinsville, Georgia, near Athens with his family for the relative safety of the remote Black community in Lickskillet, Georgia, just south of the Tennessee line. A few weeks later his home in Watkinsville, and all the structures around it, were burned to the ground.[2]

Ex-slave Alfred Richardson, an elected member of the Georgia legislature, was extremely fearless, and also extremely fortunate to have survived not one but two Ku Klux Klan attacks. Estimates range as high as forty thousand people (mostly Black men, women, and children) murdered by the Klan during Reconstruction.[3] *Southern Watchman*, the local newspaper out of Athens, blamed Richardson for the attack based on "facts, which were furnished us by respectable citizens of Watkinsville . . ."[4] Richardson later appeared before a joint committee of Congress investigating Ku Klux Klan violence against Blacks. He described Klan intimidation, whippings, and extrajudicial murders of Black men and women over voting, education, and labor issues, and how members of the Klan committed such acts with impunity.

John H. Cristy, publisher of the *Southern Watchman*, followed Richardson, in front of the committee, where he testified under oath that the attack against Richardson was the victim's fault. Later, Cristy added, "I have no idea that there ever has been an organization in the State of Georgia known as Ku-Klux, or any other sort of secret organization, except the Loyal League, since the surrender."[5]

It's hard to read of the killings of Black people by the Klan and similar paramilitary groups during Reconstruction without going back to that 1672 law, enacted in colonial Virginia, which granted immunity from prosecution for any person who committed murder in pursuit of a runaway slave. An entitlement to violence and extrajudicial killings of Blacks feels woven into the very fabric of this nation, including its great founding documents.

Violence undermined Reconstruction and ultimately forced its undoing; forced Blacks and southern society to retreat back toward slavery. Though many mark the end of Reconstruction with the 1876 presidential election, in truth, Restoration, or Redemption (as the era after Reconstruction is called), began as soon as the Civil War drew to its conclusion. In fact, the Civil War really never did end in the south, for this violence against Black citizens, who were originally the cause of the war, picked up in the months and years after the surrender at Appomattox. However, it would be irresponsible to say this violence was confined to small, isolated vigilante groups peppered throughout the south, when, in fact, the north was deeply involved. And if by violence we also mean the political violence that prepares the ground for physical violence, and vice versa, then the north was not only deeply involved but directly implicated. Reconstruction and Redemption were unfolding simultaneously. The question was which one would win.

Violence is an extreme exercise of power. Black men and women, in the decade following the Civil War, tested the bounds of American democracy. They labored to bring forth new institutions of power and wealth which finally realized the proposition that all people are created equal and endowed with certain unalienable rights—the ultimate expression of freedom dues. Yet, instead, their labors gave rise to new institutions of power and wealth based on extrajudicial murder and intimidation. The terrible effect, the awful legacy, of Reconstruction in America is that the exercise of democracy by citizens is now too often met with the exercise of violence by the state. It was certainly this way for Black folks during and after Reconstruction. And, there is a similar exercise of political violence in laws to suppress the votes of Blacks, and other Americans of color, today.

*   *   *

The Ku Klux Klan was founded in Tennessee in 1866 by Confederate general Nathan Bedford. For much of its early days, the organization was referred to as simply the Ku-Klux, derived from the Greek word *kyklos*, meaning "circle." It defined not only a circle of brotherhood among its members, but also a more general circle of who was meant to be in, and who was not, in southern White society—Black people and their allies, such as carpetbaggers (northern transplants) and scalawags (southern Reconstruction sympathizers), were targeted for exclusion. The KKK and similar groups were essentially the paramilitary wing of the Democratic Party in the south, charged with carrying out a campaign of intimidation and murder for a party whose slogan in the 1868 presidential election was "This Is a White Man's Country; Let White Men Rule."

Many southern newspapers praised the work of the Klan. The *Moulton Advertiser* published the following verse in support of the KKK, which read, in part:

> *Thadika Stevika radical plan*
> *Must yield to the coming of Ku Klux Klan,*
> *Niggers and leaguers get out of the way,*
> *We're born of the night, and we vanish by day;*
> *No rations have we but the flesh of man,*

And love niggers best—the Ku Klux Klan
We catch 'em alive, and roast 'em whole,
Then hand them around with a sharpened pole;
Whole leagues have we eaten, not leaving a man,
And went away hungry, the Ku Klux Klan[6]

Thadika Stevika is, of course, a reference to Thaddeus Stevens, and *leaguers* is a reference to members of the Union League, also known as the Loyal League. In fact, supporters of the Klan, and later their apologists, claim the KKK was necessary as a counterbalance to the league. When John H. Cristy, owner of the Athens *Southern Watchman*, told a joint committee in Washington, cited above, that he knew of no secret organization in Georgia, except the Loyal League, he was referring to a group based in New York City, Philadelphia, and Boston that sent workers to the south to help educate and organize ex-slaves, teaching them how to read and write, and most important, teaching them how to vote. Blacks, and the league, were overwhelmingly Republican, which incensed southern White Democrats, who threatened them through the Klan.

Many White southerners viewed it as an abomination that Blacks stepped into elected roles of leadership, and they were determined to reclaim the south. In fact, if Reconstruction is called "the Second American Revolution," then Redemption should be called "the Second Civil War." In all respects, it was a war against Black citizens, principally in the south, though in the terms of modern warfare it would be called a guerrilla war or low-intensity conflict.

Black voters were threatened or killed, Black schools were bombed or burned, Black elected officials, and their allies, were intimidated or assassinated. Black people were hunted, whipped, lynched, and murdered, sometimes because they asserted their freedom, and at other times simply because Whites wanted, or needed, to demonstrate their control, authority, and impunity. Principally, the Klan and similar paramilitary groups were behind this violence, often with local, state, and federal authorities looking the other way. Sometimes members of local and state governments were also members of the Klan. The goal of the violence was clear: change political power in the south so Blacks, and their Republican allies, were no longer in office and Whites, and Democrats, could restore the south to its former glory. Few spoke of bringing back slavery, but many longed for a day when only Whites ruled all affairs in the south.

In November 1871, Edward (Ned) Crosby, an ex-slave from Columbus, Mississippi, appeared before the same joint committee of Congress, investigating violence against Blacks in the south, that Alfred Richardson had appeared before several months earlier.

When asked if he had ever been visited by the Ku-Klux, he said that he had, then told the story:

> They came to my house, and came into my house. I went out to get my little child a drink of water and saw them coming. My wife asked me what they were. I said I reckoned they were what we called Ku-Klux. It looked like there were thirty odd of them, and I didn't know but what they might interfere with me, and I just stepped aside, out in the yard to the smokehouse. They came up there, and three of them got down and came in the house and called for me, and she told them I had gone over to Mr. Crosby's. They asked her if I didn't have right smart business there, and she said she didn't know; that I had gone over there to see my sister, she reckoned. She didn't know but they might want something to do to me, and interfere with me, and they knocked around a while and off they went.[7]

Luke P. Poland of Vermont, chairman of the joint committee, asked Crosby, "Have you been attempting to get up a free school in your neighborhood?"

"Yes, sir."

"Colored school?"

"Yes, sir."

"Do you know whether their visit to you had reference to this effort?"

"I had spoken for a school, and I had heard a little chat of that, and I didn't know but what they heard it, and that was the thing they were after."

Later in the testimony, Chairman Poland asked, "Who told you that unless the colored people voted the Democratic ticket it would be worse for them?"

"Several [Whites] in the neighborhood," Crosby answered.

Democrat Francis P. Blair, Jr. next took his turn to question Crosby. "Whose land were you living on, Ned?"

"Mr. Crosby's [his former owner]."

"You say Mr. Crosby asked you to vote the Democratic ticket?"

"He asked me would I do it, and I told him I would. He told my neighbor right there if Ned would vote the Democratic ticket Ned could stay where he was, but whenever Ned voted against him Ned was off."

"You told him you were going to vote the Democratic ticket?"

"Yes, sir, for fear. But my intention was the whole time to vote the radical ticket . . . All of our colored population since the Ku-Klux have been visiting about, have all been in fear of trouble. There has been nights I didn't sleep more than an hour, and if there had been a stick cracked very light, I would have sprung up in the bed."[8]

Lewis E. Parsons also testified before Poland's joint committee on the Klan. Parsons was an interesting mix. A lawyer from up-state New York, he'd come south to Talladega, Alabama, in 1840 to practice law. He served as a Confederate lieutenant during the Civil War, but was appointed provisional governor of the state by President Andrew Johnson. Parsons served as a US district attorney for northern Alabama, and began life as a Democrat, though ultimately became a Republican. He'd been asked by the governor of Alabama to prosecute members of the Klan involved in the murders of a White schoolteacher and four Black men. Though his professional and political careers were diverse, his testimony before the Poland committee was clear and direct.

When asked about whether Klan violence was directed at the Black vote, Parsons replied, "That is the conclusion I have formed, from what I have seen and heard . . . that it was intended to control the voting of the negroes . . . and also to control his labor."[9]

Questioning Parsons was John Pool, a Republican senator from North Carolina. Pool seemed surprised. "To control his labor?" Pool asked.

"Yes, sir; and I intended to state so before, if I did not."

"Without wages?" Pool asked.

"They [the Klan] meant that he should work only for such persons and upon such terms as they sanctioned."

"You then look upon it as simply a resistance to the free enjoyment of equal rights on the part of the colored people?"

"I can come to no other conclusion than that . . . The great body of the white people, I cannot state the exact number, but the great body of the white people, nine-tenths of them certainly, I reckon, were utterly opposed to making the negro a voter."

And that opposition to voting, education, and employment was the basis for White violence.

● ● ●

The testimony of ex-slaves like Alfred Richardson and Ned Crosby, and White men like Lewis Parsons and many others, before this congressional joint committee contributed to the passing, in March 1871, of "An Act to enforce the Provisions of the Fourteenth Amendment," otherwise known as the Civil Rights Act of 1871, or the Ku Klux Klan Act.[10] The act made it a federal crime to deprive US citizens of their civil rights through violence, empowering the federal government to send in troops to enforce it, and trying those arrested in federal rather than state court, where trials were more likely to have Black jurors.

In October 1871, President Grant suspended habeas corpus in nine South Carolina counties, sending in federal troops to quell violence in areas overrun by the KKK. Killing and intimidation are part of war, but in this second Civil War, many in the south may have reached for their guns too soon. By the end of that year, federal grand juries returned more than three thousand indictments. Mostly light sentences were handed down to the six hundred men convicted, though sixty-five were imprisoned for up to five years at the Albany Penitentiary, a federal facility in New York.[11] This was the first time, and the last, that such a drastic measure as the suspension of habeas corpus, combined with federal troops, was used to protect the rights of Black Americans.[12] Grant's swift and decisive actions were credited with decimating the Ku Klux Klan, and bringing to an end its first reign of terror across the south. Of course, the night riders in hoods would ride again.[13]

War is not always about counting bodies, sometimes it's about winning hearts and minds. With the latter as the battlefield objective, words, not guns, are the weapons of choice. Sustained political will is something Americans are not easily accused of, especially with regard to matters of freedom or civil rights. Although news cycles were longer in the mid-nineteenth century they certainly existed then. President Grant would soon say, "the whole public is tired of these annual autumnal outbreaks in the South."[14] But it was not only Grant holding a finger to the wind of public opinion. Newspapers and reporters in the north and south now stepped into the void left by a crippled Klan with a new weapon—a campaign of misinformation. As the 1870s headed full steam into a new century, there were other pressing matters on the minds of many Americans—new western lands to acquire, new native nations to dominate, new industrial technologies to master, and most of all, new money to make. They'd moved on from "the eternal nigger," as the *New York Herald* put it.[15] And many southern conservatives were more than glad to contribute to Americans moving on, and leaving them in control of the spoils.

Africanization became a code word for Blacks finally stepping into positions of equality and power, and for newspapers instilling fear in their White readers. "When we come to reflect that these people . . . number over four millions in this country, the majority just intelligent enough to become the readier dupes of wicked and designing men . . . who can call the Africanization danger 'a spectre'?" said the *Memphis Daily Appeal*.[16]

"The men of this country will not consent that any portion of it shall be Africanized, in order that it may be permanently Radicalized,"[17] stated the *Southern Home*, a newspaper from Charlotte, North Carolina, reprinting an article from the *Savannah News* of Georgia.

"Who Are Africanizing Louisiana?" asked the *Times-Picayune* of New Orleans.[18]

Northern newspapers spread the fear of Africanization as well. An article in the *New York Herald*, titled "Sambo in Excelsis," lavished praise on reporter James Shepherd Pike, lamenting, "With the sad prescience of fallen greatness the gentleman predicted the approaching 'Africanization' of South Carolina."[19] In an editorial, *The Perry County Democrat*, in Ohio, defined its position: "That the balance of power between political parties shall be placed in the hands of ignorant negroes, is preposterous and will not be long tolerated by a majority of the white voters in any commonwealth in the Union." The paper went on to claim that Republicans had once protested "against the Africanization of the 'People's Party'" and that the Republican Party would lament "the day when it was compelled to swallow Sambo."[20] A special correspondent for *The Cincinnati Enquirer* reported on events in New Orleans: "There is a move on foot among the colored Radicals of this city and State to turn over the government of both to the exclusive rule of the negroes . . . In order to bring about the thorough Africanization of the State, a deep scheme is now being hatched."[21]

One lone voice against this propaganda was the *New National Era*, Frederick Douglass's newspaper in the nation's capital. In a letter to the editor the alarm was sounded over a bill in the House of Representatives providing that no one who cannot read or write English shall serve on a federal jury. "The judgement of the negro is that African ignorance at the polls and in the jury-box is safer than pro-slavery rebellism and Kuklux scoundrelism . . . Leading journalists are already chuckling over it [the proposed bill] as evidence that their hue-and-cry against 'Africanization' is having its effect."[22]

Articles, editorials, and letters printed by the press have effects that follow the news cycle. But books offer a subject that can be studied and referred to over and over again. James Shepherd Pike, quoted above, stood out among the authors, most of whom were also reporters, advocating for the interests of the White south. But joining Pike were a handful of other authors including Edward King, Robert Somers, and Charles Nordhoff.

Robert Somers, in particular, was a well-known, prominent writer. Somers, a Scottish economics journalist, traveled to the US south to investigate the effects of the Civil War on the southern economy. His book *The Southern States Since the War, 1870–1*[23] was praised as recently as 1965 by Malcolm C. McMillan, a southern historian, who wrote, "Robert Somers, a Scottish journalist, was a keen and objective observer and gives a fair, detached, and balanced appraisal of economic life, politics, and race relations in the South between 1870 and 1871."[24] Yet Somers, a foreigner, still suffered from the same "White supremacism" of other writers who could not see Black people as human but merely as "darkeys"[25] possessing "wool-clad brains."[26] He celebrated the ascendancy of Democrats in Alabama. "The triumph of Democrats in this and other States has been won by hard battles against the ignorance and corruption, and marks the return of the white people of the South to a rightful and much-needed influence in the management of their affairs."[27]

As Somers alluded to, it was not just the specter of "Africanization" but perhaps more important, the idea of corruption that newspapers and writers pinned on Black folks in this propaganda campaign. The logic went something like this: The Republican Party is corrupt. The Republican Party supports Black people in the south. Therefore, Black people in the south are corrupt. It didn't matter that the logic was faulty, or the underlying premise of Republican corruption was more fiction than fact. What mattered was that corruption became a proxy for talking about race. Who's not for getting corruption out of state and local politics? In other words, who's not for getting Blacks out of office?

In terms reminiscent of Hitler's *Endspiel*, his Final Solution for the Jews, Pike supported "a satisfactory solution"[28] put forward by southern Whites, to which he added they "must rely mainly upon themselves, and mainly upon action quite outside and independent of politics, to redeem the State, if it is to be redeemed. This is the real serious work they should set about."[29] If that's not a call to insurrection, it would be hard to know what is.

Major General Adelbert Ames, then Union commanding officer of the western portion of South Carolina, knew it, and said as much in a letter to the adjutant-general of Union forces in Charleston.

My reports as to the condition of the freed people contain all I would say in the subject. The outrages upon them which have been reported speak more effectually than anything else possibly can. As with my soldiers who have been killed and wounded no effort is made by citizens to protect the freedman or punish those who trespass upon his rights or assist us in punishing them. The condition of the freedman is simply this, so long as he is subordinate after the manner of a slave and not of a freedman, and does as well he is safe from violence; but when he attempts to depart from his old discipline and assert a single privilege he meets opposition, and in localities is punished with death. This results from the fact that many especially the ignorant can see in the negro only the slave.[30]

By 1874, conservative southern Whites were smarter; saddled with a hooded but now hobbled Klan, they brought racial violence and intimidation into the light of day through public groups like the White League or the White Line, establishing a line based on race that southern Blacks crossed only at their peril. White hoods and robes may have come off, but the goals had changed little.

The New Orleans *Times-Picayune* ran an appeal to White men:

> Disregarding all minor questions of principle or policy, and having solely in view the maintenance of our hereditary civilization and Christianity menaced by a stupid Africanization, we appeal to the men of our race, of whatever language or nationality, to unite with us against that supreme danger. A league of the whites is the inevitable result of that formidable, oath-bound and blindly obedient league of the blacks.[31]

In Mississippi, the White League went under the name of the Red Shirts or Bloody Shirt, a reference to General Benjamin Butler, who'd since become a congressman in Massachusetts, rising in a fiery speech in support of the Ku Klux Klan Act, while waving a bloody shirt from a northern educator beat within a hair's breadth of his life by hooded night riders in March 1871. Allen P. Huggins, the educator, was beaten by the Klan, and Butler did rain down his wrath on the night riders, but no bloody shirt was ever held aloft during Butler's speech. Truth, however, did not matter. In modern terms, "waving the bloody shirt" went viral as a meme expressing southern contempt for northerners invoking their sacrifices in the Civil War as the basis for attempts to control the south. These leagues drew members from numerous "rifle clubs" around the south where, like the Confederate flag, the red shirt became a symbol of deep reverence for southerners lamenting their loss, and longing for return to days of southern yore.

As 1874 counted down, Adelbert Ames occupied the governor's mansion in Jackson, Mississippi, as bloody shirts waved around the state. Ames had gotten there through an 1873 election in which Republicans had overwhelmingly secured the Black vote, giving them a victory in what had long been a Democratic stronghold. Hopping mad, Democrats devised the Mississippi Plan, in hopes of retaking the state in elections to be held in 1875.

Whites were ready and ruthless, their guns were locked and loaded. And Vicksburg, a river town in the western portion of the state, became the flash point. There, ex-slave and elected sheriff Peter Crosby sought to keep the peace, and regain his office after being ousted by White citizens on trumped-up charges. On December 7, 1874, a large group of Black citizens of Vicksburg had gathered around Crosby in a show of force to help him regain his office. Red Shirts would have none of it. With the help of 160 White Leaguers, who'd crossed the Mississippi from Louisiana, they slaughtered several hundred Blacks in what is known as the "Vicksburg Massacre." Southern Whites were ecstatic.

"Raise the banner of white supremacy," said the *Mobile Register*.[32] "'Citizens' have killed off as many 'niggers' as they are ready to dispose of at present," was the opinion of the Louisville *Courier-Journal*. "When they get more ammunition they will renew the diversion. Meantime, as the telegraph informs us 'the whites are in possession of everything.'"[33]

News traveled quickly throughout the south. After the massacre, Red Shirts and White Leaguers from all over the south poured into Vicksburg, ransacking Black homes, terrorizing Black men and women, killing them.[34] Ex-slave Isaac Moseley testified that next month in front of a congressional committee visiting Vicksburg to report on the massacre. Moseley, a gravedigger, dug many burial plots for Black citizens of the Vicksburg Massacre. But he also dug a grave for one of the Red Shirts, which, he said, kept him alive. While digging that grave, Moseley heard one of the White men say, "Let us kill until we get our satisfaction."[35]

A telegram came to George W. Walton, president of the board of supervisors in Vicksburg:

TRINITY TEXAS, DECEMBER 12, 1874

To the President of the Board of Supervisors:
Do you want any men? Can raise good crowd within twenty-four hours to kill out your negroes.

J. G. GATES
A. H. MASON[36]

Ultimately, President Grant sent federal troops to broker the conflict, which resulted in Crosby regaining his office, and that was like pouring fuel on the flames of White discontent. On June 7, 1875, Crosby and Jonathan P. Gilmer were drinking together at Fred Bowman's saloon in Vicksburg. Gilmer, the former White sheriff, who was now Crosby's deputy, pulled a pistol and shot Crosby in the head. Crosby miraculously survived to see Gilmer arrested but never tried. Eventually Crosby succumbed to his wounds.[37]

Charles E. Furlong, Republican state senator from Vicksburg's Warren County, gave a floor speech titled "Origin of the Outrages at Vicksburg" eleven days after the massacre. Similar events were soon to happen around the state, Furlong said, and they would "require a stronger hand than that of Governor Ames."[38]

But the governor's attention lay somewhere faraway.

JACKSON, MISS., AUGUST 22, 1875

Dear Blanche:
. . . Need I tell you I miss you and the babies a great deal? And yet, while I would like to have you with me now I know it is best you should be where you are—and I would be the more content to be with you away from here than to have you here with me . . . I send love to you and the babies.[39]

With storm clouds on the horizon, Ames penned letters to his beautiful wife, Blanche Butler, General Benjamin Butler's daughter, who spent most of the year away from Jackson at the family home in Lowell, Massachusetts. But this was not the time for contemplating nuptial bliss.

The elections were coming and the Mississippi Plan was in full swing. Red Shirts, White Leagues, and rifle clubs roamed the countryside unchecked. The killings of Black people rose. Newspapers around the country ran with the story of Red Shirts chasing unarmed Blacks "for mile and miles, killing them as a sportsman would kill the scattered birds of a covey."[40] Requests flooded into Jackson, imploring the governor to undertake firm action in response to the mayhem and murder engulfing the state.

That's when Ames wrote to President Grant requesting federal troops. That's when Grant wrote back, through his attorney general, that the country was moving on, "tired of these annual autumnal outbreaks."[41] No troops were sent to Mississippi. Ames tried raising a militia of his own to protect Black citizens, under the leadership of a Black man, Charles Caldwell. A band of Red Shirts and White Leaguers organized under the command of former governor James Alcorn. Black men and White men, Republicans and Democrats, were headed at each other with drawn weapons.

With Mississippi about to blow up, Ames simply gave in. He brokered and signed a peace deal between the parties that required him to disband the state's militia, handing over the keys of the state to Democrats and their paramilitary thugs.

JACKSON, MISS., OCTOBER 12, 1875

Dear Blanche:
We began too late to organize and have too little means to accomplish much with the militia . . . Yes, a revolution has taken place—by force of arms—and a race are disfanchised—they are to be returned to a condition of serfdom—an era of second slavery. It is their fault (not mine, personally) that this fate is before them. They refused to prepare for war when in time of peace, when they could have done so. Now it

is too late . . . The political death of the Negro will forever release the nation from the weariness of such "political outbreaks." . . .

Last night I made up my mind to resign after the election when this revolution shall have been completed. Why should I fight on a hopeless battle for two years more, when no possible good to the Negro or anybody else would result? Why?

After all this I turn from myself to you, Beautiful—the bright, happy dwelling place of my thoughts, and send forth to you a world of love without end.[42]

"Refused to prepare for war in time of peace"? Had not the war already been settled at Appomattox? Had not the Red Shirts systematically disarmed Black people under Ames's watch? "It is their fault"? In a sad denial of responsibility, Ames blamed the victims of the violence and murder. He plotted an exit for himself, knowing full well that Black folks in Mississippi would have to live with the consequences of his indecision.

By Election Day, November 2, 1875, hundreds of Black men had been killed, thousands injured, and many that remained slept in the cane fields and woods to avoid harm. In Meridian, White Leagues had taken control of the polling stations early in the morning, even though Blacks were a majority there. Looking back across Johnson Street at the voting, a group of Black men barred from casting ballots stood "sullen and morose," watching democracy slip away.[43] Though fires had burned, and Black men were murdered the night before Election Day, when asked whether he'd seen any voter intimidation in his city, Joseph P. Billings, the mayor of Columbus, Mississippi, told a Senate panel it was "quiet as a funeral" on Election Day.[44] Quiet on the day democracy died.

Democrats routed Republicans. In some regions Black men either voted Democratic, or they did not vote at all. Grant wrung his hands, lamenting, "Mississippi is governed to-day by officials chosen through fraud and violence, such as would scarcely be accredited to savages, much less to a civilized and Christian people."[45] The

US Senate investigated, but abdicated its duty to nullify the election, calling it "one of the darkest chapters in American history."[46] And, six months later, Adelbert Ames stepped down to rejoin his beloved Blanche in Massachusetts.

The success of the plan in Mississippi set off a chain reaction, with South Carolina not far behind. Ben "Pitchfork" Tillman, a leader of the Red Shirts in South Carolina, in the elections of 1876 eventually rose to become the state's governor, then US senator. Speaking more than thirty years later at a Red Shirt reunion in 1909, Tillman fondly recalled his Red Shirt days: "Altogether in 1874 and 1876, I was a participant in four race riots. All of these were most potent influences in shaping the conflict between the whites and blacks and producing the gratifying result which brought the white man again into control of his inheritance."[47]

At least two of these race riots were outright massacres. In Hamburg, South Carolina, on July 5, 1876, and in Ellenton that September, Red Shirts, with Tillman's rifle club participating, murdered more than one hundred Blacks. Tillman and ninety-three other Whites were indicted and prosecuted but never convicted. Really, it was a rolling riot of violence against Black people extending until Election Day. In October 1876, South Carolina governor Daniel Chamberlain issued orders disbanding rifle clubs (from which the Red Shirts drew their members). He also asked President Grant for federal forces to assist him.

Like it had in Mississippi, violence against Blacks spiraled out of control. Red Shirts forced Blacks to vote Democratic at gunpoint, then forced them to turn on other Blacks to follow suit.[48] Rape of Black women was an unwritten part of the Mississippi Plan.[49] But Black women were encouraged to fight back by women like Lottie Rollin and men like Robert Smalls.

Rollin argued for universal women's suffrage on the floor of the South Carolina House of Representatives in March 1869, thus becoming the first Black woman to formally speak to a state government in the south. She organized the Women's Rights Convention that met in Columbia the following year, declaring, "We ask suffrage not as a favor, not as a privilege, but as a right based on the grounds that we are human beings and as such entitled to all human rights."[50] Black women electioneered at polling stations[51] and five were arrested for attempting to vote in the 1870 election.[52]

Robert Smalls went to the Parris Island, one of the South Carolina Sea Islands, ahead of the 1876 election, and suggested a Reconstruction-era version of *Lysistrata*[53] to the island's Black women, urging, "if their husbands voted the Democratic ticket to throw them out of the house." According to testimony before the House of Representatives, Smalls continued by saying,

> When John went to Massa Hampton and pledged his word to vote for him and returned back home his wife told him "She would not give him any of that thing if you vote for Hampton." John gone back to Massa Hampton and said, "Massa Hampton, I can't vote for you, for woman is too sweet, and my wife says if I vote for you she won't give me any." And, ladies, I think, if you all do that, we won't have a Democratic ticket polled on Paris Island.[54]

In South Carolina, David T. Corbin, US district attorney for South Carolina, wrote to Governor Chamberlain about Red Shirt violence,

> These clubs have created and are causing a perfect reign of terror. The colored men are, many of them, lying out of doors and away from their homes at night. Many of them have been killed, and many have been taken from their beds at night and mercilessly whipped, and others have been hunted with threats of murder and whipping, who thus far, by contrast watchfulness and activity, have escaped. The white men of these clubs are riding day and night, and the colored men are informed that their only safety from death or whipping lies in their signing an agreement pledging themselves to vote the democratic ticket at the coming election.[55]

Grant did send troops, but in his reply to Chamberlain's request, one senses a timidity of purpose, a hesitation of decision, and a lack of resolve to act, uncharacteristic of the great general.

> How long these things are to continue, or what is to be the final remedy, the Great Ruler of the universe only knows; but I have an abiding faith that the remedy will come, and come speedily, and I earnestly hope that it will come peacefully . . . Expressing the hope that the better judgment and co-operation of citizens of the State over which you have presided so ably may enable you to secure a fair trial and punishment of all offenders, without distinction of race or color or previous condition of servitude, and without aid from the Federal Government.[56]

The situation actually called for more than Grant's "abiding faith" or his "expressions of hope." At any rate, the troops he sent were too little, too late. When voting counting finished on November 7, 1876, only 1,100 votes separated Wade Hampton and Chamberlain—1,100 more votes for a Democratic candidate that had come through voter intimidation and murder. South Carolina's election results were thrown into chaos, and Chamberlain clung to power with the support of Grant's federal troops.

But that year also saw votes cast for a new president, with Grant not seeking a third term. The election was first called for Democrat Samuel J. Tilden, and White southerners took to the streets in wild pandemonium—firecrackers burst, guns blazed, brass bands blared. The south had risen at last! Or had it?

Tilden with 184 electoral votes was one short of an outright victory, and Republicans, backing Rutherford B. Hayes, claimed irregularities in South Carolina, Florida, and Louisiana, which happened to still have Blacks on boards of elections, still in positions of authority. Electoral boards in these states certified Hayes's electors. White southerners, having fought so hard and killed so many Blacks to suppress the vote, would not stand for it. So, for several months there were two governors, two legislatures, and two sets of electors in South Carolina and Louisiana. That meant there were also two presidents-elect. Then, Democrats mounted a filibuster in the Senate, preventing the House from counting the Electoral College votes, throwing the country into a constitutional crisis with the inauguration pending.

With the threat of another civil war looming, the country's desire to get on with business was stronger than its desire to get on with justice. "The members of the Congress are of the impression," said Lucien B. Caswell, representative from Wisconsin, "that the people wish to revive business at any political sacrifice."[57] That sacrifice? The promise of liberty and justice for all Americans, particularly for all Black Americans.

With no appetite on the part of Republicans to fight, the end came soon. In March 1877, a few days before the inauguration, the Compromise of 1877 was reached, handing the presidency to Hayes and the Republicans, but handing the south back to the former Confederate states. Within weeks of assuming office, Hayes pulled all federal troops from the south. Without support, Chamberlain fell in South Carolina, and soon a round of new constitutions in southern states would obliterate the last decade, wiping clean and turning back any strides made toward equality and freedom for "We the People" in America.

In his role as a North Carolina judge, Albion Tourgée was a fierce advocate for the civil rights of people, regardless of color. Some credit him with the phrase "color-blind justice." He stood up to White Leagues and Red Shirts and the Klan. He fined lawyers for using the word *nigger* in his courtroom. On September 3, 1879, at the end of a distinguished fourteen-year judicial career, not realizing he would go on to yet more fame as the lead attorney in the *Plessy v. Ferguson* Supreme Court case, still twenty years away, Tourgée had a front-page interview appear in the *New-York Tribune*. One senses his weariness and frustration as he pays tribute to an enemy he'd long fought.

In all except the actual result of the physical struggle, I consider the South to have been the real victors in the war. I am filled with admiration and amazement at the masterly way in which they have brought about these results. The way in which they have neutralized the results of the war and reversed the verdict of Appomattox is the grandest thing in American politics.[58]

With malice aforethought, White bloodlust savagely dismantled a decade of post-war progress made by newly freed Blacks toward creating a more perfect American union. White desires for power and wealth brutally erased new institutions of power and wealth erected from Black desires for democracy and equality. Freedom dues, first paid, were then revoked. Freedom gains, first realized, were then reversed. Black lives, which first mattered, were then cast aside. W.E.B. Du Bois summarized the post–Civil War fate of Black lives succinctly: "The slave went free; stood a brief moment in the sun; then moved back again toward slavery."[59]

And still the question lingers: Will that sun ever rise again?

AFTERWORD

August 3, 1880, was another hot, sunny day, not in Charleston this time but in Elmira, New York. By noon, a throng of hundreds milled around outside Temperance Hall, near the corner of Dickinson and Clinton streets. Almost everyone had been up since sunrise, when the firing of guns marked the start of this day of festivities and thanksgiving. Earlier that morning, most had heard either the Reverend C. E. Smith, at AME Zion, or the Reverend M. E. Collins, at AME Union, conduct rousing morning services. Afterward, they stood silently at the corner of Dickinson and Fourth streets, where Zion faced across from Union; stood silently and listened to a sixty-three-gun salute.[1]

Sunday best was called for. Women in red, and white, and blue bustled dresses wore curled and natural hair beneath wide-brimmed, feathered hats. Some men sported topcoats and tails, even under the rising summer sun. From Binghamton and Corning and Ithaca, Black folks came. From Syracuse and Geneva and Watkins Glen, they came, too. If you were Black, and within one hundred miles of Elmira, you were there, assembled at Temperance Hall to walk in a parade that marked Emancipation Day.

Almost an hour past the appointed time of noon, the marchers started walking. Taking a right turn on Lake Street and heading down toward the Chemung River. Grand Marshal Hiram Washington and his staff led the way through city streets lined with excited White residents, who decorated their homes in honor of their "colored friends and visitors." Behind the grand marshal, *oohs* rose from those watching, as a twirling baton flew high into the air, finally caught by a high-stepping drum major out in front of Elmira's A. W. La France Marching Band, sporting for the first time their neatly pressed, dark blue uniforms.

Horns blew and drums rolled as music filled the air. Next came the Palmer Guards of Syracuse, a national guard regiment under the command of Captain William H. Franklin. As the procession turned right again at Water Street and began walking west along the river, another baton went skyward, then fell into the hands of George Chapman at the head of the fifteen-member Geddes Cornet band, who swung their heads to the beat of the tune they blared. At Main Street, a third flying baton marked the coming of the Havana Cornet band, and the point at which the parade turned right, again. Black delegations from surrounding cities walked interspersed between the marching bands, waving to the onlookers they passed.

After the Havana Cornet band came Black Civil War veterans, and after them came the rumble of metal and wood from turning wheels on horse-drawn carriages carrying the reception committee and the dignitaries for the day. Only two dignitaries rode in the carriages and waved to the crowd: W. H. Lester, of Dryden, New York, who would later read in full the Emancipation Proclamation, and "the most prominent and honored colored man in the world."

Firemen, militia units, civic associations, including the Elmira Colored YMCA, then local citizens and strangers brought up the rear, as the parade turned left onto Church Street, then right at Walnut, snaking its way to the park at Hoffman's Grove. There, benches had been built but with such a large crowd many simply stood. Police on hand guarded the gathering, frustrating the attempt of a handful of White men intent on breaking it up.

After the crowd settled into their seats, more prayers and more music came from the speakers' platform. W. H. Lester, in a splendid voice, read the Emancipation Proclamation. Elmira's La France band then played again. After the band came the moment for which most had been waiting, when the US Marshal of Washington, DC, rose to address the crowd. Thunderous applause lasted for several minutes.

"I thank you for this cordial greeting," said the Honorable Frederick Douglass, "I hear in it something like the thrilling notes of a welcome home after a long absence."

August seems like a strange time for this occasion, a strange time to celebrate emancipation. Wouldn't June 19 have been better, when supposedly the last of the slaves in Texas heard about Lincoln's proclamation? Surely, by 1880, Frederick Douglass knew that day. If not then, why not January 1, when the Emancipation Proclamation actually went into effect?

But Douglass, and many others, had celebrated August 1 as Emancipation Day for nearly fifty years, and the ceremony in Elmira was the closest to that date which could be arranged. August 1 really was Emancipation Day, not for slavery in America, but for slavery in the British Empire, especially in the West Indies. On July 26, 1833, the Slavery Abolition Act was passed by Parliament, just three days before its great champion of abolition, William Wilberforce, died. On August 28 it received the official recognition of King William IV. And on August 1, 1834, it went into effect, freeing some 800,000 men and women in the West Indies, South Africa, and Canada.[2]

While much could be said about the Slavery Abolition Act in contrast to the Emancipation Proclamation, this afterword is not the place. Douglass, however, in his speech that sunny day at Hoffman's Grove in Elmira,[3] described the act as "the first bright star in a stormy sky; the first smile after a long providential frown; the first ray of hope; the first tangible fact demonstrating the possibility of a peaceable transition from slavery to freedom of the negro race." And he welcomed the combined celebration of the Slavery Abolition Act and the Emancipation Proclamation on the same day in August. "Human liberty excludes all idea of home and abroad," he said. "We may properly celebrate this day because of its special relation to our American Emancipation. In doing this we do not sacrifice the general to the special, the universal to the local. The cause of human liberty is one the whole world over."

By this time, Douglass was an elder of the freedom struggle. At sixty-two, he lamented during his speech that many with whom he'd joined, like Thaddeus Stevens, Charles Sumner, and William Wilberforce, had passed away. He understood he was now speaking to the next generation of leaders, to those to whom he would pass the torch. Douglass wanted them to understand two things—the failures of Reconstruction, and the promises of the future.

Our reconstruction measures were radically defective. They left the former slave completely in the power of the old master . . . They called them citizens, and left them subjects; they called them free, and almost left them slaves. They did not deprive the old master class of the power of life and death, which was the soul of the relation of master and slave. They could not, of course, sell them, but they retained the power to starve them to death, and wherever this power is held there is the power of slavery . . . Though no longer a slave, he is in a thralldom grievous and intolerable, compelled to work for whatever his employer is pleased to pay him, swindled out of his hard earnings by money orders redeemed in stores, compelled to pay the price of an acre of ground for its use during a single year . . . To me the wonder is, not that the freedmen have made so little progress, but, rather, that they have made so much; not that they have been standing still, but that they have been able to stand at all . . . History does not furnish an example of emancipation under conditions less friendly to the emancipated class than this American example. Liberty came to the freed men of the United States not in mercy, but in wrath, not by moral choice but by military necessity, not by the generous action of the people among whom they were to live, and whose good-will was essential to the success of the measure, but by strangers, foreigners, invaders, trespassers, aliens, and enemies.

Douglass could not know who would follow after Reconstruction. In 1880, he did not know the names Marcus Garvey, Howard Thurman, Thurgood Marshall, Martin Luther King, Emmett Till, John Lewis, Medgar Evers, Malcolm X, George Floyd, or the many thousands of others who would join the coming struggle for freedom and equality. Yet one hears in what Douglass would say next to his audience in Elmira a clear road map for the future.

> Let us, then, wherever we are, whether at the North or at the South, resolutely struggle on . . . Greatness does not come to any people on flowery beds of ease. We must fight to win the prize. No people to whom liberty is given, can hold it as firmly and wear it as grandly as those who wrench their liberty from the iron hand of the tyrant. The hardships and dangers involved in the struggle give strength and toughness to the character, and enable it to stand firm in storm as well as in Sunshine.

With a nod back to the American Revolution, Douglass also pointed a way forward, a "fight to win the prize." And who cannot hear in his words that the "hardships and dangers involved in the struggle give strength and toughness to the character," those words spoken by Martin Luther King, Jr. on another August day eighty-three years later, that "unearned suffering is redemptive."[4]

Douglass, on his sunny August day, cleaved "freedom dues" in two. On one hand, the struggle up until Reconstruction, on the other, the struggle that would come after. Most likely, Douglass did not know Anthony and Isabella's names. But he did know that the first part of freedom dues, the part which their presence began, ended poorly. And he knew the second part of freedom dues would be a protracted struggle to "win the prize."

In the beautiful poetry of his words, Douglass described why this book ends where it does; for this volume is about the first part of that struggle, the part in which Black lives mattered in creating White power and wealth, the part in which they eventually shared that power and wealth for a brief moment, but ultimately the part which ended poorly. Of course, the story of the struggle doesn't end at Reconstruction, but in some sense the tactics of the tale change there. Black Americans, who stayed in the south after Reconstruction, fought simply for their survival. Those who left for the north faced the unexpected racism of industrialization, and with it, new kinds of bondage. Take railroads, for example. While Black Americans had built them, boosting the power and wealth of their owners in the first part of the struggle, now they worked on them as servants, Pullman porters, in the second. Or take the mills of the Rust Belt. Where in the first part of freedom dues, Black labor worked plantation fields, in the second part they now worked "iron plantations," where the supervisor with a time clock replaced the overseer with a whip.

If we describe the first part of this struggle as Blacks creating White power and wealth, then the second part of this struggle should be described as Blacks challenging the very power and wealth they helped to create—the power to determine their destiny, which they had only tasted briefly, and the wealth to secure their future, and that of their descendants, which they had never really tasted at all.

Labor unions, Supreme Court challenges, eugenics, redlining, marches, protests, water cannons, dogs, sit-ins, pepper spray, rubber bullets, police violence, the Civil Rights Movement, the Black Lives Matter Movement, all the marvelous and horrific moments and events of the second part of this struggle, have antecedents in the first. This is yet another reason to end this book here. Like Anthony and Isabella, who each year prepared the earth before they sprinkled tobacco seeds on the fields of William Tucker's plantation, the first part of this story prepared the ground for the seeds of a struggle yet to come.

Looking back over that seeded earth, the main regret I have is that I couldn't tell more stories of these human seeds, more stories of why Black lives mattered in the creation of White power and wealth in America. There were times when each sentence of this book could have been easily expanded into a section, each section into a separate chapter, and each chapter into a book of its own. I found it really hard to pick and choose which stories to tell and which to leave behind. But leaving stories behind only means leaving them for others to discover and to tell, as Anthony and Isabella left us the strands of a story about why their lives mattered, strands we could then weave into this tale *Of Blood and Sweat*.

NOTES

URLs listed in these references were visited as of July 2020. Please be aware that URLs do change, even if the material still remains online. If a URL listed below is no longer valid, consider searching for the source document based on the principal author's name, the document title, or the volume the document appeared in. Another possibility is to use the "Wayback Machine" at www.archive.org and enter the URL as of July 31, 2020 or before.

INTRODUCTION

1. *Minutes of the Council and General Court of Colonial Virginia, 1622–1632, 1670–1676: With Notes and Excerpts from Original Council and General Court Records, Into 1683, Now Lost* (Richmond, VA: Colonial Press, 2011), 411.

2. See, for example, Murray Bowen and C. Margaret Hall, *The Bowen Family Theory and Its Uses* (Lanham, MD: Jason Aronson, 1981).

3. The precise linguist spelling of this word is $\sqrt{(n)}$gr, where the square root sign and parentheses have special linguist meanings apart from their meaning as mathematical symbols. See Martin Bernal, *Black Athena*, Vol. 2 (New Brunswick, NJ: Rutgers Univ. Press, 1991), 96.

CHAPTER 1: ANTONEY AND ISABELL

1. John Frederick Dorman, "Capt William Tucker His Muster, Elizabeth Cittie," *Adventurers of Purse and Person Virginia 1607–1624/25, 4th ed.* (Baltimore: Genealogical Publishing Company, 2004), 51.

2. Carter G. Woodson and Rayford Logan, eds., "Muster of Capt. William Tucker, Elizabeth City," *The Journal of Negro History*, Vol. 8, 1923, 258. In all likelihood they were baptized with the Portuguese names Antonio and Isabella. But as Heywood and Thornton note in *Central Africans, Atlantic Creoles and the Foundation of the Americas, 1585–1660* (Cambridge Univ. Press: 2007), there was a tendency in Kimbundu (a Bantu language spoken in Angola) not to pronounce

the last vowel of a name. Thus, when colonial scribes recorded their names for the 1624/25 muster, "Antoney" and "Isabell" resulted. In the 1623 census his name is spelled as "Anthony" and hers as "Isabell." See Jamestowne Society, "Lists of the Livinge & Dead in Virginia," May 8, 2017, http://www.jamestowne .org/1623-lists-of-living--dead.html.

3. John Rolfe, "Letter from John Rolfe to Sir Edwyn Sandys (1619/1620)," *Encyclo-pedia Virginia*, "20._and_odd_Negroes"_an_excerpt_from_a_letter_from_John _Rolfe_to_Sir_Edwyn_Sandys_1619_1620. For historical accuracy I have kept the period after "20," which is how John Rolfe originally recorded the number.

4. Tim Hashaw, *Children of Perdition: Melungeons and the Struggle of Mixed America* (Macon, GA: Mercer Univ. Press, 2006), 27.

5. Roberta J. Estes, et al., "Melungeons, A Multi-Ethnic Population," *Journal of Ge-netic Genealogy*, April 2012, http://www.jogg.info/pages/72/files/Estes.pdf.

6. See, for instance, Tim Hashaw, "Malungu: The African Origin of American Melungeons," *Eclecta*, July/August 2001, Vol. 5, No. 3, http://www.eclectica.org /v5n3/hashaw.html. Much like the dispute over Jefferson's paternity of Sally Hemings's children, portions of which remain even after DNA evidence proved that Jefferson did father children with this slave, the dispute over the Melungeon, and therefore African origin, of these famous people is divisive and contentious.

7. Even this reference to the "Lost Colony of Roanoke" does not exclude Melun-geon ancestry in Africa because evidence exists that, on his way back from raiding Cartagena in 1586, Sir Francis Drake stopped at the Colony of Roanoke and left with them some of the captive Africans he had on board. See, for example, Lydia Towns, "English Privateers and the Transatlantic Slave Trade," *Traversea: The Journal of Transatlantic History*, Vol. 4, 2014, https://traversea.journal.library.uta .edu/index.php/traversea/article/view/23/23, 9.

8. See, for instance, Jennifer Churchill, "The Mystery of the Melungeons," *Family Tree Magazine*, December 2003, https://www.familytreemagazine.com/premium /the-mystery-of-the-melungeons.

9. Robert W. Slenes, "'Malungu, Ngoma Vem!:' África coberta e descoberta no Brasil" ("'Malungu, Ngoma's Coming!': Africa Hidden and Uncovered in Bra-zil"), *Revista*, Vol. 12 (Luanda, Angola: Museum of Slavery, 1995), 48–67, https:// ppgh.ufba.br/sites/ppgh.ufba.br/files/1_-_slenes_malungu2001_pag_normal _-_19.04.18_0.pdf.

10. Linda Heywood and John Thornton, *Africans, Atlantic Creoles and the Foundation of the Americas, 1585–1660* (Cambridge Univ. Press: 2007), 5–48. Heywood and Thornton have impeccable and irrefutable documentation from English, Dutch, Portuguese, and Spanish sources attesting to the fact that the first wave of Afri-cans in America, prior to approximately 1660, were the Ndongo from Angola. See also Engel Sluter, "New Light on the '20. and Odd Negroes' Arriving in Virginia, August 1619," *The William and Mary Quarterly* 54, April 1997, 395–98.

11.   Pope Nicholas V, Dum Diversas, Papal Bull (Rome: 1452).

12.   Heywood and Thornton, *Africans, Atlantic Creoles and the Foundation of the Americas*, 6.

13.   Heywood and Thornton, *Africans, Atlantic Creoles and the Foundation of the Americas*, 6.

14.   Heywood and Thornton, *Africans, Atlantic Creoles and the Foundation of the Americas*, 13.

15.   John Wright, *The Trans-Saharan Slave Trade* (London and New York: Routledge, 2007).

16.   Raymond Ibrahim, "Islam's Hidden Role in the Transatlantic Slave Trade," *American Thinker*, February 6, 2020, https://www.meforum.org/60383/islam-hidden-role-in-the-transatlantic-slave-trade.

17.   See Heywood and Thornton, *Africans, Atlantic Creoles and the Foundation of the Americas*, 82–92, for an overview of the conflict between the Portuguese and the Ndongo.

18.   Heywood and Thornton, *Africans, Atlantic Creoles and the Foundation of the Americas*, 114–16.

19.   Thomas J. Deschi-Obi, *Fighting for Honor: The History of African Martial Art Traditions in the Atlantic World* (Columbia: Univ. of South Carolina Press, 2008), 21.

20.   Deschi-Obi, *Fighting for Honor*, 23.

21.   Heywood and Thornton, *Africans, Atlantic Creoles and the Foundation of the Americas*, 93–94.

22.   Heywood and Thornton, *Africans, Atlantic Creoles and the Foundation of the Americas*, 114–23.

23.   "Virgin Soil Epidemics as a Factor in the Aboriginal Depopulation in America," *The William and Mary Quarterly*, Omohundro Institute of Early American History and Culture, Vol. 33, No. 2, April 1976, 289–99, https://www.jstor.org/stable/1922166.

24.   Frank Snowden, *Epidemics and Society: From the Black Death to the Present* (New Haven: Yale Univ. Press, 2020), 102–4.

25.   Snowden, *Epidemics and Society*, 103.

26.   Snowden, *Epidemics and Society*, 103.

27.   Francis T. Bowles, "Gives the Dimensions of Pilgrims' Ship: Admiral Bowles Finds Mayflower Was 90 Feet Long With Beam of 20 Feet," *New York Times*, February 21, 1921, 3. The *Mayflower* was a fluyt. See also "Fluyt Dutch Cargo Vessel," Harrison County, West Virginia Genealogical Society, http://www.wvhcgs.com/vessel.htm.

28.   See *The William Tucker 1624 Society*, https://williamtucker1624society.org/our-story.

29.   Joseph Campbell with Bill Moyers, *The Power of Myth* (New York: Random House, 1991), 40.

30.   Violet S. de Laszlo, ed., *The Basic Writings of C.G. Jung* (New York: Random House, 1959).

31. Clyde W. Ford, *The Hero With an African Face: Mythic Wisdom of Traditional Africa* (New York: Bantam, 1999), 3–6.

32. Ford, *The Hero With an African Face*, 6.

33. Ford, *The Hero With an African Face*, 6.

34. Ford, *The Hero With an African Face*, 28–45, has a full presentation and discussion of the myth of Sudika-mbambi.

35. Wyatt MacGaffey, *Modern Kongo Prophets* (Bloomington: Univ. of Indiana Press, 1983), 136.

36. Bowles, "Gives Dimension of Pilgrims' Ship," 3.

CHAPTER 2: PIRACY AND EUROPEAN WEALTH

1. A "dynastic union" represented a federation between two monarchies, under one monarch, where the original kingdoms retained their geographical, legal, and political autonomy. Most often, the monarchies were geographically adjacent and the union often precipitated by marriage. The Anglo-Scottish Union forming the United Kingdom represents such a "dynastic union." Spain and Portugal joined under a dynastic union for eighty years (1580–1660) ruled by the House of Habsburg, a Philippine dynasty centered in Seville (Philip II, Philip III, and Philip IV). Sixteenth-century maritime predation of Portuguese ships by English, Dutch, and French privateers weakened Portugal's rule over the sea trade and was a large factor in the Portuguese crown seeking an alliance, as junior partner, with Spain, a much stronger naval power. Ultimately, the Iberian Union broke down in war between Portugal and Spain, ending in the Treaty of Lisbon in 1668, and the establishment of the Portuguese House of Braganza (the Brigantine Dynasty) as the independent rulers of Portugal and her colonies.

2. Angus Konstam and Angus McBride, *Elizabethan Sea Dogs 1560–1605* (Oxford, UK: Osprey Publishing, 2000), 6.

3. Lydia Towns, "English Privateers and the Transatlantic Slave Trade," *Traversea: The Journal of Transatlantic History*, Vol. 4, 2014, https://traversea.journal.library.uta.edu/index.php/traversea/article/view/23/23.

4. Nigel Pocock and Victoria Cook, "The Business of Enslavement," BBC, February 17, 2011, http://www.bbc.co.uk/history/british/abolition/slavery_business_gallery_11.shtml. Englishmen operated slave trading out of foreign ports, prior to Hawkins. And, Hawkins did not initiate unbroken See David Olusoga, *Black and British: A Forgotten History* (London: MacMillan, 2016), 51–2.

5. Ronald Pollitt, "John Hawkins's Troublesome Voyages: Merchants, Bureaucrats, and the Origin of the Slave Trade," *The Journal of British Studies*, Vol. 12, Issue 2, May 1973, 27–28.

6. Pollitt, "John Hawkins's Troublesome Voyages," 40.

7. Pollitt, "John Hawkins's Troublesome Voyages," 29.

8. Pollitt, "John Hawkins's Troublesome Voyages," 28–37.

9. Pollitt, "John Hawkins's Troublesome Voyages," 40.

10. Linda Heywood and John Thornton, *Africans, Atlantic Creoles and the Foundation of the Americas, 1585–1660* (Cambridge Univ. Press: 2007), 35.

11. Heywood and Thornton, *Africans, Atlantic Creoles and the Foundation of the Americas*, 40.

12. Heywood and Thornton, *Africans, Atlantic Creoles and the Foundation of the Americas*, 42–48.

13. Heywood and Thornton, *Africans, Atlantic Creoles and the Foundation of the Americas*, 6.

14. John Rolfe, "Letter from John Rolfe to Sir Edwyn Sandys (1619/1620)," *Encyclopedia Virginia*, "20._and_odd_Negroes"_an_excerpt_from_a_letter_from _John_Rolfe_to_Sir_Edwin_Sandys_1619_1620.

15. Hugh Fred Jope, Maj. USAF (Ret.), "The Flying Dutchman" (1993), cited in Tim Hashaw, "Malungu: The African Origins of the American Melungeons," *Electica Magazine*, July/August 2001, http://www.eclectica.org/v5n3/hashaw.html.

16. Jope, "The Flying Dutchman," cited in Hashaw, "Malungu."

17. Rolfe, "Letter from John Rolfe to Sir Edwyn Sandys."

18. Rolfe, "Letter from John Rolfe to Sir Edwyn Sandys."

19. The *Treasurer* and the *Bautista* arrived at Point Comfort sailing under different marques giving them permission to plunder Spanish and Portuguese vessels. The *Bautista* operated under a Dutch marque, the *Treasurer* under a marque from the Duke of Savoy (Savoy was then a state in what is now northeast France) obtained by the Earl of Warwick, Lord Rich. But in 1617, while the *Treasurer* was at sea, and presumably out of contact, the Treaty of Pavia was signed between Savoy and Spain. That meant, technically, Daniel Elfrith, captain of *Treasurer*, was operating not as a privateer but a pirate, under penalty of swinging from the gallows. It also meant that any privateering activities could bring the wrath of King James I, currently at peace with Spain, or cause a Spanish armada to appear off the Virginia coast.

   Treasurer had once visited the Virginia colony at Jamestown, prior to her second arrival in August 1619. On her first visit, she had been under the protection of Samuel Argall, then governor of Virginia, who saw to it that her looted goods were distributed to colonists and that she was provisioned in return. But Argall was part of one faction of the Virginia Company, which ran the colony, at odds with another faction over the issue of how colonists were supplied with provisions. Though welcoming of privateers' booty, the Company sold low-quality provisions to complaining colonists at high prices. Argall, a part owner with Lord Rich in *Treasurer*, saw in the ship's raids a means to provision colonists with higher-quality goods. Thus, the other faction of the Virginia Company, supported by Rolfe and Sandys, sought to get rid of Argall.

   But this second faction had a rather worrisome problem. Argall's chief benefactor was the highly esteemed Earl of Warwick, Lord Rich, himself also a shareholder in the Virginia Company. To indict Rich would be to embroil the

Company in a scandal that might also cause King James I to cancel its charter. So, this second group of shareholders focused their energies on getting rid of Argall instead. Sandys engineered the appointment of his own man, George Yeardley, as governor. Then Lord Rich sent a fast ship to pick up Argall, before Yeardley's administration arrived from England to arrest him.

This intrigue was only heightened when the *White Lion* arrived in Virginia with a cargo of slaves, followed a few days later by the *Treasurer*, also with a cargo of slaves. Jope posed no threat to these warring factions of the Company, so his ship was allowed to trade captive Africans and resupply. But Elfrith, in command of the *Treasurer*, now had no benefactor in command of the colony. He dared not call on Lord Rich's name to protect him, and the Sandys faction dared not indict Rich for fear of taking down the Company and the colony with him. So, absent a benefactor on land, Elfrith, recognizing his jeopardy, high-tailed it by sea to Bermuda, where a friendly governor, Samuel Barber, awaited the *Treasurer*'s arrival.

Later, even Jope, captain of the *White Lion*, would be ensnared in this intrigue, when in a complex and extended case before the English courts, from 1620 to 1624, Argall and Elfrith testified to Jope's primary responsibility for the capture of the *São João Bautista*.

20. Ellora Derencourt, "Atlantic slavery's impact on European and British economic development," *private paper*, https://eaderen.github.io/derenoncourt_atlantic _slavery_europe_2018.pdf. Cited with permission of the author.

21. Felipe González, et al., "Start-up Nation? Slave Wealth and Entrepreneurship in Civil War Maryland," National Bureau of Economic Research, Working Paper No. w22483, https://papers.ssrn.com/sol3/papers.cfm?abstract_id=2819868.

22. Robin Blackburn, *The Making of New World Slavery: From the Baroque to the Modern 1492–1800* (UK: Verso, 2010), 255.

23. Charles Lintner Killinger, "The Royal African Company Slave Trade to Virginia, 1689–1713," *Dissertations, Theses, and Masters Projects*, Paper 1539624680, William & Mary College, 1969, 89, https://scholarworks.wm.edu/cgi/viewcontent .cgi?article=4997&context=etd.

24. Blackburn, *The Making of New World Slavery*, 255.

25. Hugh Thomas, "The Branding (and Baptism) of Slaves," *The Review of Arts, Literature, Philosophy and the Humanities*, Vol. 12, No. 4, 1996–97, http://www.ralphmag .org/slave2.html.

26. John Micklethwait and Adrian Wooldridge, *The Company: A Short History of a Revolutionary Idea* (New York: Random House, 2003), 177.

27. Martha B. Katz-Hyman and Kym S. Rice, eds., *World of a Slave: Encyclopedia of the Material Life of Slaves in the United States* (Santa Barbara: ABC-CLIO, 2011), 259.

28. The "City of London" properly refers only to an approximately one-mile-square area of Greater London which houses London's financial and business district. See A. D. Mills, *A Dictionary of London Place Names* (London: Oxford Univ. Press), 152.

29. Blackburn, *The Making of New World Slavery*, 7, 135, 141.

30. Blackburn, *The Making of New World Slavery*, 143.

31. Filipa Ribeiro da Silva, *Dutch and Portuguese in Western Africa: Empires, Merchants and the Atlantic System, 1580–1674* (Leiden, The Netherlands: Koninklijke Brill NV, 2011), 291.

32. Mauricio Drelichman and Hans-Joachim Voth, *Lending to The Borrower from Hell: Debt, Taxes, and Defaults in the Age of Philip II* (Princeton Univ. Press, 2011), 96–101.

33. Bristol City Council, "Spain's Slavery Contract," *Bristol and Transatlantic Slavery*, http://www.discoveringbristol.org.uk/slavery/routes/places-involved/south-america/Spain-slavery-contract.

34. Charles R. Norgle, "In re AFRICAN-AMERICAN SLAVE DESCENDANTS LITIGATION," MDL No. 1491, No. 02 C 7764, US District Court, N.D. Illinois, Eastern Division, July 6, 2005. Judge Norgle issued a ruling against the litigants "with prejudice," meaning they could not file the same motion with his court again.

CHAPTER 3: SERVANTS OR SLAVES?

1. Avery Anapol, "Gayle King corrects Northam for referring to slaves as 'indentured servants,'" *The Hill*, February 10, 2019, https://thehill.com/homenews/state-watch/429335-gayle-king-corrects-northam-for-referring-to-slaves-as-indentured.

2. Federal Writer's Project, *Virginia: A Guide to the Old Dominion* (New York: Oxford Univ. Press, 1956), 483.

3. David A. Fahrenthold, "A Dead Indian Language Is Brought Back to Life," *Washington Post*, December 12, 2006, https://www.washingtonpost.com/wp-dyn/content/article/2006/12/11/AR2006121101474.html.

4. Gregory D. Smithers, "How the Kikotan Massacre Prepared the Ground for the Arrival of the First Africans in 1619," *History News Network*, September 15, 2019, https://historynewsnetwork.org/article/173032.

5. In March 1622, a group of Algonquin natives led by Chief Opechancanough mounted a series of coordinated, surprise attacks on the English settlement at Jamestown that killed 347 colonists, about one-fourth of the population there. Known popularly as the Jamestown Massacre, it provoked a sustained English reprisal that gave rise to a ten-year-long war between the English and Powhatan confederation. In May 1622, Captain William Tucker was given commission over Kecoughtan by the Virginia Company, to raise a small army to take revenge on the Powhatan, "rooting them out from being longer a people upon the face of the Earth," William S. Powell reports the note from the Virginia Company read. See William S. Powell, "Aftermath of the Massacre: The First Indian War, 1622–1632," *The Virginia Magazine of History and Biography*, Vol. 66, No. 1, January 1958, 44–75, https://www.jstor.org/stable/4246389?read-now=1&seq=8#page_scan_tab_contents. In January 1623, William Tucker was ordered by the governor of

Virginia to travel up the rivers of the Tidewater region "to take revenge uppon" the natives he found there. In May of that year, Tucker was ordered by the governor to take command of a small contigent who "uppon espetiall occasion are to accompanie him, in the shallops into Pamunckey Ryuer, neere the seate of Apponchankano [Chief Opechancanough]," Powell reports. Tucker was ostensibly to conduct prisoners that Opechancanough held back to Jamestown and to enter into a peace treaty with the Pamunkey tribe. Instead, at the peace ceremony, Tucker offered the Pamunkey poisoned wine, then opened fire, killing some 250 natives as a result. Opechancanough, a target, escaped unharmed, though the incident further opened a rift between the English and the Algonquin tribes that continued to the prolonged, ten-year war. See Powell, "Aftermath of the Massacre," 61–62.

6.   Sidney Lee, ed., *Dictionary of National Biography*, Vol. 19 (New York: Macmillan, 1909), 1212.

7.   Charles E. Hatch, *The First Seventeen Years: Virginia 1607–1624* (Scotts Valley, CA: Amazon.com, 2011), 71.

8.   There is a minor dispute about whether Anthony and Isabella were brought over as indentured servants on the *Mary & James* in 1610, when William Tucker emigrated from England, or whether they arrived on the *White Lion*. Records of the *Mary & James* in 1610 show no African indentured servants brought by Tucker. The overwhelming evidence is that Anthony and Isabella came aboard the *White Lion*. Colonial records, while sparse, show no Africans in the Virginia colony, slaves or servants, prior to the *White Lion*'s arrival in 1619. The first real census, taken in 1623, shows Tucker, and "Anthony, Negro" and "Isabell, Negro." Later a muster of Tucker's, recorded in 1624/25, shows the couple and a child. Still, it is possible to find online references to the captain of the *Mary & James* bringing indentured servants Antonie and Isabell with him, though the assertion is made lacking any source documentation. See, for instance, "Famous First," *Capt. William Tucker, of Kiccowtan*, https://www.geni.com/people/Capt -William-Tucker-of-Kiccowtan/6000000003853772881, which appears copied without attribution from a spurious page on Ancestry.com, https://www.ancestry .com/sharing/5921309?h=ce0899, purporting to show a picture of Captain William Tucker, along with a biography, though the picture is actually a painting of Meriwether Lewis.

9.   Johannes Leo Africanus, *The History and Description of Africa and of the Notable Things Therein Contained*, Vol. 1, ed. Robert Brown (Cambridge Univ. Press, 2010), 187. This account by Leo Africanus was first published in English in 1600.

10.   James H. Sweet, "The Iberian Roots of American Racist Thought," *The William and Mary Quarterly*, Vol. 54, No. 1, January 1997, 143–66.

11.   Felicia R. Lee, "From Noah's Curse to Slavery's Rationale," *New York Times*, November 1, 2003, https://www.nytimes.com/2003/11/01/arts/from-noah-s-curse-to -slavery-s-rationale.html.

12.   John Camden Hotten, ed., *The Original Lists of Persons of Quality* (London: Chatto and Windus, 1874), 244.

13.   Hotten, *The Original Lists*, 223.

14.   Hotten, *The Original Lists*, 225.

15.   Eric Williams, *Capitalism and Slavery* (Chapel Hill: Univ. of North Carolina Press, 1944), 7.

16.   David Eltis in *The Rise of African Slavery in the Americas* (Cambridge Univ. Press, 2000), 57–82, notes that economically it actually may have been more efficient and legal for Europeans to hold other Europeans as slaves but Europeans were considered cultural "insiders," while Africans were considered cultural "outsiders," and draconian measures such as slavery would not be considered for "insiders."

17.   Linda Heywood and John Thornton in *Africans, Atlantic Creoles and the Foundation of the Americas, 1585–1660* (Cambridge Univ. Press: 2007) make a useful distinction between the first group of Africans, called the "Charter Generation," and those to follow, called the "Plantation Generation."

18.   Linda Heywood and John Thornton in *Africans*, 291–331, present a very complete account of all three positions on this question of whether the first generation of Africans were servants or slaves, and they come out squarely in favor of the third position.

19.   Lerone Bennett, Jr., *The Shaping of Black America: The Struggles and Triumphs of African-Americans, 1619–1990s* (New York: Penguin Books, 1993), 62.

20.   Bennett, *The Shaping of Black America*, 62.

21.   David W. Galenson, "The Rise and Fall of Indentured Servitude in the Americas: An Economic Analysis," *The Journal of Economic History*, Vol. 44, No. 1, 3–4.

22.   Galenson, "The Rise and Fall," 4–5.

23.   Galenson, "The Rise and Fall," 6–8.

24.   John Bach McMaster, *The Acquisition of Political Social and Industrial Rights of Man in America* (Cleveland: Daughters of the American Revolution, 1903), 34–35.

25.   Don Jordan and Michael Walsh, *White Cargo: The Forgotten History of Britain's White Slaves in America* (New York: NYU Press, 2008), 128–29.

26.   Humphrey Gilbert, *A Discourse of a Discouerie for a New Passage to Cataia* (London: Henry Middleton, 1576).

27.   Cited in Marcus W. Jernegan, "A Forgotten Slavery of Colonial Days," *Harper's Monthly Magazine*, Vol. 127, (New York: Harper & Brothers, 1913), 746.

CHAPTER 4: FROM SERVITUDE TO SLAVERY

1.   H. R. McIlwaine, ed., *Minutes of the Council and General Court of Colonial Virginia, 1622–1632, 1670–1676* (Richmond: Virginia State Library, 1924), 46.

2.   H. R. McIlwaine, ed., *Journals of the House of Burgesses of Virginia 1619–1658/59* (Richmond: Virginia State Library, 1915), 12–13.

3.   Wesley Frank Craven, *White, Red, and Black: The Seventeenth-Century Virginian* (New York: Norton, 1871), 5.

4. Philip Alexander Bruce, *Social Life of Virginia in the Seventeenth Century* (Richmond: Whittet & Shepperson, 1907), 255.

5. Thomas Jefferson Wertenbaker, *Patrician and Plebeian in Virginia or the Origin and Development of the Social Classes of the Old Dominion* (Charlottesville: The Michie Company, 1910), 176.

6. Abbott Emerson Smith, *Colonists in Bondage: White Servitude and Convict Labor in America, 1607–1776* (Chapel Hill: Univ. of North Carolina Press, 1947), 306.

7. "Irish: The Forgotten White Slaves."

8. "Irish: The Forgotten White Slaves."

9. Lerone Bennett, Jr., "White Servitude in America," *Ebony*, Vol. 25, No. 1 (Chicago: Johnson Publishing, 1969), 34.

10. Craven, *White, Red, and Black*, 5.

11. Shawn Pogatchnik, "AP Fact Check: Irish 'slavery' at St. Patrick's Day myth," AP News, https://apnews.com/920e1c738df04555bccd56c09770b36d/AP-FACT-CHECK:-Irish-%22slavery%22-a-St.-Patrick's-Day-myth.

12. Shawn Pogatchnik, "AP Fact Check."

13. John Bach McMaster, *The Acquisition of Political Social and Industrial Rights of Man in America* (Cleveland: Daughters of the American Revolution, 1903), 34.

14. John Fiske, *Old Virginia and Her Neighbors*, Vol. II (Cambridge, MA: Riverside Press, 1902), 206–7.

15. The phrase "Irish Slave Trade" actually came into use decades before the internet, before it became a pawn in this trade of insults and imprecations between the many groups laying claim to its truth. One early use of the phrase regards the emergence of the English seaport town Bristol as a center for ships setting off to Ireland to capture men, women, and children to be sold and used as slaves. See William Hunt, "On the Rise of Bristol Trade," *Proceedings of the Somersetshire Archaeological and Natural History Society*, Vol. 14 (London: Longmans, Greed, Reader and Dyer, 1867), 4, https://play.google.com/books/reader?id=o1dLAQAAMAAJ.

16. Bennett, "White Servitude in America," 32.

17. Virginia General Assembly, *Colonial Records of Virginia* (Richmond: Virginia State Library: 1874), 105, https://books.google.com/books?id=qWJBAQAAMAAJ.

18. A. Leon Higginbotham, *In the Matter of Color: Race and the American Legal Process: The Colonial Period* (Oxford Univ. Press), 67.

19. George Ticknor Curtis, *History of the Origin, Formation, and Adoption of the Constitution of the United States*, Vol. 2 (Frankfort, Germany: Outlook Verlag, 2018), 419.

20. Francis J. Bremer, *John Winthrop: America's Forgotten Founding Father* (Oxford Univ. Press, 2003), 313.

21. Bremer, *John Winthrop*, 313.

22. Bremer, *John Winthrop*, 313.

23. Bremer, *John Winthrop*, 313.

24. Higginbotham, *In the Matter of Color*, 67a.

25. Higginbotham, *In the Matter of Color*, 68.

26. Oliver Perry Chitwood, *Justice in Colonial Virginia* (Baltimore: John Hopkins Univ. Press: 1905), 95. (Internal quotation marks omitted.)

27. See the Introduction to this book, and also *Minutes of the Council and General Court of Colonial Virginia, 1622–1632, 1670–1676: With Notes and Excerpts from Original Council and General Court Records, Into 1683, Now Lost* (Richmond: Colonial Press, 2011), 411.

28. The dynamic nature of this story, and the apparent genealogical links between Elizabeth Key and actor Johnny Depp, have led to much speculation, confusion, and inaccuracy regarding the historical facts. Some of that confusion I attempt to resolve in the notes of this chapter. Particularly regrettable, in this regard, is a silverpoint drawing of an African woman, said to be an image of Elizabeth Key, that has circulated widely on the internet, including by Elizabeth Key's descendants (see, for example, http://jonesandrelated.blogspot.com/2012/02 /elizabeth-key-grinstead.html). An online search shows the image was actually drawn by the German painter Albrecht Dürer, in 1521, and titled, "The Negress Katherina" (see, for example, https://curiator.com/art/albrecht-duerer/the-negress -katherina). She was the twenty-year-old servant of Dürer's Portuguese art dealer, João Brandão. Katherina's image is beautiful, and alluring. Given the year and the country she lived in, Katherina most likely came from Angola, as described earlier in this book. But under no circumstances should her image be taken as that of Elizabeth Key.

29. Contrary to most historians, and the descendants of Elizabeth Key, I strongly believe that her mother was a servant to Thomas Key, and not a slave. Elizabeth Key's case was heard in several courts. First, in the Northumberland County Court, which ruled in her favor. Next, appealed by defendants to the Virginia General Court, in Jamestown, where the court ruled against her. Then, appealed by plaintiffs to the General Council of the Assembly (the upper chamber of the legislature acting as the Virginia Supreme Court), where the case was handed back to the lower county court for reconsideration with a report from the General Assembly supporting her petition for freedom. This reversion to the Northumberland County Court was not challenged, and the Northumberland County Court issued a 1656 order granting her freedom. Only the Northumberland County Court makes reference, once, to Elizabeth Key's mother as a "woman slave." Other witnesses at the proceedings refer to Elizabeth Key's mother as "her mother," or a "Negro Woman," or that "said Negroe was the Mother of." The word *slave* does not appear in their depositions. Warren M. Billings, in a footnote to "The Cases of Fernando and Elizabeth Key," *The William and Mary Quarterly*, Vol. 30, No. 3, July 1973, 468, claims otherwise. He states, "It is significant, perhaps, that the depositions refer to Elizabeth Key's mother as a slave. Since Elizabeth Key was born circa 1630, the reference to her mother's status suggests that some blacks were already being held as slaves by

the end of the 1620s." Again, the depositions in this case state no such thing. Historians, and the descendants of Elizabeth Key, have adopted Billings's assertions without question.

Colonial courts frequently showed discrepancies in reference to the same case as it passed from one court session to the next. In *Corven v. Lucas*, cited earlier, only a short time had passed between his pleading and the court's decision. Yet, in the General Court's actual written decision his name has been altered to read "Gowen" rather than "Corven," and the name of the defendant changed from "Charles" Lucas to "Jno." (Jonathan) Lucas. The Northumberland County Court was not charged with determining whether Elizabeth Key's mother was a servant or a slave, and we cannot conclude from their single use of the word *slave* that she was, in fact, a slave, especially in light of other evidence that suggests she was not.

Billings is correct on one count: all the evidence points to Elizabeth Key's birth circa 1630. This means her mother became pregnant with her in late 1629 or early 1630. The first Africans arrived in colonial Virginia on the *White Lion* in August 1619, with another small group on the *Treasurer* four days later, then more from that same original group taken from the *Saõ João Bautista*, on the *Treasurer*, again in 1620. There's every likelihood that Elizabeth Key's mother was part of this original group of Africans. For sure, it can be said that she was part of the first generation of Africans in Virginia.

Thomas Key arrived in the *Prosperous* in June 1619. His wife, Sarah, on the *Truelove* in 1622. The 1624/25 muster of Virginia shows them as Thomas Keie and Sarah, his wife, living on, but not owning, the Chaplain's Choice plantation in Charles City County, just north of Jamestown. No servants of the Keys' are listed in that muster. Thomas Key had already married his second wife, Martha, by the time she was granted land in December 1628, which implies that somewhere between January 1625 (the date of the census) and December 1628 (the date of the land grant), Sarah Key died. At most, that leaves a four- or five-year period for Thomas Key to acquire Elizabeth Key's mother. There were no laws regarding slavery in Virginia in the late 1620s. While the first generation of Africans were more plausibly indentured servants treated as poorly as masters would later treat slaves, they were not chattel slaves.

Thomas Key was not a member of the colonial Virginia aristocracy, as some historians and genealogists assert. His passage from England to Virginia was paid for by Thomas Astley, of the Virginia Company, which alone would have disqualified Thomas Key from the ranks of the true ancient planters, who were supposed to have paid their own way (see the following note for more). A more likely scenario is that Thomas Key never purchased Elizabeth Key's mother at all. Instead, he acquired her through his marriage to Martha. Martha Key, whose birth name or first married name I cannot locate, was a member of the colonial aristocracy, probably through her first marriage. She was among the ranks of the ancient planters. So, a more plausible explanation, I believe, is that Elizabeth's mother was purchased or acquired by Martha's first husband, his estate passed on to his widow, then made available to Thomas Key through marriage. To put it simply, Thomas Key "married up."

30. Most historical accounts incorrectly describe Thomas Key as an ancient planter often simultaneously acknowledging his arrival in Virginia aboard the *Prosperous* in 1619. This 1619 arrival date patently disqualifies him from being an ancient planter, since the term and the privileges were conveyed only to those who arrived before 1616, remained for a period of three years, and paid their own passage. His second wife, Martha, however, was an ancient planter. She is listed on some rosters of ancient planters as Martha Key (or Keie); see, for example, "Ancient Planter," http://www.ancientplanters.org/ancient-planters. On other lists the reference is to "Martha Key ynd Thomas Key 1619 (sic)," though "1619 (sic)" after Thomas's name should have been a tip-off to historians and genealogists that something was amiss, since 1616 was the cutoff date for ancient planters.

31. There is also confusion among historians and genealogists regarding the grant of Algonquin land in Isle of Wight County to Martha Key and her husband. The description of the land is not in dispute for it was "lying on Warwicksqueake River, opposite the land of Captain Nathaniel Basse and adjoining that of Rice Jones." But the date, the amount, and the basis of the grant are in question. As an ancient planter, Martha Key was entitled to a land grant of 100 acres, which an original patent scanned by the Library of Virginia shows she obtained on December 2, 1628. Some genealogists, particularly the descendants of Elizabeth Key (see http://jonesandrelated.blogspot.com/2012/02/elizabeth-key-grinstead .html and http://jonesandrelated.blogspot.com/2014/07/1628-land-patent-for -martha-key.html), believe that Thomas Key "set up" his wife, Martha, with this land so that he could be in Warwick with his African mistress, Elizabeth Key's mother. The historical records do not support this conclusion, particularly since it was Martha not Thomas who was the actual ancient planter, entitled to the land. Some accounts show a land grant of 150 acres to Martha Key, wife of Thomas Key, on December 2, 1626 (see Phillip Alexander Bruce and William Glover, eds., *The Virginia Magazine of History and Biography*, Vol. 2 (Richmond: Virginia Historical Society, 1895), 68). The 1626 date is highly suspect since the original scanned patent shows the date of 1628. Regarding the size of the land granted, two principal possibilities exist: either the 150 acres is in error, or 100 acres was granted to Martha, and 50 acres to her husband, Thomas, since some colonists arriving after 1616 were entitled to land grants of 50 acres from the Virginia Company.

32. Warren M. Billings, ed., *The Old Dominion in the Seventeenth Century: A Documentary History of Virginia, 1606–1700* (Chapel Hill: Univ. of North Carolina Press, 2007), 195–96.

33. Billings, *The Old Dominion*, 197.

34. "Elizabeth Key," *Dictionary of Virginia Biography*, https://www.lva.virginia.gov /public/dvb/bio.php?b=Key_Elizabeth_fl_1655-1660.

35. Nicholas Morris was born in England in 1605 and came to Virginia well after the first colonists did, though he established a large estate in Northumberland County. In 1652, he was appointed to the bench of the Northumberland County Court. Morris was a neighbor, and apparently a friend, of Colonel John Mottrom, whose estate was litigated against by Elizabeth Key in the case. See, "Notes & Queries," *The Virginia Magazine of History and Biography* 25, No. 2 (1917), 190–200, https://www.jstor.org/stable/4243596.

36. Billings, *The Old Dominion*, 195.

37. Billings, *The Old Dominion*, 197.

38. Billings, *The Old Dominion*, 198.

39. Billings, *The Old Dominion*, 198.

40. Billings, *The Old Dominion*, 199.

CHAPTER 5: LEGISLATING FAITH, LOVE, AND LUST

1.   "Proceedings and Acts of the General Assembly January 1637/38–September 1664," Vol. 1, *Archives of Maryland Online*, 526, https://msa.maryland.gov/megafile /msa/speccol/sc2900/sc2908/000001/000001/html/am1--526.html.

2.   "Proceeding and Acts of the General Assembly," Vol. 1, 533, https://msa.maryland .gov/megafile/msa/speccol/sc2900/sc29°8/000001/000001/html/am1--533.html.

3.   "Proceedings and Acts of the General Assembly April 1666–June 1676," Vol. 2, *Archives of Maryland Online*, 272, http://aomol.msa.maryland.gov/000001/000002 /html/am2--272.html.

4.   Warren M. Billings, ed., *The Old Dominion in the Seventeenth Century: A Documentary History of Virginia, 1606–1700* (Chapel Hill: Univ. of North Carolina Press, 2007), 169.

5.   Billings, *The Old Dominion*, 169.

6.   Billings, *The Old Dominion*, 169.

7.   William Waller Hening, ed., *The Statutes at Large; Being a Collection of All the Laws of Virginia from the First Session of the Legislature, in the Year 1619*, Vol. 2 (New York: R. & W. & G. Bartow, 1823), 260, http://vagenweb.org/hening/vol02-13.htm.

8.   Hening, *The Statutes at Large*, Vol. 2, 491, https://encyclopediavirginia.org/entries /an-act-to-repeale-a-former-law-makeing-indians-and-others-ffree-1682/.

9.   Hening, *The Statutes at Large*, Vol. 2, 170, http://vagenweb.org/hening/vol02-09.htm.

10. "Proceeding and Acts of the General Assembly," Vol. 1, 533, https://msa.maryland .gov/megafile/msa/speccol/sc2900/sc2908/000001/00 0001/html/am1--533.html.

11. "Proceeding and Acts of the General Assembly," Vol. 2, 272, http://aomol.msa .maryland.gov/000001/000002/html/am2--272.html.

12. Monica C. Reed, "They are Men, and Not Beasts: Religion and Slavery in Colonial New England," PhD Thesis, Florida State Univ., 2013, 38.

13. Luke 20:20–26, Matthew 22:25–22, Mark 12:13–17, *Holy Bible: King James Version*.

14. Samuel Sewall, "The Selling of Joseph," a pamphlet (Boston: Green & Allen, 1700), https://digitalcommons.unl.edu/cgi/viewcontent.cgi?article=1026&context =etas.

15. Cotton Mather, "The Negro Christianized," a pamphlet (Boston: Green, 1706), https://digitalcommons.unl.edu/cgi/viewcontent.cgi?article=1028&context=etas.

16. Mather, "The Negro Christianized."

17. Mather, "The Negro Christianized."

18. *The Acts and Resolves, Public and Private, of the Province of the Massachusetts Bay*, Vol. VII (Boston: Wright & Potter, 1892), 537, https://play.google.com/books/reader ?id=zgpHAQAAIAAJ.

19. Cited in John Pinkerton, *Voyages and Travels in Various Parts of America*, Vol. 2 (London: Longman, Hurst et al., 1819), 262, https://books.google.com/books?id =-icZaHu5QAsC.

20. Stephen Innes, *Creating the Commonwealth: The Economic Culture of Puritan New England* (New York: Norton & Company, 1995), 272.

21. Scholars have debated how much Thomas Jefferson relied on the writings of English philosopher John Locke in incorporating the phrase "the pursuit of happiness" into the Declaration of Independence. Locke first used the phrase in his ponderous book *Essay of Human Understanding* and it was central to his political ethics but the phrase was in use throughout early-eighteenth-century England, found in the works of William Wollaston, Francis Hutcheson, Oliver Goldsmith, Richard Price, and Dr. Samuel Johnson. In his autobiography, Benjamin Franklin tells of typesetting an early edition of Wollaston's *The Religion of Nature Delineated*, while a journeyman printer in London in 1726. Neil C. Olsen in *Pursuing Happiness: The Organizational Culture of the Continental Congress* (Milford, CN: Nonagram Publications, 2013), 195, asserts that Locke, Wollaston, and the other philosophers of the day were merged by the Founders into an acceptable set of ideas summed up by phrases such as "the pursuit of happiness."

22. William Wollaston, *The Religion of Nature Delineated* (London: Beecroft, Rivington, et al., 1759), 251–52, https://books.google.com/books?id=r7gOAAAAIAAJ.

23. Joseph Sewall, *A Caveat against Covetousness* (Boston: Green for Gerrish, 1718), 5, https://quod.lib.umich.edu/e/evans/N01683.0001.001/1:2.

24. Cited in Mark H. Johnson, "God's Providence in Puritan New England: An Inquiry into the Nature of Ideas. Teacher and Student Manuals," *ERIC*, Access No. ED 032 340, Office of Education, 1966 (US Dept. of Health, Education and Welfare: 1970), 67, https://files.eric.ed.gov/fulltext/ED032340.pdf.

25. Reed, "They are Men," 142.

26. A. H. Bullen, ed., *The Works of John Marston*, Vol. III (London: John C. Nimmo, 1887), Act 3: Scene 3, https://www.gutenberg.org/files/46312/46312-h/46312-h.htm #EH_3. The playwright uses the date '79 (1579) in an incorrect reference to the Lost Colony of Roanoke, most likely first colonized by the English unsuccessfully in 1585, then again unsuccessfully in 1587.

27. William Strachey, *For the colony in Virginea Britannia: Lavves Divine, Morall and Maratiall* (London: Walter Burre, 1612), 11, https://babel.hathitrust.org/cgi/pt?id=hvd.32044024338592. Strachey was secretary of the colony from 1609 until 1611, when he returned to England to publish this compilation of colonial laws.

28. Strachey, *Virginea Britannia*, 16.

29. George Percy, *A Trewe Relacyon*, reprinted in *Tyler's Quarterly Historical and Genealogical Magazine*, Vol. III (Richmond: Richmond Press, 1922), 280, https://archive.org/details/tylersquarterlyho3tyle.

30. *Berdache* is a French term that references the practices of some indigenous North Americans, also known as *two-spirit*, that honors a third, nonbinary gender category.

31. Edward D. Neill, *History of the Virginia Company of London* (Albany, NY: Joel Musnell, 1869), 160–61.

32. Mimi Abramovitz, *Regulating the Lives of Women: Social Welfare Policy from Colonial Times to the Present* (Cambridge, MA: South End Press, 1996), 46–47.

33. Virginia General Assembly, *Colonial Records of Virginia* (Richmond: Virginia State Library: 1974), 28, https://books.google.com/books?id=qWJBAQAAMAAJ.

34. Karen M. Brown, *Good Wives, Nasty Wenches, and Anxious Patriarchs* (Chapel Hill: Univ. of North Carolina Press, 2012), 75–80.

35. Susan Fair, *American Witches* (New York: Skyhorse Publishing, 2016), 9, 30–31.

36. Hening, *The Statutes at Large*, Vol. 1, 146, http://vagenweb.org/hening/vol01-06.htm.

37. Hening, *The Statutes at Large*, Vol. 1, 552, http://vagenweb.org/hening/vol01-23.htm.

38. Until September 1752, the older Julian calendar was in use throughout Britain and her colonies. The new year began on March 25, under the Julian system, hence a date in March needs clarification of exactly which years the month spanned.

39. Hening, *The Statutes at Large*, Vol. 1, 242–43, http://vagenweb.org/hening/vol01-10.htm.

40. Hening, *The Statutes at Large*, Vol. 1, 144, http://vagenweb.org/hening/vol01-06.htm.

41. None of the Africans were killed in this raid, something that happened more than once in the colonies, causing some historians to suggest that Native Americans were well aware of the beleaguered state of Africans at the hands of the English.

42. "Proceeding and Acts of the General Assembly," Vol. 7, 177, http://aomol.msa.maryland.gov/000001/000007/html/am7--177.html.

43. John Codman Hurd, *The Law of Freedom and Bondage in the United States* (Boston: Little Brown, 1858), 250.

44. "Proceeding and Acts," Vol. 7, 177.

45. *The Acts and Resolves, Public and Private, of the Province of the Massachusetts Bay, Vol. I. 1692–1714* (Boston: Wright & Potter, 1869), 578, https://archive.org/details

/actsresolvespass9214mass/page/578/mode/2up. Note the symbol "&c" used in the title of the act is an abbreviation for the Latin *et cetera*, in this case meaning "and other similar things."

CHAPTER 6: RUNAWAYS AND REBELS

1.   H. R. McIlwane, ed., *Minutes of the Council and General Court of Colonial Virginia 1622–1632, 1670–1676* (Richmond: Library of Virginia, 1924), 466, https://www .familysearch.org/library/books/records/item/196397-minutes-of-the-council -and-general-court-of-colonial-virginia-1622–1632–1670–1676-with-notes-and -excerpts-from-original-council-and-general-court-records-into-1683-now-lost.

2.   McIlwane, *Minutes of the Council*, 466.

3.   Shirley Gay Stolberg, "Obama Has Ties to Slavery Not by His Father but His Mother, Research Suggests," *New York Times*, July 30, 2012, https://www.nytimes .com/2012/07/30/us/obamas-mother-had-african-forebear-study-suggests.html.

4.   William Waller Hening, ed., *The Statutes at Large; Being a Collection of All the Laws of Virginia from the First Session of the Legislature, in the Year 1619*, Vol. 1 (New York: R. & W. & G. Bartow, 1823), 226, http://vagenweb.org/hening/vol01-09.htm.

5.   This is the same John Mottrom whose estate would be back in front of the Council in fifteen years to argue in favor of holding Elizabeth Key, and her son, slaves.

6.   McIlwane, *Minutes of the Council*, 468.

7.   McIlwane, *Minutes of the Council*, 468.

8.   Hening, *The Statutes at Large*, Vol. 1, 254, http://vagenweb.org/hening/vol01-10.htm.

9.   Hening, *The Statutes at Large*, Vol. 2, 26, http://vagenweb.org/hening/vol02-02 .htm.

10. Hening, *The Statutes at Large*, Vol. 2, 116–17, http://vagenweb.org/hening/vol02 -06.htm.

11. "George Floyd Protests," *New York Times*, https://www.nytimes.com/news-event /george-floyd-protests-minneapolis-new-york-los-angeles.

12. My sketch of Bacon's Rebellion that follows comes primarily from James D. Rice, *Tales from a Revolution: Bacon's Rebellion and the Transformation of Early America* (Oxford Univ. Press, 2013).

13. Edward Waterhouse, *A Declaration of the State of the Colony and Affaires in Virginia* (London: George Eld, 1622), 25, https://quod.lib.umich.edu/e/eebo/A14803 .0001.001.

14. Edmund S. Morgan, *American Slavery, American Freedom: The Ordeal of Colonial Virginia* (New York: W. W. Norton, 1975), 330, https://archive.org/stream/amer icanslaveryaoomorg.

15. Alan Kulikoff, *Tobacco and Slaves: The Development of Southern Culture in the Chesapeake* (Chapel Hill: Univ. of North Carolina Press, 1986), 28.

16. William Fitzhugh, "The Letters of William Fitzhugh," *The Virginia Magazine of History and Biography* (Richmond: Virginia Historical Society, 1894), 37, https:// www.jstor.org/stable/4241732.

17. Dee Brown, *Bury My Heart at Wounded Knee: An Indian History of the American West* (New York: Henry Holt, 1970), 170–72.

18. Morgan, *American Slavery, American Freedom*, 344.

19. Rice, *Bacon's Rebellion*, 221.

20. Carrisa Harris, "A History of Wench: How a medieval word meaning 'servant' or 'child' evolved to become a racist slur," *Electric Lit.*, June 3, 2019, https://electricliterature.com/a-history-of-the-wench.

CHAPTER 7: A HOUSE BUILT ON SMOKE

1. Shannon Tushingham, Charles M. Snyder, et al., "Biomolecular archaeology reveals ancient origins of indigenous tobacco smoking in North American Plateau," *Proceedings of the National Academy of Sciences*, Vol. 115, No. 46, November 13, 2018, 11742–47, https://www.pnas.org/content/115/46/11742#ref-9.

2. Joseph C. Winter, ed., *Tobacco Use By Native Americans: Sacred Smoke and Silent Killer* (Norman: Univ. of Oklahoma Press, 2000), 305–30.

3. Iain Gatley, *Tobacco: A Cultural History of How an Exotic Plant Seduced Civilization* (New York: Simon & Schuster, 2001), 3–5.

4. J. Franklin Jameson, "Voyages of Columbus: Journal of the First Voyage," *The Northmen, Columbus, and Cabot: 985–1503* (New York: Scribner's, 1906), 117.

5. Jameson, "Voyages of Columbus," 117.

6. Columbus records in his journal on October 23, 1492, "I desired to set out to-day for the island of Cub, which I think must be Cipango (Japan) . . . ," Jameson, "Voyages of Columbus," 127.

7. Jameson, "Voyages of Columbus," 141.

8. Fernando Ortiz, *Cuban Counterpoint: Tobacco and Sugar* (New York: Alfred A. Knopf, 1947), 231.

9. David G. Sweet, "Black Robes and 'Black Destiny': Jesuit Views of African Slavery in 17th Century Latin America," *Revista de Historia de América*, Vol. 86, 1978, 94.

10. James Grehan, "Smoking and 'Early Modern' Sociability: The Great Tobacco Debate in the Ottoman Middle East (Seventeenth to Eighteenth Centuries)," *American Historical Review*, Vol. 111, No. 5, 1352–77, https://www.jstor.org/stable/10.1086/ahr.111.5.1352.

11. Yitzhak Buxbaum, *The Light and Fire of the Baal Shem Tov* (New York: Bloomsbury, 2005), 192.

12. Winter, *Tobacco Use By Native Americans*, 9–59.

13. Carol Benedict, *Golden-Silk Smoke: A History of Tobacco in China, 1550–2010* (Los Angeles: Univ. of California Press, 2011), 90–94.

14. John M. Janzen, "Central African Healing Traditions," *Representations, Ritual, & Social Renewal: Essays In Africanist Medical Anthropology* (Lawrence, KS: Univ. of Kansas, 2014), 30, https://kuscholarworks.ku.edu/handle/1808/14950 for slides accompanying the lecture see, https://kuscholarworks.ku.edu/bitstream/handle/1808/14950/3%20--%20Central%20African%20Healing%20Traditions.pdf.

15. Alfred Dunhill, *The Pipe Book* (New York: MacMillan, 1969), 20–24. I have some trouble believing that this is an actual myth from the Bushongo instead of a myth created by entrepreneur, and salesman extraordinaire, Alfred Dunhill. While Emil Torday mentions the figure Lusana Lumunbala in connection to the introduction of tobacco into the Congo in "Bushongo Mythology," *Folk-Lore: A Quarterly Review*, Vol. 22. 1911, he never once mentions this particular myth, nor does he in any of his published works. However, it is possible that Dunhill had private papers, or private correspondence with Torday, that he does not reference.

16. William Finch, "Observations of William Finch," *A General History and Collection of Voyages and Travels* . . . (Edinburgh: James Ballantyne and Company, 1813), 257.

17. R. Loddenkemper and M. Kreuter, eds., *The Tobacco Epidemic* (Basel, Switzerland: Karger, 2015), 3.

18. David Birmingham, *Central Africa to 1870: Zamezia, Saire and the South Atlantic* (Cambridge Univ. Press, 1981), 98.

19. Malyn Newitt, "Africa and the Wider World: Creole Communities in the Atlantic and Indian Oceans," *Revista Tempo*, Vol. 23, No. 3. December 2017, 473.

20. William Strachey, "A true reportory of the wracke, and redemption of Sir THOMAS GATES Knight," *Pvrchas His Pilgrimes in Five Bookes* (London, 1625), 1735, https://www.bl.uk/collection-items/stracheys-a-true-reportory-of -the-wreck-in-bermuda.

21. William Strachey, *The Historie of Travaile into Virginia Britannia* (London: The Hakluyt Society, 1819), 121, https://play.google.com/books/reader?id=fYYMAAA AIAAJ.

22. Alfred Cave, *Lethal Encounters: Englishmen and Indians in Colonial Virginia* (Santa Barbara, CA: Praeger, 2011), 103.

23. Augustine D. Selby, "Tobacco Diseases and Tobacco Breeding," *The Tobacco Leaf*, Vol. 42, No. 2,102, June 7, 1905, 58, https://play.google.com/store/books /details?id=typLAQAAMAAJ.

24. William Henry Sanders, et. al., *Vocabulary of the Umbundu Language* (Boston: Beacon Press, 1885), 50.

25. Sanders, *Vocabulary of the Umbundu Language*, 58.

26. Catherine Molineux, "Pleasures of the Smoke: 'Black Virginians' in Georgian London's Tobacco Shops," *The William and Mary Quarterly*, Vol. 64, No. 2, April 2007, 352.

27. The Summer Islands are another name for Bermuda, so called after Captain George Somers shipwrecked there with John Rolfe, whom he later brought to Jamestown, and who rose to tobacco fame.

28. William Waller Hening, ed., *The Statutes at Large; Being a Collection of All the Laws of Virginia from the First Session of the Legislature, in the Year 1619*, Vol. 1 (New York: R. & W. & G. Bartow, 1823), 210, http://vagenweb.org/hening/vol01-09.htm.

29. "Proceedings of the County Courts of Kent (1648–1676), Talbot (1662–1674), and Somerset (1665–1668)," *Archives of Maryland Online*, Vol. 54, preface, 25, http://aomol.msa.maryland.gov/000001/000054/html/am54p--25.html.

30. Hening, *The Statutes at Large*, Vol. 1, 455, http://vagenweb.org/hening/vol01-20.htm.

31. Hening, *The Statutes at Large*, Vol. 1, 196, http://vagenweb.org/hening/vol01-08.htm.

32. "Bacon's Laws of Maryland," *Archives of Maryland Online*, Vol. 75, 665, http://aomol.msa.maryland.gov/000001/000075/html/am75--665.html.

33. "Proceedings of the Maryland Court of Appeals, 1695–1729," *Archives of Maryland Online*, Vol. 77, 16, http://aomol.msa.maryland.gov/000001/000077/html/am77--16.html.

34. W. Noel Sainsbury and J. W. Fortescue, eds., *Calendar of State Papers, Colonial Series, American and the West Indies, 1677–1680* (London: Her Majesty's Stationery Office, 1896), 568.

35. Arthur Pierce Middleton, *Tobacco Coast: A Maritime History of Chesapeake Bay in the Colonial Era* (Newport News: The Mariners' Museum, 1953), 123.

36. Middleton, *Tobacco Coast*, 124.

CHAPTER 8: FOUNDING DEBTORS, FOUNDING DOCUMENTS

1. Thomas Jefferson Randolph, "Thomas Jefferson Randolph's Newspaper Advertisement for Poplar Forest and Monticello Estate Sales," *Jefferson Quotes & Family Letters*, http://tjrs.monticello.org/letter/2027.

2. Kate Mason Rowland, *The Life of George Mason, 1725–1792*, Vol. 1 (New York: G.P. Putnam's Sons, 1892), 140.

3. For an excellent summary of the "Two-Penny Act" and Patrick Henry's arguments against Maury, see Michael Kranish, *Flight from Monticello: Thomas Jefferson at War* (Oxford Univ. Press, 2010), 10.

4. Kevin Phillips, *Wealth and Democracy: A Political History of the American Rich* (New York: Broadway Books, 2002), 301.

5. Paul Leicester Ford, ed., *The Writings of Thomas Jefferson: 1784–1787*, Vol. 4 (New York: G.P. Putnam's Sons, 1894), 155.

6. George Washington, "Letter to Robert Cary & Company, 20 September 1765," *U.S National Archives: Founders Online*, https://founders.archives.gov/documents/Washington/02-07-02-0252-0001.

7. *The Magazine of American History with Notes and Queries*, Vol. 30 (Charleston, SC: Nabu Press, 2012), 122.

8. Andrew Burnaby, *Burnaby's Travels Through the Middle Settlements of North America* (New York: A. Wessels, 1904), 55.

9. T. H. Breen, *Tobacco Culture: The Mentality of the Great Tidewater Planters on the Eve of Revolution* (Princeton Univ. Press, 2009), 145.

10. Burnaby, *Travels*, 56.

11. Breen, *Tobacco Culture*, 90. Breen's short book presents an excellent discussion of the mindset of men like Jefferson, Washington, Lee, and Byrd, portraying a more honest, though less flattering, view of the Founders than that of most textbooks.

12. Breen, *Tobacco Culture*, 198.

13. Herbert Montfort Morais, *The Struggle for American Freedom: The First Two Hundred Years* (New York: International Publishers, 1944), 182.

14. This quote is frequently attributed to George Washington, but I have been unable to find an original source document or attribution. Searching the Washington papers from the National Archives turns up several letters from him discussing the sending of tobacco, but nothing with regard to a request made to send it in lieu of money for the war. There is some discussion between Washington and Jefferson of using tobacco as payment to Lord Cornwallis for prisoners, but Washington discouraged Jefferson from taking that course. Benjamin Franklin, in a pamphlet, mentions tobacco along with gold, silver, or copper as the basis of a paper currency but that was well before the Revolutionary War; see Benjamin Franklin, *A Modest Enquiry into the Nature and Necessity of a Paper-Currency* (Philadelphia: Franklin, 1729), https://founders.archives.gov/?q=%22tobacco%22&s=1111311111&r=1. I find it hard to believe Washington ever uttered these words, although tobacco was used as a means of raising funds for the war, through credit arrangements based on tobacco with European governments.

15. Silas Deane, "The Deane Papers," *Collections of the New-York Historical Society* (New York: 1889), 294–96, https://archive.org/stream/collectionsforye21newyuoft. Deane, a delegate to the Continental Congress from Connecticut, served as an ambassador to France during the war along with Benjamin Franklin and Arthur Lee. From France, Deane ran a covert operation to supply the thirteen colonies with arms in exchange for tobacco, along with his French counterpart, the playwright Pierre-Augustin Caron de Beaumarchais. Deane, essentially a US intelligence operative, died under suspicious circumstances while attempting to return from Europe to America in 1789.

16. Julian P. Boyd, ed., *The Papers of Thomas Jefferson, Vol. 1, 1760–1776* (Princeton Univ. Press, 1997), 318.

17. John Murray, the 4th Earl of Dunmore, "Lord Dunmore's Proclamation," http://www.digitalhistory.uh.edu/active_learning/explorations/revolution/dunsmore.cfm.

18. Boyd, *Papers of Jefferson*, 318.

19. Thurgood Marshall, "The Bicentennial Speech," May 6, 1987, http://thurgoodmarshall.com/the-bicentennial-speech.

20. Marshall, "The Bicentennial Speech."

21. US Constitution, National Archives, https://www.archives.gov/founding-docs/constitution-transcript.

22. William Lloyd Garrison, "No Slavery! Fourth of July! The Managers of the Mass. Anti-Slavery Soc'y," *Massachusetts Historical Society: Collection Online*, https://www.masshist.org/database/431.

23. Paul Finkelman, *Slavery and the Founders: Race and Liberty in the Age of Jefferson* (Armonk, NY: M. E. Sharpe, 1996), 1–33. The description of the Constitutional Convention and the clauses of the Constitution related to slavery are summaries of the material Finkelman presents in the first chapter of this book.

24. Finkelman, *Slavery and the Founders*. Finkelman gives an excellent overview of the debate and the constitutional clauses related to slavery.

25. Finkelman, *Slavery and the Founders*, 18–19.

CHAPTER 9: A GREAT WHITE HOPE

1. Annie Ruth Davis, "Josephine Bristow: Ex-Slave, 73 Years," *Slave Narratives: A Folk History of Slavery in the United States from Interviews with Former Slaves*, Vol. 14 (Washington, DC: Works Progress Administration, 1941), 98, https://www.loc.gov/resource/mesn.141/?sp=101.

2. The "Horn of Pain" was anything from a conch shell horn to an extremely long, trumpetlike instrument.

3. M. B. Hammond, "Correspondence of Eli Whitney Relative to the Invention of the Cotton Gin," *The American Historical Review*, October 1897, Vol. 3, No. 1, 100, https://www.jstor.org/stable/1832812.

4. National Archives, "To Thomas Jefferson from Eli Whitney, 24 November 1793," *Founders Online*, https://founders.archives.gov/documents/Jefferson/01-27-02-0407.

5. Hammond, "Correspondence of Eli Whitney," 90–127.

6. Thomas Affleck, *Affleck's Southern Rural Almanac, and Plantation and Garden Calendar for 1851* (New Orleans: Weld & Co., 1850), 5, https://hdl.handle.net/2027/umn.31951000481852h.

7. These scenes with Robert Mackay are adapted from letters he wrote to his wife from his travels to east coast US seaports and to Liverpool. See Walter Charlton Hartridge, *The Letters of Robert Mackay to His Wife* (Athens: Univ. of Georgia Press, 1949).

8. Knut Oyangen, "The Cotton Economy of the Old South," *Internet Archive*, https://web.archive.org/web/20121125045429/http://www.history.iastate.edu/agprimer/Page28.html.

9. Campbell Gibson and Kay Jung, *Population Division: Historical Census Statistics on Population Totals by Race, 1790 to 1990, and by Hispanic Origin, 1970 to 1990, for the United States, Regions, Divisions, and States*, Working Paper No. 56 (Washington, DC: US Census Bureau, 2002), 19, https://www.census.gov/content/dam/Census/library/working-papers/2002/demo/POP-twps0056.pdf.

10. Frederick M. Peck and Henry H. Earl, *Fall River and its Industries: An Historical and Statistical Record* (Washington, DC: Library of Congress, 1877), 71–72, https://play.google.com/books/reader?id=r4IlAQAAMAAJ.

11. Carol Bleser, ed., *Secret and Sacred: The Diaries of James Henry Hammond, a Southern Slaveholder* (New York: Oxford Univ. Press, 1988). Also see the review of this book, Rosellen Brown, "Monster of All He Surveyed," *New York Times*, January 29, 1989, Section 7, 22, https://www.nytimes.com/1989/01/29/books/monster-of-all-he-surveyed.html.

12. Bleser, *Secret and Sacred*, also Brown, "Monster of All He Surveyed."

13. Josiah Gilbert Holland and Richard Watson Gilder, eds., "The Atlanta Cotton Explosion," *The Century Illustrated Monthly Magazine*, Vol. 23, 565, https://books.google.com/books?id=Rf2wkXcBBnwC.

14. James Henry Hammond, *Selections from the Letters and Speeches of the Hon. James H. Hammond* (New York: John F. Trow & Co., 1866), 316, https://books.google.com/books?id=FvMeZzrWW3AC.

15. See the article on the letter by Jason Rodrigues, "Lincoln's great debt to Manchester," *The Guardian*, February 4, 2012, https://www.theguardian.com/theguardian/from-the-archive-blog/2013/feb/04/lincoln-oscars-manchester-cotton-abraham. Read the full letter at https://static.guim.co.uk/sys-images/Guardian/Pix/pictures/2013/1/31/1359635861273/Mill-workers-001.jpg.

16. Alfred P. Wadsworth and Julia De Lacy Mann, *The Cotton Trade and Industrial Lancashire, 1600–1780* (Manchester, UK: Manchester Univ. Press, 1931), 248.

17. State Street Trust Company, *Some Industries of New England: Their Origin, Development and Accomplishments* (Boston: 1923), 4–5, https://books.google.com/books?id=6mtqS-Xb7joC.

18. Hartridge, *The Letters of Robert Mackay*, 236.

CHAPTER 10: I CAN'T BREATHE

1. Richard N. Frye, Thomas von Soden Wolfram, and Deitz O. Edzard, "History of Mesopotamia," *Encyclopedia Britannica*, April 15, 2016, https://www.britannica.com/place/Mesopotamia-historical-region-Asia.

2. See, for example, Stephen R. Haynes, *Noah's Curse: The Biblical Justification of American Slavery* (New York: Oxford Univ. Press, 2002).

3. Edmund S. Morgan, *American Slavery, American Freedom* (New York: Norton, 2003), 3–24.

4. Morgan, *American Slavery, American Freedom*, 8.

5. See Chapter 1 of Morgan, *American Slavery, American Freedom*, for a full discussion of this view.

6. See "maroon," *Etymology Online*, https://www.etymonline.com/word/maroon.

7. Charles C. Mann, *1493: Uncovering the New World Columbus Created* (NY: Knopf, 2011), 331.

8. Richard Hakluyt, *The Principal Navigations, Voyages, Traffiques, and Discoveries of the English Nation*, Vol. 15 (Edinburgh: Goldsmid, 1890), 198.

9. "Ordenanzas para los negros del Yerno de Chile," *Memoria Chilena*, http://www.memoriachilena.gob.cl/602/w3-article-62279.html.

10. Sally E. Hadden, *Slave Patrols: Law and Violence in Virginia and the Carolinas* (Cambridge, MA: Harvard Univ. Press, 2001), 10.

11. Cited in John Sugden, *Sir Francis Drake* (New York: Random House, 2012), 62.

12. See Chapter 2 of this book for more on the Sea Dogs.

13. Hakluyt, *Principal Navigations*.

14. Hakluyt Society, *The Original Writings & Correspondence of the Two Richard Hakluyts*, Ser. 2, No. 76 (Cambridge Univ. Press, 1935), 142, https://archive.org/stream/in.ernet.dli.2015.172689/2015.172689.The-Original-Writings-Of-Correspondence-Of-The-Two-Richard-Haklutyts-vol-I_djvu.txtá.

15. Hakluyt Society, *The Original Writings*, 142.

16. Hakluyt Society, *The Original Writings*, 118.

17. See Chapter 5 of this book for more about Dale's Code.

18. See Chapter 6 of this book for more on Bacon's Rebellion.

19. See Chapter 8 of this book for more on the Dunmore Proclamation. The estimates for slaves taking up Dunmore's offer range from three hundred to two thousand. For the total number of slaves crossing over to the British, the estimate ranges between 20,000 to 100,000, which is actually a significant number of the slave population at the time of the Revolutionary War. See also "The Phillipsburg Proclamation" on *Black Loyalists*, and Peggy Bristow, ed., *We're Rooted Here and They Can't Pull Us Up: Essays in African Canadian Women's History* (Univ. of Toronto Press, 1994), 19.

20. Paul Finkelman, *Slavery and the Founders* (New York: Routledge, 2015), 30.

21. William M. Wiecek, "Somerset: Lord Mansfield and the Legitimacy of Slavery in the Anglo-American World," *Univ. of Chicago Law Review*, Vol. 42, No. 1, 1974, 86–146.

22. Wiecek, "Somerset," 95.

23. Horace Bertram Nelson, "The case of JAMES SOMMERSETT, a Negro," *Selected Cases, Statutes, and Orders Illustrative of the Principles of Private International Law as Administered in England* (London: Stevens & Sons, 1889), 62, https://play.google.com/books/reader?id=r_w0AAAAIAAJ.

24. Wiecek, "Somerset," 86–87.

25. Finkelman, *Slavery and the Founders*, 28–32.

26. Patrick Henry, cited in George Washington Frank Mellen, *An Argument on the Unconstitutionality of Slavery, Embracing an Abstract of the Proceedings of the Nation and State Conventions on this Subject* (Boston: Saxton & Pierce, 1841), 216.

27. Amendment II, Constitution of the United States, https://www.archives.gov/founding-docs/bill-of-rights-transcript.

28. Many popular references to policing and "slave patrols" cite Hadden, *Slave Patrols*. But Hadden clearly states that her study, originally a PhD thesis, covers the period 1700–1865. See, Hadden, *Slave Patrols*, 2. This leaves the colonial period prior to 1700 unaddressed. Slave patrols did not suddenly happen at the start of the eighteenth century, and it is important to have a better un-

derstanding of when, why, and where they first began. Hadden acknowledges as much. "Patrols were not created in a vacuum, but owed much to European institutions that served as the slave patrol's institutional forbears," Hadden, *Slave Patrols*, 3.

29. See Chapter 6 of this book for a thorough accounting of these two cases.

30. See Chapter 6 of this book for the complete text of this act.

31. George Burton Adams and Henry Morse Stephens, eds., *Select Documents of English Constitutional History* (New York: MacMillan, 1901), 76–79.

32. Adams and Stephens, *Select Documents*, 78.

33. Adams and Stephens, *Select Documents*, 77.

34. See, for example, John S. Dempsey, Linda S. Forst, and Steven B. Carter, "English Policing: Our Heritage," *An Introduction to Policing* (Boston: Cengage, 2017), 4.

35. Jonathon A. Cooper, *Twentieth-Century Influences on Twenty-First-Century Policing: Continued Lessons of Police Reform* (Lanham, Maryland: Lexington Books, 2015), 8. https://www.google.com/books/edition/Twentieth_Century_Influences _on_Twenty_F/gEawCQAAQBAJ?hl=en&gbpv=1&dq=%22statute+of+winchester %22+%22American+policing%22&pg=PA8&printsec=frontcover.

36. Hadden, *Slave Patrols*, 10.

37. Hadden, *Slave Patrols*.

38. Hadden, *Slave Patrols*, 99.

39. Hadden, *Slave Patrols*, 78.

40. Hadden, *Slave Patrols*, 167–202.

41. Hadden, *Slave Patrols*, 177–78.

42. Hadden, *Slave Patrols*, 180–83.

43. Hadden, *Slave Patrols*, 190.

44. Hadden, *Slave Patrols*, 190–96.

45. Hadden, *Slave Patrols*, 194.

46. Hadden, *Slave Patrols*, 200.

47. Works Progress Administration (WPA), *Slave Narratives: A Folk History of Slavery in the United States* (Washington, DC: Library of Congress, 1841), 18, 51, 65.

48. Hadden, *Slave Patrols*, 218.

49. Norma Torres, Congresswoman, "Torres to DOJ: Release FBI Report on White Supremacist Infiltration of Law Enforcement," June 24, 2020, https://torres.house .gov/media-center/press-releases/torres-doj-release-fbi-report-white-supremacist -infiltration-law.

50. *United States v. Kozminski*, 487 U.S. 931 (1988), https://supreme.justia.com/cases /federal/us/487/931.

51. National Public Radio, "In the Wake of Chauvin's Conviction, A Look Back At The Origins Of American Policing," *All Things Considered* (Washington, DC: April 21, 2021). https://www.npr.org/2021/04/22/989938920/in-the-wake-of -chauvins-conviction-a-look-back-at-the-origins-of-american-polici.

52. Betsy Hodges, "As Mayor of Minneapolis, I Saw How White Liberals Block Change," *New York Times*, July 9, 2020, https://www.nytimes.com/2020/07/09/opinion/minneapolis-hodges-racism.html.

53. Harvard Kennedy School, "The end of us-versus-them policing: a tough road ahead for reform," October 5, 2020, https://www.hks.harvard.edu/more/policycast/end-us-versus-them-policing-tough-road-ahead-reform.

54. Parts of this section on police reform come from my opinion column, "Reforms aren't enough to end 'us vs. them' policing in America," *Crosscut*, May 21, 2021. https://crosscut.com/opinion/2021/05/reforms-arent-enough-end-us-vs-them-policing-america.

CHAPTER 11: BEFORE THE MAST

1. Adapted from Briton Hammon, *A Narrative of the Uncommon Suffering and Surprizing Deliverance of Briton Hammon* (Boston: Green & Russell, 1760), https://docsouth.unc.edu/neh/hammon/menu.html.

2. W. Jeffrey Bolster, *Black Jacks: African American Seamen in the Age of Sail* (Cambridge, MA: Harvard Univ. Press, 1997), 6.

3. Campbell Gibson and Kay Jung, *Historical Census Statistics on Population Totals by Race, 1790 to 1990, and by Hispanic Origin, 1970 to 1990, for Large Cities and Other Urban Places in the United States*, working paper no. 76 (Washington, DC: US Census Bureau, 2005).

4. Malcolm X, "The House Negro and the Field Negro," transcript from Malcolm's famous 1963 speech, "Message to the Grass Roots." Malcolm gave a variation of this speech many times. Listen to it, for example, at https://genius.com/Malcolm-x-the-house-negro-and-the-field-negro-annotated.

5. Henry Laurens, *The Papers of Henry Laurens: Sept. 1, 1763–Aug. 31, 1765*, Vol. 4 (Columbia: South Carolina Historical Society, 1968), 319.

6. Laurens, *The Papers of Henry Laurens*, 633.

7. John Brickell, MD, *The Natural History of North Carolina* (Dublin: James Carson, 1737), 260, https://play.google.com/books/reader?id=p4c5AAAAcAAJ.

8. Elmer Turnage, ed., "Stories from Ex-Slaves," *Slave Narratives: A Folk History of Slavery in the United States from Interviews with Former Slaves*, Vol. 14, Part 3, South Carolina Narratives (Washington, DC: Library of Congress, 1941), 67.

9. William Howard Russell, *My Diary North and South*, Vol. 1 (London: Bradbury and Evans, 1863), 206.

10. Lynn B. Harris and William N. Still, Jr., *Patroons and Periaguas* (Columbia: Univ. of South Carolina Press, 2014), 56.

11. Thomas Jefferson, "Letter to James Madison," *Thomas Jefferson's Papers*, Feb. 12, 1799, https://www.monticello.org/site/research-and-collections/st-domingue-haiti.

12. Bolster, *Black Jacks*, 4.

13. Frederick Douglass, "My Escape from Slavery," *Century Magazine*, Vol. 23 (1882), 125.

14. Bolster, *Black Jacks*, 14.

CHAPTER 12: OVER COFFEE

1. Author unknown, *The Women's Petition against Coffee and The Men's Answer to the Women's Petition against Coffee*, pamphlet (London: 1674), https://www.amazon.com/Womens-Petition-against-Coffee-Answer-ebook/dp/B088X69HS5.

2. Author unknown, *The Women's Petition*.

3. Author unknown, *The Women's Petition*.

4. Ned Ward, *The London Spy Compleat* (1703) (London: J. Howe, 1703), 15. The *London Spy* was a periodical review of London public life and culture, http://grubstreetproject.net/works/T119938.

5. Pasqua Rosée, *The Virtue of Coffee Drink*, handbill (London: 1652), https://commons.wikimedia.org/wiki/File:The_Virtue_of_the_Coffee_Drink.jpg.

6. Ward, *The London Spy*, 15.

7. Robin Pearson and David Richardson, "Insuring the Transatlantic Slave Trade," *The Journal of Economic History*, Vol. 70, No. 2, June 2019, 417–46.

8. Frederick Martin, *The History of Lloyd's and of Maritime Insurance in Great Britain* (London: Macmillan and Co., 1876), 356, https://books.google.com/books?id=BEN6WlSgwxcC&pg=PA356&lpg=PA356.

9. James Oldham, "Insurance Litigation Involving the *Zong* and Other British Slave Ships, 1780–1807," *The Journal of Legal History*, Vol. 28, No. 3, 299–318.

10. Guy Faulconbridge and Kate Holton, "Update: Lloyd's of London Apologizes for Its 'Shameful' Role in the Atlantic Slave Trade," *Insurance Journal*, June 18, 2020, https://www.insurancejournal.com/news/international/2020/06/18/572696.htm.

11. See the original agreement at the "Buttonwood Agreement," *Virtual Museum and Archive of the History of Financial Regulation of The Securities and Exchange Commission Historical Society*, http://3197d6d14b5f19f2f440-5e13d29c4c016cf96cbbfd197c579b45.r81.cf1.rackcdn.com/collection/papers/1790/1792_0517_NYSEButtonwood.pdf.

12. Peter Eisenstadt, "How the Buttonwood Tree Grew: The Making of a New York Stock Exchange Legend," *Prospects: An Annual of American Cultural Studies*, Vol. 19, 1994, 75–98.

13. Ward, *The London Spy*, 289. The periodical was well-known for colorful depictions of English public life.

14. Ward, *The London Spy*, 289.

15. *Minutes of the Common Council of the City of New York, 1685–1776*, Vol. 4 (1730–1740) (New York: Dodd, Mead and Company, 1905), 85, https://hdl.handle.net/2027/nyp.33433058764709?urlappend=%3Bseq=95.

16. Francis Guy, *The Tontine Coffee House*, painting, https://en.wikipedia.org/wiki/Tontine_Coffee_House#/media/File:Tontine_coffee_house.jpg.

17. Shane White, "Slavery in New York State in the Early Republic," *Australasian Journal of American Studies* 14, No. 2, 1995, 1, www.jstor.org/stable/41053779.

18. *Minutes of the Council*, 88, https://hdl.handle.net/2027/nyp.33433058764709?urlappend=%3Bseq=98.

19. Rodney Leon, "African Burial Ground Exterior Monument," US General Services Administration. Mr. Leon, and his firm, won the competition for creating the African Burial Ground monument, https://www.gsa.gov/about-us/regions /welcome-to-the-northeast-caribbean-region-2/about-region-2/african-burial -ground/african-burial-ground-exterior-monument.

20. See, for instance, Ira Berlin and Leslie Harris, *Slavery in New York* (New York: New Press, 2005).

21. See Chapter 9 of this book.

22. See Chapter 11 of this book.

23. Edward E. Baptist and Louis Hyman, "American finance grew on the back of slaves," *The Chicago Sun-Times*, March 6, 2014, Internet Archive, *Wayback Machine*, http://chicago.suntimes.com/uncategorized/7/71/151465/american-finance-grew -on-the-back-of-slaves.

24. Thomas Jefferson, "Deed of Mortgage of Slaves to Henderson, McCaul & Company, 12 May 1796," National Archives, *Founders Online*, https://founders.archives .gov/documents/Jefferson/01-29-02-0064.

25. Thomas Jefferson, "Deed of Mortgage of Slaves to Van Staphorst & Hubbard, 12 May 1796," National Archives, *Founders Online*, https://founders.archives.gov /documents/Jefferson/01-29-02-0065.

26. Thomas Jefferson, "Deed of Mortgage of Slaves to Van Staphorst & Hubbard, 21 November 1796," National Archives, *Founders Online*, https://founders.archives .gov/documents/Jefferson/01-29-02-0167.

27. David Teather, "Bank Admits it owned slaves," *The Guardian*, January 21, 2005. JP Morgan apologized for its role in the slave trade, https://www.theguardian .com/world/2005/jan/22/usa.davidteather. In 2007, a group of shareholders for the bank rescinded that apology on grounds that it was "absurd." See Amy Ridenour, "JP Morgan Chase Slavery Apology Criticized," The National Center for Public Policy Research, May 15, 2007, https://nationalcenter.org/ncppr/2007/05/15/blog -jpmorgan-chase-slavery-apology-criticized.

28. Katie Benner, "Wachovia apologizes for slavery ties," *CNN Money*, June 2, 2005, https://money.cnn.com/2005/06/02/news/fortune500/wachovia_slavery/.

29. Michael Powelson, *Swindlers All, a Brief History of Government Business Frauds from Alexander Hamilton to AIG* (Newcastle-upon-Tyne, UK: Cambridge Scholars Publishing, 2019), 39.

30. Edward E. Baptist, *The Half Has Never Been Told: Slavery and the Rise of American Capitalism* (New York: Basic Books, 2014), 254.

31. Supreme Court of Missouri, *Milly v. Smith*, 2 Mo. 139, September 1, 1829, https:// cite.case.law/mo/2/139/.

32. See Chapter 9 of this book.

33. Baptist and Hyman, "American finance."

34. Michael Ralph and William Rankin, "Decoder: The Slave Insurance Market," *For-*

eign Policy, January 16, 2017, https://foreignpolicy.com/2017/01/16/decoder-slave
-insurance-market-aetna-aig-new-york-life.

35. Baptist and Hyman, "American finance."

CHAPTER 13: HELL ON WHEELS

1. Elizabeth Cotten, *Freight Train and other North Carolina Folk Songs and Tunes*, liner notes by Mike Seeger, 1989 (Washington, DC: Smithsonian Institution, 1989), https://folkways-media.si.edu/liner_notes/smithsonian_folkways/SFW400 09.pdf.

2. Cotten, *Freight Train*.

3. Clara Smith, recording, "Freight Train Blues," September 30, 1924, https://adp .library.ucsb.edu/index.php/matrix/detail/2000029830/140064-Freight_train _blues/.

4. Theodore Kornweibel, *Railroads in the African American Experience: A Photographic Journey* (Baltimore: John Hopkins Univ., 2010), 1–4.

5. "African American Railroad Workers: Gandy Dancers," *US Slave*, https://usslave. blogspot.com/2012/04/railroad-gandy-dancers.html. The origin of the term *Gandy* is controversial and disputed. Some claim it comes from the Chicago-based "Gandy Tool Company" but no company by that name has ever been conclusively shown to have existed. Others claim it comes from the duck-like (gander-like) movements of men running on rails. It may also be a transliteration of a West African word, or place, such as Ghana, from where many slaves came.

6. "Affairs of Southern Railroads," *Reports of the Committees of the House of Representatives*, Second Session, Thirty-Ninth Congress, 1866–67 (Washington, DC: Government Printing Office, 1867), 603. https://play.google.com/books/reader ?id=iwdVAAAAcAAJ.

7. "Affairs of Southern Railroads," 609.

8. "Affairs of Southern Railroads," 592.

9. "Messrs, G.B. Lamar and Fernando Wood," *New York Times*, November 11, 1863, 1, https://www.nytimes.com/1863/11/11/archives/messrs-gb-lamar-and-fernando-wood .html.

10. In the mid-1850s, wheat and apples were southern crops and pig iron was produced on "iron plantations," the northeastern US, which employed slave labor. See, for example, James R. Irwin, "Exploring the affinity of wheat and slavery in the Virginia Piedmont," *Explorations in Economic History*, Vol. 25, No. 3, July 1988, 295–322; Gavin Wright, "Slavery and American Agricultural History," paper presented at The Agricultural History Society, April 2003. Albemarle County, Virginia, most likely due to Jefferson's influence, had a brisk nineteenth-century trade in an apple known as the "Newtown Pippin." Much of American apple production, especially in the south, was for the production of hard cider but southern apple-growing prior to the Civil War was possible because of slave labor.

See Tim Hensley, "A Curious Tale: The Apple in North America," Brooklyn Botanic Garden, June 2, 2005, https://www.bbg.org/gardening/article/the_apple_in _north_america. In the nineteenth century, pig iron was produced in many areas of the south at iron plantations, where year-round slave laborers were overseen by White managers; see, for example, Wilma A. Dunaway, *Slavery in the American Mountain South* (New York: Cambridge Univ. Press, 2003).

11. Richard Lathers, *This Discursive Biographical Sketch: 1841–1902 of Colonel Richard Lathers* (Philadelphia: J. B. Lippincott, 1902), 85–112.

12. Mary Ricketson Bullard, *Robert Stafford of Cumberland Island: Growth of a Planter* (Athens: Univ. of Georgia Press, 1995), 288. See the footnote on this page.

13. *The Commercial and Financial Chronicle, July To December, 1901*, Vol. 73 (New York: William B. Dana, 1901), 317, https://books.google.com/books?id=DjpOAAAAYAAJ.

14. The editors, "Citigroup," *The Encyclopedia Britannica*, https://www.britannica.com /topic/Citigroup.

15. *Twenty-Second Annual Report of the Board of Public Works, to the General Assembly of Virginia with the Accompanying Documents* (Richmond: Thomas Ritchie, 1838), 74.

16. *Twenty-Second Annual Report*, 76.

17. Craig Sanders, *Amtrak in the Heartland (Railroads Past and Present)* (Bloomington: Indiana Univ. Press, 2006), 7–8. Essentially, Amtrak took over the passenger service of the Seaboard Coast Line, and CSX took over its freight service.

18. "CSX merger family tree," *Trains*, https://trn.trains.com/railroads/railroad-history /2006/06/csx-merger-family-tree.

19. William G. Thomas, *The Iron Way: Railroads, the Civil War, and the Making of Modern America* (New Haven: Yale Univ. Press, 2011), 22.

20. "A Line in Time," *Norfolk Southern*, http://www.nscorp.com/content/nscorp/en /the-norfolk-southern-story.html.

21. Kornweibel, *Railroads in the African American Experience*, 11.

22. Kornweibel, *Railroads in the African American Experience*, 23.

23. Kornweibel, *Railroads in the African American Experience*, 12.

24. Board of Public Works, *Biennial Report of the Board of Public Works, to the General Assembly of Virginia, January 22, 1859–60 & 1860–61* (Richmond, 1862), 76, 172, 269, https://play.google.com/books/reader?id=D6s4AQAAMAAJ.

25. *Railroad Gazette: A Journal of Transportation, Engineering and Railroad News*, Vol. 33 (New York: Railroad Gazette, 1901), 572.

26. Kornweibel, *Railroads in the African American Experience*, 18.

27. See "CSX merger family tree," and Sanders, *Amtrak in the Heartland*, and "History of Kansas City Southern," https://web.archive.org/web/20080709070103 /http://www.kcsouthern.com/en-us/KCS/Pages/History.aspx, and "Canadian National Railway Company," *The Encyclopedia Britannica*, https://www.britannica .com/topic/Canadian-National-Railway-Company. Note: Predecessors to today's railways may have undergone multiple name changes, mergers, and acquisitions, not all of which are referenced in the text.

28. "Tallahassee-St. Marks Historic Railroad State Trail," Florida Department of Environmental Protection, https://floridadep.gov/parks/unit-management-plans/documents/tallahassee-st-marks-historic-railroad-state-trail.

29. Colonial Society of Massachusetts, *Publication of the Colonial Society of Massachusetts*, Vol. 7, 1900–02 (Cambridge: John Wilson and Son, 1905), 195, https://books.google.com/books?id=x_8KAAAAIAAJ&pg=PA195.

30. William Page Johnson, "Richard Ratcliffe: The Founder," *The Fare Facs Gazette*, Vol. 3, No. 1, https://www.historicfairfax.org/wp-content/uploads/2012/05/HFCI31-2005.pdf. Ratcliffe's plantation was Mount Vineyard, present-day Fairfax, Virginia. In 1861, Confederate troops were headquartered at Mount Vineyard.

31. "Macadamize," Merriam-Webster Dictionary, https://www.merriam-webster.com/dictionary/macadamize. The word *macadamize* did not come into use until 1824. A modern-day variation on macadamization using tar, oil, or cement as a base is still in use for many roads today.

32. Debbie Robison, "Little River Turnpike," *Northern Virginia History Notes*, September 10, 2017, http://www.novahistory.org/LittleRiverTurnpike/LittleRiverTurnpike.htm.

33. Board of Public Works, *Fourteenth Annual Report of the Board of Public Works, to the General Assembly of Virginia. January 22, 1830* (Richmond: Samuel Shepherd & Co., 1830), 67, 212.

34. Stanley J. Folmsbee, "The Turnpike Phase of Tennessee's Internal Improvement System of 1836–1838," *The Journal of Southern History*, Vol. 3, No. 4, November 1977, 462.

35. Board of Public Works, *Thirty-Fifth Annual Report of the Board of Public Works, to the General Assembly of Virginia. 1850* (Richmond, 1850), 47.

36. Caitlin Rosenthal, *Accounting for Slavery: Masters and Management* (Cambridge, MA: Harvard Univ. Press, 2019), 122–25.

37. Board of Public Works, *Fourteenth Annual Report*, 317.

38. *Twenty-Second Annual Report*, 98.

39. Board of Public Works, *Eleventh, Twelfth and Thirteenth Annual Report of the Board of Public Works, to the General Assembly of Virginia. January 22, 1826–27, 1827–28, 1828–29* (Richmond: Samuel Shepherd & Co., 1829), 215.

40. Board of Public Works, *Seventeenth Annual Report of the Board of Public Works, to the General Assembly of Virginia. January 22, 1830* (Richmond: Samuel Shepherd & Co., 1833), 178.

41. Wayland Fuller Dunaway, *History of the James River and Kanawha Company* (New York: Columbia Univ., 1922), 131, https://archive.org/stream/cu31924022882330/cu31924022882330_djvu.txt.

42. Peter Wray, *Common Labor: Workers and the Digging of North American Canals, 1780–1860* (Baltimore: John Hopkins Univ. Press, 1997), 88.

43. Ryan A. Quintana, *Making a Slave State: Political Development in Early South Carolina* (Chapel Hill: Univ. of North Carolina Press, 2018), 68–73.

44. Wray, *Common Labor*, 126–27.

45. Quoted in "Florida History Built on Slavery," *US Slave*, http://usslave.blogspot .com/2013/06/florida-history-built-on-slavery.html. See also, Jane Landers, *Black Society in Spanish Florida* (Chicago: Univ. of Illinois Press, 1999).

46. Larry Van Dyne, "Water, Water . . . ," *The Washingtonian*, March 1, 2007, https:// www.washingtonian.com/2007/03/01/water-water/.

47. Alexander Pope, *The Works of Alexander Pope Esq. Containing his Miscellaneous Pieces in Verse and Prose*, Vol. 6 (London: J. and P. Knapton, 1751), 196, https://play .google.com/books/reader?id=QyYJAAAAQAAJ.

48. Quoted in Wolfgang Schivelbusch, *The Railway Journey: The Industrialization of Time and Space in the 19th Century* (Berkeley: Univ. of California Press, 1996), 33.

49. William and Ellen Craft, *Running a Thousand Miles for Freedom* (London: William Tweedie, 1860), http://www.gutenberg.org/cache/epub/585/pg585-images.html.

50. The Underground Railroad alone is thought to have accounted for between 40,000 to 100,000 escaped slaves a year between 1860 and 1865. See Naomi Blumberg, "Fugitive Slave," *The Encyclopedia Britannica*, https://www.britannica .com/topic/fugitive-slave.

51. James C. Cobb, "One of American History's Worst Laws Was Passed 165 Years Ago," TIME, September 18, 2015, https://time.com/4039140/fugitive-slace-act-165.

52. "Fugitive Slave Act 1850," *The Avalon Project*, Yale Law School, https://avalon.law .yale.edu/19th_century/fugitive.asp.

53. Harriet C. Frazier, *Runaway and Freed Missouri Slaves and Those Who Helped Them, 1763–1865* (Jefferson, NC: McFarland & Co., 2004), 93.

54. Court documents list only "Mr. Leib" as the Hanover, Pennsylvania, ticket agent. But see *The Official Railway List: A Directory*, 64, which lists Joseph Leib as the Hanover ticket agent, https://play.google.com/books/reader?id=JEsEAAAAMAAJ.

55. Oliver Miller, *Maryland Reports, Containing Cases Argued and Determined in the Court of Appeals of Maryland*, Vol. 16 (Annapolis: Robert F. Bonsall, 1861), 331–38, https://play.google.com/books/reader?id=VUdFAQAAMAAJ.

56. Frederick Douglass, "The Present Condition and Future Prospects of the Negro People," speech at the annual meeting of the American and Foreign Anti-Slavery Society, New York City, May 11, 1853, in Philip Foner and Yuval Taylor, eds., *Frederick Douglass: Selected Speeches and Writings* (Chicago: Lawrence Hill Books, 1999), 260.

57. Samuel F. B. Morse, *Daily Madisonian*, February 7, 1844, https://www.loc.gov /resource/sn84020074/1844-02-07/ed-1.

58. Gerda Lerner, ed., *Black Women in White America: A Documentary History* (New York: Vintage Books, 1992), 8.

59. Ervin L. Jordan, *Black Confederates and Afro-Yankees in Civil War Virginia* (Charlottesville: Univ. of Virginia Press, 1995), 40.

60. The term "drum up" business originates in the antebellum era when traveling salesmen carried their wares in boxes made of leather stretched over a wooden

frame. To announce their presence, salesmen would beat their leather boxes with drumsticks, making the sound of a muffled snare drum. In the south, during the Civil War, this practice was a way of distinguishing a salesman from a "Yankee" spy. See Ken Gassman, "Time to 'Drum Up' Business," *International Diamond Exchange*, April 12, 2020, http://www.idexonline.com/FullArticle?id=36661.

61. See A. J. Rux, "Letter from A. J. Rux to E. H. Stokes," November 17, 1860, *The New York Historical Society Museum & Library*, http://digitalcollections.ny history.org/islandora/9, and "Letter from A. J. Rux to E. H. Stokes," December 3, 1860, *The New York Historical Society Museum & Library*, and "Letter from A. J. Rux to E. H. Stokes," February 21, 1861, *Railroads and the Making of Modern America*, http://railroads.unl.edu/documents/view_document.php?id=rail .gen.0028.

62. Ninbush Young, "Ninbush Young to E.H. Stokes," telegraph, June 24, 1862. Thomas in *The Iron Way* refers to the originator of this message as "Winbush." In this author's reading of the handwritten message the first letter appears to be an *N* and not a *W*.

63. James Redpath, *The Roving Editor: or, Talks with Slaves in the Southern States* (University Park: Pennsylvania Univ. Press, 1996), 228. This was originally published in 1859.

64. Douglass, "The Present Condition."

65. Elmer Turnage, ed., "Stories from Ex-Slaves," *Slave Narratives: A Folk History of Slavery in the United States from Interviews with Former Slaves*, Vol. 7, Kentucky Narratives (Washington, DC: Library of Congress, 1941), 71.

66. Kenneth Silverman, *Lightning Man: The Accursed Life of Samuel F. B. Morse* (Cambridge: Perseus Books Group, 2003), 401.

CHAPTER 14: THE ONLY COWARDLY BLOOD

1. Unless otherwise noted, this account of Butler's interaction with Phelps and the formation of the Louisiana Native Guard is taken directly from Butler's autobiography; see Benjamin Franklin Butler, *Autobiography and Personal Reminiscences of Major-General Benj. F. Butler's Book* (Boston: A.M. Thayer & Company, 1892), 487–502, https://play.google.com/books/reader?id=0LIBAAAAMAAJ.

2. M. A. DeWolfe Howe, ed., *Home Letters of General Sherman* (New York: Charles Scribner's Sons, 1909), 252.

3. Benjamin Franklin Butler, *Private and Official Correspondence of Gen. Benjamin F. Butler, During the Period of the Civil War* (Privately Issued: 1917), 154, https:// www.google.com/books/edition/Private_and_Official_Correspondence_of_G /Ly0OAAAAIAAJ?hl=en&gbpv=1&kptab=getbook.

4. American Buttlefield Trust, "The Color of Bravery: United States Colored Troops in the Civil War," https://www.battlefields.org/learn/articles/color-bravery.

5. Ida M. Tarbell, "Lincoln and the Emancipation Proclamation," *McClure's Magazine*, Vol. 12, November 1898–April 1899, 526.

6. Abraham Lincoln, "Letter to Horace Greeley," *New York Times*, August 22, 1862, https://www.nytimes.com/1862/08/24/archives/a-letter-from-president-lincoln-reply-to-horace-greeley-slavery-and.html.

7. William Wells Brown, *The Negro in the American Revolution* (Boston: Lee & Shepard, 1867), no page numbers, https://www.gutenberg.org/files/50130/50130-8.txt.

8. Brown, *The Negro in the American Rebellion.*

9. This description of the night the Emancipation Proclamation was issued is adapted from Frederick Douglass, *Autobiographies: Narrative of the Life of Frederick Douglass, an American Slave, My Bondage and My Freedom, Life and Times of Frederick Douglass* (Varna, Bulgaria: Pretorian Books, 219), 291–94.

10. Donald M. Jacobs, *Courage and Conscience: Black & White Abolitionists in Boston* (Bloomington: Indiana Univ. Press, 1993), 22.

11. Douglass, *Autobiographies*, 292.

12. Abraham Lincoln, "The Emancipation Proclamation," National Archives, https://www.archives.gov/exhibits/featured-documents/emancipation-proclamation/transcript.html.

13. Butler, *Autobiography*, 497.

14. Butler, *Autobiography*, 497.

15. There are many sources to consult on the Black soldiers and the Siege of Port Hudson. See John D. Winters, *The Civil War in Louisiana* (Baton Rouge: Louisiana State Univ. Press, 1991); James M. McPherson, *The Negro's Civil War: How American Blacks Felt and Acted During the War for the Union* (New York: Vintage Books, 2003); and, "Black Soldiers in the U.S. Military During the Civil War," National Archives, https://www.archives.gov/education/lessons/blacks-civil-war.

16. Winters, *The Civil War*, 242–67.

17. Winters, *The Civil War*, 242–67.

18. 1844, from *berserk* (n.), "Norse warrior" (by 1835), an alternative form of *berserker*, a word which was introduced (as *berserkar*) by Sir Walter Scott in "The Pirate" (1822), from Old Norse *berserkr* (n.), "raging warrior of superhuman strength." It is probably from **ber-* "bear" + *serkr* "shirt," thus literally "a warrior clothed in bearskin" (see *bear* (n.) + *sark*). Thus not, as Scott evidently believed, from Old Norse *berr*, "bare, naked," and meaning "warrior who fights without armor." From *Etymology Online*, https://www.etymonline.com/search?q=berserk.

19. Lerone Bennett, Jr., "The Negro in the Civil War," *Ebony*, Vol. 17, No. 8, June 1962, 136.

20. "The Funeral of Captain Andre Cailloux," *Harper's Weekly*, Vol. 7, August 29, 1963, 511, https://archive.org/details/harpersweeklyv7bonn.

21. United States, *The War of the Rebellion: A Compilation of the Official Records of the Union and Confederate Armies*, Series 1, Vol. 26, Part 1: Reports (Washington: Government Printing Office, 1880–1901), 45, https://hdl.handle.net/2027/coo.31924077743049.

22. Erin Blakemore, "How an Enslaved African Man in Boston Helped Save Generation from Smallpox," *History*, February 1, 2019, https://www.history.com/news/smallpox-vaccine-onesimus-slave-cotton-mather.

23. Michael Kinch, *Between Hope and Fear: A History of Vaccines and Human Immunity* (NY: Pegasus Books, 2018), 81, https://www.google.com/books/edition/Between_Hope_and_Fear/yu8_DwAAQBAJ?hl=en&gbpv=1&pg=PT81.

24. Adam Serwer, "Why a Statue of the 'Father of Gynecology' Had to Come Down," *The Atlantic*, April 18, 2018, https://www.theatlantic.com/politics/archive/2018/04/why-a-statue-of-the-father-of-gynecology-had-to-come-down/558311/.

25. James H. Jones, *Bad Blood: The Tuskegee Syphilis Experiment* (NY: Simon & Schuster, 1993).

26. Rebecca Skloot, *The Immortal Lie of Henrietta Lacks* (NY: Random House, 2011).

27. Madeline Drexler, "Deadly Parallels: Health disparities in the COVID-19 pandemic mirror those in the lethal 1918 flu," *Harvard Public Health Magazine*, Fall 2020, https://www.hsph.harvard.edu/magazine/magazine_article/deadly-parallels/.

28. Drexler, "Deadly Parallels."

29. Michael W. Sjoding, M.D., et al., "Racial Bias in Pulse Oximetry Measurement," *New England Journal of Medicine*, Letters, Dec. 17, 2020.

30. Bennett, "The Negro in the Civil War," 136.

31. Butler, *Autobiography*, Appendix, 47.

32. Bennett, "The Negro in the Civil War," 136.

33. "Acts of Individual Bravery," "Men of Color to Arms," *Virginia Historical Society Online Exhibitions*, http://vahistorical.org/civilwar/wagingwar.htm. Butler was removed from office by executive order from President Lincoln in January 1865.

34. Read the full inscription at https://www.waymarking.com/waymarks/WMEDNW_South_Carolina_Memorial_Gettysburg_PA/.

35. Lincoln, "The Emancipation Proclamation."

36. Katherine Calos, "Black soldiers in the Civil War: Who did they fight for and why?" *Richmond Times-Dispatch*, March 14, 2015, https://richmond.com/black-soldiers-in-the-civil-war-who-did-they-fight-for-and-why/article_317568c2-1ba4-5f88-a18a-45d24a900a22.html.

37. Paul D. Escott, *"What Shall We Do with the Negro?": Lincoln, White Racism, and Civil War America* (Charlottesville: Univ. of Virginia Press, 2009), 185–86.

38. Edward Davis Townsend, Assistant Adjutant-General in "Negroes of Savannah," https://en.wikisource.org/wiki/Negroes_of_Savannah/.

39. Townsend, "Negroes of Savannah."

40. Townsend, "Negroes of Savannah."

41. Townsend, "Negroes of Savannah."

42. Townsend, "Negroes of Savannah."

43. Townsend, "Negroes of Savannah."

44. Townsend, "Negroes of Savannah."

45. John Roger Stephens and Lonnie Rashid Lynn, *Glory* lyrics (Nashville, TN: EMI Music Publishing, 2014).

CHAPTER 15: A SECOND AMERICAN REVOLUTION

1.   "The Convention," *Charleston Daily News*, January 15, 1868, 1.
2.   J. Woodruff, reporter, *Proceedings of the Constitutional Convention of South Carolina* (Charleston: Denny & Perry, 1868), 6.
3.   "The President's Last Proclamation," *The Spectator*, No. 1789, October 11, 1862. https://play.google.com/books/reader?id=DdkhAQAAMAAJ&pg=GBS.PA1124
4.   Benjamin Franklin Butler, *Autobiography and Personal Reminiscences of Major-General Benj. F. Butler's Book* (Boston: A.M. Thayer & Company, 1892), 500, https://play.google.com/books/reader?id=0LIBAAAAMAAJ.
5.   Paul M. Angle, ed., *Abraham Lincoln's Speeches and Letters 1832–1865* (New York: E.P. Dutton & Company, 1897), 220, https://libsysdigi.library.illinois.edu/OCA /Books2012-06/abrahamlincolnsspee00linc.
6.   "Appendix to the Congressional Globe," *The Congressional Globe*, Vol. 36, Part 5, 39th Congress of the United States, First Session (Washington, DC: Congressional Globe Office, 1866), 710, https://play.google.com/books/reader?id=i2M9AQAAMAAJ.
7.   John Palmer, *Personal Recollection of John Palmer: The Story of an Earnest Life* (Cincinnati: The Robert Clarke Company, 1901), 127, https://babel.hathitrust.org/cgi /pt?id=loc.ark:/13960/t77s7s742.
8.   "Appendix to The Congressional Globe," 707.
9.   William Francis Allen, Charles Pickard Ware, and Lucy McKim Garrison, *Slave Songs of the United States* (New York: A. Simpson & Company, 1867), 55, https:// archive.org/details/slavesongsunite00allegoog.
10. "Our Next Vice-President," *The New York Times*, June 16, 1864, 2, https://times machine.nytimes.com/timesmachine/1864/06/16/issue.html.
11. "Our Next Vice-President," *New York Times*.
12. "Our Next Vice-President," *New York Times*.
13. "Our Next Vice-President," *New York Times*.
14. *Journal of the Senate of the State of South Carolina Being the Extra Session of 1865* (Columbia: Julian A. Selby, 1865), 23.
15. Edmund Rhett, "Letter to Armistead Burt," cited in Richard Zuczek, *State of Rebellion: People's War in Reconstruction South Carolina, 1865–1877*, PhD Thesis (Columbus: Ohio State Univ., 1993), 32.
16. For South Carolina's Black Codes, see "The Code," *Edgefield Advertiser*, January 3, 1866, 1, https://chroniclingamerica.loc.gov/data/batches/scu_jinx_ver01/data/sn840 26897/00211101209/1866010301/0416.pdf. Most southern states' Black Codes were similar; see a survey of the Black Codes in Page Smith, *Trial By Fire: A People's History of the Civil War and Reconstruction* (New York: Penguin Books, 1990).
17. "Memphis Riots and Massacres," *Reports of the Committees of the House of Representatives, 39th Session* (Washington, DC: Government Printing Office, 1866), 1.

18. Philip H. Sheridan, "The New-Orleans Riot, Its Official History," *The Dispatches of Gens. Sheridan, Grant, and Baird*, https://tile.loc.gov/storage-services/service/rbc /lcrbmrp/t2602/t2602.pdf.

19. *Proceeding of the Pennsylvania Yearly Meeting of the Progressive Friends* (Philadelphia: John Craig & Son, 1875), 1, https://play.google.com/books/reader.

20. "Let's Have a New Divide," *Iowa Plain Dealer*, July 12, 1867, 1, https://chroniclin gamerica.loc.gov/lccn/sn83025167/1867-07-12/ed-1/seq-1.

21. Martin Luther King, Jr., "Beyond Vietnam," The Martin Luther King, Jr. Research and Education Institute, Stanford Univ., https://kinginstitute.stanford.edu/king -papers/documents/beyond-vietnam.

22. Lerone Bennett, Jr., *Black Power U.S.A.: The Human Side of Reconstruction, 1867–1877* (Chicago: Johnson Publishing Company, 1967), 31.

23. Frederick Douglass, speech, *Proceedings of the American Anti-Slavery Society, at its Third Decade* (New York: American Anti-Slavery Society, 1864), 118, https://babel .hathitrust.org/cgi/pt?id=loc.ark:/13960/t9r212f95.

24. Frederick Douglass, "The Mission on the War," *New-York Daily Tribune*, January 14, 1864, 2, https://www.loc.gov/resource/sn83030213/1864-01-14/ed-1.

25. Frederick Douglass, "The Work of the Future," *Douglass' Monthly*, Vol. 5, No. 5, November 1862, https://babel.hathitrust.org/cgi/pt?id=inu.30000007703097.

26. Charles Sumner, "Rights and Duties of Our Colored Fellow-Citizens," A Letter to the National Convention of Colored Citizens at Columbia, South Carolina, October 12, 1871, *Charles Sumner: His Complete Works*, Vol. 19 (Boston: Lee and Shepard, 1900), 165, https://www.gutenberg.org/files/50386/50386 -h/50386-h.htm.

27. F. & J. Rives, eds., *The Congressional Globe: The Debates and Proceedings of the First Session of the Thirty-Ninth Congress* (Washington, DC: Congressional Globe Office, 1866), 2459–60.

28. "Wanted—A Policy!" and "Emancipation in Russia," *New York Times*, April 3, 1861, 4, https://timesmachine.nytimes.com/timesmachine/1861/04/03/78655534.html.

29. Thaddeus Stevens, "Reconstruction," speech delivered in Lancaster, Pennsylvania. Beverly Wilson Palmer, ed., *The Selected Papers of Thaddeus Stevens*, Volume 2: April 1865—August 1868 (University of Pittsburgh Press, 1998), 25, https://books .google.com/books?id=_IjlJeXnoUAC.

30. *Proceedings of the Colored People's Convention of the State of South Carolina* (Charleston: Leader Office, 1865), 25–26, https://omeka.coloredconventions.org/files /original/fb7ce2e02cc45786fb4530926135de24.pdf.

31. *Proceedings of the Colored People's Convention*, 27–31.

32. *New-York Daily Tribune*, November 14, 1865, 4, https://www.newspapers.com/image /466694786.

33. *New York Times*, January 4, 1866, 1, https://timesmachine.nytimes.com/times machine/1866/01/04/issue.html.

34. *Cleveland Leader*, November 13, 1865, 1, https://www.genealogybank.com/doc

/newspapers/image/v2%3A125C1B91E57C8E0A%40GB3NEWS-125DE28BA2073
283%402402554–125C317DEBFF878B%400–125C317DEBFF878B%40.

35. "Black Code of Mississippi," *Chicago Tribune*, December 1, 1865, 2, https://chronicling
america.loc.gov/lccn/sn82014064/1865-12-01/ed-1.

36. Frederick Douglass, "What the Black Man Wants," *The Equality of all Men before
the Law*" (Boston: Geo. C. Rand & Avery, 1865), 38, https://play.google.com/books
/reader?id=MG9DAQAAMAAJ.

37. Wendell Phillips, "The Immediate Issue," *The Equality of all Men*, 32.

38. Elizur Wright, "Suffrage for the Blacks Sound Political Economy," *The Equality of
all Men*, 40–41.

39. *New-York Daily Tribune*, December 4, 1867, 3, https://chroniclingamerica.loc.gov
/data/batches/dlc_delphi_ver02/data/sn83030214/0020653087A/1867120401
/0671.pdf.

40. Bennett, *Black Power*, 57.

41. Woodruff, *Proceedings*, 89.

42. James S. Pike, *The Prostrate State: South Carolina Under Negro Government* (New
York: D. Appleton and Company, 1874), 10–12.

43. Pike, *The Prostrate State*.

44. Pike, *The Prostrate State*, 11.

45. Pike, *The Prostrate State*, 15.

46. Pike, *The Prostrate State*, 45.

47. Eric Foner, "Rooted in Reconstruction: The First Wave of Black Congressmen,"
The Nation, October 15, 2008, https://www.thenation.com/article/archive/rooted
-reconstruction-first-wave-black-congressmen.

48. Pike, *The Prostrate State*, 52.

49. Pike, *The Prostrate State*, 14.

50. Pike, *The Prostrate State*, 19–20.

51. Pike, *The Prostrate State*, 17.

52. Pike, *The Prostrate State*, 23.

53. "The Carolinas," *New York Herald*, June 13, 1871, 15, https://chroniclingamerica
.loc.gov/lccn/sn83030313/1871-06-13/ed-1/seq-15.

54. Woodruff, *Proceedings*, 80.

55. Woodruff, *Proceedings*, 358.

56. Barack Obama, "State of the Union," January 28, 2014, https://obamawhitehouse
.archives.gov/the-press-office/2014/01/28/president-barack-obamas-state-union
-address.

57. Woodruff, *Proceedings*, 868.

58. "The Murder of G.W. Dill in South Carolina," *New York Times*, June 13, 1868, 2,
https://timesmachine.nytimes.com/timesmachine/1868/06/13/78919321.html.
The *Times* article casts doubt on the involvement of the KKK. Hyman I. Rubin in
"Ku Klux Klan," *South Carolina Encyclopedia*, http://www.scencyclopedia.org/sce
/entries/ku-klux-klan/ and J. Michael Martinez in *Carpetbaggers, Cavalry, and the*

Ku Klux Klan: Exposing the Invisible Empire During Reconstruction (Lanham, MD: Rowman & Littlefield, 2007), 25, suggest that Dill's killing fits the pattern of KKK violence against White Republicans in the south at the time.

59. Bennett, *Black Power*, 302.

60. Bennett, *Black Power*, 302.

61. Being a Black landowner did not automatically bring compassion for poor tenant farmers. Lawrence Graham in *The Senator and the Socialite: The True Story of America's First Black Dynasty* (New York: HarperCollins, 2006), 114, tells of how Bruce employed "poorly compensated" Black sharecroppers on his plantation in Mississippi, who lived in "flimsy wooden shacks," not unlike the conditions on plantations owned by Whites.

62. Pike, *The Prostrate State*, 259.

63. Eric Foner, *Reconstruction: America's Unfinished Revolution, 1863–1877* (New York: Harper & Row, 1988), 376.

64. Woodruff, *Proceedings*, 264.

65. Woodruff, *Proceedings*, 265.

66. The description of the Rollin sisters and their work comes from Willard B. Gatewood, Jr., "'The Remarkable Misses Rollin': Black Women in Reconstruction South Carolina," *The South Carolina Historical Magazine*, Vol. 92, No. 3, July 1991, 172–88.

67. Gatewood, "'The Remarkable Misses Rollin'," 180.

68. Gatewood, "'The Remarkable Misses Rollin'," 182.

CHAPTER 16: BACK AGAIN TOWARD SLAVERY

1. This description of the Ku Klux Klan attack on Alfred Richardson is taken from his testimony before a joint congressional committee, *Testimony Taken by The Joint Select Committee to Inquire into the Condition of Affairs of the Late Insurrectionary States. Georgia*, Vol. 1, July 7, 1871 (Washington, DC: Government Printing Office, 1872), 1–19, https://archive.org/details/reportofjointsel06unit.

2. Mathew Pulver, "How Alf Richardson Fought the Klan and Became Athens' First Black State Representative," *Flagpole*, March 4, 2020, https://flagpole.com/news /news-features/2020/03/04/how-alf-richardson-fought-the-klan-and-became -athens-first-black-state-representative.

3. Claudia Isler and Barbara Jean Quinn, *Understanding Your Right to Vote* (New York: The Rosen Publishing Group, 2012), 44, place the number between 20,000 and 40,000. Herbert Shapiro in "Afro-American Responses to Race Violence During Reconstruction," *Science and Society*, Vol. 36, No. 2, Summer 1972, 1, makes reference to a figure of 20,000. Rick Selzer and Grace M. Lopes "The Ku Klux Klan: Reasons for Support or Opposition Among White Residents," *Journal of Black Studies*, Vol. 17, No. 1, September 1986, 92, cite a figure of 3,500 Blacks murdered by the Klan.

4. "Governor's Proclamation," *Southern Watchman*, February 8, 1871, 2.

5. *Testimony Taken by The Joint Select Committee*, Vol. 1, 235–36.

6. "The Ku-Klux Klan," *The Moulton Advertiser*, April 10, 1868, 3, https://www.news papers.com/image/355634019.

7. *Testimony Taken by The Joint Select Committee to Inquire into the Condition of Affairs of the Late Insurrectionary States. Mississippi*, Vol. 12, November 17, 1871 (Washington, DC: Government Printing Office, 1872), 1133, https://play.google.com/books /reader?id=tnQUAAAAYAAJ.

8. *Testimony Taken by The Joint Select Committee*, 1134–35.

9. US Congress, *Report of the Joint Select Committee to Inquire Into the Condition of Affairs in the Late Insurrectionary States, Alabama*, Vol. 1 (Washington, DC: Government Printing Office, 1872), 92.

10. The Civil Rights Act of 1871 (codified at 42 U.S.C. §1983 and commonly referred to as Section 1983). For the original act see https://www.loc.gov/law/help/statutes-at -large/42nd-congress/session-1/c42s1ch22.pdf. From civil rights to reproductive rights to child welfare and police brutality, the successful legal actions of many groups have Black Americans to thank for the violence and intimidation they suffered bringing forth this act.

11. Jean Edward Smith, *Grant* (New York: Simon & Schuster, 2001), 547.

12. In 1957, President Dwight Eisenhower sent federal troops to enforce school integration in Little Rock, Arkansas, as a result of the *Brown v. Board of Education* ruling by the Supreme Court. In 1962, President John F. Kennedy sent federal troops to enforce integration on the campus of the University of Mississippi. In 1965, President Lyndon B. Johnson sent federal troops to protect some fifty thousand civil rights marchers from Selma to Montgomery, Alabama. In July 2020, President Donald Trump sent federal troops to arrest people protesting for civil rights in major US cities. But none of these presidents has ever suspended habeas corpus for the sake of supporting or denying civil rights.

13. Most scholarship on the Ku Klux Klan cites three phases of its existence, though four may now be required. Phase I: From its inception in 1866 with founder, Confederate general Nathan Bedford, to the action of President Grant in South Carolina in 1871; Phase II: From its second founding by William Joseph Simmons in 1915 in Stone Mountain, Georgia, to the pre–World War II years; Phase III: From the early 1950s and the rise of the Civil Rights Movement until the election of 2016; and, Phase IV: From 2016 and the vocal encouragement and support given by President Donald Trump and other modern-day Republicans to "white nationalist" and "white supremacist" groups until the present.

14. Attorney General Edwards Pierrepont letter to Governor Adelbert Ames, expressing the views of President Ulysses S. Grant, "Pierrepont to Ames," *National Republican*, September 17, 1875, 1, https://www.loc.gov/resource/sn86053573/1875 -09-17/ed-1.

15. "The Eternal Nigger," *New York Herald*, June 13, 1871, 15, https://chroniclingamerica .loc.gov/lccn/sn83030313/1871-06-13/ed-1/seq-15.

16. "The Threatened Danger," *Memphis Daily Appeal*, June 28, 1872, 2, https://www .newspapers.com/image/163990564.

17. *The Southern Home*, October 31, 1871, 2, https://www.newspapers.com/image /66367849.

18. "Who Are Africanizing Louisiana?" *Daily Picayune*, July 9, 1872, 4, https://www .newspapers.com/image/27006891.

19. "Sambo in Excelsis," *New York Herald*, January 11, 1874, 3, https://www.newspapers .com/image/329390464.

20. "Defining Our Position," *The Perry County Democrat*, July 5, 1871, 2, https://www .newspapers.com/image/351531574.

21. "Letter from New Orleans," *Cincinnati Enquirer*, October 20, 1873, 2, https://www .newspapers.com/image/31307170.

22. "The Jury Box," *New National Era*, June 11, 1874, 1, https://www.newspapers.com /image/587861660.

23. Robert Somers, *The Southern States Since the War, 1870–1* (New York: MacMillan and Company, 1871).

24. Malcolm C. McMillan, "Introduction" to Robert Somers, *The Southern States Since the War, 1870–1* (Tuscaloosa: Univ. of Alabama Press, 1965).

25. Somers, *The Southern States*, 94.

26. Somers, *The Southern States*, 131.

27. Somers, *The Southern States*, 132.

28. James S. Pike, *The Prostrate State: South Carolina Under Negro Government* (New York: D. Appleton and Company, 1874), 230.

29. Pike, *The Prostrate State*, 88–89.

30. Adelbert Ames, "Letter to Lieutenant John W. Clous," cited in Stephen Budian-sky, *The Bloody Shirt: Terror After the Civil War* (New York: Penguin, 2008), 27.

31. "The White League: Its Platform in Full," *Times-Picayune*, July 2, 1874, 1, https:// www.newspapers.com/image/26993619.

32. "Opinions of the Press," *Memphis Daily Appeal*, December 13, 1874, 1, https:// chroniclingamerica.loc.gov/data/batches/tu_chet_ver01/data/sn83045160/00200 293101/1874121301/0582.pdf.

33. "Opinions of the Press," 1.

34. Albert Dorsey, Jr., *"Vicksburg's Troubles": Black Participation in the Body Politic and Land Ownership in the Age of Redeemer Violence*, PhD Thesis (Tallahassee: Florida State Univ., 2012), 109.

35. "Vicksburg Troubles," *Report No. 26, House of Representatives, 43rd Congress, 2nd Session* (Washington, DC: Government Printing Office, 1875), 291, https://play .google.com/books/reader?id=UVpHAQAAIAAJ.

36. Testimony of G.W. Walters, *Congressional Record, Containing the Proceedings and Debates of the Forty-Third Congress, Second Session*, Vol. 3 (Washington, DC: Government Printing Office, 1875), 1123, https://play.google.com/books/reader ?id=K6RmAAAAcAAJ.

37. "The Shooting of Sheriff Crosby," *Weekly Clarion*, June 9, 1875, 3, https://chronicling america.loc.gov/lccn/sn83016926/1875-06-09/ed-1/seq-3.

38. Charles E. Furlong, *Origin of the Outrages at Vicksburg* (Vicksburg Herald Press, 1874), 16, https://babel.hathitrust.org/cgi/pt?id=yale.39002014225610.

39. Blanche Butler Ames, *Chronicles from the Nineteenth Century: Family Letters of Blanche Butler and Adelbert Ames*, Vol. 2 (Clinton, MA, 1957), 142–43.

40. "The Mississippi Murder: Slaughter of Negroes by White-Leagues," *Wisconsin State Journal*, September 15, 1875, 2, https://www.newspapers.com/image/397436760.

41. "Pierrepont to Ames."

42. Blanche Butler Ames, *Chronicles from the Nineteenth Century*, 216–17.

43. W. H. Hardy, "Recollections of Reconstruction in East and Southeast Missis-sippi," *Publications of the Mississippi Historical Society*, Vol. 4 (Oxford: The Mis-sissippi Historical Society, 1901), 129–30, https://babel.hathitrust.org/cgi/pt ?id=mdp.39015039481992.

44. "Mississippi in 1875," *Report of the Select Committee to Inquire into the Mississippi Elections of 1875*, Vol. 1 (Washington, DC: Government Printing Office, 1876), 805, https://quod.lib.umich.edu/cgi/t/text/text-idx?c=moa&cc=moa&sid=95e3f6e828e1 16b80d4cccd93c806bc1&idno=AEY0467.0001.001.

45. "President Grant Replies to the South Carolina Governor," *The Reconstruction Era and the Fragility of Democracy on Facing History and Ourselves*, https://www .facinghistory.org/reconstruction-era/president-grant-replies-south-carolina -governor-1876.

46. "Mississippi in 1875," xxviii.

47. Ben Tillman, "The Struggle of '76: Address Delivered at Red Shirt Reunion of An-derson, August 25th, by Senator B. R. Tillman," *Abbeville Press and Banner*, Sep-tember 28, 1909, 10, https://chroniclingamerica.loc.gov/data/batches/scu_kingjulius _ver01/data/sn84026853/00202192932/1909092901/0388.pdf.

48. H. N. Borrey, letter, "To his Excellency Daniel H. Chamberlain," *The Miscella-neous Documents of the Senate of the United States. Second Session of the Forty-Fourth Congress*, Vol. 2, No. 3 (Washington, DC: Government Printing Office, 1877), 551.

49. For an overview of sexual violence against Black women during Reconstruction, see Rebecca A. Kosary, *To Degrade and Control: White Violence and The Maintenance of Racial and Gender Boundaries In Reconstruction Texas, 1865–1868*, PhD Thesis (Texas A&M Univ., May 2006), https://core.ac.uk/download/pdf/4272881.pdf.

50. Willard B. Gatewood, Jr., "'The Remarkable Misses Rollin': Black Women in Reconstruction South Carolina," *The South Carolina Historical Magazine*, Vol. 92, No. 3, July 1991, 184.

51. "The Georgia Election," *Charleston Daily News*, December 21, 1870, 1.

52. Melanie Susan Gustafson, *Women and the Republican Party, 1854–1924* (Urbana: Univ. of Illinois Press, 2001), 52.

53. *Lysistrata*, from the Greek *lysis*, meaning to "break apart" or "loosen," and *stratos*, meaning "army," literally means to break apart the army. *Lysistrata* is an ancient

Greek play by Aristophanes in which the main character, a woman named Lysistrata, is on an extraordinary mission to end the Peloponnesian War (an ancient Greek civil war) by convincing other women to deny sex to fighting men.

54. Testimony of John Bird before the House of Representatives on February 13, 1877, *Papers in the Case of Tillman v Small, Fifth District South Carolina* (Washington, DC: Government Printing Office, 1877), 27, https://play.google.com/books/reader ?id=pSRynWZOwroC&hl=en&pg=GBS.RA1-PA1.

55. D. T. Corbin, letter to "Governor D. H. Chamberlain," *Miscellaneous Documents*, 523–24.

56. Ulysses S. Grant, "Letter to D.H. Chamberlain, Governor of South Carolina," *Teaching American History*, https://teachingamericanhistory.org/library/document /letter-to-d-h-chamberlain-governor-of-south-carolina.

57. Lerone Bennett, Jr., *Black Power U.S.A.: The Human Side of Reconstruction, 1867–1877* (Chicago: Johnson Publishing Company, 1967), 379.

58. "Persecutions in the South," *New-York Tribune*, September 3, 1879, 1.

59. W.E.B. Du Bois, *Black Reconstruction* (New York: Harcourt, Brace and Company, 1935), 30.

AFTERWORD

1. The description of the Emancipation Day celebration in Elmira, New York, comes from "Emancipation: Why and How the Colored People Celebrate To-Day," *Daily Advertiser*, August 3, 1880, 5, https://nyshistoricnewspapers.org /lccn/sn83030951/1880-08-03/ed-1/seq-5.pdf and "The Colored People: How They Observed the Emancipation Anniversary," *Daily Advertiser*, August 4, 1880, 5, https://nyshistoricnewspapers.org/lccn/sn83030951/1880-08-04/ed-1/seq-5.pdf.

2. Read the act in its entirety at http://www.irishstatutebook.ie/eli/1833/act/73 /enacted/en/print.html.

3. Douglass's speech at Elmira is found at "Fred Douglass! His Great Speech Yesterday," *Daily Advertiser*, August 4, 1880, 8, https://nyshistoricnewspapers.org /lccn/sn83030951/1880-08-04/ed-1/seq-8.pdf. Douglass includes an extract of the speech in his third and last autobiography, *Frederick Douglass: Written by Himself, His Early Life as a Slave, His Escape from Bondage, and His Complete History to the Present Time* (Hartford: Park Publishing Company, 1882), 601–18.

4. Martin Luther King, Jr., "I Have A Dream," speech at March on Washington, August 28, 1963, https://www.naacp.org/i-have-a-dream-speech-full-march-on -washington.

INDEX

accounting practices, 252

Affleck's Southern Rural Almanac, 166–67

African Burial Ground National Monument, 230, 374n19

Africanization, 325–26

Africanus, Johannes Leo, 50

Age of Exploration, 6

agriculture, American. *See also* cotton; tobacco
    Black labor and, 4, 45, 119, 137, 139 (*See also under* cotton; tobacco)
    financial industry and, 45–46, 139
    southern crops, 375n10
    transportation infrastructure and, 138–39, 175, 231, 248
    White power and wealth from, 119, 139

Alexander II, 299–300

Algonquin tribes, 56, 97, 353n5, 362n41

Allen, Arthur, 115

American Revolution. *See* Revolutionary War

Ames, Adelbert, 327, 328–29, 330, 331–32, 333

Amoskeag tribe, 175

amphisbaena, 135

Amtrak, 248, 250, 376n17

"ancient planters," 50, 359n30

Angola, 24, 26, 39, 52, 77, 120–21, 348n10. *See also* Ndongo

Anthony and Isabella
    arrival in Virginia, 17, 18, 51, 61, 354n8
    capture of, 23, 26, 121
    descendants of, 8, 17–18, 29, 354n8
    home of, 19, 20–21
    indentured servitude/slavery of, 8, 47–48, 50, 71, 354n8
    as *malungu,* 19
    marriage of, 8
    names of, 17, 347n2
    Ndongo spirituality and, 30–33, 34, 41
    purchase of, 17, 19, 50, 51, 52, 71, 109
    tobacco and, 118–19, 121, 122, 124–29

Argall, Samuel, 351n19

Arrington, Archibald, 192

Articles of Confederation, 155, 157

asiento, 21, 33, 44

asset valuation, 252–53

Baal Shem Tov, 120

Bacon, Nathaniel, 111, 112, 113–14

Bacon, Nathaniel, Jr., 109

Bacon's Rebellion, 109–17

BaKongo mythology, 31–33, 34, 40, 41

banking industry, 45, 139, 161, 175, 176, 231–36, 248

Banks, Nathaniel, 266, 271, 272, 275

Banton, Ivie, 51

Baptist, Edward, 235, 239–40, 242

Bass, Nathaniel, 131–32

bateaux, 253–54

Battell, Andrew, 23

Battle of Jamestown, 114

Beasley, Anne, 1, 2

Beaumarchais, Pierre-Augustin Caron de, 149, 367n15

Beaver, 214

Bedford, Nathan, 319, 386n13

Benjamin, Judah, 278–79

Bennett, Lerone, Jr., 15, 53–54, 69, 304

berdache, 94, 362n30

Berkeley, Frances, 111, 145

Berkeley, William, 1, 100, 109, 112, 113, 114

Bermuda, 122–23, 365n27

berserk, 269, 380n18

bias, 8–10, 52

Bible, 177–78

Billings, Joseph, 332

Billings, Warren, 357n28

Bill of Rights, 187

ABOUT THE AUTHOR

Clyde W. Ford is the author of thirteen works of fiction and non-fiction, including *Think Black* (2019), which garnered numerous awards, among them the 2021 Washington State Book Award in creative nonfiction. In 2006, he received the Zora Neale Hurston/Richard Wright Foundation Legacy Award in fiction, and in 2019 he was a finalist for the foundation's legacy award in nonfiction. Ford was named a "Literary Lion" by the King County Library System in 2006, 2007, 2008, and 2019. He was voted "Best Writer of Bellingham, Washington" in 2006 and 2007 by readers of the *Cascadia Weekly*, and he received the 2007 Bellingham, Washington, Mayor's Arts Award in Literature. Ford is a speaker for Humanities Washington, an affiliate of the NEH, and the director of the Martin Luther King Jr. Library Publishing Project at HarperCollins Publishers.